To Betty,
With many thanks
for all of your support.
Enjoy the Reads
Thompson
4/28/00

GUIDE TO
AFRICAN AMERICAN RESOURCES
AT THE PENNSYLVANIA
STATE ARCHIVES

RG-13. Pennsylvania Historical and Museum Commission. African American Women working on an locomotive, circa 1940.

GUIDE TO
AFRICAN AMERICAN RESOURCES
AT THE
PENNSYLVANIA
STATE ARCHIVES

Ruth E. Hodge

Commonwealth of Pennsylvania
Pennsylvania Historical and Museum Commission
Harrisburg, 2000

www.phmc.state.pa.us

CONTENTS

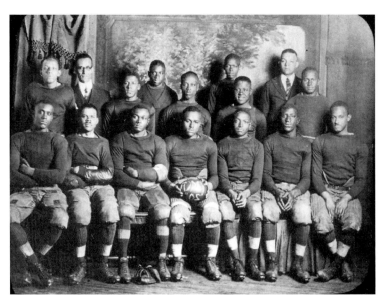

RG-22. Department of Education. State Library of Pennsylvania. Football Team of the YMCA, Broad Street Branch (Colored), Harrisburg, 1920.

FOREWORD

Years before the Pennsylvania Historical and Museum Commission produced its bumper stickers (I Brake for Historical Markers), I have traveled throughout the sixty-seven counties of the Commonwealth in search of information pertaining to African Americans for my first book *Pennsylvania Black History*, 1975. I discovered that Pennsylvania had a long and interesting history connected to African Americans, who were present among the earliest settlers, as early as 1639. History books did a credible job of recording what white Americans had contributed to society as I knew it during that period. Most books failed to record the contributions and achievements of African Americans in Pennsylvania and beyond. As one of the founding members of the Pennsylvania Black History Advisory Committee in 1976, I recommended that a survey of African American documents and other items housed by the Pennsylvania Historical and Museum Commission should be recorded and published.

Three years later in 1979, the Pennsylvania Historical Museum Commission published a thirty-six page book entitled *The Afro-American in Pennsylvania: A Critical Guide to Sources in the Pennsylvania State Archives,* written by David McBride. In recent years, with the introduction of African American studies in American education and historical institutions, archivists have been forced to re-examine closely their collections to discover unknown or uncataloged African American subject matter. Moreover, archivists and librarians today are confronted with the most pressing problems of providing researchers and news media with required information as quickly as possible.

It has been known for some time that the Pennsylvania Historical and Museum Commission has both printed and manuscript materials pertaining to African American history and culture. Much of it was inaccessible, as it had not been re-examined and cataloged. Scholars will be pleased with this new publication, *Guide to African American Resources at the Pennsylvania State Archives,* written by Ruth E. Hodge. In this impressive and diligently researched work, Hodge and her assistants included several hundred printed sources in this survey, as well as scores of manuscript collections. The purpose of this survey is to furnish an accurate and comprehensive guide to books, pamphlets, reports, day books, photographs, cash books, manumission records, organizational records, church records, periodicals, and various miscellaneous collections. The guide is filled with numerous names of African Americans both enslaved and freed, providing vital data for researchers who are compiling information for genealogy purposes.

Researchers will also discover that information relating to military records. Colored women's organizations, colored schools and soldiers', orphans schools, National Freedom Day celebrations, NAACP papers and papers of several governors and their relationships with African Americans. In addition, the guide includes information on the Pennsylvania Historical and Museum Commission's oral history tape collection that consists of interviews with African American citizens in several counties. Wholly, this material speaks as a living language that adds a greater expression to the lives of Pennsylvanians throughout the Commonwealth as well as the nation.

This present publication owes much to the work of Ruth E. Hodge and staff members of the Pennsylvania Historical and Museum Commission who participated in the planning and publishing of this guide. Publication of this guide, I am certain, documents the importance of the Pennsylvania Historical and Museum Commission in its relationship with the African American citizens. It is a splendid thought that future generations will benefit from this publication.

Charles L. Blockson, Curator
Charles L. Blockson Afro-American Collection
Temple University
Philadelphia

MG-329. Ivan L. Carter Photographs, [ca. 1922-1938]. No. 1306. "End of the Underground Railway on Woods Farm," undated.

PREFACE

It is equally important to be able to document the uniqueness of African American cultural life in Pennsylvania and the similarity of the group's activities with those of other ethnic groups throughout the state. This guide provides ample opportunity for scholars to learn about both aspects of African American life and history. On one hand, as bondspersons, workers, soldiers, and citizens, African Americans have encountered a variety of challenges working and living alongside other Pennsylvanians. Church and other organizational records, on the other hand, show how African Americans interacted with one another in their own socially segregated communities. Some documents provide insight into both the role of blacks and their interaction with the wider society. For example, the papers of Samuel Penniman Bates (MG-17) include a listing of the U.S. Colored Troops who were trained at Camp William Penn, located north of Philadelphia. Though these men were participants in the Civil War along with other Union troops, they fought in segregated regiments in which only whites were allowed to be officers.

Years ago, when I told a colleague at the National Archives that I had published an article in the *Journal of Negro History,* entitled "Black Women in Pennsylvania in the Era of the American Revolution" (1976), she replied, "Were there any?" Answering her in the affirmative did not keep me from musing on the fact that few Americans really understand the richness of the sources available for African American history. This volume by Ruth E. Hodge documents extensively the contributions of African American men and women to Pennsylvania society from the colonial period through the modern era. A close reading of this excellent volume demonstrates that African American participation in the building of the state of Pennsylvania was not occasional or sporadic, but constant and nurturing for more than three centuries. As we expect to see African Americans as we traverse the urban and rural areas of Pennsylvania today, so too would have any colonial traveler in the state. Correspondence, newspaper accounts, business records, government documents, church records, and a variety of other sources located and described by Hodge relating to African American history afford access to a wide array of record and manuscript groups containing both obvious and obscure files available in the Pennsylvania State Archives.

Because of the activities of businessmen, politicians, statesmen and community leaders, the records in the Pennsylvania State Archives also chronicle the history of African Americans in other states and even, occasionally, in other parts of the world. This work is of immense value to the research community. Those who peruse its pages and locate materials for their own use will be grateful to Hodge for many years to come. This is obviously a work of Herculean proportions and the Pennsylvania Historical and Museum Commission should be commended for its pioneering work in this arena.

Dr. Debra Newman Ham, Associate Professor
Department of History
Morgan State University

INTRODUCTION

The purpose of this guide is to assist the researcher in locating information on African Americans available in the Division of Archives and Manuscripts (Pennsylvania State Archives) of the Pennsylvania Historical and Museum Commission. The primary mission of the State Archives is to acquire, process, preserve, and provide for research and study the permanently valuable public and state records of the Commonwealth. The State Archives also acquires, preserves, and makes available private papers relevant to Pennsylvania history. This guide will give the researcher information on materials in both types of holdings that contain information on African Americans.

In 1979, Dr. David McBride prepared *The Afro-American in Pennsylvania: A Critical Guide to Sources in the Pennsylvania State Archives.* Although this was considered a preliminary effort, this guide served as a pioneer model for a most needed tool to research materials on African Americans in the State Archives. I feel extremely fortunate and honored to have had the opportunity to further this cause and especially to have followed this path first created by Dr. McBride.

Although comprehensive in scope, this guide represents only a sampling of the many record and manuscript groups, and special collections, including photographs, slides, recordings, etc., containing information on the African American experience in Penn-

1

sylvania. If information is cited in a particular record or manuscript group, it is possible that additional information on African Americans can be found in that group beyond the examples cited.

The organizational units to which the records at the Archives are assigned are designated as "Record Groups" (RGs) and "Manuscript Groups" (MGs). Record Groups represent official records of the Provincial and Revolutionary governments, the General Assembly, Supreme and Superior Courts, independent Commissions, constitutional conventions, and governmental agencies of the Commonwealth of Pennsylvania. Individual record series are cited for the agency or department of origin and are usually listed in alphabetical order within the groups or subject headings. Record groups are further classified by sub-series, usually arranged alphabetically.

Manuscript groups include papers representing the Provincial period; papers of the governors of Pennsylvania; collections of prominent Pennsylvania individuals and families, and records of social, fraternal, civic, cultural, educational, religious, political, military organizations or activities, as well as agricultural, commercial and industrial enterprises. At the beginning of each record and manuscript group is a brief history as well as a description of some of the series. This guide will serve as a companion volume when used with other finding aids and guides available at the State Archives, such as the *Guide to the Manuscript Groups in the Pennsylvania State Archives, Guide to the Microfilm Collections in the Pennsylvania State Archives, Guide to Photographs at the Pennsylvania State Archives, Guide to the Record Groups in the Pennsylvania State Archives, Guide to Genealogical Sources at the Pennsylvania State Archives and Descriptive List of the Map Collection in the Pennsylvania State Archives.*

As a general note to the researcher, he or she should be advised that a (•) represents the most detailed information available about that particular item, or items, within the structure of the record

2

or manuscript group. Not all entries are described at this level.

Generally, the term African Americans will be used in describing the prescribed records. However, the terms Afro-American, black, Negro, negroe, colored, slave, mulatto, servant, and men or women of color, will be used when those terms have been cited in the document, e.g., page, article, letter, photograph, etc., and will sometimes appear within quotation marks.

Some of the topics described in this guide are: abolition and abolitionists, affirmative action, African American colleges and universities (e.g., Cheyney, Fisk, Hampton, Howard, Lincoln, Meharry, Morehouse, Morgan); almshouses, business, census, certification and licensing (e.g.; beauticians, dentists, funeral directors, mid-wives, nurses, peddlers, pharmacists, physicians, veterinarians; charitable and beneficial organizations, civil rights, churches, corporations, county records, court records, education, governors' papers, governmental records (e.g., national, state, county, local); Habeas Corpus papers, historical events, historical markers, homes and hospitals, industries (e.g., forges, furnaces, mills, mines, railroads); legislators, marriages, migrant labor, military, music, prisons, slavery and slaves, sports, underground railroad, veterans' schools (Bridgewater and Scotland); women's activities and organizations; and the Work Projects Administration programs.

The following references were used in verifying names of people, places, professions, military units, organizations, etc.:

Altoff, Gerard T. *Amongst My Best Men: African-Americans and the War of 1812*, Put-in-Bay, Ohio: Perry Group,1996.

Blackett, R.J.M. *Thomas Morris Chester: Black Civil War Correspondent: His Dispatches from the Virginia Front*. Baton Rouge: Louisiana State University Press, 1989.

Blockson, Charles L., *Pennsylvania's Black History*. Philadelphia:

Portfolio Associates, 1975.

Brown, Ira V. *The Negro in Pennsylvania History*. University Park: Pennsylvania Historical Association, 1970.

DuBois, W.E.B. *The Philadelphia Negro: a Social Study*. Philadelphia: University of Pennsylvania Press, 1996.

Eicher, Hubert Clark. *A Century of Service: The Harrisburg Young Men's Christian Association*. Harrisburg: The Evangelical Press, 1955.

Gladstone, William A. *United States Colored Troops: 1863-1867*. Gettysburg: Thomas Publications, 1990.

McBride, David. *Integrating the City of Medicine: Blacks in Philadelphia Health Care, 1910-1965*. Philadelphia: Temple University Press, 1989.

Office of the Deputy Assistant Secretary of Defense for Civilian Personnel Policy/Equal Opportunity. *Black Americans in Defense of Our Nation*. Department of Defense,1991.

Pennsylvania Negro Business Directory, 1910: Industrial and Material Growth of the Negroes of Pennsylvania. Harrisburg: Jas. H. W. Howard, 1910.

Redkey Edwin S. *A Grand Army of Black Men-Letters from African-American Soldiers in the Union Army, 1861-1865*. New York: Cambridge University Press, 1992.

Trussell, John B. B. *The Pennsylvania Line: Regimental Organization and Operations, 1775-1783*. Harrisburg: Pennsylvania Historical and Museum Commission, 1993.

Winch, Julie. *Philadelphia's Black Elite: Activism, Accommodation, and the Struggle for Autonomy, 1787-1848*. Philadelphia: Temple University Press, 1988.

Researchers desiring a more comprehensive overview of the holdings of the State Archives and information about search room hours and reprographic and staff services should consult the Commissionís web site at www.phmc.state.pa.us or write to the reference staff at Division of Archives and Manuscripts, Post Office Box 1026, Harrisburg, PA 17108-1026. Though the web site information includes a summary list of all government records series and manuscript collections readily available for public inspection, researchers may want to clarify their research needs and interests prior to visiting the State Archives. The Archives is located at the corner of Third and Forster Streets in Harrisburg adjacent to The State Museum of Pennsylvania.

The completion of this guide is the result of the efforts of many dedicated staff members of the Pennsylvania State Archives, summer interns and volunteers. The initial seed for this publication was planted by the Commission's Black History Advisory Committee and approved by Brent D. Glass, the Pennsylvania Historical and Museum Commission's executive director. Harry E. Whipkey, former director of the Bureau of Archives and History; and Frank M. Suran, current director of the Bureau of Archives and History and State Archivist, oversaw the process of compiling this work, along with Harry F. Parker, chief, Division of Archives and Manuscripts, and Jonathan R. Stayer, head, Reference Section. I am especially grateful to Jonathan R. Stayer, Anne Marie Ickes, Sharon Nelson, and Willis Shirk for their editorial expertise which contributed significantly toward the completion of this guide. Acknowledgment is also due to other members of the staff of the Division of Archives and Manuscripts for their contribution: John Clark, Heidi Mays, Adam McKay, Linda Ries, John Shelly, Michael Sherbon, David Shoff, and Eric Ledell Smith of the Division of History. The following summer interns worked on the project: Jennifer Coleman, Cory Daly, Patricia Derstine, Kenton Emlet, Jay Lowris, Bethany Mummert, Cary Summers, Charlisa Summers and Andrea Wilson. Mary Lou Harris and Marcus Lee Hodge worked as volunteers in pulling boxes and cartons, researching and photocopying pertinent information. The staff of the Commission's Division of Publications, including Diane Reed, division chief, Harold

Myers, and Susan Gahres provided design, production and editorial services. My sincere thanks and appreciation to each of you. It has been a most rewarding, enriching, and gratifying experience for me.

Ruth E. Hodge
Associate Archivist

RECORD GROUPS

RG-1. RECORDS OF THE DEPARTMENT OF AGRICULTURE

The Department of Agriculture was created in 1895 to encourage the development of agriculture, horticulture, forestry, and related industries. A State Board of Agriculture, which had been established in 1876 to investigate subjects relating to improvements in agriculture, continued to function along with the department in an advisory capacity. Legislation passed in 1919 and 1923 abolished the State Board of Agriculture, the Agricultural Commission, and the Livestock Sanitary Board, and consolidated regulatory activities pertaining to agriculture within the department. Functions relating to forestry were transferred to the Department of Forestry in 1901.

The Department of Agriculture is responsible for promoting the efficient marketing of farm products and dealing with appropriate investigative and service problems. The department works to control animal and plant diseases as well as insect pests, and to safeguard the public against impure or misrepresented foods, fertilizers and pesticides. It also promotes the efficient marketing of farm products. The State Farm Products Show Commission and the State Harness Racing Commission are administrative commissions within the Department of Agriculture.

SECRETARY OF AGRICULTURE

Administrative Correspondence, 1941-1956, 1958-1971. (55 cartons) Grouped chronologically and thereunder alphabetically by subject of correspondence. A record of incoming, outgoing, and interdepartmental correspondence between the secretary of Agriculture and his bureau chiefs, department heads, and concerned citizens. The correspondence received and sent by Secretary Leland H. Bull, 1964-1967, contains a considerable amount of material relating to minority groups. Among these items is a 1964 Annual Report on Migrant Labor in Pennsylvania, statistical data on African American farmers in Pennsylvania, and a bibliography entitled *The Negro in the American Experience* and *A Selective List of Books on the Contemporary Negro* issued by The Pennsylvania State Library. Also present are the following booklets: *American History from the Black Viewpoint* by the Council for Human Services, September 1968; *Migrant Health Report, Pa.*, 1965; *Regulation for Migratory Farm Labor by the Department of Labor and Industry.*

Other relevant materials include: transcripts of hearings on Land Grant Colleges that cite agricultural research conducted at Lincoln University, a letter to Secretary Leland H. Bull from William G. Nagel concerning minority employment, a letter from Secretary of Health C. L. Walbor Jr., and miscellaneous letters among which is an invitation and a program from Pennsylvania's Conference to Examine the Effects of Prejudice in State Government held at Allenberry (Boiling Springs, Pa.), September 11-13, 1968. Also present is a letter from the Director of the Bureau of Markets C. W. Ford concerning proposed legislation to establish a minimum wage for migrant workers, a letter to Governor Raymond Shafer regarding a Task Force on Minority Employment, a memorandum on eligibility standards for Pennsylvania's food program for needy families, a *Miami Herald* article entitled "Union Pushes to Organize Migrants," a memorandum on surplus food distribution for migrant workers, a 1965 migrant worker health report for Penn-

RG-1. Department of Agriculture. Bureau of Markets. Lantern Slides. Women at an outside market.

sylvania, and a Pennsylvania State University Poverty Program booklet entitled *The People Left Behind*. The file also contains transcripts of testimony concerning migrant labor that was made before the United States Senate Committee on Labor and Public Welfare, Subcommittee on Migratory Labor, including testimony by James McHale regarding Senate Bill 1019, which was intended to protect the migrant workers. Finally, there are several newsletters and tracts including: *50 Years 1914-1964: The Story of the Erie County Agricultural Extension Association*, *Higher Education and the Black Atypical Student*, and *Focus on the Future: New Dimensions for 4-H and Youth Education in Pa.*

BUREAU OF MARKETS

Glass Lantern Slides of Pennsylvania Bureau of Markets, 1929. **(1 box)** Unarranged. Lantern slides providing interior and exterior views of various public markets in Pennsylvania. While most of the markets are unidentifiable, among the captioned examples are the Lancaster Farmers' Market, Harrisburg's Broad Street Market, and Pittsburgh's South Side and Diamond Markets. Within the

9

collection is a slide that depicts a group of African American women examining produce shown by a salesclerk. Other slides appear to portray African Americans at different market sites.

RG-2. RECORDS OF THE DEPARTMENT OF THE AUDITOR GENERAL

The Office of the Auditor General was created in 1809 to replace and assume many of the duties of the offices of the Comptroller General and the Register General. These offices had been originally created to liquidate claims against the state for services performed during the Revolutionary War and to assist in the final settlement of public accounts. Similarly, the Office of the Escheators General was abolished in 1821, and its duties relative to the estates of individuals dying intestate without heirs or kindred were added to those of the auditor general. The auditor general was made an elective office in 1850 and became a constitutional office with the adoption of the Constitution of 1874. The Fiscal Code of 1929 transferred the function of tax collection from the Department of the Auditor General to the newly created Department of Revenue. Under the code the department became for the first time a true auditing agency.

As the chief auditor of the state's fiscal affairs, the auditor general is responsible for insuring that the Commonwealth receives all moneys to which it is entitled and that public money is spent legally and properly. The auditor general adjusts claims against the Commonwealth, examines the settlements made by the Revenue Department, and oversees the examination of most financial transactions involving the state.

GENERAL ADMINISTRATIVE AND FINANCIAL RECORDS

Index to Churches and Beneficial Societies, transcribed 1841. (1 volume) Arranged alphabetically by name of church or society. This index contains the names of churches and beneficial societies in Pennsylvania. Information provided includes the name of the church or society and occasionally its location. African American churches and beneficial societies listed include: African Benevolent Association, African Methodist Episcopal Church of Columbia, African Zoar Methodist Episcopal Church, Colored Persons Philadelphia Library Company, and the Free Benevolent Sons of Africa.

RECORDS RELATING TO MILITARY SERVICE

Revolutionary War Pension File, 1809-1893. (4 boxes) Arranged alphabetically by surname of pensioner. A record of certifications prepared by the Orphans' Court or the state Supreme Court entitling Revolutionary War veterans and their widows to obtain compensation provided for in the Act of September 22, 1785. Information shown varies with each document. While some certifications only list the soldier's name, residence, and military unit, others also mention wounds suffered by the veteran and his rank, age, and date of enlistment.

An example of an entry for an African American is that of Griffith Smith. According to an affidavit signed by Secretary of War Lewis Cass on January 4, 1834, Smith served with his master, John Young, as an army drummer in the Revolutionary War from 1776 to 1779. As a result of his service, Smith was entitled to receive a pension of $25.60 annually from March 4, 1831 until his death. Included is a statement signed by John Frederick Weinland, Protestant minister of Germantown, certifying that Griffith Smith married Mary Brand on April 16, 1788. Also present is a petition from the General Assembly approving a widow's pension for Mrs.

Smith. Examples of other Revolutionary War pensions listed for African Americans are certificates for Edward Hector, a driver with Courtney's Company of the 4th Continental Artillery, and for Stacey Williams of Humphreys Company, 6th Pennsylvania Regiment.

War of 1812 Pension File, 1866-1896 (bulk 1866-1879). (57 boxes, 26 folders) Arranged alphabetically by surname of pensioner. A record created as a result of the legislative Act of April 30, 1866 that (with subsequent supplemental acts) granted annuities, gratuities or pensions to Pennsylvania soldiers or their widows. The legislation stipulated that the soldier must have served at least two months duty or have been wounded or otherwise disabled during the war. Files contain notarized pension applications submitted by veterans or their widows that generally show the name, signature, residence, rank, regiment, and military unit of each veteran; the name of the officer under whom he served; his period of service; and the approximate dates of his enlistment and honorable discharge. From the 1870s onward the dates of marriages and of veterans' deaths are also frequently recorded. Some applications mention widows' ages.

While many African Americans served in the War of 1812, most ship and station muster rolls do not differentiate between the races. An example of a document that does identify race is the petition for African American Jesse Walls, which includes the application of his widow Myra Walls dated September 24, 1866 for the gratuity and annuity of her husband; an affidavit dated September 26, 1866 signed by Joseph Deamer from Erie stating that Jesse Walls was a seaman who had served as a fifer on board the U.S. Brig *Niagara*; and two letters from Edward Clark dated September 26 and November 5, 1866 also stating his acquaintance with and support of Myra Wall's request and need.

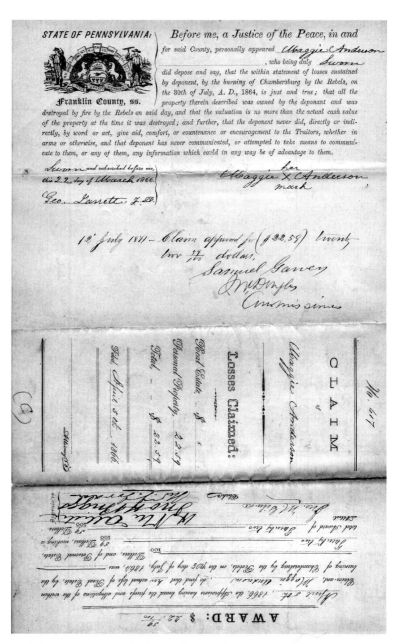

Sworn and subscribed before me, this 22 day of *March* 1866.

Geo. Garrett. J. P.

her
Maggie X Anderson
mark

12 July 1871 – Claim approved for ($22.59) twenty two 59/100 dollars.

Samuel Garver
Wm D. Wyly
Commissioners

CLAIM of Maggie Anderson No. 417

Losses Claimed:

Real Estate – $
Personal Property, 22.59
Total – $ 22.59

Filed April 5th, 1866.

AWARD: $ 22. 59/100

RG-2. Department of the Auditor General. Records Relating to Civil War Border Claims. Damage claim submitted by Jane Anderson.

13

RECORDS RELATING TO CIVIL WAR
BORDER CLAIMS

Chambersburg War Damage Claim Applications Submitted Under Act of February 15, 1866. (4 boxes) Arranged alphabetically by surname of the claimant. Indexed externally by surname of the claimant. See related series **Index to Damage Claim Applications (Submitted Under Acts Passed 1863-1871) [ca. 1871-1879]**. A record of damage claims submitted by citizens who suffered losses during the burning of Chambersburg on July 30, 1864. The applications are itemized accounts of real and personal property lost by each claimant and assign to each item a monetary value. Included are affidavits of witnesses in support of claims, a record of the award allowed each claimant by the 1866 Board of Appraisers and the 1871 commission to re-adjudicate claims, and a record of the pro rata payment given to each claimant in conjunction with the 1866 state appropriation of $500,000 for the relief of Chambersburg citizens who suffered property losses as a result of the rebel invasion.

The following African Americans submitted official claims for losses sustained as a result of the burning of Chambersburg: Jane Anderson, Maggie Anderson, Hannah Davis, John Diggs, Jane Fillkill, Eli Gates, Louisa Gates, Jesse Helm, Mary Ann Hill, Benjamin Hird, Louis/Lewis Jackson, Benjamin Jefferson, Catherine Johnston, Kitty Johnston, Eli Jones, William Jones, John Kelly, Evangeline Lewis, Sarah Mills, Caroline Morgan, Elizabeth Morgan, Louisa Nelson, Nancy Norris, Rebecca Norris, Philip Peterson, Edward Proctor, Benjamin L. Pulpress, Rebecca Robinson, Peter Slater, Charles Smith, Julia A. Standford, Diana Stevenson, Louisa Taylor, Mary Thompson, and Austin Tyler.

Chambersburg War Damage Claim Warrant Stub Books (Per Act of February 15, 1866), 1866. (4 volumes) Arranged numerically by the number of the certificate. Indexed externally by first letter of claimant's surname in the **Record of Chambersburg War Damage Final Awards Issued Under Act of February 15, 1866**. Receipts for payments that were made to Chambersburg claimants from the $500,000 appropriated by the state in 1866. Information includes the name of the claimant, the number of the certificate, the date of the payment, and the amount of the payment.

Damage Claim Applications (Submitted Under Acts Passed 1863-1871), 1871-1879. (53 boxes) Arranged by county and thereunder alphabetically by surname of claimant. A record of damage claims of residents of Adams, Bedford, Cumberland, Franklin, Fulton, and York Counties. Each application consists of a handwritten petition and a printed form called an "Abstract of Application For Damage" (primarily relating to the Acts of April 9, 1868 and May 22, 1871). Information shown includes the claim number and filing date; the name and residence (county and township) of the applicant; an inventory of the personal property and real estate lost or damaged; the estimated monetary loss incurred; and the amount and date of the award granted. Particulars, such as the names of Southern commanders responsible for the damage, are sometimes noted.

Index to Damage Claim Applications (Submitted Under Acts Passed 1863-1871), [ca. 1871-1879]. (1 volume) Arranged by alphabetically by county, and thereunder alphabetically by surname of the claimant. An index of all border raid damage claims from the counties of Adams, Bedford, Cumberland, Franklin, Fulton, and York. There is also a supplemental section concerning claims from the burning of Chambersburg that were filed separately from the rest of the border county claims. The following information for each claim is provided: the date of filing, the date of appearance, the claim number, the name of applicant, the address of applicant, the original claim under the Act of 1868, the original award under the Act of 1868, the real and personal property award under the Act of May 22, 1871, the certificate number (first or second series), the name of the attorney or assignee, the name of the administrator, and any remarks. The Chambersburg entries have additional information regarding payment amounts issued pro rata to claimants in pursuance of state appropriations of $500,000 and $300,000 in 1866 and 1871, respectively. The names of the African Americans cited under **Chambersburg War Damage Claim Applications Submitted Under Act of February 15, 1866** are included in this register.

Index to Issued War Damages Adjudicated Claim Certificates, 1872-1879. (1 volume) Grouped alphabetically by the first letter of the claimant's surname. This index lists those claimants who actually received their adjudicated claim certificates, even though the claimants never received any compensation from the federal government. Information provided includes the claimant's name and the corresponding certificate number. All of the African Americans named in the above mentioned **War Damage Adjudicated Claim Certificates** are included.

Index to Unissued War Damages Adjudicated Claim Certificates, 1872-1897. (1 volume) Grouped alphabetically by the first letter of the claimant's surname. This index lists those claimants for which adjudicated claim certificates were prepared, but were never issued. Consequently, these certificates remained in the auditor general's department. Information provided includes the claimant's name and the corresponding unissued certificate number. The following individuals are some African Americans who were not issued damage claim certificates: #25: Jane Anderson; #604: Benjamin Jefferson; #599: Lewis Jackson; #887: Benjamin Pulpress; and #1623: Louisa Taylor.

Record of Chambersburg War Damage Claim Final Awards Issued Under Act of February 15, 1866, 1866. (1 volume) Grouped alphabetically by the first letter of the surname of the claimant. A record of the pro rata payment that each Chambersburg claimant received as a result of the $500,000 state appropriation. Information in each entry includes the following information: claim number, name of the claimant, total amount claimed (in real and personal property), number of the warrant, total amount awarded (in real and personal property), and the pro rata amount received. Claim file numbers in this volume include those for such African American claimants as #617: Maggie Anderson; #594: Hannah Davis; #630: John Diggs.

War Damage Adjudicated Claim Certificates, 1872-1879. (6 boxes) Arranged numerically by certificate number. Indexed externally in two separate volumes by the first letter of the claimant's surname: the **Index to Issued War Damage Adjudicated Claim Certificates, 1872-1879** and the **Index to Unissued War Damage Adjudicated Claim Certificates, 1872-1897**. This series documents Pennsylvania's pledge to liquidate damages sustained by all claimants within the border counties. Pursuant to the Act of May 22, 1871, claimants were to receive certificates that validated their adjudicated awards within the state. Certificates were to be redeemed for their monetary value only when the federal government appropriated money for the relief of the claimants. However, not all the certificates actually made it into the hands of the claimants. Moreover, the ones that were issued proved worthless, as the federal government never allocated money to Pennsylvania for the relief of its citizens. Information found on the certificates includes the claimant's name, the certificate number, the amount of the claim, and the date the certificate was prepared. The certificates also contain the signatures of the state auditor general, the governor, and the state treasurer. The following individuals are examples of African Americans for which claim certificates were made out: #250: Hannah Davis; #254: John Diggs; #384: Jane Fillkill; #455: Louisa Gates; #457: Eli Gates; and #579: Mary A. Hill.

RG-3. RECORDS OF THE CIVIL SERVICE COMMISSION

The Civil Service Commission was created in 1939 and activated by the Civil Service Act of 1941 to promote greater efficiency and economy in government by applying merit system methods and principles to state personnel management. Civil Service had come into existence in Pennsylvania with the passage of the Liquor Control Act of 1933 that required the Liquor Control Board to select personnel under a merit system administered by the Department of Public Instruction. By 1937, two additional personnel agencies were created to administer merit systems: the Employment Board for the Department of Public Assistance and the Board of Review for the Division of Unemployment Compensation and Employment Service in the Department of Labor and Industry. The boards operated independently until the Civil Service Commission was given the authority to operate a unified program in 1941.

The Civil Service commission is a regulatory and investigative and enforcement body charged with carrying out the provisions of the Civil Service Act as amended. The commission recruits and examines job applicants, certifies employment and promotion lists, and hears appeals against actions of appointing authorities.

EXECUTIVE OFFICE

Records Relating to the Administration of Merit Systems of the Civil Service Commission and the Departments of Public Assistance and Labor and Industry, 1926-1966. (1 box)

Unarranged. These records include a classification system for positions held by civil service employees of the Commonwealth, administrative records of the Department of Labor and Industry, the Unemployment Compensation Board of Review, and the Employment Board of the Department of Public Assistance. Items related to African Americans include a booklet entitled *A Classification of the Positions Held by Employees in the Service of the Commonwealth of Pennsylvania in State-Owned Institutions*, 1936, which deals with requirements imposed upon state teachers colleges and the Cheyney Training School for Teachers. This booklet contains several photographs of African Americans. Among the records are photographs of the following Civil Service Commission employees at a National Association for the Advancement of Colored People conference: Agnes Peterson, Arlene Richardson, Rhona Ross, William "Mike" Leftwich, Linda Ashby, Louise Williams, Joyce Finley, Karen Sellers, Mel Robinson, Valeria Borrow, George "Toby" Young, and Mary Jiggetts. There is also is a photograph of a reception for Chairman Ethel S. Barrett, June 15, 1978. Ethel S. Barrett was the first African American to hold the position of chairman of the Civil Service Commission. Other photographic subjects in the files include Nancy Carter, Wilma Jones, Charles Lewis, Maude Penn, William D. Johnson, and Betty Anderson.

RG-4. RECORDS OF THE OFFICE OF THE COMPTROLLER GENERAL

The Office of the Comptroller General was created in 1782 to audit, liquidate and adjust Commonwealth accounts. After settlement, all public accounts were submitted to the Supreme Executive Council for approval. If satisfied, the council drew warrants upon the state treasurer for their payment. In 1785, appeals were allowed to the Supreme Court from the settlement of accounts by the comptroller general after the settlement had been transmitted to the Supreme Executive Council. In 1789, the comptroller general was required to submit for inspection and examination all accounts to be adjusted to the newly created Register General's Office and to take his advice and assistance in settling these accounts. The following year the duties of the two offices were reversed in that all accounts, except those specifically assigned for examination by the state treasurer, were to be examined and adjusted by the register general and then submitted to the comptroller general for his advice and approval. Under specific legislation passed in 1791 all responsibilities not inconsistent with the Constitution of 1790 for the final settlement of accounts, previously assigned to the Supreme Executive Council, were transferred to the governor. Changes were also made in 1791 in the procedures for adjusting accounts so that the comptroller general and register general had to submit accounts to the governor for final approval where they differed in opinion. When they agreed, only the balance due on each account had to be certified to the governor. Though further modifications in the methods of adjusting and settling accounts were made, it was not until 1809 that the Office of the Comptroller General was abolished and its duties transferred to the auditor general and state treasurer.

Pierce's Certificate Accounts, Consisting of Pay Roll Books, Voucher Indexes, Ownership Certificates, and an Account of Certificates Loaned to the United States, Signed by John Pierce and Relating to the Issuance of Interest Bearing Certificates to the Pennsylvania Line, [ca. 1784-1793]. (3 volumes, 1 box)

- Pay Roll Book, Volume A, 1778-1883, contains entries for the following African Americans: John Francis, Stace Williams, and Cezar Negro. The entries include the following date issued, certificate number and letter, name, amount of payment, and signature or mark.

- Pay Roll Book, Index for Volumes A and B, lists the names of the following African American Revolutionary War soldiers: Levi Burns, 10th Pennsylvania Infantry Regiment; John Francis, Epple's Company, 3rd Pennsylvania Regiment; and Stace Williams, Humphrey's Company, 6th Pennsylvania Regiment. In addition to the soldiers' names this volume provides the number of payments and the amounts to be paid.

- Pay Roll Book, Volume B, 1778-1883, includes an entry for African American Levi Burns, giving the same information as cited for Volume A.

Revolutionary War Associators, Line, Militia, and Navy Accounts, and Miscellaneous Records Relating to Military Service, 1775-1809. (99 boxes)

Navy Accounts, 1775-1794. (**6 boxes**) Grouped according to stations of duty, and arranged thereunder chronologically by date of record. Muster and pay rolls that usually give the name, rank, station and pay rate of the sailor, the period of his service, and the dates of his entry and discharge or desertion. The age of the individual is occasionally recorded as well. Included in this series are muster rolls for the various vessels that were a part of the Pennsylvania Navy, 1776-1780. Among the African Americans included on these muster rolls are "Negro Prince" and "Negro Charles," who are listed as serving on the *Ranger* commanded by John Marshall and "Negro Caesar," a drummer for Commander Thomas Houston, who served on the *Warren.*

Revolutionary War Pension Files and Related Accounts, 1785-1809. (8 boxes, 5 volumes) A record documenting pensions paid to Pennsylvania veterans of the Revolutionary War. This group of

RG-4. Office of the Comptroller General. Revolutionary War Pension Files and Related Accounts, 1785-1809. Pension Certificate for John Francis.

records includes the following materials: Pension File, 1785-1809; Pension Index Book A, 1790-1791; Pension Indexes to [Books] 1 and 2; Pension Ledger, Book 1, 1785-1789; Pension Ledger, Book B, 1790-1793, including index; and Pension Ledger, Book C, 1794-1804, including an alphabetical index prepared for reference purposes. The Index to Pension Ledger, Book 1, 1785-1789 is arranged alphabetically by surname of pensioner. An incomplete record of disabled line and militia soldiers granted pensions on orders from the orphans' court under the Act of September 22, 1785. Entries usually provide the name, age, rank and corps of soldier; the period of the pension; the amount of pension received; and a brief statement of how, when, and where the disability occurred.

Related Pension Accounts. Arranged alphabetically by surname of pensioner. Miscellaneous documents relating to Revolutionary War veterans' pensions. Included is a reference to the pension of an African American by the name of John Francis. According to the certificate, John Francis was "a Negro man aged about fifty years . . . [who] had both his legs injured at the Battle of Brandywine on the 11th September 1777," entitling him to receive a pension of three dollars a month for one year.

Tax and Exoneration Lists, 1762-1801. (47 boxes) Arranged by county, and thereunder according to political subdivision. The surnames appearing on the lists are grouped alphabetically by first letter. Lists consisting of diverse data acquired from tax (supply taxes, carriage and billiard table taxes, property returns, etc.) and exoneration returns for Allegheny, Bedford, Berks, Bucks, Chester, Cumberland, Dauphin, Fayette, Franklin, Huntingdon, Lancaster, Montgomery, Northampton, Northumberland, Philadelphia, Washington, Westmoreland, and York Counties. Depending upon the year and the type of returns, these dated lists provide such information as the name of the taxpayer, place of residence (county and township) and the type of trade in which engaged, the number of acres and type (patent, warrant, and improved) of land possessed, the number of cattle, horses and slaves owned, the tax rate, and the tax assessment. Frequently the lists also indicate whether the individual was a single free man and the valuations of distilleries, sawmills, and gristmills. Listings of slaves are found in some of the counties, including Berks, Bucks, and Cumberland.

PORT OF PHILADELPHIA RECORDS

Bonds and Papers Relating to Duties on Negro and Mulatto Slaves, 1720-1788. (1 folder) Arranged chronologically. This series documents the duties that were paid on "negro" and "mulatto" slaves imported to the City of Philadelphia. Information provided in these records includes the name of the owner(s) and the collector, the amount of duty paid, any interest incurred, and the date of the contract. Occasionally, the name of the slave is also given. These papers were originally prepared by an agent of the British crown until the Commonwealth of Pennsylvania assumed this responsibility after the Revolutionary War.

Records of the Wardens of the Port, 1776-1809. (2 boxes) Arranged chronologically by date of entry. Included in these records are accounts of work performed and the number of days charged for the board of employees at the port. The following account information pertains to African Americans:

- The accounts of Abraham Hargis for work performed on February 26, 1784 show that "Negroe Peter" was due sixteen shillings. On August 26, 1784, "Negro Jack" was listed as being due one pound and the entry ends with the statement "charge for Negro Peter getting firewood not allowed."
- The accounts for Abraham Hargis for boarding his workers in 1784 contain the following "Negro Cooper, 2 weeks; Negro Sampson, 2 days; Negro Peter, 4 days; Hired Negroes, 1 week, 2 days; board for Mr. Hazard's Negro, 2 weeks, 4 days; and board of Negro Jack, 2 weeks, 2 days." A similar account for boarded Negroes in 1784 is signed by John Pearson.
- The accounts for the contingent expenses of government for 1784 under David Rittenhouse include the following for April 26: "Negro Hampshire for sweeping the office, earned seven shillings, 6 pence." An entry for May 26 shows Hampshire earned fifteen shillings for attending the office and an entry for November 23 reveals he earned seven shillings and 6 pence for sweeping the office and fifteen shillings and 6 pence for attending the office.

Registers of Duties Paid on Imported Goods, 1781-1787. (6 volumes) Arranged chronologically by import date. Recorded at the port of Philadelphia, an entry usually gives the name of the vessel's master, the port of origin, the value of the goods imported, the name of the importer, and the duty paid. A brief description of the cargo also appears in most cases. Many of the ships transported either free or enslaved "Negroes" both before and during this period. (Refer also to Record Group 41, **Health Officer's Register of Passengers' Names, 1792-1794.**)

RG-5. RECORDS OF THE CONSTITU- TIONAL CONVENTIONS AND THE COUN- CIL OF CENSORS

Four constitutional conventions have been held since the first convention drafted the Constitution of 1776. These succeeding convention, convened in 1789, 1837, 1874, and 1967, were held in response to demands for sweeping changes to the existing constitution. Procedures for the convening of constitutional conventions have varied. The 1776 and 1789 conventions were held without any prior approval by the general electorate.

The 1776 Provincial Convention was held as a result of a calling by a conference of extra-legal Committees of Correspondence. The resulting constitution provided for an elected body known as the Council of Censors to serve as a check on the executive and legislative branches. The council was to be elected every seven years, and was to convene for a period of one year. The council was given the authority to censure public officials, order impeachment, recommend the repeal of legislation, and if necessary, call for a convention to amend the constitution. This machinery for constitutional revision was ignored in 1789 when the General Assembly called for a constitutional convention. All provisions for the Council of Censors were omitted from the Constitution of 1790

RG-5. Records of the Constitutional Conventions and the Council of Censors. Memorial of free citizens of color in Pittsburgh and its vicinity relative to the right of suffrage, 1837.

and from subsequent constitutions.

A new constitution that was adopted and signed in 1838 reduced the governor's appointive powers, increased the number of elective offices, shortened terms of office, and disenfranchised free African Americans. The Constitution of 1874 provided for popular election of judges, the state treasurer, and the auditor general; created the office of lieutenant governor and the Department of Internal Affairs; and created the position of Superintendent of Public Instruction to head the public school system. This constitution also lengthened the governor's term to four years but stipulated that a governor could no longer succeed himself, and gave the governor veto power over individual items within appropriations bills. Under this constitution the sessions of the General Assembly became biennial, the membership in the Assembly was increased and its powers were limited by a prohibition of special or local legislation on certain specified subjects and a constitutional debt limit was established.

CONSTITUTIONAL CONVENTION OF 1837-1838

Journals, 1837-1838. (8 boxes) Each journal is arranged chronologically by date of convention meeting. Journals that document the activities of the Constitutional Convention of 1837-1838. The dates are May 23-31, 1837; June 1-30, 1837; July 1-Oct. 31, 1837; Nov. 1-30, 1837; Jan. 1-16, 1838; Jan. 17-Feb. 7, 1838; Feb. 8-22, 1838; and undated.

- *Journal, July 8, 1837* includes a report titled *Memorial of the Free Citizens of Color in Pittsburgh and Its Vicinity Relative to the Right of Suffrage*. The report was prepared by a committee appointed by the "coloured citizens" of the City of Pittsburgh on June 13, 1837. It "was read, and unanimously adopted, in a public meeting of the free coloured citizens of Pittsburgh, and ordered to accompany their memorial to the

Convention of 1837." The memorial was signed by Lewis Woodson, secretary of the Free Coloured Citizens of Pittsburgh, and John B. Vashon, of Pittsburgh, Joseph Mahonney, of Allegheny town, Samuel Reynolds and Thomas Knox, of Arthursville, as well as other committee members. Included are other memorial petitions to the convention. Many of these petitions requested a hange in the constitution to recognize the rights of African Americans as legal residents of Pennsylvania and as citizens of the United States, while others petitioned against the "amalgamation" of the races.

CONSTITUTIONAL CONVENTION OF 1967-1968

Records of the Information Office, 1967-1968. (39 folders, 1 volume) Records kept by the Convention's Information Office, which distributed information about convention activities to the media. Included are copies of the *Convention Reporter,* a daily newsletter that documented the progress of the convention; copies of news releases and radio tape scripts; newspaper articles having source and date notations; and a color film entitled *A Living Constitution.* Among the items present are the following:

> *Directory of Delegates.* Contains photographs and bio-graphical information on such African Americans as Philadelphia Democrat William H. Gray, a minister and member of the Civil Service Commission, and Pittsburgh attorney K. Leroy Irvis, a Democratic speaker of the Pennsylvania House of Representatives in 1977, 1983-1987.

> *Convention Reporter, Pennsylvania Constitutional Convention, 1967-1968.* Papers prepared for each day of the convention including many articles on African Americans in Pennsylvania. Representative of some of these articles are the December 13, 1967 issue which contains an article about Jimmy

Jones who rewrote football history as a high school quarter-back. The 175 pound all-star from John Harris High School in Harrisburg served as a page for four days at the Pennsylvania Constitutional Convention. The January 8, 1968 issue contains a proposal introduced by African American delegate K. Leroy Irvis recommending that all state-related or state-aided institutions of higher learning be placed on "preferred" status, making them a part of the General Appropriation Budget each year. In the January 30, 1964 issue an article entitled "Convention Harmony" describes a special concert given by the Sixty-four-member Bright Hope Baptist Church Choir of Philadelphia, pastored by delegate William H. Gray Jr.

RG-6. RECORDS OF THE DEPARTMENT OF FORESTS AND WATERS

The Department of Forests and Waters was created under the Administrative Code of 1923 to consolidate the functions of the Department of Forestry, the Water Supply Commission, and the Bureau of Topographic and Geologic Survey. An outgrowth of the Office of Forest Commissioner, this agency was originally established as the Division of Forestry in the Department of Agriculture in 1895 and became the Department of Forestry in 1901. It was responsible for acquiring and managing state forest lands, developing state parks and roads, improving waterways, protecting the Commonwealth's water supply, supervising flood control projects, and protecting state-owned and private forest lands. The Department of Forests and Waters was absorbed by the Department of Environmental Resources in 1971.

PUBLIC RELATIONS OFFICE

Photographs and Negatives, [ca. 1890-1971]. (16 cartons, 1 box, 36 file drawers) Grouped chronologically. The following photo-

RG-6. Department of Forests and Waters. Public Relations Office. E.C.W. Camp, Licking Creek, Rothrock State Forest, May 1933.

graphs and negatives were issued by and under the Department of Forests and Waters and its predecessors:

> *Pennsylvania Department of Forestry.* A photograph shows the dedication ceremony of the Forest Academy (Conklin Hall), at Mont Alto, Franklin County, Pennsylvania. Mrs. G. H. Wirt, wife of G. H. Wirt, the first Director of the Pennsylvania Department of Forestry, laid the cornerstone for the academy. An African American is among the group of men surrounding her.

> *Pennsylvania Department of Forests and Waters.* There are many photographs of the Energy Conservation Work Camp at Licking Creek, Mifflin County, Rothrock State Forest, May 1933, featuring African Americans. Included is a photograph of Energy Conservation Workers, some of whom are African Americans, grading a road by hand at Clear Run Road, Jefferson County, Pennsylvania. There is also a photograph of a Civilian

Conservation Camp at Pine Grove Furnace, Cumberland County, Michaux State Forest District, May 1933, showing African Americans at temporary quarters and the mess tent.

RG-7. RECORDS OF THE GENERAL ASSEMBLY

Legislative power is vested in a General Assembly, which consists of a Senate and a House of Representatives. The General Assembly has the authority to enact laws, appropriate funds and levy taxes. Additional powers of the legislature include the proposal of constitutional amendments, the impeachment of public officials, investigative authority, and the confirmation of certain executive appointments. The state's original General Assembly was a unicameral body established under the Constitution of 1776 that was given vast powers that enabled it to dominate the other two branches of state government. This imbalance was corrected with the adoption of subsequent constitutions, beginning with the Constitution of 1790, which created a bicameral assembly and a popularly elected governor.

HOUSE OF REPRESENTATIVES

House File, 1790-1903. (66 boxes, 1 carton) Arranged chronologically. This series documents the legislative activity of the House of Representatives through petitions, reports, bills, and amendments. Items in the House files pertaining to African Americans include: two petitions signed by three hundred citizens of Washington County requesting a law to prohibit "negroes" from coming into the state, March 5, 1863; a petition from the citizens of Schuylkill County requesting an Act to prevent the migration of "negroes" into Pennsylvania, March 9, 1863; a petition from the citizens of Schuylkill County in favor of a law to prohibit "negroes" from coming into Pennsylvania to reside, March 20, 1863; a petition from 310 citizens of Clearfield County requesting the passage of a "law to prevent negroes from coming within our borders, also to prevent the intermarrying of the whites and blacks, and for the severe punishment of anyone performing the marriage ceremony," March 20, 1863; and 13 petitions from the citizens of Washington County praying for the passage of a law prohibiting the immigration of "Negroes and Mulattos" into the state of Pennsylvania, July 24, 1863. This flurry of 1863 legislation was probably introduced in response to an expected influx of African Americans from various seceded states freed under the provisions of Abraham Lincoln's Emancipation Proclamation. There are also two petitions from the citizens of Chester County protesting the fugitive slave laws and opposing any aid being offered to slave owners seeking to recover their slave property or allowing slave owners from slave states to retain their slaves while residing in Pennsylvania.

Septennial Census Returns, 1779-1863. (13 boxes, 2 bundles) Arranged chronologically by date of census and thereunder alphabetically by county. No state censuses were ever conducted in Pennsylvania. The so-called Septennial Census Returns, 1779-1863, merely enumerated taxpayers every seven years for the purpose of determining representation in the General Assembly. Only a few (11 percent) of these records have survived, and usually they list only the name, and sometimes the occupation, of each taxable white inhabitant. Data concerning slaves residing in the counties is often more extensive in content. Beginning with the year 1800, the name, age, gender, and residence of each slave is frequently noted, and occasionally even the owner's name is provided. The State Archives has original returns for thirty counties and the city of Philadelphia. Inhabitants are listed according to township or other political subdivision in which they resided. The following is a list of the counties and years of the census returns that contain references to African Americans:

- Bedford: 1779, 1786, 1800
- Berks: 1779, 1786, 1793, 1800
- Bucks: 1786, 1800
- Chester: 1786, 1793, 1800, 1807, 1814
- Columbia: 1821
- Cumberland: 1793, 1800, 1828, 1835, 1842, 1849
- Dauphin: 1786, 1800, 1807
- Delaware: 1793, 1800
- Fayette: 1786, 1800
- Franklin: 1786, 1800, 1807, 1814, 1821, 1828, 1835, 1842
- Huntingdon: 1800, 1821
- Lancaster: 1779, 1786, 1793, 1800
- Luzerne: 1800
- Lycoming: 1800
- Mifflin: 1821
- Montgomery: 1786, 1793, 1800, 1807, 1842
- Northampton: 1786, 1800
- Northumberland: 1800
- Philadelphia: 1793, 1800, 1863
- Somerset: 1800
- Washington: 1786, 1800
- Wayne: 1800
- Westmoreland: 1786, 1800
- Wyoming: 1849
- York: 1786, 1793, 1800, 1807

RG-9. RECORDS OF THE GENERAL STATE AUTHORITY

The General State Authority, a separate independent public corporation and governmental body, was created in 1935 to enable the Commonwealth to circumvent constitutional restrictions on its borrowing capacity. Since the state could not legally take advantage of federal grant and loan offers from the Public Works Administration, the authority was given the responsibility of negotiating for the funds needed to expand and modernize state government facilities. The objective of the authority was to build new units and remodel old ones, and then lease them to the state government until the end of their amortization period, at which time they would be turned over to the Commonwealth. The General State Authority was abolished in 1945, but the need for additional state facilities led to the creation of another General State Authority in 1949 for the purpose of "constructing, improving, equipping, furnishing, maintaining, acquiring, and operating" a wide range of public works. The Department of General Services was created in 1975 to take over the responsibilities of both the General State Authority and the Department of Property and Supplies. However, the authority continues to function as an independent public corporation until the outstanding debt from the bond proceeds spent on earlier projects is retired.

Construction Photographs and Blueprints, 1932-1939. (10 boxes, 4 folders) Arranged numerically by docket number. This series contains 8"x10" photographic prints depicting the construction, expansion, or modernization of various Commonwealth properties. The prints are labeled with the job and docket number and the subjects are almost all exterior views of construction in progress at Pennsylvania National Guard armories, hospitals, teachers colleges, prisons and other state buildings. No original negatives are present. Institutions affiliated with African Americans are:

- Teachers Colleges: Cheyney State University (first established as a school for African Americans).
- Prisons/ Industrial Homes and Schools: State Orphanages for

Soldiers' Children (a number of them accommodated children of African American soldiers) and several state hospitals and penitentiaries.

RG-10. RECORDS OF THE OFFICE OF THE GOVERNOR

The Constitution of 1790 and succeeding constitutions have placed supreme executive power in the Office of the Governor. As the chief executive officer of the Commonwealth, the governor is responsible for directing and supervising the activities of the administrative departments, boards and commissions under his authority in order to insure the faithful execution of the laws of the Commonwealth. The governor is the commander-in-chief of the military forces of the state, except when they are called into federal service. Legislative and judicial powers, including the remission of fines, the commutation of sentences, the granting of reprieves and pardons in conjunction with the recommendations of the Board of Pardons, and the right to veto bills of the General Assembly, are vested with the chief executive. The governor is also responsible for submitting the state budget for consideration by the legislature. Though Senate confirmation is required for some appointments, either directly or indirectly, the governor controls the appointment of patronage positions within the majority of state administrative agencies. The governor is elected for a four-year term and may succeed him or herself for an additional term.

Please Note: While the organizational units supporting the Governor's Office, such as the Secretary of Administration, Office of the Budget, Governor's Council on Drug and Alcohol Abuse, etc., have always been scheduled and accessioned by the State Archives under Record Group 10, it has only been since the administration of Governor Robert Casey that the actual records of the governor have been dealt with in that manner. Another exception is the **Correspondence and Issue Files** of Governor Hartranft, which were microfilmed and placed in RG-10. For the records of other governors please refer to the list of Manuscript Groups.

GOVERNOR JOHN F. HARTRANFT, 1873-1879

Correspondence and Issue Files, 1870-1879. (2 microfilm rolls) Arranged alphabetically by individual or subject. A record of incoming correspondence to Governor Hartranft. Included is a letter from Samuel J. Levok dated November 17, 1876 written on letterhead paper of the Pennsylvania Society for the Prevention of Cruelty to Animals, Philadelphia. The letter states, "Thine of 17th was rec'd today in reply will gladly give thee a verbatim copy of thy letter. Should the American people honour me with the high trust of presiding over them, I will endeavor to be just to all classes, without distinction of race, color or previous condition. My services in the field during the entire war ought to be a guarantee that I would not permit the black man to be enslaved or oppressed by unfriendly legislation."

GOVERNOR ROBERT P. CASEY, 1987-1994

Files of the Secretary for Legislative Affairs, 1987-1994. (16 cartons) The Office of Legislative Affairs serves as the principal representative of the Office of the Governor in all issues and activities related to the legislative process of the General Assembly.

Legislator File. This file, arranged alphabetically by surname of member of the Pennsylvania House of Representatives or of the Senate, contains incoming correspondence to the governor and copies of responses sent by the secretary for Legislative Affairs. The following African Americans are examples of some of the legislators who served during the Casey administration:

- Roxanne H. Jones, first African American woman elected to the state Senate, Nov. 1984; Philadelphia; 3rd District.
- Chaka Fattah, elected to the House of Representatives, 1983-88 and the state Senate, 1988; Philadelphia; 7th District.
- Andrew J. Carn, elected to the House of Representatives, Nov. 2, 1982; Philadelphia; 197th District.
- Dwight Evans, elected to the House of Representatives, Nov. 4, 1980; Philadelphia County-203 District; Democratic Appropriations Chairman.
- Harold James, elected to the House of Representatives, 1988; Philadelphia; 186th District.
- K. Leroy Irvis, elected to the House of Representatives, 1959-1988; Allegheny County; first African American to be Speaker of the House, 1977, 1983-1987.
- Thaddeus Kirkland, elected to the House of Representatives, Nov. 1992; Delaware County; 159th District.

General Correspondence, 1986-1995. (169 cartons, 1 box) Arranged alphabetically by correspondents' last name or by subject. Correspondence received by the Governor's Office and copies of the responses prepared by the appropriate agencies or staff. Topics relating to African Americans include: Black History Month, Ramona Africa, Governor's Advisory Committee on African Americans, African-American History Month, National Convention for African-American Students in Higher Education, African Heritage Month, Afro-American Historical and Cultural Museum in Philadelphia, Cheyney University (several regarding the financial state of the university), and Freedom Day Proclamations.

General Correspondence: Responses Signed by the Governor, 1986-1995. (12 cartons) Organized alphabetically by correspondent's last name or by subject. Incoming and copies of outgoing correspondence signed by the governor. The following items relate to African Americans:

- Martin Luther King Jr.: Correspondence regarding the Martin Luther King Jr. celebration. Included is a letter from Coretta Scott King asking for Governor Casey's support in expanding the Martin Luther King Jr. Federal Holiday Commission.
- The Harriet Tubman Historical Society: Letter written from the Harriet Tubman Historical Society to the United States Conference of Governors regarding the Presidential Medal of Freedom. Governor Casey responded with a letter written to President William J. Clinton supporting the posthumous awarding of a Presidential Medal of Freedom to Harriet Tubman.
- OIC International, 1989: Correspondence from Governor Casey supporting the efforts of Dr. Leon H. Sullivan and the Opportunities Industrialization Center International. Also included is a copy of the 1987 OIC Annual Report.

Issues File, 1987-1994. (213 cartons, 36 card boxes) Grouped by item, and thereunder arranged alphabetically by topic. Correspondence received by the Governor's Office dealing with topics of special public interest that generated a large volume of mail and were given special handling by the staff. Due to the volume, this file was maintained separately from the general correspondence file. The following are examples of issues associated with African Americans:

- Mumia Abu-Jamal: Correspondence written to Governor Casey regarding the imprisonment of Mumia Abu-Jamal and his death sentence.
- Philadelphia City Finances: Correspondence written to Governor Casey regarding the financial difficulties of the city of Philadelphia under the administration of Mayor Wilson Goode.

- Scotland School for Veterans Children: Correspondence written to Governor Casey regarding the February 1991 announcement of closing the Scotland School for Veterans' Children. Approximately 80 percent of the school's enrollment were African American children. "My mother had to convince several prominent people to assist her in getting me admitted to SSVC," wrote Felicenne H. Ramey, associate dean for Academic Affairs at California State University, Sacramento. "This was no small feat for a poor single 'colored' woman at that time. She was very pleased when she heard that I was accepted . . . I strongly recommend that you not cut Scotland's budget."

Proclamations, 1987-1995. (4 cartons) Official Proclamations issued by the governor that are associated with African Americans regard such topics as: Martin Luther King Jr. Day, Freedom Day, Black History Month and African American History Month

SECRETARY OF ADMINISTRATION

The Office of Administration is administered by the secretary of administration. The office serves as staff support to the governor in providing policy direction and administrative support to all agencies under the governor's jurisdiction. Robert K. Bloom served as secretary of administration from 1967 to 1971 and C. Delores Tucker served in this office from 1971 to 1979.

General Correspondence, 1969-1979. (36 cartons, 4 folders) Arranged alphabetically by topic and thereunder chronologically by date of correspondence. Incoming and outgoing correspondence of the secretary of administration for the years 1969-1979. Materials relating to African Americans include: Affirmative Action Council Minutes (1972-1973); Affirmative Action-Office of Administration records; Affirmative Action Plan, 1973, and Management Directives and Administrative Circulars, 1971-1976. Also present are materials on the American Foundation for Negro Affairs, 1974-1978; the Black Affairs Center, 1975; the Black American Racers, Inc., 1975; the Black Legislative Caucus, 1974-1978; "Black Men in Motion," 1975; statistical reports compiled by Black Opinion Research and Evaluation, Inc., 1977; the Black Perspective on the News, 1976; the Black Political Forum, 1973-1976; the Bright Hope Baptist Church, 1975; the Bureau of Affirmative Action, 1975-1976; Black Colleges and Universities, 1972-1977; Non-Discrimination Clause Contracts, undated; Correspondence of an Affirmative Action Officer, 1973 and 1974; Equal Rights Task Force, 1972; Erie County Black Democrats Association, 1977; Erie County League of Black Voters; Human Relations Commission, 1971-1973; Human Relations Commission, 1977-1979; Opportunity Industrialization Centers (OIC); National Association for the Advancement of Colored People, 1972-1978; NAACP (National Association for the Advancement of Colored People) Convention, Sharon, Pa, 1978; Negro Trade Union Leadership Council, 1976-1978; Nix, Robert N.C.,1976-1978; Official Opinions (State Civil Service and Discrimination); United Negro College Fund, 1974-1978; Urban League of Pittsburgh, Inc., 1976; Voter Registration (Erie County League of Black Voters), 1974; Welfare Rights Organization, 1975-1978; and Zion Baptist Church, 1976-1977.

BUREAU OF AFFIRMATIVE ACTION

The Bureau of Affirmative Action (BOAA) is one of the units of the Office of Administration under the governor's jurisdiction. Its purpose is to encourage and promote Commonwealth-wide programs directed at ending discrimination against protected groups in all agencies under the governor's jurisdiction. It also develops programs to involve these individuals at all levels of employment. The records of the BOAA are divided into two groups: the Commonwealth Agency Files and the General Subject File. While some files deal specifically with discrimination aimed at African Americans, many more files with relevant information are given titles of a more general nature. The files also contain information on the affirmative action plans of the specific state agencies, training units, and complaints and grievances, among other subjects. A great deal of information on African Americans can be gleaned from the BOAA files of which the following is typical:

Commonwealth Agency Files, 1972-1987. (33 cartons) Arranged chronologically by year. Contains records for the State System of Higher Education including the 1983 Affirmative Action Plan for Cheyney State College. Of special interest are the court decisions about affirmative action such as *Allan Bakke vs. Regents of the University of California* and *Ankrom vs. Commonwealth of Pennsylvania Department of Community Affairs*.

General Subject File, 1970-1985. (53 cartons) Arranged alphabetically by topic. Included in the General Subject File are numerous references to African Americans. Following is an abbreviated list of relevant topics:

- Affirmative Action, 1976-1979.
- Affirmative Action Cluster, 1978.
- Affirmative Action Desk Reference Task Force, 1976.
- Affirmative Action Discrimination Committee, 1975.
- Affirmative Action Public Relations, 1977.
- Affirmative Action - Treadway Inn, Grantville, 1976.
- Affirmative Action Work Group, 1976-1978.
- Copies of Affirmative Action Articles, 1977-1979.
- Affirmative Action Meeting, 1979.
- Affirmative Action Congress, 1981.
- Affirmative Action Plans.
- Association of Mental Health Administrators Personnel/Affirmative Action Policy, 1977.

- Affirmative Action Bureau files include several references including the Affirmative Action Advisory Committee, 1982.
- Affirmative Action (Other States), 1982.
- American Foundation for Negro Affairs, 1981-84, with a program for the Education and Research Fund dinner, plans for the establishment of an African American Hall of Fame Garden, an agenda for an African American Convention, a resolution for an African American holiday. Subjects of major concern to the Foundation, and encouragement from Governor Thornburgh for state agencies to participate in the Foundation's conferences; Bakke press releases, 1977-1978.
- Black Basic Education Conference, 1982, which includes information on the Pennsylvania Conference and a conference on "Effective Public Education."
- Blacks for Government Conference, 1981.
- Black Women's Leadership Conference (BWLC), 1991.
- Black Economists, 1980.
- Black Progress, 1976-1979.
- Bureau of Affirmative Action, 1980, 1981.
- Bureau of Affirmative Action, 1980.
- Coalition of Ethnic Groups: 1977-1979.
- Census Data - Employment, 1970-77, which has a breakdown of statistics by race, and also information on earnings and occupations.
- Council for Sexual Minorities, 1981.
- Correspondence to and from Governor Casey with reference to BWLC, including a listing of the persons honored from Philadelphia and Allegheny counties at the BWLC's reception on February 22, 1991.
- Correspondence to Governor Casey with reference to the case of Mumia Abu-Jamal, 1994.
- Correspondence to Governor Casey from officers of the Pennsylvania State Conference of the NAACP Branches.

- Correspondence to the NAACP from Governor Casey.
- Returned Correspondence from state Affirmative Action/Equal Employment Opportunity Coordinators, 1977.
- Equal Employment Opportunity Commission Program, 1976-1977.
- Equal Employment Opportunity Commission, 1977-1979.
- Equal Rights Amendment, 1971-1980; Equal Employment Opportunity Questions, 1980.
- Equal Employment Opportunity Commission for State and Local Government, 1977-1980.
- Governor's Commission for Children and Families, 1993.
- Harrisburg Alliance for Racial Justice and Community Building, 1980.
- Human Relations Commission, 1982, regarding a mini-conference on civil rights enforcement in Pennsylvania.
- Human Relations Committee, 1981.
- Human Relations Commission, 1983, regarding an effort to work together with the BOAA on discrimination cases,
- K. Leroy Irvis, 1980.
- Minorities in Public Service Projects, 1981.
- Lincoln University, 1983, with an invitation to Career Day at Lincoln and a schedule and information packet for that event.
- NAACP, 1978 and 1979, Urban League of Lancaster County.
- NAACP Conference, including pamphlets, correspondence, and newsletters, 1977.
- NAACP, 1980, Human Relations Committee, 1980.
- NAACP booklet, 1979.
- NAACP Speech, 1981.
- NAACP, 1982, with the NAACP Economic Development Survey, correspondence with Ida Belle Minnie (who worked with the Affirmative Action Office at state colleges), and documentation of a BOAA exhibit at the NAACP State Conference in Harrisburg.

- NAACP, 1983, with an invitation and information on an annual conference.
- NAACP, 1990, National Urban League.
- Prototype Affirmative Action Training Design, 1975.
- Race/Ethnic Identification Material, 1979.
- Race-Gender Data, 1979.
- *Remedies in Title VII Cases*, by Robert J. Reimstein, which was presented at the Employment Discrimination Conference at Temple University, Philadelphia, Pa., March 19, 1977.
- Urban League of Metropolitan Harrisburg, Inc., 1973-1977.
- Work Plan Affirmative Action, 1977-1978.

GOVERNOR'S COUNCIL ON DRUG AND ALCOHOL ABUSE

Subject File of the General Counsel, 1972-1975. (2 cartons)
Arranged chronologically by date of correspondence. Contains a file on the Pittsburgh Black Action Drug Abuse Center. The records in this file deal primarily with the Pittsburgh Black Action Drug Abuse Center, the Bureau of Drug Control in the Department of Justice, and the Governor's Council on Drug and Alcohol Abuse in the Commonwealth of Pennsylvania. Included are papers relating to various inspections and court cases regarding the regulation of the controlled substance methadone.

RG-11. RECORDS OF THE DEPARTMENT OF HEALTH

The Department of Health was created in 1905 to replace the State Board of Health and Vital Statistics that had been established in 1885. Charged with the responsibility of protecting the health of the citizens of the Commonwealth, the Department of Health enforces statutes and regulations pertaining to public health matters, works to insure the prevention and suppression of disease, and ensures the accessibility of high quality health care at a reasonable cost. The department provides the leadership and assistance necessary to plan, coordinate, and support a total statewide public health effort. The Department of Health operates numerous state health centers that serve as the primary public health service units within the counties.

The department's bureaus and programs deal with control and prevention of cancer, diabetes, HIV/AIDS and various communicable diseases. The department also conducts laboratory research, maintains files of health statistics, and conducts preventative and educational health programs for mothers, children and communities. It is responsible for state health care policy, quality assurance and financing, administering drug and alcohol abuse programs, Vietnam Veterans' health initiatives, and regulating the manufacture and distribution of drugs, medical devices, and cosmetics. {PATIENT RECORDS ARE RESTRICTED}

EXECUTIVE DEPUTY SECRETARY FOR PUBLIC HEALTH PROGRAMS

Elizabethtown Hospital for Children and Youth

Patient Registers, 1929-1977. (2 volumes) Arranged chronologically by date of admittance. Each register entry provides serial and unit number, name of patient, county, dates admitted and discharged, total number of days in the hospital, birthplace, date of birth, color, sex, religion, parent or guardian, and admitting diagnosis. Occasionally the parent's occupation is stated and after the year the diagnosis appears as well. Common diagnoses include scoliosis, clubfoot, cerebral palsy, and polio. {THESE RECORDS ARE RESTRICTED}

Record of Operations, 1941-1975. (4 volumes) Arranged chronologically by date of operation. Each entry provides the case number, operation date, patient name, age, sex, color, diagnosis, operator, operation performed, name of the assistant, name of the operating nurse, name of the anesthetist, the anesthetic employed, any complications that may have occurred, and results of the operation. Notes on complications and results also usually give the times the operation started and ended. (*These records are restricted.*)

BUREAU OF EPIDEMIOLOGY AND DISEASE PREVENTION

Coal Workers' Respiratory Disease Program Medical Evaluation Files, 1976-1980. (29 cartons) Arranged chronologically by processing date of each batch. Black lung medical evaluation forms document the Department of Health's program to conduct a survey of coal mining related health problems in Pennsylvania. Information furnished includes the patient's number, a county residence code, and the date the survey was completed; the patient's date of birth, race, and whether the patient was a minor; the nature of the visit to the clinic (respiratory examinations or treatments), the patient's functional level, the referral code; and information on black lung benefits, health insurance coverage, and pension benefits. Also included is information on the patient's background that might be related to the patient's symptoms such as a history of smoking, occupations, blood pressure, pulse rate, respiratory rate, tuberculin reaction, influenza vaccine status, laboratory test results, heart and lung physical examination results, hemoglobin laboratory test results, pulmonary function studies, and results of arterial blood gas analysis. Finally, a treatment history relating to medication, respiratory therapy, oxygen therapy, physical therapy, counseling given to discourage smoking, referrals made for treatment, and other diseases noticed during the examination are also noted. (*These records are restricted.*)

RG-11. Department of Health. Bureau of Health Communications. Migrant labor camp in Chester County.

BUREAU OF HEALTH COMMUNICATIONS

Photograph File, 1944-1978. (15 cartons, 46 boxes, 2 volumes, 29 file drawers) Partially indexed internally, alphabetically by topic. The first volume of the subject index, covering the period

1964-1970, is divided into the following subject categories: administration, deputy secretaries, executive office, air pollution controls, housing and environmental control, sanitary engineering, special health services, educational activities, field services, nursing programs and resources, planning, evaluation, research, retirement awards, building, conferences, copies, exhibits, miscellaneous, portraits, and scenic. Information recorded for each entry in the index includes the subject category code, photograph description, date, location, and photograph number(s). Items relating to African Americans include photographs of poor living conditions in the migrant labor camps in Chester County.

BUREAU OF HEALTH EDUCATION

Photographs, 1908, 1957-1962. (5 volumes, 7 folders) African Americans are to be found among the subjects of photographs of people and exhibits at the 8th Annual Health Conference, August 1959.

BUREAU OF HIV/AIDS (HUMAN IMMUNODEFI- CIENCY VIRUS/ACQUIRED IMMUNE DEFI- CIENCY SYNDROME)

State HIV Planning Council Minutes, 1991-1993. (1 carton) Arranged chronologically by date of meeting. The State HIV Planning Council was created by a federal act in 1990 to address the problems created by the spread of the Human Immuno-deficiency Virus (HIV). The act was effective as of 1991 and the council held its first meeting in August 1991. The primary goals of the HIV Planning Council were to advise the Departments of Health and Public Welfare on issues related to the HIV epidemic and make recommendations about the Commonwealth's response. It also sought to identify critical needs and issues that needed to be addressed at the state level and to monitor the implementation of the Department of Health's regional planning strategy. In addition, the council also sought to provide a mechanism for information sharing and networking among various coalitions and, where appropriate, for joint responses to issues. The HIV Planning Council was disbanded in 1996.

Meetings held by the HIV Planning Council dealt with issues such as the role of the Bureau of HIV/AIDS in funding, testing, and immigration. They also addressed the issues of racial and ethnic representation, state legislation relative to HIV health issues, the budget, and the compilation of HIV and AIDS statistics in the state of Pennsylvania.

BUREAU OF PROFESSIONAL HEALTH SERVICES

Migrant Health Program Patient Files, 1963-1988. (53 cartons) Arranged alphabetically by patient's name and thereunder chronologically by date of health registration sheet. Records contain a registration sheet required for treatment under this program. Medical records prepared on each visit show name of patient, home address, local or camp address, race, date of visit, and date of birth. Some records contain additional information such as patient's occupation and the names of parents, dependents, and next of kin, and of patient's employer. *(These records are restricted.)*

BUREAU OF SANITARY ENGINEERING

Sanitary Engineers' Epidemic Reports, 1904-1919. (4 boxes) The reports are organized alphabetically by county, thereunder by community, and finally chronologically by the date of investigation. Etiologies are prepared by staff from the Health Department's Bureau of Sanitary Engineering to explain why outbreaks of disease occurred in communities throughout Pennsylvania. The reports usually start with a brief history in which the population, economy, geography, environment, and social and cultural features of the municipality are described. This local history is followed by a narrative description and a statistical analysis of the problem, a discussion of possible improvements that could serve as a remedy and a series of recommendations for improving health conditions. As part of the report's content, information concerning residents who became ill or died were reported, including in some cases their names, places of residence, ages, and activities prior to the epidemic. A typical example is the East Fallowfield Sanitary Engineer Epidemic Report of 1917 which discusses typhoid fever on the farms of two African Americans, William Jones and Samuel Ruth, of East Fallowfield Township, Chester County. In addition to a large number of children in each family, there were several boarders at the home of Samuel Ruth. It is interesting to note that Ida Jones, a member of William Jones's family, became a noted Pennsylvania artist.

BUREAU OF SPECIAL HEALTH SERVICES

Records of the Genetic Disease Program, 1981-1982. (8 cartons) Arranged numerically by genetic disease program center number and thereunder by patient number. Genetic counseling forms include the following details: patient background, referral information, records of services provided, amniocentesis data, counseling site/type and number, and the disposition of the case. General data provided include the date, name of the center and the patient, the counselor number, whether the patient was a child or an adult, gender, date of birth, race, residence, income level, marital status, and pregnancy history. For children, forms include such parental information as dates of birth, parents' educational level, parents' occupations, and whether the parents were genetically related to one another and the specific nature of any such relationship. Adult patients' data include educational levels and occupations of both patient and spouse, dates of birth for both, whether patient or family was receiving services from any other department or health program, the source of the referral, and the diagnosis. *(These records are restricted.)*

ANATOMICAL BOARD OF THE STATE OF PENNSYLVANIA

Cadaver Receiving Books, 1901-1908, 1916-1925, 1942-1965. (4 volumes) Arranged chronologically by delivery date with some books having monthly groupings by areas (such as Philadelphia and Pittsburgh). A record of bodies received by the Anatomical Board of the state of Pennsylvania (now the Human Gifts Registry) and distributed to medical and dental schools in the state for teaching purposes. Entries in the books give the name, sex, color, age, nativity, marital status, and occupation of the deceased; the date and cause of death; the date the body was delivered and the tag number; the attending physician's name; dates of treatment; the name of the institution that provided the cadaver, the name of the school receiving it; and the condition of the body.

Consolidated Annual Report Books of Receipts and Distributions, 1895-1974. (4 volumes) Arranged chronologically by date of report. Statistical annual reports of cadavers received and distributed by the board. The Consolidated Report of Receipts provides a monthly account of bodies received from various hospitals, prisons, almshouses, and undertakers located in Allegheny County, Berks County, Cumberland County, Westmoreland County, York County, and the municipalities of Lancaster, Scranton, Wilkes-Barre, and Bethlehem. The Monthly Account by Categories provides the number cut and uncut, white males and white females, good and bad, claimed, substituted, buried and the totals. The Consolidated Report of Distributions provides a monthly account of cadavers distributed to the University of Pennsylvania, Jefferson Medical College, Hahnemann Medical College, Women's Medical College, Pennsylvania College of Dental Surgery, Polyclinic College, Philadelphia School of Anatomy, Western Pennsylvania Medical College, Medico-Chirurgical College, Scranton Anatomical Society, Franklin and Marshall College, and other facilities.

RG-12. RECORDS OF THE DEPARTMENT OF HIGHWAYS

A state Highway Department was created in 1903 to cooperate with the Commonwealth's political subdivisions in the improvement and maintenance of highways. Initially, the department served as a disbursing agency and was primarily responsible for administering state grants to local communities. Legislation passed in 1911 reorganized the Highway Department, providing for a system of highways to be maintained solely by the state and for a highway network financed on both the state and local level.

The Department of Highways, as it was officially designated under the Administrative Code of 1923, was given exclusive authority and jurisdiction over state highways and general supervisory powers over all roads financed in whole or in part by state funds. The Department of Highways was abolished in 1970 and replaced by the Department of Transportation.

BUREAU OF PUBLIC INFORMATION

Photograph Unit's File of Mounted and Unmounted Prints, [ca. 1915-1932]. (17 boxes)
Included in this file are some photographs showing African Americans employed in rough grading, mixing sand and stone, laying concrete, and finishing concrete in the building of roads in Crawford, Cumberland, Dauphin, Lancaster, and Washington Counties.

RG 13. RECORDS OF THE PENNSYLVANIA HISTORICAL AND MUSEUM COMMISSION

The Pennsylvania Historical and Museum Commission was created in 1945 to consolidate the functions of the Pennsylvania Historical Commission, the State Museum, and the State Archives.

RG-12. Department of Highways. Bureau of Public Information. Crawford County, Ellis Road.

Charged with the responsibility of preserving the Commonwealth's heritage, the commission administers the state archival and records management program, operates and maintains museums and historical sites, assists local historical societies and governmental agencies, and conducts research and publication programs to promote Pennsylvania history. The commission consists of the Bureau of Management Services, the Bureau of Archives and History, the Bureau for of the State Museum, the Bureau of Historic Sites and Museums, and the Bureau for Historic Preservation.

The State Archives was originally established in 1903 as an administrative unit of the State Library and was designated the Division of Public Records. A State Museum was also created under the State Library in accordance with legislation passed in 1905. As part of a general reorganization in 1919, the State Library was named the State Library and Museum. In 1923 the State Library and Museum was made an administrative unit of the Department of Public Instruction as was the Pennsylvania Historical Commission, which had functioned as an independent commission since its establishment in 1913. In 1945, the State Archives, State Museum, and the Pennsylvania Historical Commission were removed from the Department of Public Instruction to form the Pennsylvania Historical and Museum Commission.

EXECUTIVE DIRECTOR

Administrative and Correspondence Files of the Commission Chairman, 1956-1961. (3 cartons) Arranged alphabetically by topic and thereunder chronologically by date of correspondence. Administrative and correspondence files of Commission Chairman Frank W. Melvin. Included are photographs of the following African American subjects: Andrew M. Bradley, governor's office, 1956-1960; James E. Flood, secretary, M.H. Prince Hall Grand Lodge, Harrisburg, 1958; Robert N. C. Nix, United States House of Representatives, Washington, D.C.; as well as photographs of historical markers dedicated to African Americans in Philadelphia in 1960.

Administrative and Correspondence Files of the Executive Director, 1945-1988. (138 cartons, 2 boxes) Grouped chronologically by year and grouped thereunder alphabetically by topic. Correspondence documenting the administrative activities of the executive director's office. The material consists of annual reports, photographs, news clippings, correspondence, petitions, and memoranda. Included in these files are correspondence relating to Pennsylvania's Affirmative Action Plan, the Balch Institute, the Black History Advisory Committee, Black History Conferences in Pennsylvania, the Department of Community Affairs, the Cornwall Iron Furnace, the Council of the Arts, the Pennsylvania Historical Marker Program, the Pennsylvania Human Relations Commission, the Neighbor Youth Corps, and the state Program for Protection and Enhancement of the Cultural Environment.

Records of the Special Features Coordinator of the Public Resources Development Section, 1975-1986. (3 cartons) Arranged alphabetically by subject. This series contains correspondence, press releases, news clippings, brochures, minutes, and photographs of the special features coordinator of the Public Resources Development Section in the office of the executive director of the Pennsylvania Historical and Museum Commission. The special features coordinator provided public relations and publicity support to Commission programs. The subject folder includes information on the Black History Advisory Committee including minutes of its June 1983 meeting wherein the location of the next two Pennsylvania Black History Conferences were decided upon: California State College with Ida Belle Minnie as contact person and Carlisle Barracks, with Ruth E. Hodge as contact person. There are also a large number of brochures, news releases, and newspaper articles on Black History Conferences in Pennsylvania, 1980, 1982-1983; a photograph of the Black History Month Celebration, 1981-1982; and dedication programs, newspaper articles, and releases for the following historical markers: Daisy Lampkin (Pittsburgh); First Protest Against Slavery (Philadelphia); and Dr. Martin Luther King Jr. (Chester). Also included is a catalog of the Charles L. Blockson Collection, *Of Color, Humanities and Statehood: The Black Experience in Pennsylvania over Three Centuries,* showcased at the Afro-American Historical and Cultural Museum, Philadelphia, in October of 1981.

BUREAU OF ARCHIVES AND HISTORY

Administrative and Correspondence Files of the Bureau Director, 1943-1981. **(25 cartons, 1 box)** Grouped chronologically by bureau director's tenure and thereunder alphabetically by name of correspondent. Files include correspondence, ethnic culture surveys for 1966-1981, and staff reports for 1974-1976. The ethnic culture surveys contain oral history interviews, written histories on Pennsylvania's ethnic groups including African Americans, and microfilms of ethnic newspapers published in Pennsylvania. Included in the director's files is correspondence referring to the William Penn Memorial Museum exhibit for Negro History Week held February 12-16, 1975. This exhibit displayed twenty-six paintings by African American artist David Washington of Harrisburg. There is also a list of booklets, photographs, and handbills that were used in the exhibit. Included in the bureau director's correspondence is a letter dated July 1, 1976 and a monthly report for July 1976 referring to the establishment of a state advisory committee on Black history. Both were made possible by a grant from the Rockefeller Foundation. Other correspondence relates to the 1974 Association for the Study of Afro-American Life and History in Philadelphia at which annual meeting the Pennsylvania State Archives arranged to provide an exhibit booth featuring relevant publications and original documents on African American history.

Administrative and Correspondence Files of the State Historian and Staff, 1945-1973. **(10 cartons, 1 box)** In 1945, the Pennsylvania Historical and Museum Commission was given responsibility for a program to erect historical markers throughout the state. Included in the marker files are correspondence, proposals for markers, and prepared texts for markers approved for installation. Among the markers related to the African American experience in Pennsylvania are: First Protest Against Slavery, Edward Hector, Richard Henderson, Hopewell Furnace, James Family Cemetery, Daisy E. Lampkin, Joanna Furnace, Martin Luther King Jr., Horace Pippin, St. Patrick's Church (Roman Catholic School), St. Paul African Methodist Episcopal Church, St. Thomas African Methodist Episcopal Church, and Thomas Rutter. Also included in the marker file are newspaper articles opposing the nomination of Edward Hector as not being a legitimate African American.

Writings on Pennsylvania History, 1947-1949. Contains correspondence, bibliographies listing studies, theses, and dissertations relative to Pennsylvania African American history (including locations of the institutional holdings of the materials cited). One such institution is Lincoln University's Vail Memorial Library, which had *the Pennsylvania Colonization Society Papers, 1838-1912* and the *Minutes of the Executive Committee of the Young Men's Colonization Society of Pennsylvania, June 10, 1831-February 9, 1841.*

Conference on Black History in Pennsylvania Files, 1978-1995.* (2 cartons, 3 boxes)***
{Unprocessed} In 1978, the Pennsylvania Historical and Museum Commission sponsored the first annual Conference on Black History in Pennsylvania. The purpose of the conference is to educate and share with the citizens of this Commonwealth the history and culture of African Americans by meeting in communities across the state. These files include: minutes of local conference committees; correspondence of the Pennsylvania Historical and Museum Commission; budget reports;

documentation on local awards, cultural events and historical markers; addresses from keynote speakers and other conference participants; grant applications; press releases and other forms of publicity; contracts with speakers, caterers, hotels, and transportation companies; and conference brochures and posters. In addition, there are photographs of the Annual Conference on Black History in Pennsylvania, as well as reproductions of documents that were part of a Black History Month exhibit in February, 1985.

Ethnic Culture Survey File, 1948-1976. (6 cartons, 1 box) Arranged alphabetically by subject or name of correspondent. A file consisting of various types of material including brochures, newspaper articles, and correspondence relating to Pennsylvania's rich ethnic diversity. This file contains the following information on African Americans:

- A brochure on the Association for the Study of Negro Life and History, Inc. (ASNLH)
- An Arno Press catalog *The American Negro: His History and Literature, 1968-1969.*
- A program for the 1968 ASNLH conference; newspaper articles on school integration.
- *American Traveler's Guide to Negro History*
- *Pennsylvania and American History and Government for Grade 8*, prepared for the Philadelphia Public Schools.

Among the newspapers, a copy of the September 10, 1913 issue of *The Philadelphia Record*, includes the following articles on the Negro Exposition:

- "Parade and Oratory Open Negro Exposition: Vast Assemblage of Colored Race at Inauguration of Emancipation Fair."

- Addresses by ex-Governor Pennypacker, Director of Public Safety Porter, and State Representative Harry W. Bass.
- "Emancipation Fair Opens with Religious Services," with Bishop J. S. Caldwell who presided over the exposition.
- Sermon preached by Bishop I. P. Coppin of the African Methodist Episcopal Church on the theme of "The Religious Progress of the Emancipated Race."
- Emancipation Exposition building and Active Promoters" featuring the pictures of William Palmer of Pittsburgh, Julius Smith of Westmoreland County, Bishop J. S. Cadwell, executive committee chairman; and Dr. H. Y. Arnett of Philadelphia.

The correspondence includes:

- Letter from Philip S. Foner to Mr. Henry Glassie, state Folklorist.
- Letter to Professor Orrin Clayton Suthern, II, Department of Music, Lincoln University, from C. Edgar Patience.
- Photographs and art work of K. Leroy Irvis.
- Press release entitled "Museum Exhibit Will Pay Tribute to Negro Role in Pennsylvania History."
- Copy of an article entitled "Museum Spotlight Focuses on Negro."

National Historical Publications and Records Commission Regrant Project Files, 1985-1990. (1 carton, 1 box) Arranged alphabetically by name of institution.

Pennsylvania State Historical Records Advisory Board. The Pennsylvania College and University Archival and Manuscript Repository Re-grant Program operated under auspices of the Pennsylvania State Historical Records Advisory Board. The files of this program contain documentation on the grant given to Lincoln University in support of an archives processing project under the direction of archivist Sophy Cornwell of the Langston Hughes Memorial Library.

Photographs for Publications, 1950-1990. (5 boxes) Contains photographs of the "resurrection" of Henry "Box" Brown, who made his escape to freedom sealed inside a wooden box, the executive committee of the Pennsylvania Anti-Slavery Society, and Richard Allen and the leaders of the African Methodist Episcopal Church.

Photographs of Commission Properties for Publications, 1950-1990. (9 boxes) Contains photographs of Cornwall Furnace and Hopewell Furnace, which employed African Americans during their years of operation.

Reports, Correspondence, and Research File Relating to the War History Program, 1938-1947. (36 cartons) Arranged chronologically by date of report, correspondence, or research document. Includes correspondence, news releases, and many newspaper articles on African Americans. Of particular interest are copies of the addresses of General Edward Martin, then governor of Pennsylvania, given before the General Conference of the African Methodist Episcopal Church in Philadelphia, May 3, 1944, and of the commencement exercises at Cheyney Training School for Teachers on May 27, 1944, and at Lincoln University on June 6, 1944. These addresses focused on various aspects of the history of African Americans such as their strong faith in God, their zeal for education, and their commitment to serving in the country's armed forces during World War II. There are also several articles on African American servicemen who served in Europe during the war including: "Negro Aviators Have Won Fame in Anzio Battle,"

"Negro Fliers Win Fame over Anzio," "U.S.O. Aid Asked for Negro Troops," "Local Club Keeps in Touch with Colored Soldiers," "Negroes Act to Aid Air Raid Evacuees," "Negro Firms Plan Drive to Buy Bonds," and "First Negroes Take Oath Here for Service as US Seamen." In addition, newspaper clippings such as "Negroes Seek Tenement Action," and "Mulcting on Rents Charged by Negroes" reflect the National Association for the Advancement for Colored People's movement to fight for better conditions in Philadelphia's black tenement neighborhoods. Also included in this file are newspaper articles addressing the five-day employee strike against the Philadelphia Transportation Company during August 1944. This strike came about as a result of African Americans getting upgraded jobs at the Philadelphia Transportation Company. Some of the newspaper articles are entitled: "Pennsy to Hire Negroes as Dining Car Stewards," "Negroes Get Trolley Jobs Next Month," "60 Negroes Seek Skilled PTC Jobs," "State, City Heads Get Request for Immediate Action," "Plan to Find Jobs for Negroes Drawn," and "Greater Use of Colored Workers Seen."

Revolutionary War Military Abstract Card File, undated. (40 drawers) Arranged alphabetically by surname of soldier. The file consists of 4" x 6" abstract cards compiled by the Division of Archives and Manuscripts from original muster rolls, payrolls, military accounts, depreciation certificates, militia loans, and delinquent lists in its custody. Information contained on the cards differs for each individual. While some entries may only give the person's name and county of service, others may also list rank and dates of service, the name of the officer under whom he served, and the military unit to which he was attached. In a few instances, father and son relationships are also indicated. It is difficult to determine whether a soldier was an African American, and even when a racial designation appears after the name very little additional information was generally recorded. One example of an

African American who served in the Revolutionary War was John Francis. According to his card, Francis was also an invalid pensioner.

Revolutionary War Pension Index Cards, 1785-1893. (9 boxes) Indexed alphabetically by surname of soldier. Each card provides the veteran's name and volume reference for pension information. In some cases service time is also given.

PENNSYLVANIA HISTORICAL COMMISSION, 1913-1945

Reports and Miscellaneous Papers Relating to the War History Program, 1942-1945. (1 folder) Unarranged. This series contains a record of the work completed by the War History Program to document Pennsylvania's role in World War II. Documents relating to African Americans include *War Production Training Bulletins* for workers in various factories throughout the state of Pennsylvania, and bulletins addressing "Negro Women in Industry" (as production workers in aircraft factories, ordnance plants, shipyards, garment factories, and as sheet metal welders). Also included are some photographs of African American troops training for duty overseas.

Working Files of the Works Progress Administration's Pennsylvania Historical Survey, Consisting of Administrative Files, Transcripts, Photographs, Inventories, Notes, and Other Working Papers Relating to Various Projects, [ca. 1935-1950. (133 cartons, 5 boxes, 79 microfilm rolls, 40 folders, 7 volumes, 1 bundle)

Records of the Pennsylvania Writers, Pennsylvania Historical Commission, American Guide Series, 1935-1941. (27 cartons, 1 box) These records pertain to Pennsylvania's involvement with the Federal Writers Project and most notably the American Guide Series. The project was designed to employ white collar workers who were left without work by the Great Depression to write comprehensive guides for states. Project workers in Pennsylvania compiled such works as Job 11, *Pennsylvania: A Guide to the Keystone State* (1940), Job 5; *Philadelphia: A Guide to the Nation's Birthplace* (1937); and many guides for individual counties and historical subjects. Records consist primarily of field notes, manuscripts, and photographs taken or collected for a particular guide. Not all of the manuscripts and photographs prepared were actually published. The WPA historical investigations of African Americans of Philadelphia and Pittsburgh covered all periods from slavery down to the Great Depression. Most of the authors were apparently local African American journalists, writers, or social welfare workers. The articles are typed, double-spaced, and are either in pre-final or final form. Field notes are sometimes included. Below are subject outlines for the projects relating specifically relating to African Americans:

- **Job #54:** *Pennsylvania Anthracite*. In this group of stories, there is one entitled "Story of a Follower of Father Divine Hauling Bootleg Coal."
- **Job #63:** *The Negro in Philadelphia, 1938-39*, 1941. Contains manuscripts of various chapters written by different people filed in fifteen folders. Some of the topics include abolition societies, the underground railroad, cultural folkways and superstitions, education, literature, medical services, economic development, housing, professional development, interracial trends, military materials including the Colored Soldiers War Memorial, the law, personalities, railroads, religion, sports, fraternal organizations, employment (including slavery), and music. Also included

in this collection is a Directory of Negro Children. Some pertinent organizations discussed include Fellowship House, Bright Hope Baptist Church, the Negro Church of Philadelphia, Tindley Temple, Temple University Interracial Club, Colored Protective Association, American Negro Historical Society, Philadelphia Association for the Protection of Colored Women, Berean Manual and Industrial Training School, Royal Bears (a boys' club), Robert Wood Industrial Home, Charles Young Camp #27, Richard Allen Home, First Annual Convention of the People of Color, Musicians Protective Union, Debating Society of Pennsylvania, Black Affairs Center, Black Legislative Caucus, Black Ward Leaders of Pennsylvania, Black Political Forum, Public Writers' Association, the Philadelphia Library Company of Colored Persons, Demostheman Institute, Minerva Literary Association, Edgewood Literary Association, Gilbert Lyceum, Rush Library Company, Leaf Nursing Auxiliary, William A. Jackson Dental Society; *Opportunity Magazine*, *Pittsburgh Courier*, and the Armstrong Association. Also included in this collection are forty-two 8" x 10" prints showing African American housing conditions, churches, individuals, etc. The photographic subjects include the Mercy Hospital and School for Nurses located at 50th and Woodland Streets in Philadelphia, both exterior and interior views of the Home for Aged and Infirm Colored Persons at Delmont and Girard Avenues, the Monument to Negro Soldiers, St. Thomas Protestant Episcopal Church at 12th Street, Holland's Restaurant, the Allen Building, the Tindley Temple on Board Street, the First African (Cherry Memorial) Baptist Church on Christian Street, the First Colored Food Show at the Octavius Catto Lodge together with a copy of a view of Catto as it appeared ca. 1800, the Philadelphia Tribune

Building, the Bureau for Colored Children, the Berean Manual Training and Industrial School, the Philadelphia Independent building, the Susan Parrish Wharton Settlement (interior view), the Wissahickon Boys' Club, the Young Men's Christian Association, the Young Women's Christian Association, Neil's Gown Shop, and the Works Progress Administration Sewing Project.

- **Job #64:** *The Negro in Pittsburgh, 1939-1941*. Titles of the various manuscript chapters include: "Plantation Shadow," "Negro on the Frontier, the early Negro Community," "Abolition years," "Civil Rights," "Negro Wage Worker," "Middle Class and Professional Negro," "Negro Church, Negro in the Schools," "Negro and the Press," "Negro in Politics," "Community," "Folkways," "Arts and Culture," "Recreation and Athletics," "Health, Housing, Health and Social Adjustment," and "The People Speak," where twenty-four African Americans talked about their life in Pittsburgh. Also included are two poems written by George B. Vashon, a memorial titled "Memorial of the Free Citizens of Color in Political Destiny of the Colored Race on the American Continent," church registers of births and baptisms (1787), and transcriptions of newspaper articles on Pittsburgh's African Americans that originally appeared in *Pittsburgh Daily Post*, and *Pittsburgh Gazette Times* between 1841 and 1941 and the *Pittsburgh Commercial*, *Pittsburgh Leader, Pittsburgh Gazette,* and *Pittsburgh Press*.

- **Job #179:** *A Picture of Dauphin County, 1940-1941*. In this collection are portions of a manuscript making reference to Hercules," a Negro slave who belonged to the John Harris family of Harris Landing, Lancaster County (now Harrisburg, Dauphin County).

Records of the Pennsylvania Historical Records Survey,
1937-1942, 1946, 1950. (74 cartons, 3 boxes, 21 folders)

- **Inventory of Church Archives of Pennsylvania, including Records of Pennsylvania Jewish Congregations, 1937-1940, and undated.** This is the most comprehensive collection on churches throughout the Commonwealth. Since black churches were also included in the survey (they were designated "Negro" churches within the specific denominations), many details on the evolution and condition of dozens of these churches are available. The survey was carried out on a county by county basis employing a uniform four-page questionnaire. The type of information provided by these questionnaires included both the official name and the name by which the church was most commonly known in the community, the address, the date the congregation began, the date of formal organization, the name of the founder or of the mother church body, changes in the name of the church, the method of organization, any former addresses and dates of occupancy, information on properties purchased and sold including dates of transactions and the names of sellers and buyers, the type of building occupied, the date of consecration and dedication, and architectural characteristics. Also found are the name of the first settled pastor and his secular occupation, the name of the current pastor and the dates of service, the status of administrative church records and minute books, materials relating to Sunday school, published and unpublished histories and biographies, directories, registers of baptisms (marriages, members, deaths), and church cemetery information. In addition to the questionnaire, brochures, programs, and photographs may be found in the files. Some of the African American churches for which the Archives has surveys are:

W. P. A. form 20HR
Pennsylvania Supplement 1

27

Leroy J Purviance
Worker's signature

CHURCH ARCHIVES INVENTORY QUESTIONAIRE

1. County *Cumberland* ✓ City or town *Carlisle*

2. Official name of church in full *Third Presbyterian Church of Carlisle*

   (a) By what name is church known in community *Presbyterian Mission*

   (b) Exact street address *North West Corner South Bedford and East Pomfret Streets*
   (If rural give state road number, and direction and miles from nearest town)

3. (a) Date congregation first began to meet *1899* ✓
   (b) Date officially organized or recognized by higher church body *1899*

   (c) If church was chartered, give date *Record* Date of lapse if defunct *1926* ✓
   (d) Reasons for lapse if available (merged with another church, people left community etc. *Some left community - Some went to other Churches*
   (e) If church is defunct give disposition of property *Sold in 1927 to The Trustees of The Salvation Army in Pennsylvania - Deed Book-B-Vol. 6. Page 78. by the Presbytery of Carlisle*

4. (a) What church may be considered the founder or mother church of this church? *The Second Presbyterian Church, Carlisle Penna.* ✓

   (b) Has the name of this church been changed? Give former names and dates for each *No* ✓

   (c) Did congregation originate as a mission or Sunday school, or in what way *Mission and Sunday School*

5. Name of denomination in full *Presbyterian Church in the United States of America*
   Name of higher regional and district bodies (Synod, Province, Convention, Diocese, Presbytery, Association) *Presbytery of Carlisle* ✓

   (a) If church was previously affiliated with regional bodies other than the present one give names of bodies and dates of these affiliations *None* ✓

   (b) If ever affiliated with another denomination give date, name of denomination and other pertinent date *None* ✓

6. Give address and time occupied for all regular meeting places of congregation from original to present building

   Meeting place and address   Dates occupied

   ① *JORDAN'S HALL - 142 West North Street Carlisle* *February-18-1899-March 30-1900*
   ② *Northwest Corner South Bedford & East Pomfret Streets March 31-1900 - 1926*

   (a) If congregation owned any of these places of worship give also kind of material of which constructed, from whom purchased (or donated) and to whom sold.

   Bought from and date   Sold to and date   stone, brick, frame

   Congregation did not own   *See Item #3(E)*   *Brick*

7. For present edifice give:

   (a) Year erected *1854-1855* ✓ (b) If purchased, give year and from whom

   (c) Date dedicated or ~~rededicated~~ *Rededicated -1900* ✓

RG-13. Pennsylvania Historical and Museum Commission. Works Progress Administration (WPA). Inventory of Church Archives. Record of Third Presbyterian Church, Carlisle.

- *Allegheny County:* African Methodist Episcopal (A.M.E.) Allen Chapel, A.M.E. Trinity Chapel, African Methodist Episcopal Zion (A.M.E.Z.) Trimble Chapel, First African Baptist Church, First Baptist Church (one of several), Friendship Baptist Church, Gospel Hall Assembly, Homestead Second Baptist Church, John Wesley Methodist Episcopal Church, McCurdy's Presbyterian Mission, Mt. Calvary Baptist Church, Mt. Olive Baptist Church, Mt. Olivet Baptist Church, Mt. Zion Baptist Church, Park Place A.M.E. Church, Second Baptist Church, St. John Baptist Church , St. Mark's A.M.E. Church, St. Paul's A.M.E.Z. Church, St. Paul's Baptist Church, Sunrise Baptist Church, Trimble Chapel, Triumph Spiritualist Church, True Vine Church, United Free Gospel Missionary Church, Wayman A.M.E. Church, White Lily Baptist Church, etc.
- *Chester County:* Second Baptist Church, Kennett Square; St. Paul's Baptist Church, West Chester.
- *Crawford County:* Bethel African Methodist Episcopal Church, Meadville.
- *Cumberland County:* African Methodist Episcopal Church of Newville; Bethel African Methodist Episcopal Church, Carlisle; Mt. Zion Primitive Baptist Church, Carlisle; Third Presbyterian Church, Carlisle; West Street African Methodist Episcopal; Zion Church, Carlisle.
- *Erie County:* Calvary Baptist Church, Macedonia Missionary Baptist Church, Shiloh Baptist Church, all in Erie.
- *Fayette County:* Beulah Baptist Church, Smithfield; Tri-Stone Baptist Church, Georges Township; Mt. Zion Baptist Church, Connellsville; New Mt. Zion Baptist

Church, Fairchance.

- *Franklin County:* John Wesley African Methodist Episcopal Zion Church, Chambersburg; St. James African Methodist Episcopal Church, Chambersburg.
- *Lancaster County.* Colored Baptist Congregation of Columbia, Mt. Zion African Methodist Episcopal Church in Lancaster, St. Paul's Baptist Church in Columbia; Bethel African Methodist Episcopal Church in Columbia, Ebenezer Baptist Church in Lancaster, St. Paul's African Methodist Episcopal Church, Lancaster; Bethel African Methodist Episcopal Church in Lancaster, First Baptist Church in Lancaster, Wesley African Methodist Episcopal Zion Church in Marietta.
- *Philadelphia County.* First African Baptist Church, Shiloh Baptist Church, Philadelphia (City).

Records of the Philadelphia Maritime Statistics Project, Pennsylvania Historical Commission, [ca. 1937-1941]. **These records were compiled as part of a Works Progress Administration Project.**

- **Chronological List of Masters and Crews, 1798-1880.** (41 microfilm rolls) This series includes three types of records for each year. The alphabetical masters list of the names of ship captains appearing in the volume gives the page number on which they appear and the year. The ships lists give the date of travel, the name of the vessel, the name of the home port and name of the master, and the destination. The crew lists identify the names of the members of the crew serving on each vessel. The crew lists contain names of African American boys and men who served aboard merchant marine vessels. For each vessel listed as leaving or entering the Port of Philadelphia, the following information is given: name of crewman, his age, and place of birth; a physical description of the seaman (identified as free, black, mulatto, Negro, or coloured); his height; and the name of vessel. Sometimes the description is ambiguous, such as "dark complexion" which could be Caucasian as well as African American. Four specific vessels, the ship *Caroline*, the ship *Delaware*, the schooner *Industry*, and the sloop *Commerce,* are known to have carried slaves. (See also Record Group 41, **Health Officers Register of Passengers Names, 1772-1794**)

- **Slave Manifests, 1800-1841.** (1 microfilm roll) Manifests prepared by the captains of domestic slave ships list the name, gender, age, stature, class or color, and the residence of each of the slaves on board as well as the name of the shipper or owner. For example, the ship *Champlaine* carried Leah, a black female, age 37, 5' 2", shipped/owned by one Samuel Oakford who lived in Louisiana. Two ships are included that arrived from foreign ports, bringing new slaves directly from Africa. The schooner *Phoebe* brought "one-hundred and eighteen Africans men, women, and children," and the schooner *Prudence* carried "Sixteen Water Casks, One Key Tobacco, Seventeen African men, women and children."

Records of the Survey of the Federal Archives, Pennsylvania Historical Records Survey, Pennsylvania Historical Commission, 1942. (2 volumes)

- **Ships Registers of the Port of Philadelphia, Pa., Vol. 1, A-D, 1942.** (1 volume) This incomplete set of volumes documents the three specific vessels *Caroline*, *Delaware*, and the sloop *Commerce*, which are known to have carried slaves. The register provides the history of each ship including when it was built, the home port, the dimensions, date of registration, owners, master, as well as previous owners and registrations. (See also Record Group 41, **Health Officers' Register of Passengers Names, 1772-1794**)

RG-14. RECORDS OF THE DEPARTMENT OF INTERNAL AFFAIRS

The Office of the Secretary of Internal Affairs was created by the Constitution of 1874. Under the constitution and subsequent legislation, the secretary's department was assigned all the duties of the surveyor general, as well as duties involving the supervision of the activities of business organizations and charitable institutions, and responsibility for establishing a Bureau of Industrial Statistics. The department also included a Bureau of Mines, which was abolished upon the creation of the Department of Mines in 1903.

The Department of Internal Affairs contained five major bureaus, which were transferred to other agencies at the time of its abolition in 1968. The Justice Department received its Bureau of Standard Weights and Measures, while the Bureau of Statistics became part of the Department of Commerce. The Bureau of Topographic and Geologic Survey was initially transferred to the State Planning Board, and later to the Department of Environmental Resources. The Bureau of Land Records became part of the Department of Community Affairs, which had also received the Bureau of Municipal Affairs from Internal Affairs in 1967.

BUREAU OF STATISTICS

Record of Marriages, 1885-1891. (4 volumes, 1 box) Arranged alphabetically by surname and thereunder by date of marriage. A record of marriages in Pennsylvania. Information provided about husband and wife includes: full name, occupation, residence, place of birth, age, color (white or black), date of marriage, and county in which license was purchased. Examples of entries for African Americans include:

- Lulu Hodge from Carlisle, who married Nathan Cooper, a waiter from Carlisle, on October 10, 1885. Both parties are identified as "black."
- Clara Hassler of Chambersburg who married Gabriel Nunse, a laborer from Chambersburg, on January 28, 1886. Clara is listed as "black" while Gabriel is identified as "white."
- Annie E. Hall from Chambersburg who married William H. Gates, a laborer from Chambersburg, on October 24, 1886. Annie is listed as "white" while William is identified as "black."

Some of the counties in which African-American marriage records were found are: Adams, Beaver, Berks, Blair, Bradford, Centre, Clearfield, Cumberland, Fayette, Franklin, Greene, Pike, Union, and Warren.

Registration Record of Practitioners of Medicine and Surgery, 1881-1889. (1 volume) Entries are grouped by county and thereunder grouped alphabetically by first letter of physician's surname. A record of registered Pennsylvania physicians. Information provided for each practitioner includes the doctor's name; date and county of registration; sex, color, and place of birth; place of residence; medical and other degrees (institutions and dates); and places of continuous practice in Pennsylvania since 1871. Documented in this volume are eight African American physicians/practitioners: Rebecca J. Cole, David C. Foster, William Greene, Edwin C. Howard, Sarah Jane Phoenix, Charles S. Schadd, Harriet J. Sweeny, and Silvia White.

RG-15. RECORDS OF THE DEPARTMENT OF JUSTICE

The Department of Justice represented the government in litigation involving the Commonwealth and is responsible for providing legal advice to the governor and all departments, boards and commissions. The head of the department and chief law enforcement officer of the state was the attorney general, whose appointment is first mentioned in the Constitution of 1776. Prior to 1923, the Department of Justice was known as the Attorney General's Department. Included in the Department of Justice was the Board of Pardons, first established in 1874, and the Bureau of Correction, which was created in 1953 to administer the state correctional institutions formerly maintained by the Department of Welfare. The attorney general became an elected officer in accordance with a constitutional amendment approved in 1978. The first elected attorney general assumed office in 1981, and the functions of the Department of Justice were transferred to the office of the Attorney General, and to the governor's office Bureau of Corrections, which later became a department in its own right.

The Commonwealth was one of the first political entities to abolish the use of corporal punishment for crime and to replace it with a system of rehabilitation through incarceration. In 1818 the legislature provided funds for the construction of the state's first penitentiary, the Western State Penitentiary in Pittsburgh. Subsequently, approval for the erection of the Eastern State Penitentiary at Philadelphia in 1821 and for the Industrial Reformatory at Huntingdon in 1878 was granted.

ATTORNEY GENERAL

General Correspondence, 1958, 1963, 1965, 1967-1970. (83 cartons) Arranged chronologically by year and thereunder alphabetically by individual or subject. A record of incoming and out-

RG-15. Department of Justice. Bureau of Correction. Press Office History File, 1829-1981. Pennsylvania Industrial School Camp Hill basketball team.

going correspondence of the attorney general. For the years 1967-1970 there are several letters relating to African Americans. Relevant subjects include the 1970 Black Panther Convention at Temple University, the investigation into the Get Set Day Care program where an African American woman was found to be embezzling money, and the 1971 investigation into the status of Black special agents in the Bureau of Investigation. Especially notable in the latter investigation is the case of George Howard, who was fired and then rehired with back pay after winning his claim of racial bias. Also included is a file discussing the details of the 1971 requirements of the State Human Relations Commission, requiring all employment applications to ask the race of an applicant for a job. A 1969 survey of non-white employees in Pennsylvania provided support for this measure.

BUREAU OF CORRECTION

Press Office History File, 1829-1981. (22 boxes) Arranged alphabetically by prison name. Newspaper clippings, photographs, annual reports, and miscellaneous articles pertaining to the state prison system. Examples of items relating to African Americans are photographs taken at the Camp Hill prison facility showing a men's choir singing at a dinner or banquet function, two ministers including African American minister Rev. George N. Spells of York, a large group of African American prisoners singing at an event, an inmate going into a building wearing a graduation robe, an inmate receiving his diploma, a graduating class, a graduate speaker, inmates in the audience, a band playing, a choir singing for a Christmas program, a cafeteria and its workers, a religious service with an African American minister speaking, and Joe Louis and Gill Turner boxing in Harrisburg on October 20, 1952.

State Prisoner Statistical Reports of Weekly Admissions and Discharges, 1953-1962. (13 cartons) Arranged chronologically by week. A record of criminal institution statistical reports maintained by the director of research and statistics. The files are broken down into three categories: Population Counts, Admissions and Discharges. Information on the population counts (categorized as white and negro) include the number of adults, juveniles, lifers (murderers), habitual criminals (lifers), defective delinquents, death house criminals, and infants. The admission and discharge statistics are broken down into the following categories: institution number, name of the convict, parole number, date of admission, county that committed the convict, offense, sentence time, race, county of birth, age, and marital status.

BOARD OF PARDONS

Clemency File, 1874-1900, 1906-1907, 1948-1962. (3 boxes, 70 cartons) From 1790 to 1873 the documents are filed chronologically. All other materials are arranged alphabetically according to petitioner's surname. Individual case files contain diverse documents (summary sheet, letters, petitions, court transcripts, newspaper notices, copies of death warrants, pardon proclamations or respites) about persons seeking pardons from the president of the Supreme Executive Council, the governor, or the Board of Pardons. The information found in the file varies with each dossier and the time period. While one case file may merely provide a person's name and reason for being imprisoned, another may also list the incarcerated individual's occupation and particulars about his or her life and family. Records concerning African American prisoners include the file for Mamie Alexander, who was imprisoned for larceny in the Philadelphia County Jail. Requests dating from February 18, 1895 cite the condition of her deteriorating health and the lack of available health care as the cause for her pardon.

Pardon Books, 1874-1934. (23 volumes) This series is broken down into two categories: applications and proclamations. The application volumes are, in most cases, a complete record of the progress of an application for pardon. Information provided includes a brief case history, usually in a narrative form, and a written recommendation by the Board of Pardons. The Board of Pardons only provides the reasons for its recommendations for the period 1874-1877. During the period from 1882 to 1930 records of commutation actions are included. For 1931 to 1934, only the dates of the application, hearing, re-hearings and actions are provided. Unlike previous records, these consist mostly of commutation records with only a few pardon actions. The proclamation volumes contain Board of Pardons recommendations and the reasons for its judgments. A separate volume dated April 25, 1889-February 27, 1895 and labeled No. 1 contains only the Board's reasons for their judgments. There are many accounts of African Americans being sentenced and paroled, such as:

• Junius Alston was tried for murder on April 26, 1916 and sentenced to be electrocuted the week of December 11, 1916. He had come to Pennsylvania from North Carolina in February

1916 and was employed at a lime quarry in Cedar Hollow, Pennsylvania.

- Armistead Randolph of Philadelphia was sentenced January 1913 to be hanged.
- James Frazer from South Carolina moved to Steelton, Pa. and was employed at Bethlehem Steel Co. He killed Charles Smith Hopper at Brougher's Hotel, Walnut and Cowden Streets, Harrisburg.
- Isaiah Croson, a thirty-seven year-old black coke drawer, was sentenced August 4, 1914 to be hanged for first degree murder. On December 22, 1914, the sentence was commuted to life in prison.

EASTERN STATE PENITENTIARY

Although construction of the Eastern State Penitentiary at Philadelphia was authorized by the state legislature in 1821, the first inmates were not received until 1829. The Act of April 10, 1826, stipulated that prisoners sentenced from Adams, Berks, Bradford, Bucks, Centre (as of 1833), Chester, Columbia, Cumberland, Dauphin, Delaware, Franklin, Lancaster, Lebanon, Lehigh, Luzerne, Lycoming, Montgomery, Northumberland, Perry, Philadelphia, Pike, Schuylkill, Susquehanna, Tioga, Union, Wayne, and York Counties were to be incarcerated at this penal facility.

Prison Population Records

Admission and Discharge Books, 1844-1888. (3 volumes)
Entries are arranged numerically by prisoner number. A record of prisoners admitted and discharged at the Eastern State Penitentiary in Philadelphia. Normally the books list the name (after July, 1866), prisoner number, race, age, sex, marital status, nativity, occupation, date of admission, length of sentence, and date of discharge of the prisoner; the amount of time that was spent in jail;

and the number of previous convictions. Information concerning the inmate's moral habits, hereditary diseases, vaccinations, and physical and mental health (at the time of commitment and discharge) is also included. The admission and discharge of African American photographer Glenalvin J. Goodridge, charged with rape, appears in the first volume, *Admission and Discharge Book, 1844-1865*.

Commitment Papers, 1841, 1861-1904. (7 boxes) Arranged chronologically by date of the fine. A record of individuals convicted of a crime in the Court of General Sessions, Court of Oyer and Terminer, and Court of Quarter Sessions from various counties in Pennsylvania. Information provided includes the convict's name, prisoner number, type of crime committed, court date, and the court's verdict. A sample entry is: Commitment no. 4763, received February 19, 1863, whereby Glenalvin J. Goodridge, son of the William Goodridge of York, was charged with rape and sent to prison for five years. To locate records of African Americans the series **Admission and Discharge Books, 1844-1888**, which shows the convict's race, must be consulted first.

Descriptive Registers, 1829-1903. (5 volumes) Arranged and numbered according to date of admission. Alphabetical indices are available for prisoners received from October 22, 1829, to June 13, 1895. A descriptive record of prisoners entering the Eastern State Penitentiary. Information provided includes date of admission and prison number; name, age, and nativity; occupation; complexion, eyes, hair, stature, distinguishing marks and length of foot; crime, sentence, where sentenced, and number of convictions; when and how discharged, time expired, when received, and remarks. Included is information on Glenalvin Goodridge who was committed on February 19, 1863.

Discharge Descriptive Dockets, 1873-1934. (4 volumes) Arranged chronologically by discharge date. A register of prisoners discharged from the Eastern State Penitentiary. Information provided includes prisoner number, name, color (white, mulatto, black), weight, age (at discharge), sex, crime, and sentence of the prisoner; the dates of admission and discharge; the method of discharge; the period of incarceration; the occupation practiced (until 1917) and the education (until 1906) received during imprisonment; the intended residence after release; and the amount of money that was earned in overwork (until 1907) and received upon discharge (from 1908 onward). From 1882 and beyond, the county responsible for sending the criminal to the penitentiary is noted, and occasionally the date on which the person might have been returned to custody is recorded. The amount of property owned by the individual is also sometimes mentioned in the dockets. Examples of African Americans include prisoner number 6892, John Agnes, a mulatto, imprisoned in 1871 at age 29 for murder in the second degree and prisoner number 2392, Mary Hamilton, an eighteen year-old black woman imprisoned for larceny in 1884.

Medical Statistics Books, 1883-1900. (3 volumes) Arranged numerically by prisoner number. A prisoner record kept by W. D. Robinson, resident physician at the Eastern State Penitentiary. Information provided includes each convict's name (until January 30, 1886), prisoner number, age, color, sex, occupation, nativity, marital status, social habits (temperate or not), date of reception, sentence, number of convictions, the state of the inmate's physical and mental health, and whether the person had any hereditary diseases in his family or had been protected against small pox. Occasionally the person's crime and physical location within the prison are also mentioned.

Reception Descriptive Book, 1879-1884. (1 volume) Arranged and numbered in order by admittance date. Indexed internally, alphabetically by name of prisoner. A descriptive list of inmates from January 2, 1879 to November 27, 1884. Basic information provided for each inmate includes name, number, age, marital status, color, occupation (before and after arrest), county of birth, and physical description (complexion, color of eyes and hair from November 19, 1884 onward).

Scrapbooks, 1884-1893, 1908-1917, 1925-1926. (3 volumes) The clippings are grouped by the date of publication and thereafter labeled with a prisoner number. Newspaper clippings that contain data about inmates, including particulars about their crimes and trials. At times photographs or newspaper sketches are also affixed. Examples of such articles are: "Colored Citizens Register Protest," "Prison for Negro Slayer," "Negro Women Rob and Kill Farmer in Den," "Arrest Negroes for Robbing Gypsy Woman," "Negro Woman Is Guilty of Murder," and "Negroes Admit Plot to Rob the Turners."

Statistical Books, 1835-1852, 1871-1909, 1911-1913. (7 volumes)

Medical Statistics Book of W. P. Robinson, House Physician, 1835-1852. A statistical record kept by the by the house physician. Information provided about each prisoner includes name, reception date, color and sex, age, bodily health, social habits (drunk or sober, marital status,), whether or not inoculated for small pox, hereditary diseases, number of convictions, length of sentence, and occupation. One sample entry is: Mary Johnson, received January 23, 1884, convict number 2002, 23 years of age, in good bodily health, colored female, abstainer, married, vaccinated against small pox, hereditary disease - gout, one conviction, sentenced to 1 to 6 years, Pennsylvania native, houseworker.

Statistical Books, 1871-1879, 1899-1915. Volumes which record the number of crimes committed per year per county. Information includes the number of convicts received by sex and color, age of the convicts, marital status, parental status (living or dead), level of education, and type of conviction.

Statistical Book, 1880-1883. A record of the number of crimes committed per month, the number of convicts received by sex and color, level and type of education, age of the convicts, and type of crime committed.

Medical Statistical Record Book, 1883-1886. A volume which records the number of crimes committed per month, the number of people who committed those crimes, the number of people received to date at the Eastern Penitentiary by sex and color, the marital status of the convicts, their social habits, level of education, the type of crimes committed, the location of crimes committed by county, and the location from which they were sent to the penitentiary.

Statistical Book, 1884-1892. A record of the number of crimes committed per year per county. Information includes the number of convicts received by sex and color, age of the convicts, marital status, parental status (whether living or dead), level of education, type of crime, the number of convictions received per year, nationality, and occupation.

PENNSYLVANIA INDUSTRIAL REFORMATORY, HUNTINGDON

In reaction to public pressure for the creation of a middle penitentiary district the state legislature in 1878 authorized the construction of such a facility at Huntingdon. In 1881, however, because of

Governor Henry Martin Hoyt's reforming influence, the legislature converted the institution from a prison to a reformatory for first-offender males between the ages of fifteen and twenty-five.

Prison Administration Records

Scrapbook, 1889-1929. (1 volume) Unarranged. Consists of newspaper clippings that contain data about inmates, including particulars about their crimes and trials. Items relating to African Americans include printed programs for prisoner entertainment events such as: "Entertainment by the inmates of the Pennsylvania Industrial Reformatory," Huntingdon, Pa., Friday, November 28, 1890 (Part II cites "Colored Quartet and Solo . . .The Old Home Ain't What It Used to Be"); a program dated June 30, 1893 citing "Negro Melody - Old Joe's Dream - Washington"; a program dated June 29, 1893, Descriptive Fantasia "On the Plantation," Orchestra and Colored Quartet; a program dated June 29, 1897 citing "Colored Quartet Uncle Tom's Cabin" by Numbers 1838, 1084, 101, and 2151; a program dated May 30, 1903, Recitation, "The Negro Soldier" by No. 3365; and Commencement Exercises of the School of Letters and Exhibit of the Industrial Departments, June 28, 1923. A few of the printed programs will give the last name of the inmate participating in the productions, but in most cases prisoners' numbers are given. Included in this scrapbook are also newspaper "wanted" and "reward" advertisements for slave runaways.

Prison Population Records

Biographical and Descriptive Registers, 1889-1932. (12 volumes) Arranged numerically by prisoner number. These registers contain biographical data and physical descriptions of inmates confined at the Industrial Reformatory at Huntingdon. Some of the registers indicate race or color for African Americans who are identified in the **Registers of Prisoners, 1889-1899, 1901-1925.** Biographical and descriptive information can be obtained by researching the prisoner's number and name in these records.

Conduct Ledgers, 1889-1898, 1903-1905, 1916-1918. (5 volumes) These ledgers give the following information for each prisoner: number, name, age, offense, maximum years to be incarcerated, age when received into the prison, county, year and month, report number, marks and scars, weight loss or gain, and remarks.

Physicians' Record of Prisoners, 1889-1910. (10 volumes) Organized chronologically by examination date. Two types of records comprise the series:

Physicians' Record of Prisoners Examined, 1889-1896, 1903-1907. Information includes the name, prisoner number, age, color, nativity, occupational training, occupation before conviction, schooling, habits, marital status, number of any children, sentence, names of any relatives, parental relations (i.e., living or dead, cause of death and age at death), and his state of physical and mental health. Diverse information about hereditary diseases and parental traits also appears.

Additional Physicians' Record, July 25, 1898-February 7, 1910. Besides listing the name, prisoner number, age, color, date of birth, and date of examination of the inmate, the record gives a grief medical history of the person and mentions the birthplaces (state or country) of his parents, the occupation of his father, and the parent that he most resembled.

Prisoners' Record, 1889-1921. (4 volumes) Arranged numerically by prisoner number which was assigned chronologically by reception date. A listing of inmates at the Pennsylvania Industrial Reformatory. Information found includes each inmate's name, age, alias, prison number, age, color, nativity, crime and maximum sentence of the offender; the dates that he was convicted, sentenced and received; the name of the court and county where he was tried; and the dates that he was discharged, paroled, reparoled, or escaped (when pertinent) from prison.

Registers of Prisoners, 1889-1899, 1901-1925. (2 volumes) Arranged numerically by prisoner number, which was assigned chronologically by reception date. Register that provides the name and prisoner number of each convict, the crime for which convicted, the sentence imposed, the dates of sentencing and reception, and the name of the county and court where tried and convicted. Occasionally, the age, color, and nationality of the individual are given along with the date discharged or paroled. The following are examples of prisoners identified as African Americans: Alonzo Maso, #2944; Albert Moore, #1945; John Stuart, #2096; LeRoy Profater, #3308; Arthur Goens, #3309; Robert Lane, #3916; Robert Carter, #4045; Thomas Durnin, #4132; Robert Henson, #4630; and George Moore, #4734.

WESTERN STATE PENITENTIARY

Although the state legislature authorized the erection of the prison on the outskirts of Allegheny City (now part of Pittsburgh) in 1818, the first inmates were not received until 1826. The Act of April 10, 1826 stipulated that prisoners sentenced from Allegheny, Armstrong, Beaver, Bedford, Butler, Cambria, Clearfield, Crawford, Erie, Fayette, Greene, Huntingdon, Indiana, Jefferson, Juniata, McKean, Mercer, Mifflin, Potter, Somerset, Venango, Warren, Washington, and Westmoreland Counties were to be incarcerated at this penal facility.

Admission and Discharge Books, 1872-1900. (3 volumes) Arranged numerically by prisoner number which was assigned chronologically by date of admission. A record of admissions and discharges from 1872-1900. From 1872 to 1891, entries show prisoner number, color, marital status, age, nativity (state or country), sex, occupation, and habits (whether temperate or not) of the convict; the admission and discharge dates; the amount of time that was spent in county jails; the length of the sentence; the time that was actually served in prison; the number of convictions; and the individual's physical and mental health before, during, and after imprisonment. In addition the books indicate when the prisoner was vaccinated or paroled. After 1891 the discharge sections of the books were not completed. Entries in these latter volumes simply record the convict's name, prisoner number, color, age, sex, marital status, and mental and physical health.

Commutation Books, 1917-1958. (4 volumes) Arranged chronologically by month of commutation. A record of sentence reductions granted each month to inmates of the Western State Penitentiary. The four volumes overlap in dates as follows: Vol. 1, 1917-1958; Vol. 2, 1919-1945; Vol. 3, 1928-1950; and Vol. 4, 1941-1958. Data contained in Volume 1 for each prisoner listed include inmate number, minimum or maximum expiration of sentence, action of the board (paroled, rejected, or continued), discharge number, day of the month, and remarks. Also listed are occasional delinquents and violators. Data contained in the other three volumes include prisoner name and number, date of sentence, minimum and maximum terms, minimum and maximum expiration of sentence, date prisoner was transferred to Rockview, date prisoner was returned from Rockview, date of release, date of return for violation of parole, date of maximum sentence to be served for violation, date final discharge was granted, date declared delinquent, and remarks (paroled, died, etc.).

Convict Description and Receiving Dockets, 1872-1957. (7 volumes) Arranged numerically by prisoner number which was assigned chronologically by reception date. Descriptive register of prisoners entering the Western State Penitentiary. From 1872 to 1926, entries normally give the name, prisoner number, age (when received), color, sex, nativity (up to October 30, 1926), physical description (complexion, stature, scars, foot size, height, weight, color of eyes and hair), occupation, mental condition (until October 27, 1927), schooling, physical health, habits, parental relations, civil condition (marital status and number of living progeny where appropriate), industrial relations (data on apprenticeship and trade skills), crime and sentence of the inmate; the dates of sentencing, reception and discharge; the number of previous convictions; and the name of the county and courts where he or she was convicted. Information regarding the method by which the prisoner was released appears, and sometimes the amount of property that he or she possessed is included. From 1873 to 1926, data about whether the person served in the army or navy are also recorded.

Convict Docket, 1826-1859. (1 volume) Arranged chronologically by date. Indexed internally by surname of prisoner. The docket records the name, prisoner number, and sentence of the convict; the dates of sentencing, admittance, and discharge; the method of discharge; and the name of the court where he or she was tried. Physical descriptions sometimes appear that may indicate the person's age and race, while in other instances the record may state that the offender was a young man or woman. Between April 10, 1837, and February 22, 1839, the docket contains a brief account of the prisoner's trial and sentence instead of descriptive data.

Descriptive Books, 1826-1873. (4 volumes) Arranged numerically by prisoner number which was assigned chronologically by reception date. Descriptive lists which, in most instances, record the name, prisoner number, age, sex, color, nativity, mental condition, occupation, marital status, number of any living children, religious affiliation, physical health, residence, habits (abstainer or not), physical description (build, scars, height, foot size, complexion, and eye and hair color), fingerprint classification (from March 31, 1922, onward), and sentence of the prisoner; the dates of sentencing and reception; the number of convictions, former prisoner numbers; the places of previous imprisonment; the nativity of the person's parents (from January 17, 1897); and the name of the court where he or she was convicted. In addition these books mention whether the inmate served in the army or navy, worked as an apprentice, was naturalized or an alien (as of September 24, 1897), could read and write, or attended a public or private school. From 1876-1939, detailed physical measurements (length of arms, trunk, left middle finger, forehead, etc.) of the convict are given. After August 16, 1922, the prisoner's place and date of birth are recorded.

Descriptive Register, 1826-1876. (1 volume) Arranged numerically by prisoner number which was assigned chronologically by date of reception. A register that lists the name, number, age, occupation, nativity, stature, complexion, foot size, marks (scars), and eye and hair colors of the inmate; the dates of sentencing and reception; the crime and sentence; the method of discharge; the number of previous convictions; and the date that the sentence was due to expire. Remarks recording the date on which the imprisoned person died or escaped are sometimes found as well.

Discharge Descriptive Dockets, 1873-1957. (9 volumes) Arranged chronologically by prisoner discharge date. A record of discharges at the Western State Penitentiary. Information includes the prisoner's name, number, age, color, physical condition, mental state, sex, crime, sentence, and occupation (up to February 27, 1923 only); the date of sentencing and discharge; time served in prison; weight when admitted and discharged; and from 1930 onward parole statistics.

Record of Parole Violators, 1942-1954. (1 volume) Arranged chronologically by date parole violator was returned. A record of parole violators at the Western State Penitentiary. Information given includes the prisoner's name, number, and color; whether or not paroled or returned as a parole violator; county from which returned; by whom returned (sheriff, patrol agent, State Police, etc.); the maximum time for parole, and remarks.

RG-16. RECORDS OF THE DEPARTMENT OF LABOR AND INDUSTRY

The Department of Labor and Industry was created in 1913 to enforce the laws of the Commonwealth relating to the welfare and safety of industrial employees. It replaced the Department of Factory Inspection, an outgrowth of the Office of Factory Inspector, which had been established in 1889. The department administers the laws and programs relating to workmen's compensation, workmen's unemployment insurance, labor relations, mediation, minimum wages for women and minors, conditions of labor, fair employment practices, and employment security.

SECRETARY

Annual Reports of the Commissioner of Labor and Industry, 1913-1916. (7 volumes) Arranged chronologically by year. Reports compiled by the Bureau of Statistics and Information for the Commissioner of Labor and Industry and sent to the General Assembly. These annual reports include employment and pay data charts on males, females, Negroes, Americans, and foreigners for various classes of industry. Information provided on the industries includes their average capital market value, number of days of operation, number of male and female employees, average daily wages, and the percentages of males, females, Negroes, and foreigners employed by the firms. Accident statistics are listed by industry and show the cause and nature of the mishap. Statistics on disease rates by industries are also given and later reports provide a breakdown of weekly wage rates. Narrative reports relate to Industrial Board standards and codes adopted, "timely tips" for employers and employers, and mediation and arbitration activities that occurred during the year. For the year 1915, reports from the Workmen's Compensation Bureau and the state Workmen's Insurance Fund were appended to these annual reports.

Biennial Report of the Department of Labor and Industry, 1919-1920. (1 volume) Report contains narratives from each of the bureaus within the department: Employment, Inspector General, Mediation and Arbitration, Workmen's Compensation, Industrial Hygiene, and Engineering. The Industrial Board section summarizes petitions for approval of safety devices and industrial codes and rulings on labor practices. Examples of such practices include allowing minors to run motion picture machinery or to work with explosives and allowing women to work on railroads or on streetcars. Studies and surveys conducted by the Board include one on the "Colored" population of Pennsylvania and a cooperative study with Bryn Mawr College on safety. There is also a sketch detailing the wartime activities of the Industrial Board. The Workmen's Compensation section of the reports shows the amount of money spent. The Mediation and Arbitration section discusses wages and capital lost from the 555 recorded strikes in 1920. The Employment report has statistics on soldiers returning to work and discusses the employment of immigrants. Finally, the report for the new Bureau of Rehabilitation contains a narrative description of the goals set for aiding the disabled.

BUREAU OF MEDIATION

Labor Dispute Case Files, 1938-1943, 1951-1953. (12 boxes) Arranged chronologically by year and thereunder alphabetically by name of company. A record of staff mediators' preliminary, progress, and final reports on labor dispute cases handled by the Bureau of Mediation. Although the information furnished varies with the type of report, data provided generally include the filing date, file number and name of the company; location; type of industry; date of assignment; date dispute began and type of dispute; union affiliation; cause of dispute; number of employees of company by sex and number of employees directly or indirectly affected; status of negotiations prior to arrival, the location and date of the mediation conference; the names and organizations of the conference attendees; and a summary of the results of the conference. An example of the type of information that can be found relating to African Americans is a letter dated August 7, 1939, from A. Bernard Vogel, executive and vice president of the Rolling Green Memorial Park, at 18th and Christian Streets, Philadelphia. Mr. Vogel requested from Mr. James A. Newpher, director of the Bureau of Professional Licensing of Philadelphia, a re-examination for African American salesman Harry Weiner who had failed to pass his real estate examination. The letter stated, "as you know, our business is the sale of burial lots on an installment basis to members of the Colored Race only."

BUREAU OF REHABILITATION

Biennial Report, 1921. (1 volume) The Bureau of Rehabilitation was created in 1920 to respond to the employment needs of wounded soldiers coming home from the war. The report describes the general principles of the Bureau, discusses the use of federal funds for civilian rehabilitation, and contains statistics on employees aided in finding new work. Data found include an enumeration of age, race, sex, marital status, whether illiterate and number of years of schooling, and the number of dependents. An interesting report on the rehabilitation problem in the coal mining industry is also present.

RG-17. RECORDS OF OFFICE OF LAND RECORDS

The Proprietary Land Office began functioning in 1682 with the appointment of Thomas Holme as surveyor general. The agents of the Penn family who were responsible for surveying, receiving purchase money, and selling land were collectively known as the Land Office. After the outbreak of the Revolutionary War in 1776, the Land Office ceased to function. Ownership of the Proprietary lands, with a few exceptions, was transferred in 1779 to the Commonwealth by an act of the General Assembly. In 1781, a state land office was created by the Revolutionary government, which consisted of a secretary of the Land Office, a receiver general and a surveyor general, who were assigned the records and responsibilities of their Proprietary predecessors of the same title. A Board of Property, similar to one that had functioned under the Penn government, was also created in 1782 to hear and determine cases of controversy arising from the transaction of Land Office business.

In 1809, the offices of receiver general and master of rolls were abolished. Their duties of collecting purchase money and enrolling state laws were assigned respectively to the secretary of the Land Office and the secretary of the Commonwealth. In turn, the functions of the secretary of the Land Office were inherited by the surveyor general in 1843. The Constitution of 1874 transferred the duties of the surveyor general and the Land Office to the secretary of Internal Affairs. The Land Office Bureau, or as it was later designated, the Bureau of Land Records, remained in the Department of Internal Affairs until 1968, when it was assigned to the Department of Community Affairs. In 1981, the Land Office functions were transferred to the Historical and Museum Commission where it continues to serve as the depository of original titles and conveyances, and as the custodian of all deeds and instruments relating to real estate owned by the Commonwealth. The early records are available on microfilm.

Commission Books, 1733-1809. (6 volumes) Arranged chronologically by date commission was recorded. Indexed internally, alphabetically by name or subject. This series contains a record of commissions to office holders in the Commonwealth of Pennsylvania as well as oaths of allegiance, lotteries, charters, corporations, proclamations, purchasers of arms, pardons, manumissions, and other items relating to the function of the executive branch of state government.

- *Commission Book No. A-4* contains a commission recorded July 26, 1773 to appoint Justices of the Peace George Bryan and James Biddle as justices of the peace in Philadelphia. The commission was issued by "George, the Third of Great Britain, France, and Iceland to . . . be chosen and legally sworn or affirmed to hear, examine, convict, or acquit according to law all and every such Negroe or Negroes in the said City and County as have been or hereafter shall be guilty of committing any murder, manslaughter, bugging, burglary, rapes, . . . and upon due proof and conviction such judgment or sentence in the premises to pronounce as is agreeable to the laws in that case made or provided or other ways to acquit and discharge such

Negroe or Negroes in case the Evidence shall not be sufficient for a conviction therein and or this to do or cause to be done all acts and things that may be necessary for the trying, judging and execution of such Negroe or Negroes as by virtue of this Commission and a law of our State Province instituted An Act for the Tryal of Negroes you are required and impowered to do as fully and amply as if the same were herein expressly and particularly mentioned - and all officers of the said City and County are hereby required to give due attendance and obedience . . . Signed, Richard Penn; recorded 26 July 1773."

• ***Commission Book No. 1*** contains the following manumission: "the Negro man Henry Thomas, formerly a slave to Col. Robert Knox, deceased . . . is now a free man" as a result of his master's last will and testament, witnessed August 12, 1785. The certificate for Henry Thomas to enter the state of Maryland was issued on August 13, 1785. Other examples of Philadelphia manumissions include the following: William Lewis freed a "Negro boy named Caesar," January 1, 1795; Robert Field freed "Negro man named Mirlin"; Lewis Vallette freed his slaves Lewis, Wishesta, John Charles, Franksay, and Maria Theresa; James Cox freed "Negro man Amboy"; Daniel Rundle freed his "Negro man named Charles, who intends from henceforth to go by the name of Charles Rodgers"; William Hamilton freed James and Paul Richmond; Richard Nottingham of Long Island, New York, freed a number of "Negroes on the Island of Tortola in the English West Indies"; the will of Thomas Lawrence, Esquire of Philadelphia provided that his slave Cesar be freed at the end of his eighth year; John Cox freed "Negroe boy Tom"; Mary Hamilton freed Scipio Africanus; and William Gray, born in Barbados and imported into Philadelphia by Robert

RG-17. Office of Land Records. Materials Related to Capitol Buildings and Capitol Buildings and Grounds,1911-1917, 1956. Lincoln School.

Gray, was granted his freedom at Pitts Town, New Jersey. Many other manumissions are included in these volumes as well.

- ***Commission Book No. 2E2*** contains a charter for the African Methodist Episcopal Church of Zoar in the Northern Liberties of Philadelphia dated December 11th, 1806.

Letters of Attorney, 1685-1812. (22 volumes) Arranged chronologically. Letters of attorney issued most often for the settlement of the estates of deceased persons who died intestate, or to protect the interests of individuals who were unable to act on their own behalf. The letters generally specify the name or names of the person or persons for whom the power of attorney was issued, the name of the person or persons acting as attorney, and the reason the letter was issued. The following is an example from volume 1 of a letter of attorney relating to a contract marriage in 1782 between John Black, a shopkeeper of Philadelphia, and Ruth Leonard, a free mulatto woman of Philadelphia." The contract states that "John Black shall and will within the space of half a year after the said marriage shall be celebrated between them, lay out the sum of five hundred pounds in the purchase of a house in the said city of Philadelphia."

Materials Related to Capitol Buildings and Grounds, 1911-1917, 1956, undated. (14 folders) This series contains information on the Capitol Park Extension Commission, 1911-1917, which acquired additional property for expanding the capitol complex in Harrisburg. Many of the buildings demolished to make way for the expanded capitol complex were owned or rented by African Americans. Included are minutes, photographs, and listings of property owners. Information provided about properties includes location, city valuation, and appraiser's valuation. Among the properties owned by African Americans were: Old Lincoln School, North

Street; Brotherly Love Lodge, 432 South Street; Corona Hotel (former home of the YMCA and the Red Lion Hotel), 644 Broad Street; Fry's Hotel, North 5th and State Streets; Wesley Union African Methodist Episcopal Zion Church, South and Tanner Streets; African Methodist Episcopal Church; and the residence of Dr. Morris H. Layton Sr., 518-520 5th Street.

RG-19. RECORDS OF THE DEPARTMENT OF MILITARY AND VETERANS AFFAIRS

The Department of Military and Veterans Affairs is responsible for administering the Pennsylvania National Guard, the Pennsylvania Veterans' Commission, the State Armory Board, the Scotland School for Veterans' Children, and veterans' homes in Erie, Hollidaysburg, Spring City (Chester County), Scranton, and Pittsburgh. The department also operates various programs of assistance to veterans. It was established in 1793 as the Adjutant General's Department and under the Administrative Code of 1923 it became the Department of Military Affairs. It assumed the name Department of Military and Veterans' Affairs in 1995 and the head of the department is the adjutant general, whose office and duties were also first defined in 1793. Included in the department at one time were the State Athletic Commission, which was placed in the Department of Revenue in 1937, and the Pennsylvania Aeronautics Commission, whose functions were transferred to the Department of Transportation in 1970.

ADJUTANT GENERAL

Civil War Muster Rolls and Related Records, 1861-1866. (135 cartons) Arranged by regiment and thereunder according to company. In the files are the following types of muster rolls which included the United States Colored Troops who trained at Camp William Penn. (See Appendix)

Muster-In Rolls. Entries usually list the soldier's name, age, rank, military unit, and the date and place where enrolled, the name of the person who mustered him in, the term of enlistment, the date of mustering in, and the name of his commanding officer. Remarks concerning promotions and assignments are sometimes recorded.

Muster-Out Rolls. The lists ordinarily give the soldier's name, age, rank, military unit, regiment and company; the date, place and person who mustered him in; the period of enlistment; and the name of his commanding officer. Particulars concerning pay earned, promotions, capture by the enemy and related information regularly appear as well.

Muster and Descriptive Rolls. Generally the rolls show the name, age, place of birth (town, county, state or country), occupation, physical description (complexion, height, color of eyes, and hair) and rank of the soldier; the unit, regiment, company, and commanding officer to which he was assigned; and the amount of money received for pay, bounties, and clothing. Rolls for unassigned United States Black troops are included in this group.

Alphabetical Rolls. Following a list of officers by rank, the names of enlisted men on the rolls are arranged alphabetically by the soldier's surname. Entries usually indicate the name, age, rank, occupation, and residence of the soldier; the unit, regiment, company, and commanding officer to which he was assigned; and the date and place where the roll was taken. Particulars about sickness or injury suffered by the soldier are sometimes noted.

A review of the Civil War records reveals that many African Americans were born in the South as well as in the North. These alphabetical rolls not only contain the muster rolls of the United States Colored Troops who enlisted in Pennsylvania but also of units which had African Americans associated with them. Examples of African Americans appearing on the alphabetical rolls include:

- 47th Pennsylvania Volunteer Infantry Regiment mustered in Morganzia, Louisiana on June 22, 1864: Aaron Bullard, John Bullard, James Bullard, Presto Garris, John Hamilton, Thomas Haywood, Abraham Jassum, Edward Jassum, and Samuel Jones.
- 12th Cavalry, 113th Pennsylvania Volunteers: Company muster rolls cite African American servants who served with the regiment.
- 103rd Regiment of the Pennsylvania Volunteers (mustered in at Harrisburg on February 24, 1862 and mustered out on June 25, 1865). African American Crowder Edgar Patience (Pacien) was enlisted as a cook at Plymouth, North Carolina on April 4, 1864.

Civil War Veterans Card File, 1861-1866. (373 card boxes) Arranged alphabetically by the soldier's surname. This series consists of 3" x 5" cards initially prepared to serve as an index to Samuel Penniman Bates' *History of Pennsylvania Volunteers, 1861-1865* (Harrisburg, 1869-71). These cards document the United States Colored Troops who trained at Camp William Penn. The Office of the Adjutant General later expanded the scope of the project by transcribing data found on the original muster rolls to the cards. Among the information that appears on the cards are the soldier's name, military unit, age at enrollment, description (complexion, height, color of hair and eyes), residence and birthplace;

the date and place where he was enrolled; the date and place where he was mustered in; and the date of discharge. An example of an African American citation is John Bullard, who enrolled on April 5, 1864 in Company I of the 47th Infantry at Natchitoches, Louisiana. He mustered in June 22, 1864 as an eighteen-year-old "colored" cook and was mustered out December 25, 1865.

Draft Board Records, Consisting Primarily of Lists of Persons Whose Registration Cards Were in the Possession of Their Local Board, [ca. 1917-1918]. (56 letter drawers)
Arranged alphabetically by county, and thereunder numerically by draft board number. A record of Pennsylvanians drafted into military service during World War I whose registration records were in the possession of local draft boards. The records are in the form of registration and induction lists. Information usually appearing on the lists includes the draftee's name, postal address, and age. At times the occupation of the draftee is also recorded. Typical references to African Americans found in the Cumberland County files include:

- *Western Union Telegram* received in Harrisburg on December 11, 1917 and sent to the sheriff of Carlisle at Local Board No. 2 stating, "Your Board should have eighty percent of quota plus Negroes in Camp, if you have less men than this number in Camp wire this Office immediately the amount of shortage."
- *Monthly Report of Status of All Registrants* includes induction statistics indicating "White" and "Colored" registrants.
- Lists of *Names of Persons Whose Registration Cards Are in the Possession of the Local Board*. The Lists for 1917 give only the registration number, name, and address while the lists for 1918 give the registration number, name and address, and color designation. Examples of African Americans from the

June 1917 List include: Charles Leslie Brown Sr., George Corbin, John Henry Cuff, Clarence Edward Drew, Peter Andrew Hodge, Carl Victor Profator, and William David Thompson. The June 1918 list provides the names of Henry Crocker and Elliot Johnson of New Cumberland and Samuel Smith of Marsh Run.

- *Induction and Final Induction Reports.* Listed in chronological order based on the date of induction, information includes order number, name of registrant, date of induction, draft call number, name of post, station or camp, acceptance status, date of acceptance or rejection; whether registrant was discharged after having been accepted at camp, and the date of discharge. There is no indication of race or color, but names of known African Americans on the list include: John Cary Ahl, Charles L. Brown, Alexander Coleman, John H. Cuff, Harold Cook Gatewood, Richard Leslie Hinton, Clarence Hopewell, Moses Charles Lane, Philip Mackey, and Thomas Henry Sipes.
- *List of 5-D Registrants.* Included on this listing is the registration number, name, and address. Although race is not specified, known African Americans are: William Haines Jr., Frank Stackfield, and Richard Thompson.

General Correspondence, 1793-1935. (30 boxes) Correspondence regarding the returns of election of officers, requisitions for arms and military stores, copies of general orders, and papers concerning the formation of military companies. Of primary interest are letters referring to African Americans serving in various wars, especially the Civil War. Some examples are:

- Letter, May 20, 1861, from G. E. Stevens, Commandant of lst Regiment of Colored Pennsylvania Volunteers to Governor A. G. Curtin telling him that "any number of able Colored men can be ready at an hour['s] notice" to fight in the war.

- Letter, July 16, 1863, from William Eliot Furness to George L. Stearns, telling Stearns that he had received permission to appear before the Board of Examinations for a commission with a Colored Regiment. In order for him to be freed from his present position with the government, he would need approval from the governor.
- Letter, July 18, 1863, from Thomas Webster, chairman of the Office of the Supervisory Committee for Recruiting Colored Regiments, Philadelphia, to Governor A. G. Curtin requesting to have orders transmitted for the "honorable discharge of Private William Elliot Furness of Company D, . . . in order that he may obey a summons to appear before the Board of Examiners at Washington, D. C. to determine an application for commands in US Colored Troops"
- Letter, July 18, 1863, Thomas Webster to Governor Curtin stating "our first Regt. of Colored Troops, i.e., the 3rd Regiment, US Colored Troops, is full and we want officers badly - Furness is to be one of them."

Records of the Scotland School for Veterans' Children, 1868-1995. (10 cubic feet) {unprocessed} In 1893 the legislature passed an act authorizing the purchase of land on which to erect the Pennsylvania Soldiers' Orphans Industrial School. One hundred acres were purchased in the Cumberland Valley for $12,000 from Colonel Alexander Stewart and the facility erected on this site became the Scotland School for Veterans' Children. In the early years, the enrollment was all white but as time went on African Americans entered the school. Today, the school is heavily populated with African American students. The records include bound annual reports of the Commission of Soldiers' Orphans Schools, 1870-1918; lists of names of soldiers' orphans to be discharged,1893-1912; a time ledger, 1895; a student death register, 1868-1905; *Industrial School News* (student newspapers), 1897-1970; yearbooks, 1943-

1995 (not inclusive); and minutes, 1921-1987. Also included are anniversary booklets and videos of the 75th and 100th anniversaries illustrating the success of African American graduates from the Scotland School.

Spanish American War Muster Rolls and Related Records, 1898. (16 boxes, 12 folders)
Arranged by regiment and thereunder by company. The records include the following types of muster rolls:

> *Muster-In Rolls*. Entries usually list the name, age, place of birth (town or county, state or country), occupation, residence, description (height, complexion, eye, and hair color), marital status and rank of soldier; the date and place where he was mustered in and enrolled; the period of enlistment; the location of the station of general rendezvous; the number of miles traveled to reach the rendezvous; and the date and location of the muster. Data regarding the physical disabilities of recruits and the names and addresses of parents or guardians of single soldiers are routinely included.

> *Muster-Out Rolls*. The dated lists generally give the name, rank, and residence of the soldier; the military unit, regiment, and commanding officer to which he was attached; the date and place where he was enrolled; the name of the enroller; the period of enlistment; the date of last pay; the date and place of the muster; and the place where he was discharged. Remarks concerning the physical disabilities of the person or changes in the soldier's rank are oftentimes mentioned as well.

Spanish American War Veteran's Card File of United States Volunteers, undated. (1 carton) Arranged alphabetically by veteran's surname. The series consists of 4" x 6" cards containing information abstracted from official records of the United States War Department between 1940 and 1941. Data appearing on the cards usually include the name, race, age, birthplace, residence, and rank of the veteran; the date and place where enlisted; the dates and places of service; and the military unit to which attached. Remarks concerning the date and place of discharge and information about prior military service are also often noted. An example of information provided for an African American who fought in the Spanish American War is:

- Jeremiah E. Crabb was a resident of Pine Valley, Pennsylvania who was born in Pine Valley on January 11, 1856. Crabb enlisted on November 19, 1899 at Fort Wright, Washington as a Private in Company M, 24 United States Infantry, and died of wood alcohol poisoning at Fort Wright on December 20, 1899.
- Thomas Bruff was a resident of Norristown, Pennsylvania who enlisted as a Private on May 10, 1898 in the Band of the 10th United States Cavalry at Lytle, Georgia. Bruff served in Cuba from June 14,1898 to July 20, 1898. He died on July 20, 1898 at Santiago, Cuba of illness under honorable conditions.

Spanish American War Veterans' Compensation File, [ca. 1934]. (35 cartons) Records created by the state Adjutant General's Office in 1934 to document compensation provided to veterans who served in the Spanish American War and in the occupation of the Philippines from 1898 to 1904. Included in the file are:

Veterans' Compensation Applications. Normally, these forms provide the veteran's name, rank, color, address, date and place of birth, date and place of enlistment, dates of service and the regiment to which he was attached, his legal address at the time of enlistment and the date and place of discharge. Information regarding engagements participated in, wounds suf-

Commonwealth of Pennsylvania

VETERAN'S COMPENSATION APPLICATION

1058

NUMBER 242406 (1)

Read instructions and then type or print answers to the following questions striking out words that do not apply. Numerals in parenthesis refer to corresponding numerals in the instructions.

COMMONWEALTH OF PENNSYLVANIA

COUNTY OF ___Delaware___ } ___Solomon Bouldin___

being duly sworn, deposes and says: I am the veteran named in the following descriptive information; I served in the military or naval forces of the United States from __Aug. 3 1918__ to __July 23 1919__; I claim veteran's compensation as authorized by Act No. 53, approved January 5, 1934; I was a resident of Pennsylvania at time of entry into service; I make this claim with full knowledge of the penalty for making a false statement relative to a material fact concerning this claim and the answers to the following questions and descriptive information are true:

(2) ___Bouldin___ ___Solomon___ ___3540332___ ___Negro___
    (Last name) (First and middle name) (Serial number) (White or colored)

(3) Legal residence at entry into service ___117 Lloyd st. Chester Del.Co. Penna.___
    (Street and number, City, County and State)

(4) Present residence: ___1727 Verdun Ave. Chester Del.Co. Penna.___
    (Street and number, City, County and State)

(5) Enlisted, commissioned or inducted in RA; ANC; NA; NG; ERC; Navy; NRF; MC; ORC; Pa. Vols; US Vols; at
    __NA Phila.,Penna.__ on __Aug. 3 1918__

(6) On active duty in Navy or in Reserve from ___--------------___ to _____

(7) Place and date of birth ___Amityville Penna. June 40 1893___

(8) Names and addresses of dependents: Wife (full name) __Nellie G(Morgan) Bouldin same as husba__
    Minor children ___Floyd Henry(step-son) same address___
    Mother (full name) ___Deceased___
    Father ___Rev. A.L.Bouldin 256 W.King st. York Penna.___

(9) Service in organizations, at stations or on vessels in the order named as follows:
    ___Co. B 813 Pioneer Inf.___ from _____ to _____
    _____ from _____ to _____
    _____ from _____ to _____

(10) Grades or ratings with dates of appointments or promotions: __Pvt. to Supply Sgt.__

(11) Engagements: __Meuse-Argonne__

(12) Wounds or other injuries received with dates: __None__

(13) Served overseas from __Sept. 15 1918__ to __July 15 1919__

(14) Honorably discharged on __July 23 1919__ at __Camp Dix N.J.__

(15) Did you ever apply for or receive a bonus or veteran's compensation from any other State? __No.__

(16) Did you ever refuse on conscientious, political or other grounds to perform full military duty or to render unqualified service? __No.__

Subscribed and sworn to before me this __13__ day
of __March__ 193 4.

(17) ___Casper H Green___
    (Signature and seal of officer administering oath)

(18) ___Solomon Bouldin___
    (Signature of Applicant)

My Commission Expires December 31, 1940   CERTIFICATE OF IDENTIFICATION   __March 13. 1934__
                                                                              (Date)

(19) I, __Casper H Green__, do hereby certify that I am __Alderman__
    (Name of person certifying to)   (Title of officer
    __7 ward Chester Pa.__; that __Soloman Bouldin__ applying for Veteran's
    and position)   (Name of applicant)

Compensation is known to me to be the applicant named in the application; that __he is mentally competent; that the signature of the affidavit is the signature of the applicant.

Signature and impression
of seal or stamp indicat-
ing office or position held.

Read Instructions (19) before signing.   X __Casper H Green__
                                             (Signature of person identifying applicant)

(1) __12__ Months at $10.00 per month; Total $ __120__

(1) Computed by __P.T. Meredith__   Reviewed by __W.T Brennan__

(1) Checked and approved by __G. Muller__

For The Adjutant General.

RG-19. Department of Military and Veterans Affairs. Adjutant General. World War I Compensation Application for Solomon Bouldin

fered, the dates of overseas service, and the names and addresses of dependents is also included. Examples of African American veterans covered by these files are William Achforth, Co. G, 25th US Infantry, and Thomas Henry Alexander, Co. D, 24th US Infantry.

World War I Veterans' Service and Compensation File, 1917-1919, 1934-1948. (555 cartons) Arranged by service branch (Army, Navy, or Marines) and thereunder alphabetically by the veteran's surname. Records created by the adjutant general's office in 1934 to provide compensation for World War I veterans during the Great Depression. An "Out of State" category also exists for persons who applied to the Commonwealth for a bonus but who were unable to substantiate Pennsylvania residency. Included in this series are:

> *Service Statement Cards.* Entries may show the name, rank, serial number, race, birthplace, age (and sometimes date of birth), and residence of the soldier; the military organization or unit to which he was attached; the dates of assignments and transfers; the engagements served in; the date of any wounds received; and the dates of overseas service and discharge.

> *Compensation Applications.* Contains such information as the name, rank, serial number, race, date of birth, and place of birth of the veteran; legal residence at the time of application and enlistment; the place and date where he was enrolled and discharged; and the period for which he served. Data concerning engagements in which involved, wounds suffered, the dates of overseas service, and the names and addresses of dependents are also included. The documents are signed and dated by the applicant.

> *War Service Record of Soldiers, Sailors, and Marines.* Survey questionnaires filled out by World War I veterans in 1920 for the Pennsylvania War History Commission. Normally the questionnaire gives the name, postal address and county of residence of the person; his age at entry into the service; and

the military unit, regiment and company with which he served. Data about the veteran's next of kin (their address and relationship to him) and particulars regarding the dates and places of his residency since beginning service are also provided.

World War II Veterans' Compensation Applications, [ca. 1950]. (3,082 cartons) Arranged alphabetically by surname of veteran. A record of veterans who applied for the World War II bonus provided for by the Act of June 1, 1947. Information contained on the applications includes the name, signature, residence, birth date, place of birth, sex, and serial number of the individual; the dates of domestic and foreign service rendered; the branch of the service in which enlisted; the dates and places where the applicant entered and left active service; the applicant's residence at the time of his enlistment; the name and location of the applicant's draft board; the dates that the application was received and processed; the amount of compensation awarded; the name and address of wife and addresses and ages of minor living children and stepchildren; and the names and addresses of living parents. The notarized application also records the ages of all dependents, whether the applicant was still on active duty in the armed forces at the time of filing the application, and whether he had ever received sea duty pay or a bonus. Though race is not mentioned, the file contains records of known African Americans. *These records are restricted* to veterans, their families and authorized veterans agencies.}

NATIONAL GUARD OF PENNSYLVANIA (1867-[ONGOING]), PENNSYLVANIA RESERVE MILITIA (WORLD WAR I), AND PENNSYLVANIA RESERVE DEFENSE CORPS (WORLD WAR II)

Enlistment Records, Including "201 Files," 1867-1945. (194 cartons) Arranged alphabetically by surname of guardsman. Enlistment papers of men who served in the National Guard of Pennsylvania from the end of the Civil War through the end of World War II. The "201 Files" are detailed personnel records kept on servicemen since World War I. Information given varies with the type of form utilized. Among the information likely to appear is the name, signature, age, date and place of birth, occupation, marital status, education and residence of the recruit; the date of enlistment or application; and the name and address of the nearest relative. A brief medical history and physical description including weight, height, eye, hair color, and complexion (African Americans are described as "black" or "dark complexion") is usually included, as well as the number of children for married guardsmen. Some of the older applications record the nationality as well. Examples of African American enlistees are: Bernard Brown, Co. I, 218th Infantry; and Joseph E. Brown, Co. F, 9th Infantry.

Mexican Border Campaign Muster Rolls and Related Papers, 1916-1917. (10 boxes) Arranged by military organization and regiment. Enlistment papers and muster rolls for members of the National Guard of Pennsylvania who participated in the Mexican Border Campaign of 1916-1917. The enlistment papers show the recruit's name, city or county of birth, age, address and occupation at time of enlistment, height, complexion, eye and hair color, unit assignment, and the recruit's signature. The reports of medical examination note evidence of any nervous or vascular diseases, the circumference of the chest measured under wearing apparel and during moments of forced inspiration and expiration, circumference of the abdomen, and evidence of piles, hernia, varicocele, or varicose veins. Also included in the file are descriptive lists and payrolls. The descriptive lists provide the names of guardsmen mustered into each company, together with their grades, dates of enlistment, places of residence, and whether they entered United States service. The payrolls contain the voucher number, name and rank of disbursing officer, date of payment, organization and regiment, station, period covered by the voucher, appropriations information, name and rank of payee, whether present or absent, date of enlistment, number of years served, and remarks affecting pay. Scattered throughout the files are various types of correspondence that frequently include letters from servicemen or their spouses requesting exemptions from service due to economic hardship or other reasons. While African Americans can not be fully identified in the muster rolls, reference to race is made in the "Medical Examination Reports" found among the regimental papers. An example of such an entry is a report for Company I, 10th Regiment, dated July 1, 1916, providing the following information: "John Checks, cook, Rejected Negro; "Charles Flemming, cook, Rejected Negro," and "George E. Munick, Rejected Negro." The designation "Rejected Negro" is used instead of the normal designations of "qualified, disqualified, not examined."

Muster Rolls, Payrolls, Quarterly Returns and Related Papers, [ca. 1867-1917]. (52 cartons) Arranged according to unit designation, and thereunder chronologically by the date of the document. Records of muster, daily roll call, and pay roll for soldiers who served in various Pennsylvania military units.

Abstracts of Daily Roll Call and Muster and Payroll. The rolls are dated and provide the name, rank, signature, age, height, occupation, and residence of each guardsman; the company, organization (infantry, artillery, and the like), and brigade to which attached; the date of most recent enlistment; and total number of enlistments. Particulars concerning the amount of pay earned and received, whether the federal oath of allegiance was taken, and comments concerning early discharge are also frequently found.

Applications for Company Organization. An application that records the type of company (infantry, artillery and the like) to be formed, the county where the company was being organized, the name of the person forwarding the application, and the dates on which the application was filled out and received. The documents are signed by each volunteer and list the individual's name, residence, and place of birth.

Inspection Rolls. The rolls are dated and give the name, rank, age, height, residence, and occupation of each guardsman; regiment; brigade, company, station, and commanding officer to which he was assigned; the date of enlistment; and the number of drills and parades in which he participated. Comments revealing whether the guardsman was absent without leave are also included.

Muster Rolls. The rolls provide the name, rank, height, complexion, hair and eye color, age, birthplace, marital status, occupation, residence, and signature of each member of the company; the date and period of enlistment; the name of the commanding officer; and the station, regiment, and unit to which he was attached. Discharges and transfers, or the fact that a recruit might not have been naturalized, are also recorded. In 1870 the Adjutant reported that a provisional brigade of "colored" troops in Philadelphia was assigned to the 11th, 12th, and 13th Regiments. In addition, ten other companies of African Americans were organized throughout the Commonwealth. Examples of three such units are:

- 5th Division, "Russell Guards" (Colored), under the command of Captain Edward Davis, from Dauphin County, Pennsylvania, mustered on May 23, 1870. The company disbanded on August 1, 1873. There are thirty-seven African Americans listed on the muster rolls.

- 11th Infantry, Company A, "Wagner Zouaves," under the command of Captain Walter T. Morris, mustered May 31, 1870, and disbanded May 12, 1874.
- 1st Regiment (1st Provisional Battalion), Company A, 3rd Division, "Reeves Rifles," under the command of Captains William P. Widdicombe and John R. Dobson began March 19, 1870 and disbanded September 23, 1878.

Veterans' Card File, [ca. 1867-1921]. (53 boxes) Arranged alphabetically by surname of veteran. 4" x 6" cards originally maintained by the Office of the Adjutant General for veterans who served in the Pennsylvania National Guard. Generally the cards show the name, rank, age, physical description, (height, complexion, hair and eye color), occupation and residence of the guardsman; the date and place of his enlistment; the date and reason for his discharge; and the unit (company and regiment) to which he was assigned. Although the cards do not designate race per se, African Americans are identified by the name of the unit and by physical description (i.e., Negro, colored, or black). Typical records relating to African Americans include: Charles Armstrong, Pvt., Colored Company of Titusville; John Edward Berry, Pvt., Co. L, 3rd Infantry, "Negro complexion;" William, Pvt., Union Guards of Shippensburg, P.N.G., "black complexion."

World War II Pennsylvania State Defense Corps Auxiliary Cards, 1941-1946. (16 boxes) Arranged alphabetically by surname of soldier. Under state and federal law, the State Defense Corps Auxiliary can be activated by the governor when the National Guard, in whole or part, is on active duty. During World War II, the National Guard was called overseas and the Commonwealth established a State Defense Corps Auxiliary. These cards are records of participants in that force. The information contained on these cards is as follows: name, military branch, residence, place of birth, date of birth, occupation, hair and eye color, height, weight, complexion, and history of service from enlistment to discharge, including date of each advancement in rank. African Americans have been identified by the designation of their complexion being "colored." Examples are: Samuel Morgan, Special Weapons, 1st Engineering Brigade; Vincent G. Hutchinson, Co. A, 1st Engineering Brigade; James E. Morrison, Quartermaster and Maintenance Co.; and John Morrison, Co. C, 1st Engineering Brigade.

RG-20. RECORDS OF THE DEPARTMENT OF GENERAL SERVICES

The Department of General Services is the central construction, purchasing, publishing and maintenance agency for the Commonwealth. It was created in 1975 to replace the Department of Property and Supplies and the General State Authority. The Department of Property and Supplies was created in 1923 to take over the duties formerly assigned to the Board of Commissioners of Public Grounds and Buildings, the Bureau of Information, the Department of Public Printing and Binding, the Division of Documents, the Director of Publications and several other commissions. Like its successor, the Department of Property and Supplies was the chief purchasing and distributing agent for the Commonwealth's departments, boards, commissions and related institutions. Included among the services offered to state agencies was the procurement of materials and supplies, the provision of real estate space and facilities, the management of state-owned vehicles, control of the construction, maintenance and protection of buildings and grounds, and the disposal of surplus property. The Board of Public Grounds and Buildings, originally established in 1885, continued to function within the Department of Property and Supplies along with the state Art Commission, which was responsible for examining and approving the design and location of public buildings and monuments.

RG-20. Department of General Services. Secretary of General Services. Capitol Park Extension Files, 1951-58, Hooper Funeral Home.

SECRETARY OF GENERAL SERVICES

Program Correspondence, 1959-1963, 1967-1971, 1974-1979. (6 cartons) Grouped chronologically, and thereunder arranged alphabetically by subject. Correspondence and reports of the secretary of General Services regarding departmental administration and programs. Relating to African Americans are the files on the President's Commission on Equal Employment for 1962. Among the items found in these files are correspondence between Andrew Bradley, secretary of Property and Supplies, and Vice President Lyndon Johnson regarding a meeting of the commission; an invitation to Secretary Andrew Bradley; and information provided to participants in various workshops.

DEPARTMENT OF PROPERTY AND SUPPLIES, 1923-1975

Building Demolition Files of the Bureau of Real Estate and Insurance, 1951-1966. (3 boxes)

Capitol Park Extension Files, 1951-58. Included in this subseries are correspondence, listings, agreements, and photographs of properties acquired by the state for the extension of the Capital Park. A large portion of these properties were occupied by homes, churches, and businesses belonging to or patronized by African Americans. Examples include: Abe Fortune's gas station, Bethel African Methodist Episcopal Church, and the Phyllis Wheatley Young Women's Christian Association.

General Correspondence of the General State Authority, 1957-1962. (20 folders)

Andrew M. Bradley, 1957-1960. The Honorable Andrew M. Bradley was appointed as secretary of Property and Supplies in 1957. He was the first African American ever to serve in the cabinet of a Pennsylvania governor. Prior to his appointment as secretary, he was the second African American in Pennsylvania to be certified as a public accountant. He held his post until 1960. Included in the general correspondence file is an invitation from the African Methodist Episcopal Church of Philadelphia for Bradley to become a member of a proposed Citizens' Committee of Philadelphia that was preparing for the two hundredth anniversary Celebration of the AME Church. Also present is a news release concerning Bradley's appointment by Governor Lawrence to an international convention of the American Academy of Political and Social Science together with a list of African American magazines and newspapers notified of the appointment. Other items include a request from Temple University Sociologist Edwin Eames for information concerning housing for African Americans in Harrisburg and a biography and letter of gratitude from Hugh Gloster, author of *Negro Voices in American Fiction*, for submitting his name for the position of president of Lincoln College. Finally, the collection contains a letter regarding a scholarship to Lincoln University from Virgil Hammond, a list of the names of prominent African American leaders invited to Governor Lawrence's inauguration, a letter from Governor Lawrence's secretary responding to a resolution by the Philadelphia Chapter of the Association for the Study of Negro Life and History, a letter from Governor Lawrence's secretary acknowledging a brochure from the National Chairman of Equal Opportunity Day of the National Urban League, and a letter from Dick Kent to a reporter at a Philadelphia publication regarding an article on Bradley that appeared in the magazine *Ebony*.

RG-21. RECORDS OF THE PROPRIETARY GOVERNMENT

William Penn assumed proprietary rights over the Province of Pennsylvania under the Charter granted him in 1681 by King Charles II of England. Basic charters or frames of government adopted in 1682, 1683, 1696 and 1701 largely determined the organization and administration of the colonial government. The last of these constitutions, the Charter of Privileges, remained in effect until the Revolution. The 1701 Charter provided for a unicameral assembly composed of four members from each county. A Provincial Council, which had exercised powers associated with all three branches of government, no longer functioned as a legislative body. Originally an elective body, the council later continued in existence as an appointed board in an advisory capacity to the Provincial Governor and exercised executive powers in the absence of the governor.

PROVINCIAL COUNCIL, 1682-1776

Executive Correspondence, 1682-1775. (22 boxes) This series has several items that relate to the African American experience in Pennsylvania. They are as follows:

- Proclamation for "Commission [to be] Formed to Try Negroes, etc., Lower Counties [originally part of Pennsylvania but now composing the state of Delaware], King George III to Government of the Counties of New Castle, Kent and Sussex, Delaware, February 1763." This proclamation called for a special body to prosecute and punish "Negroe and Mulatto Slaves."
- Record of conviction of Mulatto Daniel and Negro Harry Bedilow, signed by George Bryan and James Biddle, Philadelphia, September 18, 1773. This document is a court statement of the conviction of these two slaves for burglary. The slaves were to be transported to a place of execution and hanged. Their monetary value was also to be determined and their masters were to be compensated by the Province for their loss.
- Record of the murder conviction on September 22, 1773 of Negro George, a slave owned by James Sykes, Dover, Delaware. In this document there is a reference to the commission to try "black and mulatto slaves."

RG-22. RECORDS OF THE DEPARTMENT OF EDUCATION

The Office of Superintendent of Public Instruction was established under the Constitution of 1874. It replaced the Office of Superintendent of Common Schools, which had been created in

1857, to assume the duties relating to the administration of public schools originally lodged with the Secretary of the Commonwealth by the Free School Act of 1834. By 1876 the superintendent's office was known as the Department of Public Instruction. The powers and duties of this department were greatly increased in 1923 when the State Library and Museum, the State Board of Censors, the Public School Employees' Retirement Board, the Pennsylvania Historical Commission, and the various state professional examining boards were made administrative units of Public Instruction.

In keeping with its responsibility for administering the state's educational policies, the Department of Public Instruction supervised the public school system, distributed state subsidies to school districts, administered teachers' colleges and vocational-education programs, issued licenses for certain professions, and operated the State Library. Several administrative units were eventually separated from the department. In 1945, the Historical Commission, the Museum and the State Archives were merged to form an independent agency, the Pennsylvania Historical and Museum Commission. The State Board of Censors was abolished in 1956 when the act creating it was declared unconstitutional by the state Supreme Court, and in 1963 the professional examining boards were transferred to the jurisdiction of the Department of State. In 1969 the name of the Department of Public Instruction was changed to the Department of Education.

BUREAU OF STATISTICS

Higher Education General Information Surveys on College Enrollments, 1960-1971. (1 carton, 3 boxes) Arranged chronologically by year, thereunder by type of institution, and finally alphabetically by name of institution. Annual reports relating to enrollment in institutions of higher learning filed with the Department of Education. Information furnished includes the name of the institution, the signature of the administrator, the date of the report, and the date the report was received by the Bureau of Statistics. Reports filed from 1960 to 1968 provide documentation of both full-time and part-time enrollments. Freshmen full-time student enrollments are broken down by gender. Reports filed from 1969 to 1971 document full-time and part-time enrollments and credit hours registered and these are broken down by gender for undergraduates, graduate students, non-degree students, and first-time freshmen. Enrollment statistics are given for the following African American institutions: Cheyney State College, Crozier Theological Seminary, and Lincoln University.

Higher Education General Information Surveys on College Faculty and Staff, 1967-1968, 1970-1971. (2 cartons, 2 boxes) Arranged chronologically by year, thereunder by type of institution, and finally alphabetically by institution. United States Department of Health, Education and Welfare reports filed with the Pennsylvania Department of Education relating to employees in institutions of higher education. Information furnished for each institution includes the name and signature of the administrator, date of the report, and date the report was received by the Bureau of Statistics. Reports document full-time and part-time personnel totals and are broken down by functions such as instruction, research, library, and public service. Faculty totals are further broken down by rank and area of teaching or research. Other information provided includes salaries and benefits of faculty, library staff, and administrators and statistics regarding the educational levels of faculty members. Cheyney State College, Crozier Theological Seminary, and Lincoln University are among those institutions documented by the file.

Higher Education General Information Surveys on College Financial Statistics, 1968-1972. (2 cartons) Arranged chronologically by year, thereunder by type of institution, and finally alphabetically by institution. Annual reports filed with the Pennsylvania Department of Education relating to financial statistics of institutions of higher learning. Information furnished includes name and address, signature of administrator, date of report, and the date the report was received by the Bureau of Statistics. Reports show revenue by source, expenditures by functions, physical plant assets, indebtedness on physical plant, and endowments. Reports for Cheyney State College, Crozier Theological Seminary, and Lincoln University are included within the file.

Reports of Degrees and Other Formal Awards Conferred, 1962-1965, 1968-1972. (5 cartons) The 1962-1965 reports are arranged chronologically by year, thereunder by type of degree, and finally alphabetically by institution. The 1968-1972 reports are arranged chronologically by year, thereunder by type of institution, and finally alphabetically by institution. Annual reports relating to degrees, certificates and diplomas conferred by institutions of higher education filed with the Department of Education. The reports for 1962 to 1965 are broken down into such categories as certificates and diplomas, associates' degrees, bachelors' degrees, and higher degrees. Information furnished includes name and location of institution, name of administrator and date of report, date received by the Bureau of Statistics, and the type and number of degrees conferred by gender for each program. The reports for 1968 to 1972 are broken down by type of institution. Reports are available for Cheyney State College, Crozier Theological Seminary, and Lincoln University.

COMMISSIONER FOR HIGHER EDUCATION

Administrative Correspondence, 1972-1978. (1 carton) Arranged alphabetically by subject or name of correspondent. Administrative correspondence of the Commissioner of Higher Education. Included in this series is "Lincoln University Special File, 1977-1978," consisting of correspondence, newspaper articles, and memoranda referring to a crisis that occurred at Lincoln University during the presidential administration of Dr. Herman R. Branson. Owing to administrative actions taken at the time, which included the dismissal of some faculty, five trustees resigned. These resignations resulted in a campaign for the removal of the president. Also included in this file are the bylaws of Lincoln University of the Commonwealth System of Higher Education, Chester County, Pennsylvania, Draft, November 19, 1977; *Faculty Handbook*, September 1969; and a report issued by "The Boston Consulting Group" which analyzed Lincoln University's goals, financial needs, and fundraising capabilities.

Minutes of the Board of Normal School Principals, 1920-1931. (1 carton) Arranged chronologically by date of meeting. A record of the official proceedings of the meetings of the Board of Normal School Principals. Information typically found includes the date, time, and location of the meeting, a list of those members attending the meeting; and the topics discussed. Typical subjects discussed included admission requirements, committee appointments, committee reports, courses of study, curricula, finances, length of school year, redistricting, summer school sessions, and school vacation dates. Files relating to Cheyney State College are included.

Minutes of the Board of Presidents of State Colleges, 1931-1977. (3 cartons) Arranged chronologically by date of meeting. A record of meetings of the Board of Presidents of State Colleges and Universities. Prior to 1960, the state colleges were known as State Teachers' Colleges. Information provided varies for each of the thirteen state-owned schools. A typical entry includes the date, time and campus location of the meeting and a list of those members attending the meeting. Topics discussed frequently included athletics, committee appointments, budgeting, committee reports, curricula, enrollment, faculty, fees, finances, salaries, school year calendars, and academic standards. Files relating to Cheyney State College are included.

Minutes of the Board of State College and University Directors, 1971-1975. (1 carton) Arranged chronologically by date of meeting. A record of meetings of the Board of State College and University Directors. A typical entry includes the date, time and location of the meeting and a list of those members attending the meeting. Topics discussed included budgets, capital projects, committee appointments, committee reports, faculty, fees, legislation, programs, purchasing, residency requirements, and salaries. Files relating to Cheyney State College and Lincoln University are included.

Minutes of the Board of Trustees of State Colleges and Universities, 1954-1965, 1971-1977. (9 cartons) Arranged alphabetically by name of institution and thereunder by date of meeting. A record of meetings of the Board of Trustees of State Colleges and Universities. Information provided varies for each of the thirteen state-owned schools. A typical entry includes the date, time and campus location of the meeting and frequently lists the names of the members and invited guests. Reports submitted generally include the president's report on the budget, and reports by the athletic committee, budget and finance committee, institutional development committee, personnel committee and the public relations committee. Common topics include faculty appointments, retirements, accreditation, building development, gifts, grants, tuition fees, and student assistance. Files relating to African American institutions of higher learning include those for Cheyney State College and Lincoln University.

Specialized Correspondence, 1965-1977. (3 cartons) Arranged alphabetically by subject. This series contains specialized correspondence of the commissioner of Higher Education. Among the topics documented are the Commonwealth University System, faculty development, Servicemen's Opportunity College, tenure, State College Missions, and student problems. One example of African American source material is correspondence regarding the admission of a African American student with health problems to Cheyney State College.

OFFICE OF EQUAL EDUCATION OPPORTUNITY

Records of Equal Rights Program Activities, 1965-1977. (1 carton) Arranged alphabetically by subject. Records documenting the activities of the Office of Equal Education Opportunity designed to ensure school desegregation and access by minority students to higher education. Files include memoranda, correspondence, testimonies, reports, agendas, news clippings, grant applications, press releases, minutes, service purchase contracts, general invoices, programs, and registration forms. Among the items found are the following: *Afro-American Mandate, 1968*; *Curriculum Inclusion of Minority Group Content in the Schools of the Commonwealth of Pennsylvania*, prepared by Dr. Neal V. Musmanno, September 19, 1968; materials relating to the participation of female students and black students in approved vocational education courses and programs for School Year 1973-74; and a 1975 State Board Report regarding School Desegregation.

OFFICE OF SCHOOL EQUITY

The Office of School Equity directs the implementation and monitoring of all basic education and Equal Employment Opportunity (EEO) compliance plans. It also provides curriculum assistance in equity in the areas of age, sex, national origin, and race, and coordinates and directs statewide assistance to school districts in implementing the Teacher Expectation and Student Achievement (TESA) programs.

Emergency School Aid Act Applications, 1980-1996. (5 cartons) {unprocessed} Applications for federal assistance grants under the Emergency School Aid Act of 1980-1996, also known as Title IV of the Civil Rights Act of 1964. Included in this collection are documentation for workshops and conferences of the Office of School Equity which held workshops on multi-cultural education throughout the school systems in the Commonwealth.

School Desegregation Files, 1964-1996. (28 cartons) {unprocessed} Arranged alphabetically by county. Reports, letters, and memoranda for the various school districts throughout the Commonwealth documenting implementation of Title IV of the Civil Rights Act of 1964. This legislation changed the previously existing policy for awarding funds to public schools and to desegregation assistance centers. The original regulations implementing Title IV provided for financial assistance to personnel operating public schools who requested assistance in eliminating discrimination on the basis of race, sex, and national origin. The regulations were amended in 1987 in such a way that "funds for national origin and race desegregation assistance may not be used to provide assistance in the development or implementation of activities, or the development of curriculum materials for the direct instruction of students, except that assistance may be provided in the development or implementation of activities or development of curriculum materials for the direct instruction of students of limited English proficiency."

STATE BOARD OF CENSORS (MOTION PICTURE)

Applications for Examination, 1915-1951. (4 boxes) Arranged chronologically by date of application. This series contains applications submitted by motion picture film companies requesting the State Board of Censors to review their films. Each application lists the title of the film, manufacturer, names of leading actors and actresses, number and length of reels, style of film, and whether the film was approved without changes, approved with the elimination of some material, or condemned in total. If the film was approved contingent upon the elimination of some scenes, an elimination form is attached which lists the specific changes that needed to be made. Often there is a memorandum of changes form that indicates the nature of the requested changes, when the changes were made, and when the board approved the film. Some applications have copies of the script attached. Representative of motion pictures having content related to African Americans are: *King of the Carnival, Native Son, One Stormy Night, Schulamite, Tarzan,* and *Zululand.*

STATE LIBRARY OF PENNSYLVANIA
Glass Lantern Slides, 1890-1960. (300 cu. ft.)

Pennsylvania History, Dauphin County, Harrisburg:

- YMCA Broad Street Branch (African American YMCA): A group of slides with images of the following: Dr. George Reed's Bible class, the hiking club, the Montakama Business Club, and the first and only football team of the "Y" organized in 1920 at the 644 Broad Street location (Corona Hotel). Also included is a slide of the branch's second and last YMCA building on Forster Street.

United States History:

- Music-Negro Spirituals: These slides contain music scores for the following Negro spirituals: "Deep River," "Keep

Me From Sinking Down," "My Lord's Writing All the Time," Nobody Know the Trouble I Seen," "Steal Away," "Swing Low, Sweet Chariot," and "Turn Back Pharaoh's Army."

- Slave Life and the Civil War: This collection includes four lantern slides relevant to the African American in Pennsylvania: #20: "A Group of Contrabands - Negro Slaves"; #35: "First Reading of the Emancipation Proclamation"; #37: "Scene of the Emancipation Proclamation"; and #56: "Emancipation Statute in Lincoln Park, Washington, D.C."

- Slave Life and Lincoln: In this section are included sixteen lantern slides depicting slave life during the administrations of Zachary Taylor and Millard Fillmore including: #4: "Slaves of the Northern Sweatshops"; #5: "A Typical Slave Family Around Cabin-Fire Place with Home Made Furniture"; #6: "Fugitive Slave Arriving at House of Levi Coffin"; #7: "Uncle Tom on the Auction Block as Various Types of Buyers Crowd Around"; and #10: "Slaves Escaping Through the Underground Railway with Bundles." A second grouping depicting scenes from the administration of Abraham Lincoln includes one labeled "Men From All Walks of Life Answer Lincoln's Call for Volunteers," and one labeled "Emancipation."

PROFESSIONAL AND OCCUPATIONAL BOARDS

Though race is not indicated in these records, the author was able to recognize the names of a number of individuals of whom she has personal knowledge. Other individuals were identified because the school from which they graduated was known to be a historically Black college or university.

Record of Dental Licenses, 1897-1923. (11 volumes) Arranged numerically by license numbers that were assigned chronologically. Recorded copies of dental licenses designated by law to be kept in the archives of the Dental Council. The certificates, which are signed by each of the examiners who reported the candidate as having passed the dental examination, list the name of the dentist, the date and place where the examination was passed, the date issued, and the agency and officials conferring the license. African American dentists in this series include Dr. Stephen Johnson Lewis, No. 2754, who passed examination June 9-12, 1909 and was licensed on July 26, 1909, and Dr. Joseph N. Dunston, No. 5012, who passed his examination on June 1920 and was licensed on January 24, 1921.

Summary of Examinations, 1897-1971. (6 volumes) Arranged chronologically by date of examination. This series records the examination scores of applicants applying for dental and dental hygienist licenses. The date, location and type of examination are listed, as are each applicant's name, residence, test score on the written examination, grades for practical work completed, and overall result (pass or fail). The column titled "Remarks" frequently provides the name of the college or university from which the applicant received his or her degree. Examples of African Americans who applied for and received dental licenses include Howard University Medical School graduate Dr. Joseph J. B. Mason and Meharry Medical College graduate Dr. Joseph Dunston.

No. 6491

Commonwealth of Pennsylvania

MEDICAL COUNCIL.

To all to whom these Presents shall Come, Greeting:

Whereas, It appears by the report of the BOARD OF MEDICAL EXAMINERS representing the

STATE MEDICAL SOCIETY

of the State of Pennsylvania that

Morris Hallowell Layton, Jr.

having given satisfactory evidence of fitness as to age, character, preliminary education, medical instruction and all other matters required by law, was fully examined by the members of the Board of Examiners whose signatures are hereto attached, and found duly qualified for the practice of medicine, he *is hereby, in accordance with the provisions of the Act of Assembly approved May 18, A. D. 1893, granted this* LICENSE TO PRACTICE MEDICINE AND SURGERY *in the State of Pennsylvania.*

EXAMINERS:

Henry Beates, Jr., M. D., Pres.

W. D. Hamaker, M. D., Sec.

Morton P. Dickeson, M. D.,

R. W. Ramsey, M. D.,

Adolph Koenig, M. D.,

Francis R. Packard, M. D.,

J. B. Walker, M. D.,

In Witness Whereof, *We have hereunto set our hands and caused the Seal of said Medical Council to be affixed at Harrisburg the* first *day of* August, 1910

Henry Houck,

President

Hon. an C. Stober,

Secretary

Passed Examination June 21-24 1910

It

RG-22. Department of Education. Medical Council. Record of Medical Licenses Recommended by the State Medical Society, 1894-1911.

Record of Certificates Accepted in Lieu of Preliminary Examination, 1904-1911. (3 volumes) Grouped chronologically by date of certificate, and thereunder alphabetically by first letter of applicant's surname. A registry kept by the Medical Council of Pennsylvania to provide proof that candidates for medical study had received adequate preliminary academic grounding for their chosen field. Entries generally give the name of the applicant, the high school attended, the date of graduation, the date that the certificate was issued, and the name of the examiner approving the certificate. Affidavits from school officials are frequently included. Examples of certificates issued to African Americans are: July 20, 1906, Frisby C. Battis Jr., Wilberforce University; March 5, 1908, Samuel Clyde Wilson, Lincoln University; March 23, 1908, Joseph J. B. Mason, Howard University; October 21, 1908, Ernest R. MacDonald, Lincoln University; May 25, 1909, Thomas J. Miller, Lincoln University; May 25, 1909, William Willoughby, Shaw University; January 26, 1910, Charles Anthony Lewis, Lincoln University.

Record of Medical Licenses Recommended by the State Medical Society, 1894-1911. (15 volumes) Arranged chronologically by date of license and thereunder by license number. Copies of medical licenses designated by law to be kept in the office of the Medical Council. The State Medical Society served as the examining board that recommended the issuance of these certificates. Information found includes the name of the physician, the date and place where the examination was passed, the agency conferring the license, and the date the license was issued. Many of the licenses bear signatures of officers of the Medical Council and the physician examiners. Among the African Americans in this group are: #4611, Edward Mayfield Boyle, January 25, 1906; #4624,

James Edward Foster, January 25, 1906; #5919, Charles T. C. Nurse, January 6, 1909; #6491, Morris Hallowell Layton Jr., August 1, 1910.

State Board of Funeral Directors
(Under Health Department from 1935 to 1959)

Minute Books, 1895-1963. (15 volumes) Arranged chronologically by date of meeting. A record of the meetings and proceedings of the State Board of Funeral Directors. Entries list the dates, locations, and names of participants present at meetings. Typical subjects discussed or reported upon are the organization of the board, the formulation of rules for governing the profession, the establishment of fees, the holding of hearings, and matters dealing with the examination and registration of morticians. Financial reports are regularly recorded, and extensive lists of applicants requesting examinations and licenses frequently appear. Included in the minutes is information on several African American funeral directors including James F. Hill, Webster D. Jackson, and Frances B. Jones of Philadelphia; Helen M. Hunt of Chester and Pauline H. L. Gordon of Johnstown. Included also are entries regarding the Colored Funeral Directors Association of Philadelphia and Vicinity.

State Board of Medical Education and Licensure

Known as the Bureau of Medical Education and Licensure prior to 1923, on July 1, 1963, this bureau was transferred from the Department of Public Instruction to the Professional and Occupational Affairs Commission in the Department of State.

Minute Books, 1911-1962. (12 volumes) Arranged chronologically by date of meeting. This series documents the meetings and proceedings of the State Board of Medical Education and Licensure in compliance with the legislative directive that it meet at least twice annually in Harrisburg to transact business. The minutes show the date and location of the meeting and a record of attendance. Matters addressed include decisions concerning the revocation, suspension, or restoration of licenses; the licensing of applicants on the basis of endorsement or reciprocity agreements; the formulation of rules and policies regulating medical conduct; the scheduling of examinations; and the review of applications for entry into various medical training programs. Reports on inspections of medical training facilities and lists of Pennsylvania physicians certified to practice medicine in other states are also included. Information relating to African Americans includes:

- Minute Book for December 12, 1911-December 1, 1920 showing an examination list for Howard University, Washington, D.C.
- Minute Book for April 9, 1953 to December 14, 1956 containing many approved statements of acceptance of Medical Licenses for African Americans. Information found generally includes the name of the applicant, the name of the college or university attended, and the dates of attendance; an endorsement to practice medicine in Pennsylvania; and the National Board Licensing certificate number, date of issue, the name of the interviewer and the name of the doctor recommending the license. Examples of African Americans granted licenses include Howard University graduates Jane V. Williams, Osward J. Nickens, and George E. Blackman.

Records of Licenses Issued on Licenses from Other States, 1912-1963. (13 volumes)

Arranged chronologically by date of license and thereunder numerically by license number. A record of licenses issued by the

State Board of Medical Education and Licensure on the basis of the applicant having already been accepted as a qualified physician in another state. Entries list the name of the physician, the date licensed, the examining board that licensed the applicant, and the agency and officials conferring the license. Many African American medical doctors are documented in the records but some are not easily identifiable because they attended integrated medical colleges. A large number, however, received their training at established African American institutions such as Howard University's Medical School (Washington, D.C.), Leonard Medical College (Raleigh, N.C.), and Meharry Medical School (Nashville, Tennessee).

Records of Medical Licenses, 1912-1964. (42 volumes) Arranged chronologically by date of license and thereunder numerically by license number. Copies of medical licenses designated by law to be retained in the archives of the Department of Public Instruction. The certificates list the name of the physician, the date the license was issued, and the agency and officials conferring the license. To find a record of an African American who passed the exam for a medical license, the name of the individual licensee must be known. An example of an entry for an African American is # 24949, Morton Onque Blake, licensed on September 13, 1951, who practiced in Athens and Wilkes-Barre.

Registers of Physicians, 1870-1917. (3 volumes) Prior to 1913 entries are arranged in strict alphabetical order, but after 1913 they are only grouped alphabetically by surname of physician. A record of physicians who were registered in Pennsylvania from 1870 to 1917. Normally, the doctor's name, license number (from 1895 onward), postal address, county where registered, and date of registration are given. Information concerning the death or change of address of the doctor is also frequently included. Some known

African Americans are: Forrest Hunter Battis, Philadelphia, #5454; Frisby Battis, Harrisburg (no license number), 1911; T. Clifford Boston, Philadelphia, #1551 (no date); George William Bowles, York, #5040, 1907; Edward Mayfield Boyle, Williamsport (no license number),1908; Cornelius Lennon Carter, Harrisburg, #4613, 1905; James Edward Foster, Harrisburg, #4624, 1906; Walter H. Scudder, 910, Philadelphia, #5792, 1912; and Hiram Tobias Williams, Chester (no license number), 1902.

State Board of Nurse Examiners

Known as the State Board of Examiners for Registration of Nurses prior to 1951, effective July 1, 1953 the State Board of Nurse Examiners was transferred from the Department of Public Instruction to the Professional and Occupational Affairs Commission in the Department of State.

Licensed Practical Nurse Registration Book, 1923-1965. (1 volume) Arranged numerically by certificate number. A record of Licensed Practical Nurses registered by the Pennsylvania State Board of Examiners for Nurses from February 9, 1923 to December 23, 1965. Information provided for each nurse includes the certificate number, applicant's name, and the date the certificate was granted. The book is arranged to indicate whether the applicant was registered by examination, waiver, or endorsement. Representative of African American practical nurses are: #2145, Eunice Smallwood, December 22, 1957; #315651, Sarajane Roebuck, May 22, 1957; #19781; and Evelyn Louise Foster of Carlisle, November 18, 1959.

Registered Nurse Certificate Books, 1917-1969. (7 volumes) Arranged numerically by certificate number. This series contains a listing of individuals certified as either licensed attendants or registered nurses. Records for 1917 through September 9, 1923 show the individual's name and date certified, but do not list a certificate number. The records from September 10, 1923 through 1969 provide the certificate number, the individual's name, and the date certified. Representative of an African American entry is that for a nurse who was certified #28,317, Mary Elizabeth Thompson, November 8, 1929.

State Board of Pharmacy

Known as the State Pharmaceutical Examining Board, 1887-1917, and as the Pennsylvania Board of Pharmacy, 1917-1923. Effective July 1, 1963, the Board was transferred to the Bureau of Professional and Occupational Affairs in the Department of State.

Index of Qualified Assistants, 1887-1941. (2 volumes) Grouped alphabetically by first letter of surname of assistant pharmacist. Index lists the names and registration numbers of assistant pharmacists certified to practice in Pennsylvania. The index only provides the name and registration number of the person with no other personal information. To find an African American pharmacist you must know the individual's name. An example is Henry Edwin Parsons who appears as #5475 in Volume 1.

Registration Books for Assistant Pharmacists, 1887-1978. (3 volumes) Arranged numerically by register number and partially indexed externally, alphabetically by surname of assistant pharmacist in **Index to Qualified Assistants, 1887-1941**. A record of qualified assistant pharmacists registered with the Pennsylvania State Board of Pharmacy. A typical entry contains the registration number, name, address, county of residence, and age of the applicant, the amount of experience in the profession, and the date of registration. Prior to 1899, the registers have renewal dates and state whether the assistant was examined or in practice before May 24, 1887. The grades earned by the registrants are recorded from November 25, 1907 onwards and after June 30, 1922 a preliminary certificate number was assigned. From 1963 to 1978, a record of the registrant's examination scores and the college that he or she attended appears in lieu of professional experience. To find a record of an African American, the name of the pharmacist must be known. An example of such an entry is #5475 for Henry Edwin Parsons of 814 South 18th Street, Philadelphia, registered March 23, 1906.

Registration Books for Pharmacists, 1887-1963. (5 volumes) Arranged numerically by register number and indexed externally, alphabetically by the pharmacist's surname in **Pharmacist Index, 1887-1967**. A record of persons registered as pharmacists by the Commonwealth. Entries ordinarily show the registration number and date, the name and address of the pharmacist, and the county of residence. Prior to 1911 the registers list renewal dates and whether a registrant was examined or in practice prior to May 24, 1887. After June 29, 1911, the registers record the age of the individual, the college attended and the grades attained. Information such as whether a pharmacist was registered because of a reciprocal agreement with another state, or whether the registrant died or moved, is periodically indicated as well. To find a record of an African American, the name of the pharmacist must be known. An example is #9356 for H. Edwin Parsons, 1162 South Cameron Street, Harrisburg, registered June 1, 1908.

State Board of Veterinary Medical Examiners

Veterinary Registration Books, 1905-1961. (5 volumes) Arranged numerically by certificate number. A record of veterinarians registered in Pennsylvania. Information recorded in these volumes varies over time. The earlier books give the registrant's name, address, date of birth, the college of graduation and the dates attended, the certificate number (during the 1930's), the date and county of first registration, and the dates that registration fees were paid. The more modern books do not record the birth date (after 1951), data regarding first registration (from the 1940's on), or the dates fees were paid. The date of death is also sometimes recorded on the registration page. Book 2, page 960 contains the record for Basil George Edward Curry, an African American veterinarian who first lived in Gettysburg and later moved to Huntingdon. He graduated from Ontario Veterinary College in 1909.

State Dental Council and Examining Board

Record of Dental Licenses, 1923-1965. (21 volumes) Arranged chronologically by date of license and thereunder numerically by license number. Consists of recorded copies of dental licenses designated by law to be kept in the archives of the Dental Council. The certificates, which are signed by each of the examiners who reported the licensee as having passed the dental examination, list the name of the dentist, the date and placed where the examination was passed, the date issued, and the agency and officials who conferred the license. African American dentists are documented in the records. One is Dr. Walter Thurston Dunston, who passed the examination in June 1960 and was licensed on July 12, 1960.

SUPERINTENDENT OF PUBLIC INSTRUCTION, 1874-1969

The Office of Public Instruction was established under the Constitution of 1874. It replaced the Office of Superintendent of Common Schools which had been created in 1857 to assume the duties relating to the administration of the public schools originally lodged with the secretary of the Commonwealth by the Free School Act of 1834. In 1969, the name of the Department of Public Instruction was changed to the Department of Education.

Applications for Teaching Certificates, 1866-1922. (35 cartons) Arranged alphabetically by surname of teacher. Application forms for permanent, provisional, temporary, special, and continuation certificates submitted by teacher candidates to the superintendent of Public Instruction. The type of data varies with the forms utilized. Application forms for provisional college certification contain the name, age, address, county of residence and college of the candidate, the college courses that he or she studied, the date that the diploma was issued, and the dates that the application was received and the certificate granted. Application forms for permanent certification, on the other hand, usually only indicate the name, address, number of semesters of teaching experience, the school district of the applicant, the date that the application was received, and the date that certification was granted. Included in these records are applications from African Americans. Application # 4227 is that of Oscar N. Frey, a resident of Philadelphia and a graduate of Lincoln University, May 7, 1918.

General and Administrative Correspondence, 1936-1964. (8 cartons) Grouped chronologically by year. Incoming and outgoing correspondence of the Department of Education includes the following material pertaining to Cheyney State Teachers' College: a report of visitation to Cheyney State College by the National Council for the Accreditation of Teacher Education Team (NCAT), February 19-22, 1961; a list of the members on NCAT Education Team; letters from the college's President James H. Duckrey to Richard F. Shier, deputy superintendent, Department of Instruction, concerning the NCAT Education Team's visit; a 1960-61 *Catalogue of Cheyney State College* which includes pictures of Bibble Hall (administration building), Portica Brown Hall (home

August 2, , 1918

To Dr. N. C. Schaeffer,
Superintendent of Public Instruction.

I hereby certify that I am 31 years of age, and that I am a graduate of Lincoln University College, located at Lincoln University in the county of Chester State of Pennsylvania and that I hold a diploma from the said college dated May 7, 1918, duly granted upon the completion of a four years' College Course.

I now reside at 3443 Filbert Street and my Post Office address is W. Philadelphia P. O., Philadelphia County.

Oscar N. Frey,
Applicant for a Provisional College Certificate.

FORM No. 51.

APPLICATION

OF

College Graduate for Provisional College Certificate.

No. 4227

Name of Applicant, Oscar N. Frey

P. O. Address, Philadelphia County.

Lincoln University College,

Diploma issued May 7, 1918

Application received Sept. 5, 1918

Certificate granted, Sept. 6, 1918

Duplicate issued Mar. 27, 1919

RG-22. Department of Education. Superintendent of Public Instruction, 1874-1969. Teaching certificate #4227 for Oscar N. Frey.

economics building), Yarnall Hall (women's dormitory), Waring Hall (dining hall), Burleigh Hall (men's dormitory), Coppin Laboratory, Vaux-Hall (industrial arts building), and an architect's sketch of the new physical education building; an *Evaluator's Handbook of the Middle States Association of Colleges and Secondary Schools'*

Commission on Institutions of Higher Education; a 1961 master class schedule; a list of periodicals currently received; a letter to President James H. Duckrey from Nathaniel H. Evers, assistant director of the National Council of Accreditation of Teacher Education, dated January 6, 1961; *Faculty Handbook: Policies and Procedures, 1960-61*; miscellaneous correspondence dated from October 1950 through September 1951 concerning changing the name of the institution from Cheyney Training School for Teachers to Cheyney State Teachers' College, including a letter dated November 29, 1950 from Henry Klonower; copies of House Bill # 850 and 851 (Session of 1951) addressing the legality of the name change of the college; correspondence (May 14 and 18, 1948) regarding the extension of the lease of the Tanglewood property for the use of State Teachers' College at Cheyney; correspondence between James M. Brittan, attorney at law, and Ruth B. Dowling, secretary of the State Council of Education, with reference to a copy of the charter of Cheyney before it was acquired by the state (January 12 and 21, 1944); and correspondence from Cheyney President Dr. Leslie Pinckney Hill requesting approval for the college to participate in the National Defense Education Program.

General Correspondence including Miscellaneous Minutes and Reports, 1932-1933, 1935-1964. (12 cartons)

Reports of Higher Institutions of Learning, 1936-1964. Contained among these records are "Reports on Progress in Implementing Statewide Higher Education Desegregation Plans pursuant to Title VI of the Civil Rights Act of 1964." These materials provide information on African Americans as students, employees, and employers in such Pennsylvania institutions of higher learning as Cheyney State College and Lincoln University. Representative examples of the types of reports included are:

- Reports on the Progression of Students in Higher Education Programs. These reports give information on student academic progress as well as reasons for students not returning to higher education. Thirteen reasons are listed and the students are classified as either black or white (meaning not of Hispanic origin) and male or female.
- Reports on Employees of State Agencies and Governing Boards for Higher Education. These reports are broken down by gender into six racial categories: Black, American Indian, Asian, Pacific Islander, Hispanic, and White.
- Reports of the Division of Data Services provide information on staff employed by institutions of higher learning. Information generally found includes the name of the instructor or staff person, gender, the field of preparation, and the name and address of the institution.

Minute Books of the State Board of Education, 1911-1920. (2 volumes) Arranged chronologically by date of meeting. A record of meetings of the State Board of Education. A typical record includes the date, time, and location of the meeting, a list of members attending the meeting, and the official proceedings of the meeting. Topics discussed include admission requirements, committee appointments, curricula, appropriations, expenses, investigations, school room lighting, graduation requirements, conditions of school buildings, legislation, physical education, vocational education, and federal education reports and plans. On November 8, 1918, Stanley Y. Yarnell, president of Cheyney State Teachers' College, and Leslie Pinkney Hill, a principal of Cheyney, appeared before the Board of Education in Philadelphia to comment on the legal standing of certificates and diplomas issued by Cheyney State Teachers' College. Both individuals requested the board to investigate their concerns regarding the matter.

Record Book of State Certificates for College Graduates, 1893-

1911. (1 volume) Arranged numerically by certificate numbers. A registry of college graduates who were granted certificates to teach by the State Board of Education. Data entered include the name, town and county of the teacher, the college attended, the degree received, and the date the certificate was issued. Notations concerning the subjects majored in frequently appear as well. The following are examples of African Americans who received certificates: #625, Gilbert H. Jones, Wilberforce University, AB, May 1906; #1325, J. E. Maxwell, Wilberforce University, BA, June 1900; #1480, William K. Valentine, Lincoln University, AB, May 1907; #446, Samuel D. Wingate, Lincoln University, AB July 1898

Record Books of Permanent Teaching Certificates , 1868-1908. (2 volumes) Arranged numerically by certificate number and indexed internally, alphabetically by first name of surname. A record of persons granted permanent teaching certificates by the State Board of Education. Entries for the 1868-1896 volume shows the recipient's name, post office and county of residence, the date the certificate was issued, and the volume and page number of the *Pennsylvania School Journal* wherein the certification is recorded. A description of the subjects studied is also frequently given. The 1897-1908 volume shows the recipient's name, post office and county of residence, the date the certificate was issued, and a list of subjects studied. Included in this series are entries for the following African Americans: #2469, Vernon R. James, Steelton and #1425, Helen E. Taylor, a graduate of Lincoln University.

Record of Examinations for Permanent Certificates, 1897-1919. (2 cartons) Arranged alphabetically by name of county, and thereunder chronologically by date of examination. A record of the examination results of applicants for permanent teaching certificates filed with the Department of Public Instruction. Information contained on the forms includes the names of the members of the examining committee, the number of applicants, the number of applications approved, the names and occasionally the addresses of the applicants, the number of terms each applicant taught, each applicant's examination score, the percentage score in each of several subjects such as spelling, reading, writing, arithmetic, history, government, hygiene, algebra, geography, and pedagogy; and either the certificate number issued or the date the certificate was issued to each successful applicant. Contained in this series is a certificate for African American Alice B. Butcher (#4698), who taught in the Carlisle School District for many years.

Reports of Degree Granting Institutions to the State Council of Education, 1938. (7 cartons) Included in this series is the Report of Cheyney Training School for Teachers, 1938. This report consists of a number of sections covering faculty and other professional staff, student personnel and programs, graduation requirements, curricula, buildings and grounds, and finances.

School District Annexation and Appropriation File, 1924-1966. (18 cartons) Arranged alphabetically by school district. Records relating to proposals for, and opposition to, the creation of new school districts, new school construction projects, and the locations of new schools. Typical items found include correspondence, requisitions, court documents, agreements, financial statements, reports, petitions, and hearing minutes. A representative sample of material found in the series includes a file entitled "Cheyney Training School for Teachers, 1930-1939" that contains correspondence and other documentation relating to a transfer of property between the Home for Destitute Colored Children, Cheyney Training School for Teachers, and the Commonwealth of Pennsylvania. Included is a blueprint of the properties prepared by C. M. Broomall, Media, Pennsylvania, dated January 16, 1928. Correspondence concerning authorization of a four-year curriculum offering degrees in such subjects as elementary education, industrial arts, and home economics is also present.

RG-23. RECORDS OF THE DEPARTMENT OF PUBLIC WELFARE

The Department of Public Welfare administers a vast array of human services programs, promotes local social services and planning activities, and distributes federal and state funds to local social service agencies. The Department of Welfare was established in 1921 to take over the responsibilities of the Board of Public Charities, the Commission of Lunacy, and the Prison Labor Commission among others. The Board of Public Charities was originally created in 1869 to inspect all charitable and correctional institutions in the Commonwealth and the Committee on Lunacy was originally established in 1883 to examine facilities for the confinement of the insane. The Administrative Code of 1929 further defined the powers of the new department as a social service agency. In 1937 the Department of Public Assistance was established to provide direct cash relief to Pennsylvanians through 67 county boards of assistance during the Great Depression. In 1953 the supervision of penal and correctional institutions was transferred from the Department of Welfare to the Department of Justice. The Department of Welfare and the Department of Public Assistance were merged in 1958 to form the Department of Public Welfare. As the primary state agency concerned with the social welfare and financial needs of the citizens of the Commonwealth, the department today provides public assistance, medical assistance, and aid to the handicapped, administers mental health and retardation programs, and provides licensing and inspection of nursing homes, day-care centers, and hospitals.

OFFICE OF MENTAL HEALTH

(All of the following records are restricted. Permission must be obtained from the corresponding hospital Superintendent or the Office of Mental Health before access is permitted.)

Danville State Hospital

Construction of the Danville State Hospital was authorized by an act of the Pennsylvania State Legislature dated April 13, 1868 and the governing board for the institution was created by a separate act on March 27, 1873. Located in Mahoning Township about one mile east of Danville, the institution was originally called the Danville State Hospital for the Insane and still operates as a state mental facility.

Female Admission Registers, 1884-1923. (2 volumes) Arranged chronologically by date of admission, and indexed externally by surname of patient in **Alphabetical Register of Female Patients, [ca. 1886-1926]**. These volumes document the admission of female patients into Danville State Hospital. Information given about each patient includes name, age, marital status, color (white, black, or mulatto), occupation, county of residence, country or state of birth, number of children, number of siblings, admission number, any previous admission numbers, census of hospital at time of admission, and the admission date. Other commitment information found in these registers includes the name of the person who was financially responsible for the patient; whether the patient was committed by friends, court, or overseer of the poor; whether the patient was an insane convict or was classified as criminally insane; the patient's physical condition and the nature of any or mental physical disorder; the perceived cause of the insanity; any complications (epileptic, paralytic, suicidal, homicidal, idiot, imbecile); the duration of the attack in years, months and days; the number of attacks; and the age of the patient at the time of the first attack. The register also provides information on the date of discharge and reason (death, restored, improved, not improved); the cause of death; the number of years, months or days in the hospital; and the names of relatives who were also diagnosed as insane.

Male Admission Register, 1884-1923. (1 volume) Arranged by date of admission and indexed externally, alphabetically by surname of patient in Alphabetical Register of Male Patients [ca. 1886-1926]. These volumes document the admissions of male patients into Danville State Hospital. Entries list the admission number, any previous admission numbers, the population of hospital at the time of admission, the admission date, patient's name, age, marital status, color (white, black, or mulatto), county of residence, country or state of birth, number of children, number of siblings, and occupation. Other commitment information includes the name of the financially responsible person; whether committed by friends, court, or overseer of the poor; whether the patient was an insane convict or diagnosed as being criminally insane; physical condition; the nature of any physical disorder, the nature of the mental disorder, the supposed cause of insanity, complications (epileptic, paralytic, suicidal, homicidal, idiot, imbecile); duration of attack in years, months and days; the number of attacks; and age of the patient at the first attack. The register also provides information on the date of discharge and the reason (death, restored, improved, not improved); the cause of death; the duration of stay in the hospital; and the names of any relatives who were also diagnosed as insane.

Patient Register and Record of Burial Plots, 1872-1937. (1 volume) Arranged numerically by patient registration number. Although the spine of the volume is labeled as burial plot records, the volume primarily contains information similar to that found in the Male and Female Admission Registers. Each patient entry shows a register number, name, sex, color, age, place of birth, residence, occupation, and marital status. Information on the patient's condition includes the name of the person by whom committed (court order, friend, or family member) and who will pay for keep, cause and form of insanity, names of insane relatives, number of attacks and admissions, and the duration of attacks before admission. Data regarding release include date of discharge, type of discharge, time in hospital, by whom removed and remarks. At the end of the volume is a diagram of burial plots from approximately 1872 through 1937 showing on the grid where each person is buried, the name, and when he or she died. Occasional notations reveal status as veterans or if moved elsewhere for burial.

Dixmont State Hospital

Dixmont State Hospital was originally founded in 1848 in Pittsburgh as the Western Pennsylvania Hospital. It was a general hospital that treated all types of illnesses, including mental illness and as such it was the first institution for the insane in western Pennsylvania. In 1862, the Insane Department at the hospital was moved to a new building outside of Pittsburgh and was named the Western Pennsylvania Hospital for the Insane at Dixmont. The name Dixmont was given to honor the social reformer for the insane, Dorthea Dix. The Dixmont Hospital was legally separated from the Western Pennsylvania Hospital in 1908 when it was individually incorporated as the Dixmont Hospital for the Insane. Supported by private contributions since 1852, it had a nine-decade tradition of state appropriations that enabled the hospital to expand its facilities and care for the increasing number of mentally ill persons. Despite the state appropriations, it continued as a private corporation until 1945 when it was taken over by the state and placed under the Department of Public Welfare. From that date, it operated under the name Dixmont State Hospital until it closed in July 1984.

Admission Books, 1883-1944. (3 volumes) Arranged chronologically by date of admission. This series documents all admissions to the Dixmont State Hospital. Information given about each patient includes name, age, color, gender, place of birth, marital status, place of residence and previous register number; dates of current and previous admission, discharge and/or death; how committed; reason for discharge; form of mental disorder; duration and number of attacks; age at first attack; condition at time of discharge; and any remarks.

Autopsy Records, 1920-1939. (1 folder) Arranged in reverse chronological order by date autopsy was performed. A postmortem record of male and female patients of the Dixmont Hospital. Information given about each patient may include name, age, sex, and race; the form of mental disorder; the dates of admission, death and autopsy; clinical diagnosis and cause of death; the name of the physician who performed autopsy; and specific details of the postmortem examination.

Death Certificates, 1909-1912. (1 folder) Arranged chronologically by date of death. Certificates that recorded deaths occurring at the Dixmont Hospital. Information contained about each decedent includes name, gender and race; dates of birth and death; age at time of death; marital status; occupation; names of parents; places of birth of decedent and of parents; cause of death; date and county of burial; name of undertaker and name of the attending physician.

Discharge Books, 1883-1930. (3 volumes) Arranged chronologically by date of discharge or death. A list of persons who were released from the hospital or who died there. Information provided includes each patient's name, register number, date of admission, date of discharge or death, age at time of discharge or death, race, gender, social class, condition at time of discharge as a result of treatment, cause of death, and name of institution to which transferred if applicable.

First Admission and Re-Admission Cards, 1891-1935. (8 folders) Arranged alphabetically by surname of patient. Cards that document the first admission and re-admissions of patients to Dixmont Hospital. Information given about each patient may include name, date of admission, form of mental illness, age at admission, marital status and number of children, occupation, race, religion, place of birth of patient and patients' parents, residence by county and city, a brief family medical history, information about present and past attacks, and by whose authority the patient was committed.

Hospital Record Books, 1856-1895. (3 volumes) Arranged chronologically by date of admission. These volumes provide a record of admissions to and discharges from the Western Pennsylvania Hospital for the Insane. Information given about each patient includes name and registration number, age, race gender, marital status, occupation, residence, date of admission, date of discharge or death, duration of illness before admission, cause and form of insanity, number of attacks, name of the person by whom committed, reason for discharge, length of time at the hospital, and remarks.

In-Patient Record Cards for World War I, 1919-1920. (1 folder) Arranged alphabetically by surname of patient. These 5" x 8" cards provide a record of World War I soldiers who were provided with mental treatment at Dixmont Hospital. Information given about each patient may include name and address of patient and nearest relative; compensation number; rank and unit designation; age at time of admission; gender, race, religion, occupation, and place of birth; diagnosed form of mental illness; dates of admission, diagnosis, and transfer or release; whether patient was transferred or released; and condition at that time.

Male Patients' Clothing and Property Books, 1895-1904. (2 volumes) Arranged by date of patient's admission to the hospital. Indexed externally, alphabetically by name of patient in the **Male Patient's Clothing and Property Book Indexes**. A record of the property that belonged to patients while in the care of the Western Pennsylvania Hospital for the Insane at Dixmont. Information provided includes patient's name and race, date of admission, a description of the items on their person at that time, dates and descriptions of additional items that were later acquired, where they were acquired and location where stored. Also included are receipts for items that were placed in the safe or that were transferred to another institution.

Patient History Books, 1859-1950. (64 volumes) Arranged chronologically by date of admission. Books that document the medical history of patients and their families. Information provided about each patient includes name, age, gender, color, and religion; occupation of patient, patient's spouse, or parents; places of birth and residency; marital status and number of children; places of residence and nativity of parents; names of physicians who certified commitment; diagnosis of mental disorder; personal characteristics; date of admission; and agency or persons who committed the patient.

Patient Population Statistical Tables, 1936-1946. (3 folders) Unarranged. Loosely grouped by year. Statistical data on the patient population for each year. Data appearing on approximately eighteen separate tables relate primarily to patients' first admissions and compare a specified data element to the primary diagnosed psychoses. Data elements that were charted include race, age, degree of education, economic condition, use of alcohol, marital status, cause of death, age at time of death, and total duration of hospital life. In addition, other related information can be obtained such as the patient's country of birth, citizenship, financial status, and the number and gender of officers and employees for the year. Also present is a list of names of private patients residing in the hospital who became wards of the Commonwealth when the state assumed responsibility for the hospital in 1945.

Record of People to Be Notified, 1855-1952. (8 volumes) Arranged chronologically, and thereunder alphabetically by surname of patient. These volumes provide a record of contact persons or organizations for patients residing in the hospital. Information provided includes name and color of each patient; register number; date of admission, discharge or death; how committed; whether patient was transferred, escaped, paroled, or died; and name, address, and relationship of nearest relative. If no relative was listed, the agency that committed the person was to be notified.

Will Book of Charles Brewer, 1860-1878. (1 volume) Arranged by type of material. Charles Brewer was born in Taunton, Massachusetts, moved to Pittsburgh in 1814, and died in Allegheny County in 1860 at the age of 76 years. Mr. Brewer bequeathed over $6,000 to both the Western Pennsylvania Hospital and the Western Pennsylvania Hospital for the Insane. The total amount of contributions Mr. Brewer gave to various institutions totaled over $370,000. This volume was compiled from the court records of Allegheny County by John B. McFadden, one of the managers of the Western Pennsylvania Hospital and member of the Committee of Managers for the Distribution of the Annual Income Accruing from the Brewer Fuel Fund Amongst the Poor of the Cities of Pittsburgh and Allegheny. This volume outlines assets, names of executors, and persons or institutions to which Mr. Brewer wished to leave a bequest and the amount per annum of the bequest, a summary of the amounts in several accounts, a recapitulation of amounts received and dispersed by the executors, summary of bequests and payments to institutions, and a listing to bequeathed institutions in Allegheny County and the total amount they received. Some of the other institutions Brewer supported included the Young Men's Bible Society, the Protestant Orphan Asylum of Pittsburgh and Allegheny County, the Pennsylvania Colonization Society (the sum was to be applied "by the said society to defray the expense of the passage of colored persons wishing to emigrate from the United States to the Republic of Liberia in Africa"), the Seamen's Aid Society (to address the moral condition of the seamen of the port of Philadelphia), and the Association Mission of Minnesota Among the Indians.

Harrisburg State Hospital

The Harrisburg State Hospital was authorized in 1845 to provide care for mentally ill persons throughout the Commonwealth. A nine-member board of trustees was empowered to appoint a superintendent, purchase land, and construct facilities near Harrisburg for the "Pennsylvania State Lunatic Hospital and Union Asylum for the Insane." In 1848 the name of the hospital was changed to the Pennsylvania State Lunatic Hospital and construction began on the facility. The first patient was admitted on October 6, 1851. Initially, every poor district was charged a weekly maintenance fee for the care of each indigent patient. The board for each private patient was based on his or her ability to pay.

In 1869, the Board of Public Charities was created to inspect all public and voluntary charitable institutions in the Common-wealth and to report to the legislature with recommendations concerning their operation. For four decades, the unpaid board and its small staff had no authority to correct the conditions it found, but by persuasion and publicity they were able to improve the quality of care in public institutions. A major objective in the beginning was the removal of the insane from almshouses to the Pennsylvania State Lunatic Hospital and other state hospitals. A Committee on Lunacy was created within the Board of Public charities in 1883 to oversee mental institutions.

In 1921, the name of the facility was changed to the Harrisburg State Hospital. Also in that year, the Board of Public Charities was abolished and the Department of Public Welfare was created to administer all state hospitals. Up until 1955, certain administrative responsibilities, such as the selection of the hospital superintendent and the enactment of rules and regulations governing the hospital, were vested in the Board of Trustees of the Harrisburg State Hospital. In 1955 an amendment to the Administrative Code authorized the Department of Welfare to assume administrative responsibilities for the Harrisburg State Hospital, relegating its Board of Trustees to specific advisory duties. This act also provided for the appointment of a Commissioner of Mental Health within the Department of Welfare to assume overall responsibility for Pennsylvania's mental health program. As of 2000, the institution still operates as a state hospital.

Admission Card File, 1885-1952. (3 cartons) Arranged numerically by admission number. A record of individuals admitted to the Harrisburg State Hospital. These 5" x 8" index cards provide each patient's name, date of admission, name of the physician, the case and admission numbers, age, marital status, number of children, and place of birth for both the patient and their parents. Also recorded are the year of arrival in United States when applicable, citizenship status of both the patient and their parents, race, educational level, occupation, religious affiliation, a description of their living environment and economic condition, their place of residence, and the length of time they have lived in Pennsylvania. Clinical information includes etiological factors other than heredity, the nature of the psychosis, the patient's mental characteristics (temperamental and intellectual), and any family history of mental and nervous diseases, mental deficiency, and inebriety (alcohol or drugs). The cards also provide information on alcoholic habits of the patient (whether an abstainer, temperate, or intemperate), any accompanying physical diseases that were not an integral part of the psychosis, and the duration of the present attack prior to admission.

Admission Registers, 1851-1969. (8 volumes) Arranged numerically by patient's admission number. A record of individuals admitted to the Pennsylvania State Lunatic Hospital. For the years 1851-1955 the information provided includes each patient's name and admission number, the date of admission, age, race, class (whether indigent or private), place of birth, marital status, number of children and living siblings, patient's occupation prior to the onset of insanity, previous place of residence (county, city, and township), the name of the person by whose authority the patient was admitted, the date of medical certificate, the name of the person by whom the certificate was signed, the nature of disorder, the suspected cause of the insanity, any complications, whether the patient exhibited suicidal or homicidal tendencies, whether the patient was paralytic or classified as a congenial idiot, the date of discharge, whether patient died or improved, the total period of residence, and remarks. The registers for the years 1956-69 give only the patient's name and admission number, the date of admission, admission class (whether indigent or private), county of residence, commitment form number, and the date of discharge or death.

Annual Reports of the Board of Public Charities, 1870-1882, 1885-1906. (32 volumes) Arranged chronologically by date of report. Annual reports of the Board of Public Charities of the state of Pennsylvania. The board's mission was to gather information on the conditions of all charitable and correctional institutions within the state, to inspect all of their books and papers, and to observe and criticize procedures when necessary. Information provided includes names of the officers of the board, board of directors report (documenting powers and duties of the board, organization, members and officers, subjects of inquiry, minutes, institutions visited, board expenses and a general view of state institutions), a secretary and general agent's report (documenting institutions interrogated, duties performed by the corresponding secretary, Charitable Institutions and Almshouses, and County Prisons), and an appendix. Statistical data on penitentiaries, reformatories, hospitals for the insane, criminal courts, county jails, almshouses, township poor farms, and medical charities were compiled at the end of each yearly report from 1873 on and many of these statistical breakdowns contain information on African Americans.

Court Order Books, 1883-1924. (19 volumes) Arranged numerically by admission number. For the years 1889-1893 the books are indexed internally, alphabetically by surname of the patient. Copies of orders by which courts sent individuals to the Harrisburg State Hospital. Information provided includes patient's name, admission number, and date that the defendant was ordered by the court to Harrisburg State Hospital. African Americans are documented in this series but the admission number of the patient must be known.

Medical Case Book, 1851-1867. (1 volume) Arranged chronologically, and indexed internally by first letter of patient's surname.

A case book documenting treatments and observations of male and female patients at the Pennsylvania State Lunatic Hospital. Information given includes name, age, sex, and previous occupation of each patient; whether married, single or widowed; appearance of the patient upon admission; and habits and temperament. Also included is a description of the mental disorder, the manner and period of the attack, the changes produced in the patient's temper or disposition (specifying whether the malady displayed itself by delusions or irrational conduct, morbid or dangerous habits or propensities), and whether the patient had experienced any failure of memory or understanding or was affected by epilepsy or ordinary paralysis such as tremulous movements of the tongue, defect of articulation, or weakness or unsteadiness of gait. The case book lists any affliction related to the patient's previous health history, what was believed to be the predisposing cause of the illness, whether the patient had experienced any former illness, whether the present illness had been preceded by any premonitory symptoms such as restlessness, unusual elevation or depression of spirits, or any deviation from ordinary habits and conduct, and whether the patient had undergone any previous treatment or had been subject to personal restraint. Many African Americans are documented in this series but individual patient names must be known in order to locate them.

Medical Case Books of the Female Department, 1880-1922. (30 volumes) Arranged chronologically by observation date. Case book documenting observations and treatments of female patients at the Pennsylvania State Lunatic Hospital and Harrisburg State Hospital. Information given includes name, age, sex, and previous occupation of each patient; whether she was married, single or widowed; an accurate description of the external appearance of the patient upon admission; habits and temperament; the appearance of the eyes, countenance or expression and any peculiarity in the form of the head; the condition of the vascular, respiratory, and abdominal organs, and their respective functions; information on the pulse rate and appearance of the tongue, skin, urine, etc.; and the presence or absence of bruises or other injuries. Also included is a description of the mental disorder, the manner and period of the attack, a minute account of the symptoms, changes produced in the patient's temper or disposition, and whether the malady was accompanied by memory loss, epilepsy, paralysis, confusion, defect of articulation, unsteady gait, illusions, irrational conduct, or morbid or dangerous habits or propensities. The case book lists any affliction related to the patient's previous health history, any predisposing cause of the illness, whether the patient had experienced any previous mental illness, whether the present illness had been preceded by any premonitory symptoms such as restlessness, unusual elevation or depression of spirits, or any remarkable deviation form ordinary habits and conduct, and any previous treatments or episodes requiring personal restraint. Entries were made either weekly or when the nature of the case required it. In all cases an accurate record was to be kept of the medicines administered, and other remedies employed along with the results, and also of all injuries and accidents. Many African Americans are documented in this series but individual patient names must be known.

Medical Case Books of the Male Department, 1881-1924. (42 volumes) Arranged chronologically by admission number. Case books documenting observations and treatments of male patients at the Pennsylvania State Lunatic Hospital and Harrisburg State Hospital. Information given includes name, age, sex, and previous occupation of each patient; marital status, an accurate description of the external appearance of the patient upon admission, habits and temperament, the appearance of the eyes, countenance or expression, and any peculiarity in the form of the head. Also gives information on the condition of the vascular, respiratory, and abdominal organs, pulse rate, the appearance of the tongue, skin, urine, etc., and the presence or absence of bruises or other injuries. In addition, there is a detailed description of the mental disorder, the manner and period of the attack, a minute account of the symptoms, and the changes produced in the patient's temper or disposition such as whether the malady displayed itself by illusions or irrational conduct, morbid or dangerous habits or propensities, occasioned any failure of memory or understanding, or was associated with epilepsy, paralysis, tremulous movements of the tongue, defects in articulation, or weakness or unsteadiness of gait. The case book also lists any afflictions in the patient's previous health history believed to be the predisposing cause of the illness, whether the patient had experienced any former illness, whether the present illness had been preceded by any premonitory symptoms such as restlessness, unusual elevation or depression of spirits, or remarkable deviation from ordinary habits and conduct; and any previous treatments received. During the first month after admission, entries were to be made at least once in every week or, in certain cases, whenever the nature of the case required it. In all cases an accurate record was to be kept of the medicines administered, the observed results, and any injuries and accidents. Many African Americans are documented in this series but individual patient names must be known.

Patient History Books, 1893-1916. (19 volumes) Arranged numerically by admission number. A record of personal and medical histories of patients at the Pennsylvania State Lunatic Hospital. Information given includes each patient's date of admission, patient number, case book number, name, age, sex, weight, height, hair and eye color, temperament, marital status, birthplace, occupation, educational level, family history, past mental history, present state of mind, and whether or not violent, dangerous, destructive, homicidal, or suicidal. Other information found includes whether or not the patient was an alcoholic, had syphilis, or any drug problems; a description of the patient's physical condition (facial expression, articulation, skull conformation, ear measurements, palate, motor function of muscles, reflexes, secretion, special senses, trophic disturbances, temperature, pulse, circulation, respiration, sugar level (tongue and albumin); the patient's mental state; doctor's diagnosis and the quality, color and odor of urine samples. Many African Americans are documented in this series but individual patient names must be known.

Register of Female Patients, 1852-1884. (1 volume) Arranged numerically by admission number and indexed internally, alphabetically by surname of the patient. A record of female patients admitted to the Pennsylvania State Lunatic Hospital. Information provided about each patient includes name, number, and admission date; the condition of the patient; age, nativity, residence and occupation; the duration of symptoms prior to admission; how the patient was committed and supported; the cause and form of the disease; any complications and results of treatment; period of residence, date of discharge, and remarks.

Register of Male Patients, 1851-1895. (1 volume) Arranged numerically by admission number and indexed internally, alphabetically by surname of the patient. A record of male patients admitted to the Pennsylvania State Lunatic Hospital. Information provided about each patient includes name, number, and admission date; the condition of the patient; age, nativity, residence and occupation; the duration of symptoms prior to admission; how the patient was committed and supported; the cause and form of the disease; complications and results of treatment; period of residence, date of discharge, and remarks.

Mayview State Hospital

Located in Allegheny City to the north of Pittsburgh, Mayview State Hospital is a state-operated mental institution for the poor and insane. The Borough of Pittsburgh had established a home for the care of paupers as early as 1804, which institution was replaced by the Allegheny City Almshouse in 1818. A City Poor Farm was erected in 1852 to which a building for the treatment of the insane was added in 1879. As a result of overcrowding, a new institution named Marshalsea was constructed in 1892. Allegheny City is located on Pittsburgh's north side and also maintained a separate institution for the poor and insane at Claremont, now known as Blawnox. When Allegheny City became part of the city of Pittsburgh in 1907 the mental patients at Claremont were transferred to Marshalsea. In 1916, the state legislature gave its consent to change the name of the hospital from Marshalsea to the Pittsburgh City Home and Hospital at Mayview. In accordance with an act of 1938 requiring the state to take over all institutions for the care of the mentally ill, Mayview came under state control in 1941. The Commonwealth took over control of the mental section (Mayview State Hospital) and the City of Pittsburgh continued to administer the indigent section of the hospital (Pittsburgh City Home and Hospital at Mayview). In March 1973, the Department of Public Welfare made plans to move patients judged to be criminally insane from Fairview State Hospital to Mayview. In 1982, an adolescent center was transferred from Woodville State Hospital to Mayview. During the closing of Dixmont State Hospital in 1984, the deaf unit was transferred to Mayview. As of 2000, Mayview State Hospital is still in operation.

Admission Book of the Insane Department of the Pittsburgh North Side City Home, 1911-1916. (1 volume) Arranged chronologically by date of admission. A record of admissions to the

Insane Department of the Pittsburgh North Side City Home. This volume provides the following information about each patient: name, age, color, gender, social class, place of birth, marital status, former place of residence and previous register number of the patient; admission, discharge and/or death dates; name of the person who ordered the commitment; reason for discharge; and form of mental disorder.

Admission Registers, 1925-1941. (3 volumes) Arranged chronologically by date of admission. These registers document the admission of all patients into Mayview State Hospital. Information includes each patient's name, case number, age and gender; date of admission; and who ordered the commitment. Additional information recorded before September 24, 1929 may include marital status and color of the patient.

Alms House Registers, 1876-1884. (2 volumes) Arranged chronologically by date of admission. Registers documenting admission of destitute persons to the City Poor Farm in Pittsburgh. Information given about each individual may include each person's name, age, gender, marital status, place of birth, various places traveled, religious affiliation, color, occupation, and previous address; dates of admission, discharge or death; where patient was transferred from; length of residence in Pittsburgh; number and ages of dependents; and circumstances surrounding his or her arrival at the City Poor Farm.

Alphabetical Admission and Discharge Register, 1850-1881. (1 volume) Arranged alphabetically by surname, and thereunder chronologically by date of admission. This record documents the admissions and discharges at the City Poor Farm. Information given about each inmate includes name, age, and place of birth, and admission and discharge dates. The remarks column provides information regarding the circumstances of the admission and discharge. There is no column designated for color or race, however, "col'd" is written beside the names of several patients.

Case Book of Allegheny City Farm, 1884-1887. (1 volume) Arranged chronologically by date of admission, and indexed internally by surname of patient. Case book documenting the history of patients at the Allegheny City Farm from their time of admission until their time of release. The book contains a series of entries made on different dates charting the medical progress of patients. The entries are not made in a consistent fashion and primarily consist of observations rather than descriptions of treatments applied. Information given may include name, age, gender, color, place of birth, and marital status of the patient; date of admission; condition upon admittance; and cause of illness.

Case Books of Pittsburgh City Home and Hospital, 1879-1912. (23 volumes) Arranged chronologically by date of admission. Case books documenting the history of patients at the Pittsburgh City Home and Hospital from their time of admission until their time of release. The books contain a series of entries made on different dates charting the medical progress of patients. The entries are not made in a regular fashion and primarily consist of observations rather than descriptions of treatments applied. Information given may include name, age, gender, date of birth, color, place of birth, occupation, marital status, and case number of the patient; names and nativity of parents; a physical and mental assessment; and diagnosis.

Death Registers, 1939-1956. (3 volumes) Arranged chronologically by date of death, and indexed internally by surname. These registers document the deaths of patients at Mayview State Hospital. Information provided may include name, age, place of former residence, gender, color or race, marital status, date and place of birth, and occupation of the patient; names of parents; length of time at hospital; age of spouse; date and cause of death; and date and place of cremation, burial, or removal.

Patient History Books, 1879-1884. (2 volumes) Arranged chronologically by date of admission. Books that document the medical history of patients and their families. Information may include patient's name, age, gender, nativity, color, place of residence, amount of education, marital status, number of children, age of youngest child, occupation, and religion; place of residence and nativity of parents; cause of commitment; duration of insanity; details of attacks; personal habits; date of admission and discharge; and name of person by whom patient was committed.

Register of Discharges and Deaths, 1950-1958. (1 volume) Arranged chronologically by date of discharge or death. A record of persons who were discharged or died at Mayview State Hospital. Information includes name, gender, and case number of the patient; discharge and/or death number; discharge condition, with result of treatment; and disposition notes regarding the discharge of the patient. Totals are given for discharges and deaths by month and year.

Norristown State Hospital

In 1878 construction began on a new mental hospital to serve the southeastern population of Pennsylvania. Prior to this time, the only other state mental hospitals were located in Warren County, Danville, and Harrisburg. The Norristown Hospital was built to relieve the overcrowding of the psychiatric wards of the Philadelphia Almshouse and other hospitals. When the hospital opened for patients in 1880 it was divided into men's and women's departments. In 1924, however, the hospital was reorganized under a single superintendent. As of 2000, Norristown still operates as a state hospital.

Annual Reports of the Board of Public Charities and Committee on Lunacy, 1894, 1897, 1907. (3 volumes) Arranged chronologically by year. Annual reports documenting the activities of the Board of Public Charities and Committee on Lunacy. Information found in these reports includes statistics on mentally ill persons residing in county jails and correctional institutions, almshouses, and private homes and asylums; operating expenses of institutions for the insane and their hospital bed capacity; and the numbers of immigrants residing in such institutions. Other statistics provide data on patients' gender and race, the reasons they were committed, diseases, and deaths. The Committee on Lunacy report contains statistics on the five state hospitals for the mentally ill located in Harrisburg, Danville, Norristown, Warren County, and Dixmont, and contains information on the weekly diet, admissions, and discharges.

Annual Reports of the Committee on Lunacy, 1885, 1887-1890. (5 volumes) Arranged chronologically by year. Printed volumes containing narrative accounts and statistical breakdowns on the populations residing in both private and state mental hospitals. Information found includes data on the patients' occupations, gender, race, physical and mental condition, diseases, and causes of mortality. Also found are data on geographical areas served by the various institutions, the names of managers, the value of real estate, the construction of new buildings and their capacities, receipts and expenditures for each institution, and records of admissions, discharges, and population sizes.

Annual Reports of the Norristown State Hospital, 1882-1959.

(**47 volumes**) Arranged chronologically by year. Printed volumes containing narrative accounts of the year's activity. Included are general lists of expenditures and receipts, statistics on number of patients admitted and discharged, nativity of the patients, county they lived in, occupation, marital status, age, how committed (by friends, overseers of the poor, or the courts), form of disease of those admitted, alleged causes of insanity (old age, sunstroke, scarlet fever, domestic trouble, religious excitement and others), duration of the disease before admission, cause of death, and the number of private patients. There are also lists of those that recovered and those that died, showing age, sex, race, country of origin, form of sanity, cause of sanity, period of residence, whole duration of attack, number of attacks, and age at first attack of insanity in the family. Some reports show expenses and income from the farm, and soap and brush factories and are divided into the following sections: the report between the men's and women's departments, staff names and occupations, reports of the pathologist on medical problems, amusements, and religious instruction. The reports from 1929 on discuss occupational therapy, psychosis and psychopathic conditions, and community services. Though not part of the reports, photographs of the hospital taken in 1924 are found at the end of the series.

Philadelphia State Hospital

Founded in 1906 as the City Farms at Byberry, this facility originally functioned as a Philadelphia city institution. In 1928 the facility was renamed the Philadelphia Institution for the Feeble Minded, and in 1931 the name was again changed, this time to the Philadelphia Hospital for Mental Diseases. It became a state mental hospital on October 22, 1938.

Annual Report Book, 1928-1935. (1 volume) Arranged chronologically by date of report. For the year 1928 and the period 1931-1934, the Annual Reports contain narrative accounts of operations of the Philadelphia State Hospital as well as the Annual Statistical Reports which were submitted to the Department of Statistics of the National Committee for Mental Hygiene. For years 1928 through 1931, only an Annual Statistical Report is provided. The difference between the two types of report is that the Annual Reports contain a narrative, while the Annual Statistical Reports only contain tables of information. The latter all contain the same type of information describing characteristics of the institution's population with regard to sex, age, race, citizenship, country of origin, cultural environment, economic condition, marital status, education, illness, and whether improved. Other information about the hospital includes financial data, number of employees, and their racial and gender groupings by job classification. This volume also contains a summary of activities during 1932 through 1935.

Census Book, 1940-1941. (1 volume) Arranged chronologically by month. This book was designed to monitor the patient population at Philadelphia State Hospital. Information given about each patient includes name; dates of admission, discharge, parole, escape, or return; sex and color; and register and case numbers. Handwritten notations include date of death, date transferred, and to which institution.

Death Registers of Females, 1909-1942. (4 volumes) Arranged chronologically by date of death. A record of female patient deaths at Philadelphia State Hospital. Information provided about decedents may include name, register number, date of admission, form of mental disorder, age at death, color, religious affiliation, marital status, place of birth, occupation, length of time at hospital, date and cause of death, and by whom committed.

Death Registers of Males, 1920-1942. (**3 volumes**) Arranged chronologically by date of death. A record of male patient deaths at Philadelphia State Hospital. Information provided about decedents may include name, register number, date of admission, form of mental disorder, age at death, color, religion, marital status, place of birth, occupation, length of time at hospital, date and cause of death, and by whom committed.

Discharge Registers of Females, 1907-1942. (**2 volumes**) Arranged chronologically by date of discharge. These registers contain information regarding the discharge of female patients from the Philadelphia State Hospital. Information given about each patient includes name, register number, date of discharge and last admission; age when discharged, removed or die; color and social condition; form of mental disorder; condition when discharged with a result of treatment; and where the patient went after release.

Discharge Registers of Males, 1907-1942. (**2 volumes**) Arranged chronologically by date of discharge. These registers contain information regarding the discharge of male patients from the Philadelphia State Hospital. Information given about each patient includes name, register number, date of discharge and last admission; age when discharged, removed or died; color and social condition; form of mental disorder; condition when discharged with a result of treatment; and where the patient went after release.

General Registers of Female Patients, 1895-1908, 1920-1939. (**4 volumes**) Arranged chronologically by date of admittance. This record documents female patient information for the Philadelphia State Hospital. Data given about each patient may include name, race, and date or register number of previous admission; current register number; dates of admission and discharge or death; place of birth; marital status and number of living children; ages when admitted and at time of first attack; number of attacks; previous city and county of residence; occupation prior to insanity and degree of education; form of mental disorder and supposed cause; by whom committed or removed; and relatives who were insane.

General Registers of Male Patients, 1895-1939. (6 volumes) Arranged chronologically by date of admittance. This record documents male patient information for the Philadelphia State Hospital. Information provided about each patient may include name and race; date or register number of previous admission; current register number; date of admission, discharge or death; place of birth; marital status and number of living children; age when admitted and at first attack; number of attacks; previous city and county of residence; occupation prior to insanity and degree of education; form of mental disorder and supposed cause; by whom committed or removed; and relatives who were insane.

Medical Journals, 1932-1933, 1938-1939. (4 volumes) Arranged chronologically by date. A daily census accounting for all residents of the Philadelphia Hospital for Mental Diseases. Information provided includes the average number of patients, the total number of patients, and the average number of patients on parole. All of these classifications are broken down by gender. Notes are given regarding who was paroled, discharged, admitted, transferred, eloped, died, or returned from parole.

Patient Characteristics and Statistical Register Book, 1940-1942. (1 volume) Arranged chronologically by day, month and year. For each date, two entries are found. One is for the Philadelphia State Hospital, and the other is for the children's "camp" program. Information given includes census data on the following categories of persons: children, epileptics, feebleminded (not insane), tubercular, and colored. The register gives information on the number of persons admitted, discharged, and died for each day and totals for the year. Also included is a daily account of the number of males and females paroled, escaped, and returned; the number of patients on the census and on parole; and the total number of patients on the registers.

Retreat State Hospital

The Central Poor District was established in 1860 on a 146 acre tract of land in Luzerne County about fourteen miles from Wilkes-Barre. Originally equipped only with outdoor pavilions, these were later replaced by permanent buildings. The first of these was the Female Ward, erected in 1878. This was followed by the construction of the Male Ward in 1884, to which an addition was made in 1895. Together, these composed the Luzerne County Almshouse. In 1890 the Central Poor District also assumed responsibility for the care of the mentally ill, opening the Hospital for the Insane in 1900. By 1924 the facility was identified as the Retreat Mental Hospital in the annual reports although it was still governed by the Central Poor District of Luzerne County. By an act of the legislature in 1937, the haphazard system of poor districts was abolished and county institution districts were set up. Although county commissioners assumed control of poor and indigent sick relief in the counties, management of individual institutions remained the same. In accordance with an act of 1938 requiring the state to take over all institutions for the care of the mentally ill, Retreat came under state control September 16, 1943. The almshouse buildings, whose purpose had been superseded by federal and state relief programs during the Depression, were emptied in 1945 and remodeled as patient dormitories. In 1980, due to decreasing use of hospital facilities and cutbacks in the overall Department of Welfare budget, Retreat State Hospital was forced to close.

Annual Reports, 1902-1921, 1924, 1926-1936, 1944-1949. (43 volumes, 3 folders) Arranged chronologically by date of report. Annual reports of the Board of Directors from the Luzerne County Central Poor District and of the superintendent of Retreat State Hospital. Types of information provided in the reports include names of the members of the board of trustees, officers, staff, and consultants; documentation regarding changes in personnel; and patient treatment, activities, and hospital entertainment. There is also a statistical breakdown of the institution's population documenting first admissions, diagnoses, places of birth of patients and their mothers, citizenship, economic conditions, marital status, educational levels, religious affiliations, use of alcoholic beverages and cause of death where applicable. Other information about the hospital includes documentation on the amount of food produced on the farm and in workrooms, the amount of food and supplies consumed, number of employees and their salaries, and photographs of the institution. The annual reports contain overall financial statements of the poor district and the annual reports and financial statements to the board by the superintendents of the hospital, the almshouse, and the farm.

Biennial Reports of the Board of Trustees, 1948-1964. (4 folders) Arranged chronologically by date of report. Information in the reports includes names of the trustees, officers, staff, and consultants; documentation regarding changes in personnel; general conditions in the hospital, including activities, treatment, and entertainment; and various departmental reports. Also found are tables regarding first admissions which show hospital population, diagnosis, nativity and mother's nativity, citizenship, economic condition, marital status, degree of education, and use of alcoholic beverages; and various tables regarding religious affiliation, cause of death, psychoses, age, and length at hospital of deceased patients.

General Registers, 1900-1968. (2 volumes) Arranged chronologically by date of admission. The general registers provide detailed information about each patient. Entries may show name, register number and any former register numbers, age, country of birth, country of parents' birth, county of residence, occupation, legal status, sex, color, marital status, mental diagnosis, cause of illness, religious affiliation and educational level of the patient; date admitted, source of support and by whom committed; whether naturalized; duration and number of attacks; and date and reason for discharge or death. Men and women are listed separately.

Historical File, 1900-1978. (13 folders) Arranged alphabetically by subject. This series contains the original insane hospital admissions list of July 1900; memoranda and programs relating to the hospital's centennial; miscellaneous court papers (petitions, appointments and reports of investigative commissions, and commitment orders) from the 1920s and 1930s; a 1902 guide to the Pennsylvania laws governing the Central Poor District and its institutions; drafts of a history of the hospital; several issues of the Retreat State Hospital newsletter, *Riverview Echo*; and two aerial photographs of the buildings and farm. Also included is correspondence covering such matters as flood damage.

Warren State Hospital

Warren State Hospital was Pennsylvania's third state mental institution. The State Hospital for the Insane at Warren, Pennsylvania was established by an act of the legislature approved on August 14, 1873, and admitted its first patient on December 5, 1880. In 1920, the name of the institution was officially changed to Warren State Hospital. As of 2000, Warren State Hospital is still in operation.

Female Case Books, [ca. 1883-1913]. (17 volumes) Arranged chronologically by date of admission and indexed internally, alphabetically by surname of patient. Case books documenting the history of female patients from the time of admission until the time of release. The books contain a series of entries made on different dates charting patients' progress. The entries were not made regularly and primarily consist of observations rather than descriptions of treatments. Information may include name, age, marital status, native state, and previous county of residence of patient; date of admission; husband's occupation; and cause of illness. Miscellaneous loose sheets are contained within the volumes, including correspondence from patients to their doctors and other medical documentation.

Male Case Books, [ca. 1883-1913]. (19 volumes) Arranged chronologically by date of admission and indexed internally, alphabetically by surname of patient. Case books documenting the history of male patients from the time of admission until the time of release. They contain a series of entries made on different dates charting the patients' progress. The entries were not made regularly and primarily consist of observations rather than descriptions of treatments. Information may include name, age, marital status, native state, and previous county of residence of patient; date of admission; and cause of illness.

Woodville State Hospital

The Allegheny County Home was a municipal corporation, established and chartered in 1852 for the care, treatment, and maintenance of indigent persons with a physical illness. Control of the home was vested in a board of Poor Directors. In 1900 the Allegheny County Home became known as the Allegheny County Home and Hospital for the Insane. The Insane Department was opened on October 1, 1900, with a total of 226 patients, some of whom were transferred from other Pennsylvania institutions for the insane. In 1938, an act of the legislature vested control of the institution in the Allegheny County commissioners. The Allegheny County Home and the Hospital for the Insane then became known as the Allegheny County Institution District Hospital. On June 1, 1941, as the result of the Goodrich Act which brought all mental patients in Pennsylvania under the control of the Commonwealth, the Mental Department of the Allegheny County Institution District Hospital came under the control of the Department of Welfare of the Commonwealth of Pennsylvania, and was renamed Woodville State Hospital. In 1991, because of the overall decrease in facility use and budget cuts to the Department of Public Welfare, Woodville State Hospital closed.

Account Book for Patients, 1974-1982. (1 folder) Arranged chronologically by year. A record of discharges, deaths, and transfers of patients at Woodville State Hospital. The books list number; name of patient; whether or not discharged, died or transferred; and in many instances age, physical condition, sex, and race.

Admission and Discharge Registers, 1900-1962. (2 volumes) Arranged alphabetically by surname of patient and thereafter by date of admission. A record of admissions and discharges at the Woodville State Hospital. The 1900-1941 register lists name of patient, register number, date of discharge, and date of death. The 1913-1962 register lists patient name, date of discharge, date of death, register number, residence, color, age, and marital status.

Discharge, Death and Transfer Books, 1942-1984. (1 box) Arranged chronologically by year. Books pertaining to the discharge, death, and transfer of Woodville State Hospital patients. These books list each patient's number and name; whether the patient was discharged, died or transferred; and, in many instances, the patient's age, physical condition, sex, and race.

New Admissions Registers, 1959-1970. (1 carton, 2 volumes) Arranged chronologically by year. A record of patients admitted to Woodville State Hospital. Information given about each patient includes admission number, name, date of admission, and in many instances race, sex, religion, and home address.

Return Admissions Register, 1970-1984. (2 folders) Arranged chronologically by date.
Register of patients who were readmitted to Woodville State Hospital. Entries provide date of re-admittance, patient's name, age, race, gender, birth date, religious affiliation, home address, marital status, and citizenship status.

BOARD OF PUBLIC CHARITIES

The Board of Public Charities was created in 1869 to inspect all charitable and correctional institutions in the Commonwealth of Pennsylvania. This board was abolished in 1921 and its charitable responsibilities became merged with those of the Department of Welfare that was created in 1923.

Committee on Lunacy

The Committee on Lunacy was established by the Board of Charities in 1883 to examine facilities for the confinement of the insane in the Commonwealth of Pennsylvania. It was abolished along with the Board of Charities in 1921.

Institutional Population Records, [ca. 1882-1920]. (49 volumes, 18 boxes) Grouped alphabetically by name of institution. A record of admissions, discharges and deaths of patients or inmates at the

Pennsylvania State Lunatic Hospital, Harrisburg; Philadelphia Hospital Department of the Insane; and the Pittsburgh City Home and Hospital. Each hospital's records are arranged uniquely and contain varying amounts of information. Typical information provided about each patient may include name; dates of admission, transfer, death or discharge; occupation and gender (African Americans are usually denoted with "col'd" next to the name); register number; a detailed medical history; and a description of psychological state upon commitment.

DEPARTMENT OF WELFARE, 1923-1958

Bureau of Community Work

Reports on County Homes, 1917-1935. (6 boxes) Grouped alphabetically by name of county, and grouped thereunder in rough chronological order. Inspection reports written by field representatives of the Bureau of Assistance and submitted to the secretary of the Department of Welfare to facilitate the preparation of recommendations to the county homes. Also included in this series is inter-agency correspondence. Information given in each report includes name of the institution, city and county where the institution was located, name of field representative conducting the inspection, patient population statistics, names and titles of various institutional officers and personnel, information about the buildings and grounds, and recommendations. Records are available for the following institutions: the Pennsylvania State Lunatic Hospital, Harrisburg; Philadelphia Hospital Department of the Insane; and the Pittsburgh City Home and Hospital.

Reports on County Poor Relief, 1932-1939. (3 boxes) Arranged alphabetically by name of county. Reports compiled by field representatives of the Bureau of Assistance and submitted to the secretary of the Department of Welfare to facilitate the preparation of recommendations to the directors of the poor of each county. The reports consist of evaluations of the county homes, almshouses, children in foster care, and the children's programs. Information contained within these reports includes names, titles, and salaries of staff, population statistics, information on plants and equipment, care and treatment of residents, and evaluation of special patients' cases. Additional types of information found include menus for various weeks, newspaper articles, and investigative reports prompted by complaints filed. County population statistics refer to African American inmates both individually and as a segment of the population. For example, some African American inmates are recorded in the censuses of Berks County Poor Relief, 1932-1938; Bloom Almshouse in Cambria County, 1933-1937; and Lehigh County Almshouse, 1933.

RG-24. RECORDS OF THE OFFICE OF THE REGISTER GENERAL

The Office of the Register General was established in 1789 to serve as a check on the comptroller general. Initially the comptroller general was required to submit all public accounts before final settlement to the register general for his advice and assistance. The duties of these offices were reversed in 1790 when the register general was given the responsibility for examining and adjusting accounts and then submitting them to the comptroller general for his approval. In 1809, the auditor general's office was created to replace and assume the functions of the register general.

Day Books, 1789-1809. (27 volumes) Arranged chronologically by date of transaction and indexed externally in **Ledgers, 1789-1815**, alphabetically by name of account. These volumes provide a record of the daily transactions of the Office of the Register General. Information provided about each transaction includes name of the firm or individual involved, date, circumstances of payment, amount of payment, and the account number. Types of activities documented include the payment of widows' pensions, militia fines and expenses, forfeited estates, and the surveying and improvement of roads. Included in some of the day books are references to African Americans. Day book entries dated May 20, 1791 and June 2, 1791, for example, show the amount of money due to "John the Negroe" from the comptroller general's office.

RG-25. RECORDS OF SPECIAL COMMIS-SIONS

The records of temporary independent commissions have been placed in one record group. These commissions were created to perform a specific function and they were terminated at the completion of that function. Being independent, they were not established under the purview of an on-going executive department. As can be ascertained from their names, these commissions were formed to serve primarily as investigative or planning bodies, or as vehicles to erect public monuments and promote the official commemoration of historic events.

COMMEMORATIVE, MONUMENT AND EXPOSITION COMMISSIONS

Fiftieth Anniversary of the Battle of Gettysburg Commission

General Correspondence, [ca. 1909-1914]. (4 volumes) Grouped alphabetically by first letter of correspondent's surname. Correspondence exchanged between national, state, and local officials and private citizens involved in planning the 50th anniversary of the Battle of Gettysburg in 1913. Also included are addresses given at the anniversary celebrations. At the New York veteran's celebration on July 3, 1913, the Rev. Dr. Newell Dwight Hillis spoke on the history of slavery, its role in the division between the North and the South, and the consequent reconciliation between Union and Confederate soldiers.

Pennsylvania Constitution Commemoration Committee

General Correspondence, 1935-1938. (11 boxes, 6 folders) Grouped by type of material and arranged thereunder chronologically. Contains minutes, general correspondence, and miscellaneous papers of the executive, regional, and special committees organized to plan Pennsylvania's 150th anniversary commemoration of the ratification of the U.S. Constitution. Included in this series is a folder entitled "Negro Participation, June 20, 1938." Materials found include letters and papers documenting the participation of African Americans in ceremonies in Philadelphia. Constitution Commemoration Committee members included the following African Americans: Robert L. Vann, chairman of the Pennsylvania Negro Committee, Pittsburgh Region, W. T. Poole, Richard F. Jones, P. J. Clyde Randall, Homer S. Brown, and Ivory Cobb. Also present in the file are many letters to and from Dr. John P. Turner, chairman of the Pennsylvania Negro Committee, Philadelphia Region, containing references to the celebration. Despite opposition to "negro" participation, the celebration was held at Convention Hall in Philadelphia on Monday June 20, 1938. The program included a choir, a pageant dramatizing the death of Crispus Attucks, and addresses by Philadelphia Mayor S. Davis Wilson, the Rev. Dr. Robert Bagnoll, pastor of the St. Thomas Presbyterian Episcopal Church, and former Mayor Harry Mackey. Bagnoll's address reiterated the theory that Alexander Hamilton's mother was a "negro" from the Virgin Islands. There are also letters of invitation to various African American churches and organizations to participate in the celebration parade. These organizations included the Charles

RG-25. Special Commissions. Pennsylvania Constitution Commemoration Committee. Crispus Attucks Pageant on June 20, 1938, In Philadelphia.

Young Company #27 of United Spanish War Veterans; George Bratcher Post #3614, Knights of Pythias; Colonel Charles Young Post #682; Quaker City Lodge, Elks #720; O. V. Catto Lodge, Elks #20; Holly Briggs Post VFW #2168; Leon Spencer Reid Post #547, American Legion; Pyramid Temple Shriners; Clarence Hill Post #1297; Crispus Attucks Post #151; and Cris Perry Lodge of Elks. The files include a listing of African American magazines and newspapers published in the District of Columbia, Maryland, New Jersey, New York, and Pennsylvania.

Publicity and Newsclippings, 1936-1938. (7 boxes, 32 folders) Unarranged. Included in this collection are 372 photographs relating to activities celebrating the 150th anniversary of the United States Constitution. The prints were collected from newspapers throughout the state, especially from the Philadelphia and Pittsburgh presses. In a folder labeled "Publicity-Photographs, 1937-1938" are several photographs of African American celebrations including parade scenes, contestants gathered in the William Penn School for Girls, images of bands and choruses performing at a June 18, 1938 birthday celebration for Dr. John P. Turner, and the Crispus Attucks Pageant held on June 20, 1938. A copy of a Wilkes-Barre *Times-Leader* article entitled "Program Gives Actual Picture of Washington" provides background information on George Washington. This article contains a paragraph headed "Slavery" that quotes Washington's sentiments with regard to slavery: "I shall never purchase another slave, but I cannot sell them, because I have principles against this tragedy in the human species. It is the wish nearest my heart that some way might be found to abolish slavery by law. It would prevent much future mischief."

Pennsylvania Three Hundredth Anniversary Commission
(Swedish Tercentenary)

Historical Data, undated. (7 folders) Grouped by subject, and thereunder alphabetically by first letter of correspondent's surname. A record of general correspondence and miscellaneous papers and financial accounts of the anniversary commission established to celebrate the arrival of the first Swedish settlement on the Delaware River. Included in the folder is the following item relating to African Americans: "Bibliography and Books, 1937-1938," in the August 1938 issue of *The Delaware County Advocate*, which contains an article "From Shanties to a Park: The Restoration of John Morton's Birthplace." Accompanying this article is a photograph of the home in Prospect Park, Chester, in which John Morton was born, surrounded by "negro shanties."

Sesqui-Centennial Commission of the Commonwealth
of Pennsylvania

Correspondence Relating to Exhibits, 1926. (3 folders) Grouped by type of material. Reports and general correspondence of the commission that oversaw the exhibits for the 1926 state Sesqui-Centennial Exposition in the state building in Philadelphia. Included are letters from State Archivist H. R. Shenk requesting information from various groups in order to represent "all racial and religious elements" in the Pennsylvania Building at the Sesqui-Centennial. Additionally, the file holds a report from Shenk to Dr. Clyde L. King outlining six "achievements of the colored race."

PLANNING AND OTHER COMMISSIONS
Pennsylvania Post-War Planning Commission

General Correspondence, [ca. 1943-1947]. (8 boxes) Arranged chronologically by date of correspondence. This Commission was created in 1943 to undertake studies in order to prepare for the economic dislocations expected in the post-war period and to devise measures to prevent the kind of mass unemployment that resulted at the end of the First World War. Included in this file are letters to and from Joseph V. Baker, chief of the Division of Negro Research and Planning in the Department of Labor and Industry. The letters are dated 1943 and allude to working toward meeting the needs of the black community in Pennsylvania after World War II.

RG-26. RECORDS OF THE DEPARTMENT OF STATE

The Department of State is headed by the secretary of the Commonwealth, whose office was established under the Constitution of 1776. The secretary is the keeper of the Great Seal and the initial custodian for many of the official documents of state government. Election returns, the laws and resolutions of the General Assembly, and proclamations, veto messages, and other recorded acts of the governor are all filed with the Department of State. The department is also responsible for issuing commissions to elected and appointed officials, receiving and examining documents relating to the incorporation and regulation of corporations, regulating professional boxing and wrestling matches, and administering legislation relating to election procedures, professional licensing, and the operation of charitable organizations.

SECRETARY OF THE COMMONWEALTH

Attorney General's Correspondence, 1791-1894. (1 box) Arranged chronologically. Correspondence received and sent by the attorneys general of Pennsylvania. Among the items found is a cache of eleven letters dated May 17-24, 1838 relating to the disturbances in Philadelphia that resulted in the destruction of Pennsylvania Hall, a large structure built for public meetings that served as a gathering place for the African American community and as a center of abolitionist activity. Among the correspondence are two letters to Governor Joseph Ritner from Pennsylvania Adjutant General William B. Reed, two letters to the governor from Samuel Webb stating that the riots caused African Americans in Philadelphia to fear for their lives, a resolution of the board of managers of the Pennsylvania Hall appointing Charles Harris as the messenger to inform the governor and others as to the status of the rioting, letters between Adjutant General Reed and Secretary of the Commonwealth Thomas H. Burrows, letters between Adjutant General Reed and Mayor John Swift, and letters from John G. Watmough to Adjutant General Reed and Governor Ritner.

Clemency File, 1790-1873. (68 boxes) Arranged chronologically. Individual case files that may contain diverse documents about persons seeking pardons from the president of the Supreme Executive Council, the governor, or the Board of Pardons. Types of documents for each case may include summary sheets, letters, petitions, court transcripts, newspaper notices, death warrants, pardon proclamations or respites. The information found in the file varies with each dossier and the time period. While one case file may merely provide a person's name and reason for being imprisoned, another may also list the incarcerated individual's occupation and particulars about his or her life and family. In a few instances photographs of prisoners are included. Some examples of cases involving African Americans are:

- April 1791. *Commonwealth vs. Phoebe Douglas.* Phoebe Douglas, a "Negroe," was convicted of taking property valued at thirty shillings from Ralph Izard for which she was sentenced to make restitution and serve six months of hard labor. Included are four petitions for pardon based upon Phoebe's good moral character.
- September 7, 1791. *Commonwealth vs. Negro Perry.* Negro Perry was convicted of fraud, sentenced to one year's hard labor, and fined one pound, seventeen shillings, and six pence. Included is a petition for pardon with pardon statement and fine cancellation dated April 18, 1792.
- December 1791. *Commonwealth vs. Andrew Wilson.* Andrew Wilson, a black man, was fined ten pounds "for fornication and bastardy on a Negro girl," Rebecca Knowles. The court adjudged him to pay thirty shillings fine and two shillings, six

pence per week in support until the child turned five years old.

- November 1792. *Commonwealth vs. Benjamin, a Negro.* Benjamin was convicted of burglary and sentenced to hard labor until December 25, 1792. Included is a petition of Benjamin which also notes "pardoned December 1, 1792."

- November 1792. *Commonwealth vs. Bello Robinson, Negro.* Bello Robinson was convicted of manslaughter and sentenced to be branded on the "brown of the left thumb with the letter "M," to pay a fine of five pounds, and to undergo a servitude of hard labor for three months. Includes petition and a notation of pardon given February 26, 1793.

- January 12, 1793. *Commonwealth vs. Negroe Virgil Williams.* Virgil Williams was convicted of fornication and bastardy. Includes petitions for remission of his fine, which was forgiven February 9, 1793.

- November 1863. *Commonwealth vs. Frances Wilson, Gillmore Hull, Sylvester Gordon, Edward Stuckey, and Franklin Bostick.* John Brown, a free African American accused of robbing a store and, though he protested his innocence, he was nonetheless banished into Maryland from his home in Salisbury Township, Lancaster County where he was physically abused and almost sold back into slavery by the defendants in this suit. This file contains testimonies of many people who saw John Brown being abused and beaten, one of whom was his wife, Susan Brown.

- December 1864. *Commonwealth vs. Glenalvin J. Goodridge.* Glenalvin Goodridge was accused of raping a white woman named Mary E. Smith. Mary E. Smith claimed that she went to his photography studio to have a photograph taken and that he pulled her into a darkroom and raped her. This file contains a copy of the record in the Court of Oyer and Terminer and General Jail Delivery for the County of York. Information includes statements as told by Mary E. Smith and other witnesses and several letters of testimony from people who wrote to Governor Andrew G. Curtin, requesting a pardon for Goodridge. The Governor pardoned Glenalvin J. Goodridge on December 13, 1864. The certificate of pardon is also in this file.

Executive Correspondence, 1790-1969. (108 boxes) Arranged chronologically date of letter. Executive correspondence of the Pennsylvania secretary of the Commonwealth containing both official correspondence and election returns. The following items are representative of materials that relate to African Americans:

- Undated list of illegal voters dated February 15, 1799. Heading the list is Benjamin Mengole, a "bad voter," a "foreigner" and a "Mulatto boy." The paper states that while his father became a citizen, Benjamin did not. He had immigrated with his father from Port-au-Prince in 1793.
- Correspondence dated January 8, 1805 from the Legislature of North Carolina to the governor of Pennsylvania. The letter asked for Pennsylvania's concurrence in a proposed amendment to the federal Constitution that would "prevent the further importation of Slaves, or People of Colour, from any West-India Islands, from the Coast of Africa, or elsewhere, into the United States, or any part thereof."
- Letter, dated April 24, 1811, and an enclosure, both informing the Commonwealth that a black man, Thomas Lock, had reported the death of another African American, John Lloyd, whose material possessions now belonged to the Commonwealth because he had no heirs.
- Letter dated April 26, 1839 from George Sanderson to Secretary of the Commonwealth Francis R. Shunk informing him of the new library that would be open by summer 1840 in Carlisle. Connected with the Equal Rights Society, the library

was incorporated in 1837 as the Equal Rights Library and contained 348 volumes. The Library would be a public library with every citizen to have access to it upon payment of $1.00.

- Letter dated May 11, 1861 from W. McCauley to Governor A. G. Curtin regarding the enlistment of the first "colored" soldiers to offer their services during the Civil War. McCauley refers to the noble history of Negro soldiers in the American Revolution and the War of 1812.

- A resolution dated October 20, 1861 from the citizens of Coudersport, Potter County, to the president of the United States protesting the use of Pennsylvania soldiers to capture and return fugitive slaves.

- Letter dated October 26, 1863 from the Provost Marshal General's Office, Washington, D.C., signed by the following: James B. Fry, provost marshal general; Henry Stone, assistant adjutant general; and C. C. Gilbert, major, 19th US Infantry, acting assistant provost marshal general of Philadelphia. The letter, addressed to Brigadier General R. A. Pierce, assistant provost marshal general of Massachusetts, was written in response to certain recruitment questions including whether or not colored volunteers would be credited to the state's quota and paid the offered bounty. The response was that they would be accepted but that it was uncertain whether or not the bounty would be paid.

- Letter dated May 15, 1865 from Governor A. G. Curtin to State Treasurer William H. Kemble, instructing him to pay five hundred dollars to the treasurer of the Home for Destitute Colored Children of Philadelphia.

- Letter dated June 5, 1865 from Governor A. G. Curtin to President Andrew Johnson that makes reference to a policy of paying a one hundred dollar bounty to recruits "white or colored."

- Letter dated December 12, 1866 addressed to Governor A. G. Curtin regarding the Pennsylvania Soldiers' Orphans Schools, the presence of "colored soldier's orphans" in the schools, and the possibility of appointing a "colored man to travel the state and locate additional colored orphans."

- Report bearing the notation "1867" addressed to the Committee on Out Wards lists the names of Pennsylvania soldiers being cared for in an almshouse that was apparently located in the city of Philadelphia. The report names the "colored soldiers" and reports a total of "thirty colored soldiers in residence at the almshouse."
- Letter dated February 23,1867 from Governor J. W. Geary to Major General George G. Meade regarding the arrival of "colored troops" in the state for discharge and the need to provide them with "rations, quarters and transportation."
- Letter dated November 30, 1868 from Samuel Jeanes, treasurer of Home for Destitute Colored Children, to Governor J. W. Geary requesting payment of state appropriation for the facility.
- Letter dated June 19, 1869 from George F. McFarland, superintendent of the Soldiers' Orphans School, noting clothing requirements for a total of 2,133 children, which included 124 "colored" children at the Bridgewater school.
- Letter dated July 10, 1869 from Samuel Jeanes, treasurer of the Home for Destitute Colored Children to Governor J. W. Geary requesting payment of a financial appropriation made by the state legislature to the institution.
- Report dated September 14, 1869 regarding the number of soldiers' orphans to be clothed including those at the "colored" school at Bridgewater.
- Letter dated November 30, 1869 from Samuel Jeanes to Governor J. W. Geary applying for payment of the state appropriation funds to the Home for Destitute Colored Children.
- Letter dated January 7, 1870 from Samuel Jeanes to Governor John W. Geary repeating request for payment of the state ap-

propriation for Home for Destitute Colored Children.

- Letter dated May 5, 1870 regarding the new treasurer of the Home for Destitute Colored Children.
- Letter dated June 1, 1872 from the trustees of the Governor Library in Buffalo, New York, requesting the donation of various materials for their collection. The trustees reported that the library would be accessible to all patrons regardless of age, sex, or color. One of the trustees whose signature appears on the letter was former United States President Millard Fillmore.
- Letter dated June 12, 1873 to General Babcock from Frederick Douglass. The author requested that his friend, George Hill, be considered for a postmaster position and that the matter be brought to the attention of President Grant.
- Document dated April 7, 1885 recording an inquiry into the conduct of the 18th Regiment, Pennsylvania National Guard while in Washington, D.C. for the inauguration of President Cleveland in March 1885. It states that a "colored boy" was dancing for the troops. Also included is the testimony of Gilbert Williams, "a colored servant."
- Document dated July 15, 1885 from the Adjutant General's Office, Washington, D.C., providing statistics on the number of Pennsylvanians who served in the Civil War: a total of 337,936, which included 8,612 "colored troops."

Executive Minute Books, 1790-1943. (44 volumes) Arranged chronologically. A daily record chronicling the official activities of the governor of Pennsylvania, such as appointments and commissions of state and local officials (most often justices of the peace, notaries public, and police); the issuance of warrants, mandates, orders, paroles, commutations, respites, and requisitions for arrest and prisoner delivery; the certification of incorporations; account approvals given; the delivery of messages and addresses to the General Assembly; the approval of acts and resolutions of the assembly; and the receipt of official reports. The following is an example of an entry pertaining to African Americans:

- On Monday, March 20, 1837, Adam Klinefelter, Esq., sheriff of York County, was appointed an agent of the Commonwealth of Pennsylvania to transport Nathan S. Bemis, Edward Prigg, Jacob Forworth, and Stephen Lewis from Maryland to Pennsylvania for trial. Fugitives from justice, they were charged with having seized and taken away without lawful authority the wife and six children of Henry Morgan, a free "colored" man living in the Lower Chanceford Township, York County.

Pardon Books, 1791-1877. (12 volumes) Arranged chronologically by date of entry. A record of pardons granted to convicted felons by Pennsylvania's Governors. The following items are typical of references to African Americans:

- Pardon Book for January 28, 1861 through November 30, 1866: a pardon certificate dated January 12, 1864 for Robert Thomas of Lancaster County who had been charged with "larceny." At the request of several affluent citizens, Governor Andrew G. Curtin pardoned Thomas in order that he could "enter the military service of the United States in a Regiment of Colored Troops."
- Pardon Book for January 28, 1861 through November 30, 1866, a pardon dated December 13, 1864, for Glenalvin J. Goodridge of York, who had been charged with a rape of Mary E. Smith. At the request of several affluent citizens, Governor Curtin pardoned Goodridge in order that he could return to teaching school and supporting his family.

BUREAU OF ELECTIONS, COMMISSIONS, AND LEGISLATION

Engrossed Laws, 1700-1968. (526 boxes) Arranged chronologically by date of legislation. The original laws created and established by the Commonwealth of Pennsylvania. One of the most important pieces of legislation is the Act for the Gradual Abolition of Slavery passed March 1, 1780 and amended March 29, 1788 and December 8, 1789. Among its various provisions, the act ensured that no slave could be held in servitude for more than seven years past his twenty-first birthday. Although the act did not immediately prohibit slavery, it was the first legal action taken in the country to implement a policy of gradual abolition of slavery. This series contains the official copies of other acts relating to African Americans in Pennsylvania.

State Campaign Expense Account Files, 1974-1990. (349 cartons, 1 box) Arranged chronologically by year, and thereunder alphabetically by name of committee or candidate. The state campaign expense files consist of campaign income and expense reports of candidates for state judicial offices and political action committees. Information found includes the name and address of the candidate and of the political action committee. In addition, the expense reports contain a summary of receipts and expenditures for the dates listed on the report. The summary includes a list of contributors from whom the committee or candidate received funds and a list of recipients who received money from the committee or candidate for printing, postage, advertising, etc. The report also contains the dates for the period being reported and a notarized affidavit section completed by the individual submitting the report. Expense accounts for African American legislators include Dwight Evans and K. Leroy Irvis among others.

RG-26. Department of State. Bureau of Elections, Commissions, and Legislation. Engrossed Laws, 1700-1968. Gradual Abolition Act of 1780.

BUREAU OF PROFESSIONAL AND OCCUPATIONAL AFFAIRS

The records of the Bureau of Professional and Occupational Affairs also include the records of the following state boards: the Real Estate Commission, the State Board of Chiropody, the State Board of Cosmetology, the State Board of Examiners and Public Accountants, the State Board of Funeral Directors, the State Board of Medical Education, the State Board of Nurse Examiners, the State Board of Optometrical Examiners, the State Board of Physical Therapy Examiners, and the State Dental Council and Examining Board. All African Americans who have been licensed by any of these professional boards are documented in these records.

Bureau Commissioners' Correspondence, 1961-1984. (55 cartons) Arranged in alphabetical order by institution, organization, or individual and thereunder chronologically. Incoming letters to the commissioner of the Bureau of Professional and Occupational Affairs. This series documents the commissioners' interactions with other state agencies, individuals, and organizations both professional and vocational. The majority of information concerns public grievances, complaints, and legal action taken by each profession's board of examiners. Included in this file are correspondence and memoranda from Secretary of State C. DeLores Tucker, the first African American woman to hold this position, and Barton A. Fields, deputy secretary. Information found includes Tucker's stated position on a proposed work stoppage, her explanation of the pay roll situation in light of the budget crisis, and a statement of her support of the Governor's Affirmative Action Program.

State Board of Cosmetology

Minute Books, 1967-1975. (11 volumes) Arranged chronologically by date of meeting. A record of the minutes of the meetings of the State Board of Cosmetology. Information found generally concerns enforcement of rules regulating the proper training and licensing of cosmetologists in Pennsylvania. Documented is the December 1974 investigation into why African American cosmetologists Ms. Carolyn Desmond and Ms. Daisy Restenberger failed to file the proper forms for a transfer student. Neither woman actually appeared before the board because "a satisfactory explanation was received by telephone from Ms. Restenberger."

State Board of Funeral Directors

Minute Book, 1963-1964. (1 volume) Arranged chronologically by date of meeting. A record of the minutes of State Board of Funeral Directors meetings. In 1963 this board was transferred from the Department of Education to the Department of State. Information found generally concerns enforcement of licensing procedures and practices of funeral homes in Pennsylvania. Included is an inspector's report for the investigation of the Laws Funeral Home, Chester, Pa.. This investigation was initiated by a complaint received from a competing funeral home alleging that an unlicensed employee had been performing embalmings at the funeral home owned by Mrs. Laws. The board ruled that both funeral homes would be sent a copy of the laws governing funeral homes in Pennsylvania, specifying the activities that are allowed under a license.

State Board of Medical Education and Licensure

Index of Licensed Practitioners of Medicine in Pennsylvania, 1894-1981. (10 volumes) Arranged alphabetically by first letter of surname. An index of physicians licensed to practice medicine in Pennsylvania. Information recorded includes the physician's name, the date of license, license number, institution, and occasionally the date of death for each doctor. The following are some African Americans who received Pennsylvania licenses:

- George Goyle Adams, #13594, a graduate of Howard University, licensed on August 26, 1931.
- Gladstone Wesley Allen, #2504, graduate of Meharry Medical College, licensed October 17, 1947.
- Felix Adolphus Anderson, #12355, a 1926 graduate of Howard University, licensed February 23, 1928 , died April 15, 1964.
- Edward Stanley Abbott, #10246, a graduate of Howard University, licensed February 23, 1921.
- Clyde Harrison Anthony, #11677, a Meharry Medical College graduate, licensed February 11, 1926.
- Charles Theophilus Atkinson, #21500, who transferred into Howard University in 1944 licensed December 12, 1946, died March 2, 1980
- Burl Bassette, #996, who also transferred to Howard University, licensed November 1, 1927.

COMMISSION ON CHARITABLE ORGANIZATIONS

Charitable Solicitations Registration File, 1924-1961, 1963-1987. (234 cartons) Grouped loosely by date of approval and thereunder alphabetically by name of organization. The Solicitation Act was passed by the General Assembly in 1925 to protect citizens from illicit charity drives. Registration was required of fund-raising groups that planned to solicit contributions. Some applications contain only the names of the organization and its officers, and the name of the proposed program. Many application files, however, are rich with information on the formation and work of the organization, as well as correspondence from officers, bureau officials, boards of directors, or supporters of the organization's proposal.

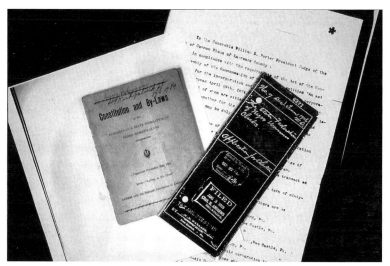

RG-26. Department of State. Commission on Charitable Organizations. Charitable Solicitations Registration File. Pennsylvania Federation of Negro Women's Clubs.

Cited below by county are some of the African American organizations' applications who sought registration:

- *Allegheny:* African Orthodox Science Church, Pittsburgh; Bethel African Methodist Episcopal (A.M.E.) Church, Pittsburgh, 1942; Beulah Baptist Church, Pittsburgh, 1942-1945; Buena Vista Friendship Home for Indigent Colored Masons, Pittsburgh, 1951-1955; Brown Chapel A.M.E. Church, Pittsburgh, 1942-1943; Coleman Industrial Home for Colored Boys, Pittsburgh, 1931-1945; Ebenezer Baptist Church, Pittsburgh, 1947; Golden Link Society, Pittsburgh, 1948; Grace Hope Tabernacle, Pittsburgh, 1951; Grand Order of Eastern Star, Pittsburgh, 1946-47; Inter-Racial Action Council, Pittsburgh, 1945-1949; Inter-Racial Hospital Association, Pittsburgh, 1939; Moore Athletic Association, Pittsburgh, 1947-1948; Morning Star Baptist Church, Pittsburgh, 1946; Mother's Club of Etna, Pittsburgh, 1946; National Association of Negro Musicians,

Inc., Pittsburgh, 1941; National Negro Hospital Foundation, Inc., Pittsburgh; New Pilgrim Baptist Church, Pittsburgh, 1948; Omega Grand Order of Eastern Star, Pittsburgh, 1946-1947; Order of Independent Americans, Pittsburgh, 1948; Pennsylvania Federation of Negro Woman's Clubs, Sewickley, 1949; St. Mark A.M.E. Church, Pittsburgh, 1950-1951; St. Philip's Orthodox Christian Science Church, Pittsburgh; John Wesley A.M.E. Zion Church, Pittsburgh, 1934-1950; and Mary E. Wilson Rebekah Lodge, Pittsburgh. Of special note is the Pennsylvania Federation of Negro Women's Clubs' file which contains the charter, dated the 28th day of July, 1906, and the earlier constitution and bylaws, November 10th, 1903, when it first became affiliated with the National Association of Colored Women.

- *Beaver:* Aliquippa Youth Cooperation Council, 1947.
- *Chester:* Cheyney State Teachers' College Alumni Association, 1947; Downingtown Industrial and Agricultural School, Downingtown, 1948; Tabernacle Baptist Church, Coatesville, 1925-1928 .
- *Cumberland:* Social Service Welfare Club, Carlisle, 1951.
- *Dauphin:* Church of God in Christ, Harrisburg, 1950.
- *Lycoming:* Aged Colored Women's Home, Mary Slaughter, founder, Williamsport, 1953; Bethune-Douglass Community, Williamsport, 1953; and Williamsport Community Welfare Corporation.
- *Philadelphia:* Richard Allen Statue Committee Fund, 1949; Bethel A.M.E. Church, 1928; Center for Older Adults, Northwest, 1978; Committee for Racial and Religious Tolerance, 1939-1941; Community Home for the Aged Colored People, 1946-1947; Independent Order of Odd Fellows, 1947-1948; Negro Veterans' Association, 1949; Philadelphia Metropolitan Council, National Council of Negro Women, 1949; YMCA, Christian Street Branch, 1947-1948.

- *Washington:* Eva Mae Brown Home for Negro Delinquent Girls, Canonsburg, 1938-1943; Washington County Welfare League of Negro Women, Washington, 1940.
- *York:* Citizens Committee to Open Municipal Swimming Pool (Regardless of Race), York, 1949.

CORPORATION BUREAU

Charter Books, 1812-1875. (8 volumes) Arranged chronologically. A record of charters granted to private corporations and organizations in the Commonwealth. These volumes contain charters from the following African American organizations as well as corporations and institutions that supported African Americans. The following are examples of materials containing references to African Americans:

- **Volume l, 1812-14:** African Humane Society of Philadelphia, African Farmers' and Mechanics' Society, and the Benezet Philanthropic Society of Philadelphia.
- **Volume 2, 1815-19:** African Friendly Society and Female Benevolent Society of St. Thomas African Episcopal Church of Philadelphia, Rush Beneficial Society of the Free Sons of Ethiopia of Philadelphia, First African Baptist Church of Philadelphia, Society of the Sons of Africa, Friendly West Indian Society, African Washington Benevolent Society of Pennsylvania, and the African Warner Mifflin Society of Philadelphia.
- **Volume 3, 1819-25:** Angolian Society of the City of Philadelphia, Female Benezet Society of Philadelphia, Granville Harmony Society of Philadelphia, African Benevolent Association, Wilberforce Benevolent Society of Philadelphia, Society of the Daughters of Ethiopia, Benezet Philanthropic Society of Philadelphia, Brotherly Union Society of the County of Philadelphia, African Methodist Episcopal Wesley Church of the City of Philadelphia, Benevolent Sons of Bethel and Union

Churches, Tyson Benevolent Association of the City and County of Philadelphia, African Union Society, and the Female Baptist Assistant Society of Philadelphia.

- **Volume 4, 1825-32:** Female Granville Society of Philadelphia, First Colored Wesley Methodist Church in the City of Philadelphia, Benevolent Daughters of St. Thomas, Daughters of Absalom, Daughters of Zion of the Angolian Ethiopian Society of Philadelphia, United Daughters of the Wesley Society of Philadelphia, United Brethren Society of Philadelphia, United Benevolent Daughters of Zion, Second African Presbyterian Congregation of Philadelphia, Benevolent Daughters of Wesley of the City and County of Philadelphia, Society of the Friendly Benevolent Sons of Zion, Coachmen's Benevolent Society of Philadelphia, Association for the Care of Colored Orphans, First African Baptist Female Union Society of Philadelphia, Wilberforce Association of Philadelphia, Society of the Sons of St. Thomas, Society of the Female Daughters of Hosea, Pennsylvania Colonization Society, African Porter Benevolent Society, Female Methodist Assistant Society of Philadelphia, United Sisters' Society, Daughters of Aaron, Harrison Benevolent Society of Philadelphia, Society of the Daughters of Isaiah, Daughters of Africa, African Methodist Episcopal Church of York, Benevolent Daughters of Tyson, and United Shipley Beneficial Society of Philadelphia.
- **Volume 5, 1832-36:** Philadelphia Association for the Moral and Mental Improvement of the People of Color.
- **Volume 6, 1836-41:** Philadelphia Library Company of Coloured Persons, Rush Librarian Debating Society of Pennsylvania, Benevolent Sons of Africa, African Methodist Episcopal Church of Columbia, African Zoar Methodist Episcopal Church, Benevolent Sons of Bethel and Union Churches, Citizen Sons of Philadelphia Association, Brotherly Union Society of the County of Philadelphia.

- **Volume 7, 1841-52:** Brown Beneficial Society of the City and County of Philadelphia, Rising Sons and Daughters of Lucretia Mott, First African Baptist Church of Philadelphia, Union Sons of Industry of the City and County of Philadelphia, Beneficial Sons of Clayton Durham, Union Sons of the Borrows Beneficial Society of the City and County of Philadelphia, Association of the Benevolent Daughters of Borrows, Female Rush Assistant Society of Pennsylvania, Union Benevolent Daughters of Elijah Society of Philadelphia, Guardian Samaritan Society of the City and County of Philadelphia, Joseph Cox Beneficial Society of the City and County of Philadelphia, African Methodist Episcopal Mount Pisgah Church of the Borough of West Philadelphia, Lombard Street Central Presbyterian Congregation of Philadelphia, United Sons and Daughters of the Lovejoy Society of the City and County of Philadelphia, United Sons and Daughters of Joseph Henderson Society, Union Sons and Daughters of Peter Spencer Association, African Union Church.
- **Volume 8, 1856-75:** St. Thomas's African Episcopal Church and American Union Church.

RG-27. RECORDS OF PENNSYLVANIA'S REVOLUTIONARY GOVERNMENTS

The Constitution of 1776 vested limited administrative and executive powers of the government of the Commonwealth in an elected council of twelve members known as the Supreme Executive Council. The primary function of the council was to oversee the proper execution of the laws of the state. The council was composed of one member from Philadelphia and one from each county. A president and vice president of the council were selected from among the twelve by joint vote of the General Assembly and the council.

Prior to the formal organization of the Supreme Executive Council in March 1777, executive and military powers were exercised by the Committee of Safety (1775-1776), and the Council of Safety (1776-1777). The Committee of Safety was appointed by resolve of the Provincial Assembly to supervise all military activities and matter relating to the defense of the state. The committee first met on July 3, 1775, and continued to function until July of the following year, when it was replaced by the Council of Safety. The council was created by the state Constitutional Convention of 1776 to assume executive responsibilities until the new constitutional government could be organized.

Functioning under the revolutionary governments was the Board of War, the Navy Board, and the second Council of Safety, which had been created in 1777. The Constitution of 1790 provided for a popularly elected governor with expanded executive powers to replace the Supreme Executive Council.

SUPREME EXECUTIVE COUNCIL, 1777-1790

Clemency File, 1775-1790, and undated. (12 boxes) Arranged alphabetically by surname of petitioner. Individual case files of persons seeking pardons from the president of the Supreme Executive Council that contain such diverse items as summary sheets, letters, and respites about persons seeking pardons. The information found varies with each dossier and the time period. While some case files only provide a person's name and reason for being imprisoned, others list the incarcerated individual's occupation and particulars about his or her life and family. References are made to African Americans from several counties. Representative of these are the following:

- November 1785, Philadelphia County-a petition for Negro Sarah, who was convicted of stealing the goods of Ruth Black.
- November 1787, Philadelphia County-Alice Clifton, slave of

John Barthlomew, was convicted of murdering her female child on April 5, 1787. She was sentenced to be hanged by the neck until dead.

- January 1789, York County-In *Pennsylvania vs. Negro Harry*, Negro Harry was found guilty of stealing money from Jacob Wertz. He was charged to pay back the money as well as a fine, and to serve three months of hard labor.
- June 1789-In *Commonwealth vs. Negro Cuff, Slave to Cornelia Cross*, Negro Cuff was convicted of larceny of the property of Benjamin W. Morris. He had to restore the goods stolen or the value of them. In addition, Cuff was fined forty-five shillings and sentenced to a servitude of hard labor for six weeks. He was later granted a pardon.
- August 1789-Petition of John Irwin of Westmoreland County requesting release of his servant boy, who had committed felonies in Bedford County and been fined twenty pounds. Because he was unable to pay the fine, he was to be sold at a public sale. The petition requested a remission of the fine on the grounds that the servant would not sell for even a fifth of the fine and the owner would therefore take a great lost.
- September 1780-Petition of James Oellers, of Philadelphia, on behalf of his slave Sarah Craig, read on September 25, 1780. Sarah Craig had knowingly received stolen goods from Alice Wiley, who had taken them from John Fry. As a result of this petition, Sarah was granted a pardon in October 1790.

Forfeited Estate File, 1777-1790. (4 boxes) Arranged chronologically. This series documents the property of colonists deemed loyal to the British Crown during the Revolutionary War that had been seized by the revolutionary authorities. Cited here are some examples representative of references to African Americans:

- ***Bucks County:*** An inventory and assessment of the forfeited goods and chattels and property of Gilbert Hicks taken August 28, 1778., lists "a Negro 12 years old" valued at 112 pounds and ten shillings.

- **Chester County:** An inventory of lands, tenants, goods and chattels of Christopher Wilson taken July 6, 1778 lists a "Negro Wench 19 years old" valued at 75 pounds.
- **Lancaster County:** A petition of John Swanwick read in Council October 21, 1777, regarding the protection of the estate of his father W. Swanwick, who had died and left his estate to John's mother, Mary Swanwick. A militia captain had taken some of her property, which included a "Negro girl."
- **Philadelphia County:** An inventory of household goods and property of John Tolly appraised August 8, 1778, lists "one black wench named Betty, two female children," valued at forty pounds.
- **York County:** A petition, read in Council in September 1778, for Negro Ralph who had been purchased by John Rankin from Robert Power. Rankin declared his intention to free Negro Ralph after he had served Rankin for a fixed term. Shortly after Negro Ralph obtained his freedom, however, Rankin died. Negro Ralph feared being sold as part of the Rankin estate and this petition was made on behalf of Negro Ralph.

RG-30. RECORDS OF THE PENNSYLVANIA STATE POLICE

The Department of State Police was created in 1905 to help preserve law and order throughout the Commonwealth and to cooperate with and assist local law-enforcement officers in the apprehension of criminals. It was the first uniformed police organization of its kind in the United States. The original compliment number was limited by law to 228 officers who were expected to patrol the 45,000 square miles of Pennsylvania. The State Highway Patrol in the Department of Revenue, which had originally been established in the Department of Highways in 1923 to enforce motor vehicle laws, was merged with the department in 1937 to become the Pennsylvania Motor Police. The name of the agency was changed to Pennsylvania State Police in 1943. In keeping with its responsibility to assist local police departments, the State Police administer professional training programs for municipal police and provide direct assistance to state law enforcement agencies wishing to utilize the technical, scientific, and data resources of the department. They have jurisdiction in all political subdivisions in the state.

COMMISSIONER OF STATE POLICE

Ku Klux Klan General Correspondence, 1922-1929, 1932, 1934-1940. (5 boxes) Grouped chronologically by year of correspondence. Includes correspondence, membership lists, orders for supplies, telegrams, registration cards, photographs, and meeting minutes of Ku Klux Klan units in Pennsylvania. The bulk of the information contained within this series deals with membership issues and membership recruitment. Correspondence between officers of the Pennsylvania Klan relates to various events as well as issues with the Klan's hierarchy. Notable events documented are rallies in Carnegie, Lilly, and Reading and the 1934 Thomas Abbott case. Most of the correspondence contained in the files is either addressed to or from Pennsylvania's King Kleagle Samuel D. Rich or his successor Samuel G. Stouch III. Two photographs dated 1924 show the Hanover Klan and a flag raising by Klansmen in full Klan regalia in Shrewsbury, Pennsylvania.

Ku Klux Klan General Files, 1923-1940. (3 boxes) Arranged alphabetically by subject. This series is a miscellaneous grouping of files that include papers about each Klavern's election returns, enlistment papers for various counties, mailing lists, countersigns and passwords, official bulletins, newspapers, publications, and information provided by the State Police regarding the acquisition of these records. Data provided by the election returns include county and city or town; Klavern name, local Klavern number and the locations of meetings; and name, office and addresses of elected Klan members and the year of the election. Enlistment papers show name and marital status of each enlistee, city and county of residence, age, occupation at time of enlistment, length of enlistment, physical description, amount of education and military service, and whether or not each was approved for membership. The mailing lists contain the names and addresses of Exalted Cyclops or Kligrapps and their respective Klaverns in Pennsylvania or New Jersey. Some of the records, such as the official bulletins and a sampling of conservative newspapers, were compiled for administrative use. The General Files include enlistment papers from the following counties: Adams, Allegheny, Beaver, Carbon, Clarion, Crawford, Erie, Indiana, Lawrence, Mercer, Northumberland, Venango, Washington, and Westmoreland; as well as mailing lists and special issues of the following newspapers: *American Free Press*, October 15, 1940; *American Protest*, 4th Special Edition; *American Protestant*. July 1940; *The Fiery Cross*, October 1940; *The Free American*, August 1, 3, 15, 1940; *New York Journal*, Editorial page, July 26, 1939; *New York Times*, Business page, September 29, 1939; *The Philadelphia Inquirer*, September 29, 1940; and *The Ulster Protestant*, May and June 1940.

Strike Reports, 1922, 1932-1964. (29 boxes) Grouped by labor dispute and arranged thereunder chronologically by date of disturbance. Contains strike duty reports prepared by State Police officers, along with interdepartmental teletype messages relating to labor disturbances in industries ranging from coal and hosiery to construction and steel. Also included are annual Departmental manpower utilization reports that provide statistics on the use of officers for strike duty between fiscal years 1938-1950. Information found in the strike reports may differ with each reporting officer, but usually includes the date and the name, title, and address of the officer to whom the report is being sent; the subject of the report; a brief synopsis of any police activity; a short account of the officer's observations; a record of mileage; and the signature of the reporting officer. The annual strike manpower reports provide, for each month, the number of strike days, the number of police dogs, the percentage of time spent on strike duty, and the average number of men used. In addition, the total number of police dogs, the number of strike days, the average number of men per day, the percentage of time on strike duty, and the average number of days on strike duty per month are calculated for each year. The manpower reports are frequently accompanied by related reports such as an annual list of industrial disturbances, a record of boarding and lodging, and a monthly report of the number of men from each troop involved on a daily basis on strike duty. Examples of reports and correspondence relating to African Americans are:

- A Special Report, dated April 29, 1922, concerning racial threats and retaliation investigated by State Police agent #607 at Orient Station pertaining to a riot at Tower Hill No. 1. According to this report, "upon my arrival in Orient I noticed many men and women about who appeared to be enraged and were very loud in their talk, making many threats about what they intended to do to the State Police and deputies about. In conversation with a party named Spaike, he stated that the people, especially the foreigners, were either going to cripple or possibly kill a colored deputy named King, who is doing deputy work in this vicinity."
- Correspondence concerning a race riot at the Philadelphia Transportation Company in August 1944. During the month

of August, the emergency troops of the various squadrons were mobilized to suppress this riot. Among this correspondence is a memo dated August 1, 1944 that contains the following text: "telephone call received by commissioner from Major Henry, . . .I thought I would call and let you know in Philadelphia all trolleys, buses and elevators are down this morning. Today is the day the colored people are supposed to go on as operators, motormen and conductors, and everything went out this morning." Included in this correspondence are statements issued by the National Association for the Advancement of Colored People (NAACP) and Philadelphia Mayor Bernard Samuels.

PERSONNEL DIVISION

Diary and Photographs of Wallace K. Keely, 1905-1949. (1 volume, 3 photographs) Arranged in chronological order. A personal scrapbook of State Police Officer Wallace K. Kelly, who served with the force from 1906 to 1940. The diary has newspaper clippings, postcards, and photographs of state troopers as well as "mug" shots, biographical profiles, and background information pertaining to criminals and cases involving the State Police, with emphasis on the activities of Troop C which was headquartered at Pottsville, Pennsylvania. The "mug" shots are usually accompanied by descriptive cards that provide the name, residence, occupation, race, age, height, weight, hair and eye color, and build of the person; the date and place of arrest; the nature of the crime (date, place, means, object); the date and time of the crime; and the names of any associates, places frequented, or peculiarities that might make apprehension of the person easier. Included in the diary is a photo and information on Newton Young, alias Frank Johnson, an African American who was arrested June 3, 1921.

RG-31. RECORDS OF THE DEPARTMENT OF COMMERCE

The Department of Commerce was created in 1939 to promote the development of business, industry and commerce in the state. Under the enabling legislation, the Pennsylvania State Publicity Commission was abolished and its function of attracting tourists to the Commonwealth was transferred to the Department of Commerce, while the State Planning Board was made an administrative board within the department and remained there until 1955. In 1968, the Department of Internal Affairs' Bureau of Statistics was assigned to the Department of Commerce, along with administrative responsibilities for the newly created Bicentennial Commission.

The Department of Commerce served industry and various community industrial development organizations by administering and coordinating federal and state aid programs, and by making available pertinent technical and statistical information. Agency urban planning and redevelopment functions were transferred to the Department of Community Affairs in 1966. In 1996, the Departments of Commerce and Community Affairs were merged to create the Department of Community and Economic Development.

SECRETARY

Secretary's Subject File, 1973-1977. (10 cartons) Arranged chronologically by date of document.

Non-Discrimination Clause for State Contract Files. Contains correspondence, executive orders, regulations, agreements, and other forms of documentation with reference to the "non-discrimination clause" for state contracts. A memorandum dated January 6, 1972 and addressed to "Heads of all Administrative Departments, Independent Administrative

Boards and Commissions and Other State Agencies under the Governor's Jurisdiction" states that "all Commonwealth contracts must include anti-discrimination clauses which not only prohibit discrimination on the grounds of race, color, religion, ancestry or national origin, but also prohibit discrimination on the grounds of sex or age." Also included are copies of the non-discrimination clause.

Charitable Foundations Files. These files contain guidelines for foundations that were interested in applying for state grants for site development programs. Such grants were designed to promote such varied programs as education; health; civil and cultural development; the welfare of children, youth, the handicapped, and the aged; historic preservation; and urban affairs with special emphasis on projects originating in the Pittsburgh area. One foundation documented is the Ford Foundation. It stated that its "interests included community development addressing the following: intergroup relations; conflict resolution; social, economic and educational opportunity for minority groups; housing; social and economic resources and other initiatives.

BUREAU OF MINORITY BUSINESS DEVELOPMENT

Subject File, 1975-1983. (18 cubic feet) {unprocessed} Contains loan applications, business summaries, notes, technical assistance documentation, correspondence, insurance information, income tax returns, credit information, and financial information, with reference to African American businesses such as the Unity Broadcasting Company, WCXJ Radio, Pittsburgh.

RG-33. RECORDS OF THE SUPREME COURT

The Supreme Court was created in 1722 by an act of the Provincial Assembly and was originally required both to hold sessions in Philadelphia and to travel on circuit for the trial of cases. Appellate sessions were formerly held in several different locations, but now the court sits only in Philadelphia, Harrisburg, and Pittsburgh. In addition to its appellate jurisdiction, the Supreme Court also has original, but not exclusive, jurisdiction of habeas corpus cases, mandamus or prohibition of courts of inferior jurisdiction cases, and quo warranto cases involving any Pennsylvania officer holding state-wide jurisdiction. As part of its general administrative authority under the Commonwealth's unified judicial system, the court is responsible for establishing rules governing the practices and conduct of all state courts.

EASTERN DISTRICT

Affidavits of Defense, 1784-1808. (2 cartons) Arranged chronologically by date of oath. These handwritten forms were used to show whether there was a just and legal defense to be made by the defendant against the claims of the plaintiff. This process was completed for hearing before the Pennsylvania Supreme Court. The affidavits typically show the dates of the oath and of the Supreme Court hearing, and the names of the litigants, and alderman or justice of the peace who witnessed the swearing. The following court case includes an affidavit of defense referencing an African American: *Burke vs. Allen*, case no. 149, December 1800.

Autograph File, 1683, 1767-1815. (3 boxes, 1 folder) Arranged alphabetically by surname. The documents within this series were extracted from their original files in 1925 due to their unique historical value. Included in this series is "A Return of Prisoners Con-

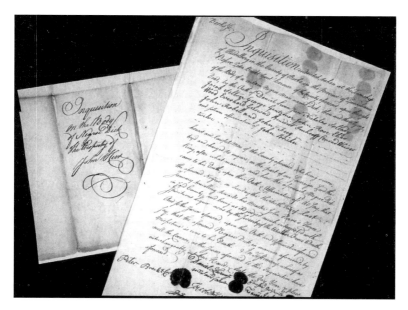

RG-33. Supreme Court. Eastern District. Coroners' Inquisition Papers, 1751, 1768-1796. Inquisition for Negro Dick.

fined in the Gaol of Lancaster County the 14th Day of May, Anno Domini 1781," which provides the prisoner name at time of commitment, the name of the person by whom committed, and the nature of the crime. Included on this list is "Negroe Abraham, a runaway Servant to James Brown" and "Negroe Mishich, a runaway slave property of Jos Irwin of Conogogig."

Certiorari and Habeas Corpus Papers, 1753-1775, 1777-1787.
(**4 cartons**) Arranged chronologically by court term. These papers were used to appeal a lower court verdict. The certiorari papers requested transcripts from a lower court to be given to a higher court for review of the proceedings. The habeas corpus papers were writs used to bring a person before a court. Many of the writs that were used to compel appearance of slaves before the court provide the slave's name, place of residence and name of his master. In some instances familial relationships are mentioned and details

are entered such as where the slave worked and when he or she was purchased. The following are some examples of writs involving African Americans:

- *Chester County:* Cato, "a Negro man," was charged with stealing his wife Mary and their three children, Betse, Cato, and Isaac, from their owner and master, Samuel Moore of Chester County, on March 13, 1786. He was discharged April 1, 1786.
- *Philadelphia County:* Pompey, "a Negro man," the property of Mr. Isaac Wihoff, was charged with disorderly conduct on May 29, 1786, but was later discharged on July 19, 1786.

Coroners' Inquisition Papers, 1751, 1768-1796. (1 carton) Arranged chronologically by filing date. Reports of inquisitions conducted by a county coroner and a twelve-man panel who had viewed a body to determine the cause of death. These inquests investigated the need for criminal prosecutions and were used as the basis for indictment at the grand jury inquest if needed. Inquisition papers are signed by the coroner and several witnesses. When possible, the name of the victim, the approximate date and manner of death, the date and place of the inquiry, and the location of the body of the deceased are given. The occupation, age and race of the deceased person also sometimes appear and, in the case of a slave, the name of his or her master is provided. In one case a white male criminal was allegedly killed by "a Negro male criminal." Several of the documents report "unknown Negroe men" found in the "work houses" in Philadelphia where the cause of death was reported as follows: "the aforesaid departed this life by the visitation of God in a natural way and not by any violent ways or means whatsoever to the knowledge of the said Jurors."

Escheat Papers, 1796-1822. (11 folders) Arranged by court term and case number. This series was arranged originally in chronological order by the earliest document date with some case papers added. On September 29, 1787, "An Act to Declare and Regulate Escheats" established a process by which the Commonwealth acquired the real and personal property of persons who died intestate or without heirs. For the execution of this law, a Supreme Council was commissioned consisting of John Nicholson (also comptroller general) as escheator general, Clement Biddle and William Irwin who in turn appointed a deputy for each county. These officers held inquisitions and rendered decisions concerning escheated property. Inquisitors were warranted by the county sheriff and witnesses' testimony taken. If the escheators court found no claim or will, the property was turned over to the state. Otherwise, claimants were to appear at the next session of the Supreme Court. This process was changed by an Act of April 2, 1821, whereby the auditor general assumed the duties of the escheator general and the Courts of Common Pleas replaced the Supreme Court. The following is a sampling of relevant materials regarding African Americans:

- May 18, 1780, Marriage license issued to "Negro Sam Bevis with the leave of his Mullatoe Catherine Johnston," recorded by Archibald McClean, in York County.
- July 24, 1780, Indictment of John, "a Negro man," in Philadelphia, for a felony; fined two thousand pounds and committed to prison.
- August 1780, Indicted with trespass and assault on two occasions, Negro Tom, a slave. Thomas Patton was fined five pounds for each account, before William Henry, Esquire, of Lancaster County.
- September 20, 1780, Negro Jim, Negro Daniel, Negro Not, Negro Cato and Negro James under the Court of Oyer and Terminer were fined 2,000 pounds for larceny in Philadelphia.
- November 1780, Negro Sol, slave to William McIntire, of

Lancaster County, was charged with larceny and fined one hundred and fifteen pounds.

- January 28, 1782, Negroe Violet, a spinster indicted for larceny, was convicted and fined two pounds and committed to jail in Philadelphia,
- January 28, 1782, Negroe Lucy, a spinster, indicted for keeping a disorderly house and a tippling house was fined twelve pounds and ten shillings and was committed to jail.
- October 25, 1782, Robert Cochran, late of the City of Philadelphia and "main person" of Negroe Barney, was charged with larceny in Philadelphia .
- February 25, 1783, Negro Richard and Negro Took were charged with fornication and battery and each fined ten pounds in Chester.
- October 28, 1783, Sam Zachery, late of the City of Philadelphia, "Negroe," was fined one shilling for larceny and committed to jail.

Insolvent Debtor Papers, [ca. 1789-1805, 1812-14]. (7 cartons) Arranged chronologically by first letter in surname of debtor, and thereunder chronologically by date of filing. Papers relating to insolvency cases brought before the Supreme Court of Pennsylvania in the Eastern District. Types of papers filed include petitions, bonds, assignments, renunciations of assignments, debt schedules, and certificates of discharge, reference, and naturalization. The petition of Samuel Butcher, July 7, 1791, lists all of his property, including his slaves: a Negro man named Fortune, and a Negro girl five years of age. Butcher transferred all of his property to the designated assignees in order to pay his creditors.

Miscellaneous Records of the Supreme Court of Nisi Prius, [ca. 1786-1800]. (45 volumes) Arranged by the Genealogical Society of Pennsylvania as follows: "Beyond a partial attempt to arrange them by counties they are here presented in a chaotic condition, with the hope that the index may enable the searcher to find the wheat concealed among much chaff." Indexed internally in volume 44, alphabetically by surname of person involved in Supreme Court proceedings. This index inaccurately and incompletely references the previous volumes. Volume 45 is indexed internally, alphabetically by surname. These records were originally presented to the Genealogical Society of Pennsylvania after the basement of the State House in Philadelphia was cleared out in 1895. These records were then compiled and later deposited by the Genealogical Society with the Pennsylvania State Archives. The volumes contain a wide variety of miscellaneous Supreme Court records, including court minutes, coroner's inquisitions, proceedings in cases, lists of marriage, public housekeepers, and tavern licenses issued. Some pre-Revolutionary records exist, identifying George III as the reigning monarch. An example of the type of materials found relating to African Americans is a 1782 deposition by Michael Shafer of Berks County who on several occasions sold slaves to Charles Carr, an employee of John Lesher. Shafer's deposition alleged that John Lesher never paid Michael Shafer.

Writs of Habeas Corpus for Negro Slaves, 1786-1787. (2 folders)
Arranged chronologically by date of writ. Dozens of writs resulting from the Act for the Gradual Abolition of Slavery and responding memoranda concerning detained African American men, women, and children were filed with the Supreme Court. These contain diverse types of information that vary with each writ. Many of the documents provide the slave's name, place of residence and name of master. In some writs, the age and/or date of birth is given, familial relationships are mentioned, and particulars are entered about where the slave worked and when he or she was purchased. Documents are present for cases filed in various counties including Chester, Cumberland, Lancaster, Philadelphia, and York. Some examples are:

Chester County: Writs concerning the case of Negro girl named Phobe English who was allegedly purchased by Alexander McMonigel of Chester, Pennsylvania from George Taylor of the Borough of Wilmington. The earliest of these reads: "The Commonwealth of Pennsylvania to [Alexander M. Monagale of New Garden Township in the County of Chester,] GREETING, You are commanded, that the Body of [Phobe English - a Negro Girl about seven or eight years of age] under your custody detained, as it is said, together with the day and cause of [her] being taken and detained, . . . " (1785). Other proceedings in this case are dated 1787 and 1789 and result in a decision of the state Supreme Court "that the said Phobe English was born free and is now free from any slavery or servitude; that her mother Elisabeth English, her Grandmother and Great Grandmother appear to me to have been also born free." It is signed by Thomas M. Kean, September 19, 1789.

Cumberland County:
- 1780, John Calhoon registered the following Negroes: Diana, Nell, Pegg, Fanny, Phobe, and Tom.
- 1780, John Herron registered Jerry, Sall.
- 1780, John Young had one "Negro wench named Pegg."
- 1780, John Creigh of Carlisle owned Jean.
- 1780, Robert Miller of Carlisle registered Darby, Violet, Toy and Abraham.
- 1780, property of Stephen Duncan, a Negro man named Frank.
- 1781, property of James Steward of Georgia, Negroe Frank, 21 and Dinah, 16 years old, held in Carlisle by James Langston..
- 1783, property of Richard Bitler, a Negro female called Charlotte, daughter of a wench called Mott.

- 1787, property of John Moore of West Pennsburg, a Negro female born 1785 and Tobias, a male born Oct. 1787.
- 1787, Property of William Brown, a Negro girl named Sidney.
- 1787, Property of Reverend James Johnston, a Negro girl named Tamar.
- 1789, Property of William Robinson, a Negro girl named Lucy.
- 1789, Frank West of Tyrone Township owned Sligo, Jacob, Poll, Chamont, Mila, Lewis, John, and Debby.
- 1789, Negro child called Nell belonging to Frank Campbel.

York County: Writs relating to the case of "Negro Hannah" who had been brought into Pennsylvania by her master, Robert Crawford, and kept longer than the six months allowed under Pennsylvania's Act for the Gradual Abolition of Slavery. On May 26, 1787, William Askew reported that in the year 1781 he had purchased the estate owned by Robert Crawford in "Hambleton" Township, York County. Askew complained that Robert Crawford would not comply with the contract respecting Askew's title, and in consequence Askew brought a suit against Crawford on the 22nd day of February 1782. Askew testified that "the Saturday following, I had the writ served on Crawford and it was the Monday following that Negro Hannah applied to William McClean, Esq. for a pass and although I do not at this time remember what time Crawford brought the Negro and her children from Maryland to Pennsylvania yet I do know and will remember that the aforesaid Negroes were held as Crawford's slaves by him in Pennsylvania after they came from Maryland more then six months." On May 25, 1787, William Cochran stated that "Negro Wench Hanah, came to his hous and handed him a paper signed by William McClean, Esq., setting forth that the said Negroe

Wench had right to hire herself as any other free woman where she might find employ; from this time that Said Crawford came into this county from Maryland, I new the Negro Wench to be in the service of Mr. Crawford as a slave, which was above six months, when I saw the paper."

THE COURTS OF OYER AND TERMINER

Court Papers, 1757-1761, 1763, 1765-1776, 1778-1782, 1786-1787. (7 boxes) Arranged alphabetically by name of county, and thereunder by court term and case number. These documents from the Oyer and Terminer Courts include case files, judicial administrative papers, and diverse records from the Mayor's Court of Philadelphia; minutes from Nisi Prius courts of Northampton and York; and tavern license petitions from Philadelphia. Among those pertaining to African Americans are:

- Berks County, 1772. Elizabeth Bishop, wife of John Bishop was charged with the murder of their slave Louis[e].
- Berks County, 1775. An inquisition into the death of Peter, the slave of John Patton of Heidelberg Township. Thomas Roach was charged with the murder.
- Berks County, 1776. The jury's decision in the case of the King versus Thomas Roach.
- Berks County, 1761. The testimony of Margaret Stuyter in regards to her husband, an African American man named Charles, who was suspected of murder.
- Lancaster County, 1767. Testimonies involving the murder of Dinah, a slave of William Crawford. Two men were tried separately for the same crime.
- Lancaster County, 1781. York, a slave of Michael Ego was charged with the rape of Elisabeth Snyder.
- Lancaster County, 1781. Phobe, a slave of James McCally, and Matty, more commonly known as Patty and formerly called

Charity, a slave of Amos Slaymaker, were charged with the burning of Slaymaker's barn.

- Northampton County, 1780. Negro Abraham was charged with murder.
- Philadelphia County, 1768. Richard Wild was tried in the murder of one of his slaves, Cloe. When asked to pay funeral expenses Wild claimed Cloe was really Rosanna, a slave of Sylvera Liguance, Jamaica.
- Philadelphia County, 1774. An unmarried mulatto Elizabeth was indicted and tried for the murder of her newborn baby.
- Philadelphia County, 1775. Mulatto George was charged with the manslaughter of William Rice.
- Philadelphia County, 1778. Joseph Head, a Negro boy, was charged with stealing a mare owned by Arnold Kramer.
- Philadelphia County, October 1781. Negroe Fanny was charged with murder but was found "not guilty."
- Philadelphia County, September 1782. A Negro slave owned by William Parker, named Peter, was found guilty of murder and was sentenced to be "hanged by the neck till he be dead."
- Philadelphia County, 1782. The case of the Commonwealth of Pennsylvania versus Negro Peter in the murder of Negro James.
- Philadelphia County, 1782. Testimonies involving the breaking and entering of William Ball's house. Those on trial included John Dorset, a slave of Samuel Hillegro, Lot and Luz Suzey, two free mulattos, and John Freeman, alias Samuel Nurick.
- York County, 1780. Testimonies concerning the robbery of McSherry's store and house. The testimony involves George Weaver, Jacob Sherman, and his slave Dick.

MIDDLE DISTRICT

Appeal Papers, 1799-1981. (80 boxes, 20 cartons) Arranged by court term and case number. Papers filed with the Supreme Court of Pennsylvania in the Middle District for appeals from lower courts, including petitions for certiorari, petitions for extension of time, acknowledgments of record, notices of appeal, judgments, opinions of the justices, praecipes for appearance (which call for the appearance of interested parties before the court), and petitions for appeal. The petitions for appeal enumerate the arguments in support of an appeal and also list the questions raised in the case due to the decisions of the lower courts. Appeals relating to African Americans include:

- Adams County, 1812. Deposition of widower Christiana Bittinger with regard to the changing of the name of her slave from Coll to Sall and a deposition of Elizabeth Baum, daughter of Nicholas Bittinger, regarding this slave girl named "Sall." Later in the same year, several documents from Franklin County refer to this same Negro slave woman called Sall who was registered from birth as Collin and called Coll by her first owner, Nicholas Bittinger, even though her mother, family, and friends called her Sall. There are several depositions from Bittinger's widow, daughters, and the son-in-law who last owned her stating that Sall was indeed named Collin (Coll). Included in the Franklin County file is a deposition of Barbara Lehr, also a daughter Nicholas Bittinger, verifying that the slave called "Sall" was also recorded as "Collie, Coll, and Collin." A deposition from York county dated 1819 has "slave ownership register certificates" of Richard McCallister and Nicholas Bittinger relating to the deposition concerning Sall, Collin or Coll of Franklin County. In addition to Sall (Coll), other slaves are listed for Richard McCallister and Nicholas Bittinger.
- Franklin County, 1812. Lydia Furguson, "a woman of color,"

was charged as a runaway. She had belonged to Lord Fairfax in nearby Alexandria, Virginia and claimed she was to be freed upon his death and left $100 in his will.

- Lancaster County, 1818. Daniel Haines took Negro Tom to jail for refusing to go to New Jersey with Mr. Isaac Low. Mr. Low then sold Tom to a Mr. Philips to take to Kentucky; Tom then refused to go to Kentucky.
- Franklin County, 1819. Negro Sal gave her daughter, Mulatto Mave, to William Holiday's daughter Ruth Somerville. Ruth's husband James Somerville, claimed that Mave had left him and was no longer in his possession.
- York County, 1840. Appeal no. 52 contains several documents connected with the case of the *Commonwealth vs. Prigg*, an important case used as an anti-slavery weapon to create new fugitive slave laws in Pennsylvania. In 1837, Edward Prigg, a professional slave catcher from Maryland, seized Margaret Morgan and her children. She was the wife of Henry Morgan, a free African American who lived in the Lower Chanceford Township, York County.

RG-34. RECORDS OF THE DEPARTMENT OF COMMUNITY AFFAIRS

The Department of Community Affairs was created in 1966 to assist local governments and to enable the state to provide important services necessitated by expanding intergovernmental relationships involving all levels of public jurisdiction. Plans relating to the abolition of the Department of Internal Affairs resulted in the transfer in 1967 of its Bureau of Municipal Affairs and in 1968 its Bureau of Land Records to the Department of Community Affairs.

Community Affairs was responsible for providing technical and training assistance to local governments, and administering

UNION AME
CHURCH

CAMPBELL AME CHURCH

RG-34. Department of Community Affairs. Bureau of Community
Development. Community Plans and Studies, 1963-1968, Media, Pa.

218

appropriate state and federal aid programs. The department directed programs in the areas of housing and development, urban renewal, community planning, and recreation and conservation. In 1996, the Departments of Community Affairs and Commerce were merged to create the Department of Community and Economic Development.

SECRETARY

Records of the Governor's Committee on Migratory Labor, 1953-1972. (4 cartons) Grouped by subject and thereunder arranged chronologically by year. These records consist primarily of award ceremony speeches, letters, photographs, minutes, and annual reports, and also contain miscellaneous materials regarding migrant labor. Types of materials found regarding the Camp and Crew Award Ceremonies include speeches, letters, photographs, programs, and recommendations for awards. Information contained in the minutes of the Governor's Interdepartmental Committee on Migratory Farm Labor meetings include names and titles of the members present and the date, time, and place of meeting. Various topics discussed include health, welfare, crime, and education. The annual reports of the Committee of Migratory Labor document the activities of the year as prepared by the Governor's Committee on Migratory Labor. They contain reports by interdepartmental members of the committee, various tables, and information regarding community outreach. The files of minutes and annual reports of the Governor's Committee on Migratory Labor, 1953-72, contain letters, reports, and newspaper articles that include references to African Americans. An article from the Harrisburg *Patriot News*, dated April 15, 1964, features the state Secretary of Labor and Industry, William P. Young, an African American, reviewing the work of Pennsylvania's migratory labor program in recent years at a two-day Conference on Migrant Health at the Harrisburger Hotel. Included are photographs taken during the conference.

BUREAU OF COMMUNITY DEVELOPMENT

Community Plans and Studies, 1963-1968. (9 cartons) Included in these records are comprehensive plans for various improvement projects for communities, cities, and boroughs throughout the state. An example of material relating to African Americans is charts citing percentages of the non-white population in the predominantly African American community of Media in Delaware County, as well as information on various organizations, churches, and educational facilities in that community.

RG-36. RECORDS OF THE LEGISLATIVE REFERENCE BUREAU

Legislation passed in 1909 originally provided for a Legislative Reference Bureau to be maintained by the trustees of the Pennsylvania State Library. A new bureau independent of the State Library was created in 1921, and it remained an agency of the executive branch with a director appointed by the governor. In 1923, it was abolished and a new Legislative Reference Bureau was established under the legislature with a director elected by the General Assembly. Though created to serve the members of the legislature, the heads of state agencies, and in some cases private citizens, the basic function of the Legislative Reference Bureau is the drafting of bills and other instruments needed by the General Assembly. The bureau acts as a legal advisor to the legislature and its members, prepares digests, analyzes bills, compiles and edits the *Pennsylvania Code*, *Pennsylvania Bulletin* and *Pennsylvania Consolidated Statutes*, and oversees publication of the Pamphlet Laws. Under the Commonwealth Documents Law passed in 1968, administrative regulations are not valid until filed with the bureau.

DOCUMENTS LAW SECTION

Rules and Regulations Issued by State Agencies Originally Filed with Department of State, 1931-1969. (7 cartons, 1 box) Arranged in chronological order by year and thereafter by rule/regulation number. Rules and regulations adopted by state agencies. Among these are two reports used in drafting legislation that document the African American experience in Pennsylvania: "Governor's Commonwealth Conference on Higher Education, July 28, 1966" lists college presidents and administrators, including those at Lincoln University, Cheyney University, and Crozier Theological Seminary; and "Employment Practices in Pennsylvania, February 1953" is a report of the Governor's Commission on Industrial Race Relations.

RG-38. RECORDS OF THE SUPERIOR COURT

C reated in 1895 to relieve the workload of the Supreme Court, the Superior Court was made a constitutional court in 1968. An intermediate appellate court, the Superior Court hears all appeals from the Courts of Common Pleas that are not exclusively assigned to the Supreme or Commonwealth Courts. At present the court hears cases in Philadelphia, Harrisburg and Pittsburgh, and until the mid 1960s it also sat in Scranton.

EASTERN DISTRICT

Appeal Papers, 1895-1956. (105 cartons) Arranged chronologically by court term, and thereunder numerically by case number. Appeals filed with the Eastern District of the Superior Court. Information provided about each case includes the names of the parties involved, the name and county of the lower court from which the case was being appealed, the court term and case number, the date the appeal was filed, and a sworn statement by the appellant affirming that the appeal was not merely a frivolous filing. The following papers are available for Case No. 145 of the October 1946 term in the Superior Court regarding *Incorporation of the Most Worshipful Widows' Sons Grand Lodge of Ancient Free and Accepted Colored Masons of Pennsylvania, vs. Most Worshipful Prince Hall Grand Lodge of Free and Accepted Masons of Pennsylvania*: Notice of Appeal, Acceptance of Service, and Praecipe for Appearance; Appeal and Affidavit; Acknowledgment of Record, Remittitur, etc.; Order to Take Record Out of Court; Withdrawal of Motion to Discharge Appeal; Petition to Discharge Appeal; Affidavit of Service of Notice and Petition to Discharge Appeal; Assignments of Error; and Order and Decree Reversed and Application Refused at the Cost of the Appellee.

Appearance Dockets, 1895-1954. (55 volumes) Arranged chronologically by court term, and thereunder numerically by case number. Records of Superior Court proceedings in the Eastern District. For each case brought before the court, information given includes: names of parties and attorneys involved, a description of the proceedings and the actions of the court, original court of jurisdiction, dates of argument presentations, nature of the judgment, and the name of the justice who wrote the opinion. The docket for the October term, 1946, records Case No. 145, described above under the appeal papers, regarding *Incorporation of the Most Worshipful Widows' Sons Grand Lodge of Ancient Free and Accepted Colored Masons of Pennsylvania (Plaintiffs) vs. Most Worshipful Prince Hall Grand Lodge of Free and Accepted Masons of Pennsylvania (Exceptants).*

Minute Books, 1895-1951. (19 volumes) Arranged chronologically by date of session. Records of the daily activities of the Superior Court in the Eastern District. Information provided about court sessions includes dates and times the court convened and adjourned, names of justices present, listings of cases heard, and the judgments held. An example of the type of material found is the entry for Thursday, November 14, 1946 for Case No. 145, mentioned above in the appeal papers and the appearance dockets, concerning the "Colored Masons" with John F. Williams, appellant, and William T. Connor, appellee which was heard during October 1946 term.

RG-40. RECORDS OF THE DEPARTMENT OF INSURANCE

The Insurance Department was created in 1875 to execute the Commonwealth's insurance laws. All powers previously vested with the auditor general relating to the licensing of insurance agents were assigned to the department. Legislation passed in 1921 re-established and reorganized the Insurance Department and amended, revised, and consolidated existing statutes pertaining to insurance companies. The department reviews and regulates insurance rates, audits companies, supervises and oversees the incorporation and licensing of companies and agents, and investigates consumer complaints.

BUREAU OF REGULATION OF INSURANCE COMPANIES

Annual Statements of Domestic Insurance Companies, 1961-1973. (4,559 volumes) Arranged chronologically by year and thereafter numerically by Insurance Department number. A record of annual financial statements for insurance companies headquartered in Pennsylvania. The "oversize" data sheets show date that report was received by the Department of Insurance; name of the company; signature of the president, secretary-treasurer, and/or other representative; company code number; employer's identification number; date of incorporation; lists of officers and directors/trustees; date of the statement and signature/seal of notary public. Financial information provided by the reports includes assets, liabilities, surplus and other funds, underwriting and investment income, changes in financial position, analysis of non-admitted assets, reconciliation of ledger accounts, exhibit of premiums and losses, notes to financial statements, special deposit schedule, schedule of all other deposits, schedule of examination fees and expenses, five year historical data, real estate owned for the current year, mortgages owned, collateral loans in force, collateral loans discharged, bonds owned, preferred stocks, bonds and stocks acquired for the current year, bonds and stocks sold, bonds and stocks redeemed and other related facts. The following list is a sampling of insurance companies owned by African Americans: Atlantic Life and Accident Insurance Company; Liberty Life, Health and Accident Insurance Company; Mutual Assurance Company of Philadelphia; Mutual Life Insurance Company of America; Pilgrim Life Insurance Company of Philadelphia; Provident Home Industrial Mutual Life Insurance Company; Provident Mutual Life Insurance Company of Philadelphia; Tribune Association of Philadelphia; and Union Mutual Life, Health and Accident Insurance Company.

RG-41. RECORDS OF THE NAVIGATION COMMISSION FOR THE DELAWARE RIVER AND ITS NAVIGABLE TRIBUTARIES

The regulation of shipping on the Delaware River can be traced back to the passage of an act by the Provincial Assembly in 1766 which provided for the appointment of wardens for the Port of Philadelphia. The wardens were responsible for issuing pilots' licenses and making rules and regulations governing their service. Legislation passed in 1803 provided for a Board of Wardens consisting of a master warden and six assistants. This act defined the powers of the board to grant licenses to pilots, to make rules for their conduct, to decide disputes involving masters of vessels and ship owners, to direct the mooring of vessels and their loading and unloading, and to publish rules and regulations relating to these duties.

The Board of Commissioners of Navigation for the River Delaware was created in 1907 to assume those duties previously assigned to the wardens for the port, and the offices of the harbor master and master warden. In 1937, the Commissioners of Navigation were replaced by the Navigation Commission for the Delaware River and Its Navigable Tributaries. Originally established in the Department of Forests and Waters, the Navigation Commission was transferred to the Department of Transportation in 1970 and to the Department of Commerce in 1976. The commission is currently located within the Bureau of Professional and Occupational Affairs in the Department of State.

PORT OF PHILADELPHIA

Health Officer's Account of Passenger Entries, 1789-1794. (1 volume) This register contains an account of vessels arriving at the Port of Philadelphia and a record of passengers submitted by captains to the health officer of the port. Information provided includes the date of arrival, a description of the vessel, the name of vessel, the name of commander, the port from which last sailed, the name of the vessel visited, and the number of passengers and servants. Vessels included in this register are also listed in the *Health Officer's Register of Passengers' Names, 1792-1794*. Some of these vessels carried African Americans as cargo, including the sloop *Sally* and the sloop *Lark*.

Health Officer's Register of Passengers' Names, 1772-1794. (1 volume) This register contains names of passengers and seamen arriving at the Port of Philadelphia as reported by the commanders of the vessels to the health officer. The following information is included in the register: date of arrival, name of vessel, name of captain, where ship sailed from, and other pertinent information. Many of the vessels carried "negroes" and "servants." For example, the sloop *Sally*, commanded by Amherst Bartlett from Cape Francois, transported "Peter Desmarier and Mulato Jacob, Negro wench Mary and boy Azore"; on April 16, 1793 the brig *Industry*, commanded by William Brewster, from St. Thomas transported Augustis Thomas and a Negro servant; and on August 9, 1793 the sloop *Lark* commanded by John Burrows from St. Martins transported "John Richardson and negro servant."

Tonnage Registers, 1784-1789. (6 volumes) These registers show the date of each ship's entry into Philadelphia, name of vessel, master's name, place bound, name of owner or consignee, tonnage, and fees. Vessels such as the sloop *Polly* and the brig *Phoebe* are listed as having "negroes, mulattos, and servants" included in their cargoes.

RG-42. RECORDS OF THE DEPARTMENT OF REVENUE

The Department of Revenue was created in 1927 to serve as general tax and revenue collecting agency of the Commonwealth. The department administers laws and regulations relating to the collection of taxes, though it does not collect taxes for return to local governments except in certain specific cases. The Department of Revenue began to function after the passage of the Fiscal Code of 1929, at which time it assumed tax-collection duties previously carried out by the auditor general, the Treasury Department and other state agencies. The Highway Department's Bureau of Motor Vehicles and state Highway Patrol were transferred to Revenue that same year. In 1937, the Highway Patrol was removed from the department and merged with the State Police to form the Pennsylvania Motor Police. The shift of responsibility in this area was completed when legislation passed in 1970 assigned the powers and duties involving traffic safety programs and the registration and licensing of motor vehicles and operators to the Department of Transportation.

BUREAU OF COUNTY COLLECTIONS

Record of Direct Inheritance Tax Appraisements and Receipts, 1917-1950. (19 volumes) Arranged alphabetically by county, and thereunder chronologically by date of appraiser's return. A record of appraisements of estates subject to direct inheritance tax. Information provided includes name and county of decedent; appraised values of real and other property; tax rate; amount of tax due per appraisment; dates of appraisers' return and register's receipt; date charged, sealed and countersigned at the auditor general's office; total value of appraisements filed; debts and expenses of administration; whether a 5 percent discount for prompt payment was granted; penalty of interest due; amount of tax paid to register of wills; date and amount of payment into the state treasury; a stamp and statement verifying the closure of the account; the name of the register of wills handling the account; and miscellaneous notes and remarks. The names of individuals known to the author are following examples of African Americans who were subject to the direct inheritance tax: John T. Stanton, Margaret C. Mackey, Mary Rice, Catherine Brady, J. Phillip McCard, Robert Thompson, George Rice, Jacob Gantz, Mary K. Thompson, Eugene Rice, Elizabeth Ruth Snowden, George Peck, Daniel Hodge, Laura Settlers, and Elizabeth and William Byers, all of Cumberland County.

CHIEF COUNSEL

General Correspondence, 1955-1968. (7 cartons) Correspondence is arranged alphabetically by topic, while the legislative file is arranged chronologically by year. A record of incoming and outgoing correspondence of the chief counsel of the Department of Revenue. One case involving an African American pertains to a discrimination case between Department of Revenue employee Edward C. Kennedy and the State Civil Service Commission. On November 18, 1965, the chief counsel rendered a final decision in the discrimination case.

RG-43. RECORDS OF THE DEPARTMENT OF ENVIRONMENTAL RESOURCES

Functions relating to the management and protection of the natural resources of the Commonwealth were centralized in the Department of Environmental Resources in 1971. Under the terms of legislation passed in the previous year, the Department of Forests and Waters and the Department of Mines and Mineral Industries were then abolished and their powers and duties assigned to Environmental Resources. In addition, specific responsibilities for the protection of environmental resources previously vested in the Departments of Agriculture, Health, and Labor and Industry, and the State Planning Board were also transferred to the department. In 1996, the functions of the Department of Environmental Resources were split between two newly created agencies: the Department of Environmental Protection and the Department of Conservation and Natural Resources.

BUREAU OF COMMUNITY ENVIRONMENTAL CONTROL

Agricultural Migrant Labor Camp Program Files, 1969-1976. (2 boxes) Arranged alphabetically by subject. Committee meeting reports, correspondence, statistics, and training materials relating to the program to monitor environmental conditions in labor camps. File entries relating to African Americans include: an evaluation of the migrant labor camp program for the 1973-1974 season; minutes and reports of the Governor's Committee on Migrant Services, 1970-1973; reports of the Governor's Interdepartmental Council on Seasonal Farm Workers, 1974-1976; migrant labor camp files, 1969-1976; *20th Century Slavery: Report on Migrant Workers in Pennsylvania* by James J. A. Gallagher; applications for migrant labor camp registration certificates; tables and charts of migrant populations; lists of contact persons for migrant education in Pennsylvania; and letters and reports on migrant camp awards violations.

ENVIRONMENTAL QUALITY BOARD

Public Hearing Transcripts, 1971-1982. (13 cartons) The Environmental Quality Board formulates, adopts and promulgates rules and regulations under which the Department of Environmental Resources operates. These rules and regulations ensure environmental protection of the state's water, air, mining and land resources. Included with these transcripts are Rules and Regulations, Title 25-Environmental Resources. Those that directly relate to African Americans are "Subpart D, Environmental Health and Safety, Article II, Institutions and Housing, Chapter 177," and "Migrant Labor Camps" in which African Americans were employed. Included also are several proposals and amendments to Chapter 177 concerning environmental conditions in the labor camps, and "notices of violations" of environmental regulations with regard to migrant labor camps.

RG-45. RECORDS OF THE DEPARTMENT OF MINES AND MINERAL INDUSTRIES

The Department of Mines was created in 1903 to succeed the Bureau of Mines, which had been established in the Department of Internal Affairs in 1897. The name of the department was changed in 1956 to Mines and Mineral Industries. In keeping with its primary responsibility of protecting coal miners from unsafe working conditions, the department enforced the coal mining laws of the Commonwealth, inspected mines and collieries, investigated serious accidents, and supervised the examination and certification of applicants for certain mining jobs. The department also supervised the restoration of strip-mine areas, promoted research relating to new uses and markets for coal, and published the annual reports of the coal mine inspectors. In 1971, the Department of Mines and Mineral Industries was abolished and its powers and duties were transferred to the newly created Department of Environmental Resources.

SECRETARY

Registers of Mine Accidents for Anthracite and Bituminous Districts, 1899-1972. (39 volumes) Arranged by coal mining district, and thereunder according to the date of the accident. A registry of persons who were involved in coal mining accidents in the anthracite and bituminous coal fields. In addition to giving the name of the mine where the accident occurred, information listed about the victim includes his name, age, nationality, marital status, number of children, job in the mine, and whether he was a citizen or an alien. After 1972, the books are further divided into fatal and non-fatal coal mining accidents (1973-1989) and fatal (1973-1986) and non-fatal (1973-1981) non-coal mining accidents. With the exception of the person's nationality, all of the data found in the earlier registers also appear in the accident books categorized as fatal coal mining accidents. Other information shown includes the name of the operator; the victim's previous experience (both in and about the mines and in the occupation engaged in when killed) and exact date of death; the number of children left that were under thirteen years old; and particulars about the accident/death (whether inside or outside the mine, whether due to natural or accidental causes, whether a chargeable offense, and the county and time that the fatality took place). The registers list African Americans who were working in mines when accidents occurred. In an accident on May 29, 1925 in the eighteenth anthracite district at Silver Creek, Jesse Garvin, and James Brown were identified under nationality as USA (Colored).

Registers of Mine Accidents for the Bituminous Districts, 1899-1972. (20 volumes) Arranged numerically by district, and thereunder chronologically by date of report. These registers provide documentation on mining accidents for the numerous bituminous coal districts. Information within each report includes the name of the inspector, the name of the mine, and the name of the individual injured; the district number; date of the accident; the extent of the injuries (whether fatal or not); whether the accident occurred inside or outside of the mine; whether the victim was a citizen or an alien; the victim's nationality; the job classification, marital status, and number of children; and the cause of the accident. Corrie Ford, who died on Aug. 20, 1899 is identified as "Colored American."

RG-46. RECORDS OF THE VALLEY FORGE PARK COMMISSION

The Valley Forge Park Commission was created in 1893 to preserve, improve, and maintain as a public park the site on which General George Washington's Army encamped at Valley Forge during the winter of 1777-1778. The Park Commission operated the state park independently until 1923 when the Commission was placed under the Department of Forests and Waters. In 1971, the Park Commission was transferred to the jurisdiction of the Pennsylvania Historical and Museum Commission. Administrative and operational responsibility for Valley Forge Park was formally transferred to the federal government in 1977.

Minute Books, 1893-1977. (35 volumes) Arranged chronologically by date of meeting. A record of the meetings of the Valley Forge Park Commission from its inception in 1893 until it was turned over to the federal government in 1977. In the minute books for 1975 are facsimile copies of the "Bicentennial Broadside from Valley Forge Park," No. 4 and 5, dated July 1775 and August 1775, respectively. In the July 2, 1777 broadside Alexander Hamilton declares: "The Congress has declared that no slaves should be enlisted, but several have already played an active part. The southern colonies most dependent on slavery have put no blacks in the field, while men in the northern and middle states frequently send slaves as substitutes, giving them their freedom with their muskets." In a biographic note on James White, it states "tax records for Chester County show James White owned property from December 17, 1771 to September 10, 1778, to include ownership of one Negro slave." The August 2, 1775 issue states, "Slaves try to enlist: Returned by British—Norfolk—the town has been greatly disturbed lately by the behavior of the slaves, who run off in the mistaken notion of finding shelter on the British men of war in the harbor. The naval officers have repeatedly assured the populace that no encouragement is given to slaves trying to join the English forces, and Captains McCartney and Squires receive the thanks of the community for the many they've returned."

RG-47. RECORDS OF THE COUNTY GOVERNMENTS

Pennsylvania comprises 67 counties, including the consolidated city-county of Philadelphia. The constitution establishes a basic organization, but counties can adopt their own form of government. Six counties have adopted home rule charters: Philadelphia, Delaware, Erie, Lackawanna, Lehigh, and Northampton.

Counties continue to serve in their traditional role as agents of the state for law enforcement, judicial administration, and the conduct of elections. The county is also responsible for the property assessment function. Counties become involved in regional planning, solid waste disposal and public health. They perform welfare functions, such as those relating to mental health. Counties also can establish housing and redevelopment authorities and conduct community development programs. Counties maintain hospitals and homes for the aged, and they may support local libraries and community colleges.

Legislation enacted in recent years has strengthened the policymaking role of the county commissioners, granting them greater control of and responsibility for county government. The geographic size of counties enables them to cope with functions that can be better performed on an area-wide basis, that is, mass transportation and environmental protection.

County government in Pennsylvania, as provided for in the county codes, may be described as of the non-executive type. The chief governing body is generally a three-member board of county commissioners, but numerous other elected officials can function to a large extent independently of the county commissioners. These include the sheriff, district attorney, prothonotary, clerk of courts, register of wills, clerk of the Orphans' Court, coroner, recorder of deeds and jury commissioners. Additionally, there are the elective offices of either a controller or three auditors and the treasurer who serve as the county finance officers. A public defender is appointed as provided by law. The county commissioners, the elected officers and the county court individually or jointly appoint a number of other county officials and employees needed to carry out county functions by law.

Whereas the eleven elected county officials are enumerated in the Pennsylvania Constitution, their powers and duties are prescribed by statutes that are scattered throughout the county codes and general state laws. Consolidation of certain elected offices is provided by state law in the smaller class counties involving the offices of prothonotary, clerk of courts, register of wills, clerk of the Orphans' Court, and recorder of deeds.

ADAMS COUNTY

Prothonotary

Register of Negroes and Mulattoes, 1800-1820. (1 microfilm roll) Grouped alphabetically by surname of slave owner and thereunder chronologically by date of registration. This register is a record of children born to slaves in Adams County. Information provided for each child includes name, occupation, and place of residence of the slave owner; name, date of birth, and gender of the child; whether negro or mulatto; and the date registered.

BEDFORD COUNTY

Prothonotary

Record of Negro Mulatto Slaves, 1780, 1798. (1 microfilm roll) Arranged chronologically by date the slave was registered. This roll documents slaves held in Bedford County. Information provided by each entry generally includes name and occupation of slave owner; slave's name, age, and length of servitude; the classification "negro" or "mulatto"; and the date registered.

Record of Negro and Mulatto Children, 1821-1825, 1828. (1 microfilm roll) Arranged chronologically by date register was filed. Register of children born into slavery. Information provided for each child includes name and occupation of owner, date of birth, name of child and mother, date return was filed, and date petition was filed with the Quarter Session Court.

Record of Negro and Mulatto Children and Miscellaneous Slave Records, [ca. 1780-1834]. (1 microfilm roll) Arranged chronologically by date of document. Petitions to keep the services of slaves past age twenty-eight; certificates of claim to runaway slaves; court orders to remove runaway slaves; a bill of sale; an apprentice indenture; and a record of "negro" and "mulatto" children registered.

BUCKS COUNTY

Board of County Commissioners

Applications for Burial of Deceased Soldiers and Their Widows, 1909-1923. (1 carton) Grouped chronologically by year of applications. These applications and their related records pertain to "An Act authorizing and requiring the County Commissioners of each county in the State . . . at the expense of the county, to look after, bury and provide a headstone for the body of any honorably discharged solder, sailor or marine who served in the army or navy of the United States during the late rebellion and any preceding war, and shall thereafter die in their county, having insufficient means to defray the necessary burial expenses" (May 12, 1885) or to "An Act Relative to the Burial of the bodies of certain indigent deceased widows at the county expense" (April 12, 1917). Information provided by these application forms includes name of the soldier and/or soldier's widow; rank of the soldier; company, regiment or unit information; dates of discharge and death; place of burial, occupation immediately preceding death; various remarks; an affirmation statement made by people who knew the decedent; and a statement of the costs to bury the body, including the laying out of body, coffin, grave, hearse hire, and other expenses. In addition, canceled checks and headstone order receipts are found within these records. Applications for known African Americans from the United States Colored Troop list include: James D. Brown, Lewis R. Burns, Matilda Conn (widow of Charles A. Conn), Anna E. Derry, Elizabeth Derry, John Derry; William Hampton, Samuel Holt, Abraham Johnson, Emer Johnson, Levi Leboo, William Perry; Henry Preston, Gustavus Russell, Sarah F. Ryan, widow of Samuel P. Ryan, Jonathan Smith, Lewis E. Taylor, Joseph Van Horn, William Washington, and Susanna Wells (widow of Richard Wells).

Prothonotary

Register of Slaves, [ca. 1783-1830]. (1 microfilm roll) This volume documents the births of "negro" or "mulatto" children to slave mothers. Information provided about each child includes name, occupation, and township of residence of the slave owner; name, gender, and either the age or date of birth of the child; and the date registered. This volume also contains records of manumissions, which may include information regarding names of the individuals, dates slaves were set free, physical descriptions, and circumstances regarding emancipation.

CENTRE COUNTY

Prothonotary

Birth Returns for Negroes and Mulattoes, 1803-1820. (1 microfilm roll) Unarranged. A record of slaves born in Centre County. Information includes the name of the slave and slave owner; his occupation of slave owner and township. One document records: "One male mulatto child named Peter, born on the twenty second of March one thousand eight hundred and three," signed by owner James Rankin. The document further states, "Chester County, Pennsylvania: Before me Richard Miles, Esquire, Clerk of the Court of General Quarter Session at the Peace of Said County appeared

James Rankin of Potters Township, farmer, being duly sworn according to law deposith and saith that on the twenty second day of March one thousand eight hundred and three his negroe wench named Sall was delivered of a male mulatto child he calls by the name of Peter."

CUMBERLAND COUNTY

Board of County Commissioners

Returns for Negro and Mulatto Slaves, 1780-1781, 1788-1811, 1813-1821, 1824-1826, 1833. (1 microfilm roll) Unarranged. Loose returns for negro and mulatto slaves in Cumberland County. Information includes slave owner's name, township, occupation, and the name and age of the slave. Examples are:

- Robert Gibson of Carlisle in the County of Cumberland, Pennsylvania, came before me John Agnew Justice of the Peace for said County and delivered to me the names and age of all his slaves and desires the same be recorded as such: Phillis a mulatto slave for life blind of both eyes aged about 25 or 20 years, Poll a slave for life aged 3 years and one month," signed by Robert Gibson, carpenter, August 22, 1781.
- John Smith of Carlisle, Innkeeper, returned two mulatto servants; Humphrey aged two years and six months, and James, aged two years and three months, as "my property," signed John Smith, March 31, 1789.

The individual returns are preceded by a typed listing of the returns prepared by the count, giving the names of slave owner and slave/indenturer, and the slave's date of birth. Examples of entries African Americans are:

- No. 38; 1780, General William Thompson: James, born 1743;

Name in Full.	Joseph N. Dunston
Place of Nativity.	Raleigh, North Carolina
Place of Residence.	216 Harrisburg St. Steelton. Pa
Dental Degrees, Institutions and Dates.	D.D.S Meharry Dental College, Nashville Tenn May 20 1920
Other Degrees, Institutions and Dates.	
Place or Places of Continuous Practice in Pennsylvania. Dates.	
Date of License by Pennsylvania State Medical Council.	January 25 1921
Remarks.	

STATE OF PENNSYLVANIA, } ss:
County of Dauphin,

RG-47. County Governments. Dauphin County. Prothonotary. Dentist Registers, 1883-1934. Entry for Dr. Joseph N. Dunston.

Nell, born 1744; Betty, born 1757; Venus, born 1760; Jacob, born 1774; Perus, born 1774; and Sam, born 1779.

- No. 2; 1780, Robert Gibson: Phillis, born 1780.
- No. 43; John Smith, Carlisle: Humphrey, mulatto, born October 1787; James, born January 1788.

Clerk of Courts

Slave Returns, 1780, 1789, 1814. (1 microfilm roll) Unarranged. Loose returns for slaves living in Cumberland County. Information includes name of slave owner, county and township, slaveowner's occupation, and name, sex, and age of slave. An example: William Duncan of Hopewell Township in Cumberland County reports Toma, a female slave for life, aged about 22 years. Signed by William Duncan on October 11, 1780.

DAUPHIN COUNTY

Prothonotary

Dentist Registers, 1883-1934. (3 volumes) Arranged chronologically by date of entry. Indexed internally, alphabetically by surname of dentist. Dentists were required to register within the county in which they practiced by an Act of the General Assembly of Pennsylvania passed on April 17, 1876. These volumes document dentists who had recently graduated from dental colleges and were recording their diplomas, as well as the affidavits of dentists who had practiced dentistry previously in places other than Dauphin County. Information provided within these records includes names of dentist, recorder, and secretary; number of years in practice of dentistry and the locations; and the date recorded. Most of the diplomas that were registered were written in Latin. One method of locating African Americans in the records is to search for the names of individuals who graduated from traditionally Black colleges and universities. One African American registered who is known to the author was Joseph N. Dunston, who began his practice in Harrisburg and later moved to Williamsport where he remained until his death.

Liquor License Dockets, 1895-1924. (2 volumes) Arranged by political subdivision and thereunder by number on license list. These dockets list individuals who requested licenses from the county to sell liquor as wholesalers, tavern owners, or retailers, or to produce liquor as distillers, brewers or bottlers within Dauphin County municipalities. Information provided includes the type of license applied for, the location of the establishment, the name of the applicant(s), the name of the attorney(s), the date the transfer occurred, and the number of the applicant on the license list. Notations also record whether the application was denied, continued, or withdrawn. Following are examples of the names of African Americans known to the author who applied for licenses in Dauphin County: Frank Woodfork and Charles Jackson at 523 State Street, Harrisburg, retailers; and Benjamin A. Striplin at 523 State Street and 945 North 7th Street, Harrisburg

Midwife Register, 1921-1924. (1 volume) Entries are arranged in chronological order. Indexed internally, alphabetically by surname. A record of women from Dauphin County who, in compliance with the Act of June 5, 1913, registered their certificates to practice as midwives with the Court of Common Pleas. The affidavits in the register were signed by midwives and show their names and residences, the dates that their certificates were issued by the Bureau of Medical Education and Licensure, and the place in Harrisburg where recorded. The dated and subscribed forms were signed by the prothonotary. Elizabeth Alexander (Aunt Liza), Certificate #6804, issued January 1, 1920, 114 Balam Street, Harrisburg, was one African American woman who practiced as a midwife in Dauphin County.

Midwife Registration Receipt Book, 1921-1924. (1 volume)
Arranged chronologically by certificate number. A record of certificates issued by Dauphin County to individuals who practiced midwifery. Information includes registration number, registrant's name, date of registration, and the name of the clerk of the prothonotary's office. Elizabeth Alexander (Aunt Liza), Registration No. 2, was one African American woman registered to practice as a midwife in Dauphin County.

Petitions for Peddlers' Licenses, 1796-1881. (7 folders) Arranged in chronological order by date license was granted. Information varies with each petition, but normally the person's name, residence, and reason for seeking a license (e.g., deformity, disability) to peddle or hawk appears along with the date of license. The petitions were signed/marked by the applicants. One peddler was John W. Pinkney, who served in Co. D., 22nd Regiment of the United States Colored Troops and had been wounded at Petersburg, Virginia during the Civil War.

Physicians' Registers, 1881-1928. (3 volumes) Arranged chronologically by date of registration. Indexed internally, alphabetically by surname. A record of registrations of Dauphin County practitioners of medicine and surgery. A typical listing shows the name, signature, place of birth, date of birth (until March 12, 1883), and residence of the physician; the date that he received his medical degree; the name of the institution from which he graduated; and the date that he registered. Particulars concerning the person's medical experience are sometimes provided as well. The following are typical of African Americans registered in Dauphin County:

• Dr. William H. Jones, of Hamburg, graduated from Howard University on March 10, 1887 and registered October 3rd of the same year.

- Dr. Benjamin Butler Jeffers, of Steelton, graduated from Howard University in May 1897 and was licensed July 16, 1898.
- Dr. Edward Mayfield Boyle, registered March 1, 1906.
- Dr. James Edward Foster, registered March 5, 1904.
- Dr. Benjamin Butler Jeffers, registered July 19, 1906.
- Dr. William H. Jones, registered October 3, 1887.
- Dr. Francis H. King, registration date unknown.
- Dr. Morris Hallowell Layton Jr., registered August 5, 1910.
- Dr. Alexander L. Marshall, registered August 5, 1910.
- Dr. James Edwin Tyndull Oxley, registered August 12, 1910.

For other licensing records, **see RG-22, RECORDS OF THE DEPARTMENT OF EDUCATION**, and **RG-26, RECORDS OF THE DEPARTMENT OF STATE**.

Soldiers' Burial Records Books, 1902-1933. (7 volumes) Arranged chronologically by date of application. Indexed internally, alphabetically by surname of soldier. These volumes contain applications for burial of deceased soldiers and their widows in Dauphin County. Information provided includes the name of the soldier and/or the soldier's widow; rank, company, regiment or unit; dates of discharge and death; place of burial; occupation immediately preceding death; various remarks; an affirmation statement made by people who knew the decedent; and a statement of the costs to bury the body, including the laying out of body, coffin, grave, hearse hire, and other expenses. An estimated 150 applications for African American soldiers and their widows are found in these records.

Emergency Relief Board Records, 1932-1941. (41 cartons) {unprocessed} Arranged alphabetically by surname of applicant; carton one remains unarranged. This series consists of correspondence and records relating to the Dauphin County Emergency Relief Board and the Talbot Bill (House Bill #70 of special session held in 1931 that became law December 27, 1931), and includes unemployment relief applications. The applications document such varied circumstances as desertion by a husband, spousal abuse or neglect, and hardships brought on by old age, unemployment, or the lack of sufficient income. Other types of documents found within the application files include applications for assistance to the directors of the poor, records of poor relief granted, reports of investigation, Harrisburg Social Service Exchange forms, family records, application blanks [Commonwealth of Pennsylvania], and miscellaneous correspondence. Information contained on these types of applications includes name of applicant, names and ages of persons living in the household occupations, employers, weekly income of the household, date of application, and the amount of equity in property. Additional information may be obtained from these records in some cases, such as race, religion, and names of other relatives.

FAYETTE COUNTY

Records for Negroes and Mulattoes, 1785, 1830, & undated. (1 microfilm roll) Arranged chronologically by date of document. This series primarily documents the records of births of "negro" or "mulatto" children in Fayette County. In addition to birth returns and certificates of slave registry from other counties, miscellaneous single items are also included. The birth returns were prepared after the passage of the 1780 Act for the Gradual Abolition of Slavery in Pennsylvania. Information provided includes the township of residence, date of birth, the names of the mother and the children born, the name and occupation of the individual whose property they were considered, and the name of the notary. These records were filed years after the individual's birth and numerous individuals could be listed on one return. The certificates of slave registry from other counties document slaves brought into the county from Cumberland, Lancaster, Washington, and Westmoreland Counties. Information includes the date registry information was filed with the appropriate courthouse, the names and township of the owner, the sex and age of the slave, and sometimes the slave's date of birth and mother's name. The group of miscellaneous single items includes such materials as a request of name alteration (the slave's registered name was "Lucy," however, her mother called her "Luisa"), an extract from the record of slaves registered by Hugh Laughlin, a petition of George Mannypenny for extension of his slave's servitude because she had a child, and an exemplification indenture, which was a legal office copy of a deed that was recorded to be as valid in a court of law as the original deed. Information provided in such documents includes the names of parties involved and the dates of the documents or court actions.

LANCASTER COUNTY

Clerk of Courts

Returns of Negro and Mulatto Children Born after the Year 1780, 1788-1793. (1 microfilm roll) Unarranged. A record of individual slave returns for Lancaster County. Information includes name of slave owner and his occupation, township, name of slave or servant, sex, and color. Some returns may further describe the slave's color and sex. For example, William Smith, a farmer living in Earl Township, owned one mulatto boy named Benn who was born on December 19, 1787. According to this return, Benn actually belonged to William Smith's daughter, Margaret Smith, who was underage and residing with Smith.

Index to Slaves, 1780-1834. (1 microfilm roll) Arranged chronologically by date of return and thereunder alphabetically by slave owner's name. An index to slave returns in Lancaster County. Information includes slave owner's name, and page number on which original return can be found.

WASHINGTON COUNTY

Recorder of Deeds

Negro Register, 1782-1851 (bulk 1782-1820). (1 microfilm roll) Arranged alphabetically by surname of slave owner. Provides the name of the slave owner, his township, and the name and age of the slave. An example: James Bell of Peters Township, one boy named Flanders, 9 years of age; William Campbell of Hopewell Township, one girl named Hajar, 14 years of age.

RG-48. RECORDS OF MUNICIPAL GOVERNMENTS

In addition to living under a county government, every Pennsylvanian also lives in a municipality. Municipal governing bodies make policy decisions, levy taxes, borrow money, authorize expenditures, and direct administration of their governments by their appointees. The scope of their functions and responsibilities is broad. Many powers given to local governments are not exercised in every place, while others are shared with the state and even national government. All of the various municipalities in Pennsylvania share the same basic responsibilities with respect to provision of public services at the local level and have similar statutory powers. Although cities have more specifically enumerated powers than boroughs and townships, similar powers may also be exercised by boroughs and townships under general grants of power. Home rule provides equal opportunity for all classes of municipalities to exercise new powers

Mayor's Registry of Colored Persons, 1820-1849. (1 microfilm roll) Arranged chronologically by date of entry. Contains entries in accordance with a borough "ordinance prescribing regulations concerning free persons of colour" passed May 9, 1820. Information includes date of entry; name of head of household; names of wife, children, servants and any other occupants; ages of occupants; and occupation of head of household. Other information may also be given, i.e., mulatto, whether a person owned the property, street address, etc. For example, John Larris is listed as a "negro, about 29 years of age" who worked as a laborer and was married to a wife named Anne who resided in the house of Dennis O'Donnald, Adamstown, Pennsylvania.

RG-50. RECORDS OF THE PUBLIC SCHOOL EMPLOYEES' RETIREMENT SYSTEM

The Pennsylvania Public School Employees' Retirement System was created in 1917 and commenced operation in 1919 with a seven member Public School Employees' Retirement Board. Prior to the establishment of a statewide system, there were local teacher retirement systems in thirteen school districts. During the period 1919-1975, the Retirement System operated within the Department of Public Instruction, which was renamed the Department of Education in 1969. In 1975, the Pennsylvania School Employees' Retirement System became an independent state agency. At that time the board membership was increased to eleven members to include three ex-officio members, three members to be elected by the active professional members of the system, one member to be elected by annuitants, one member to be selected by the active non-professional members of the system, one member to be elected by the members of the Pennsylvania public school boards, and three at-large members. In 1991, the voting membership of the board was further increased to include two senators and two representatives.

Administrative and Board Action File, 1918-1965. (2 cartons) Grouped by type of record. Administrative and legal records of the executive offices of the Public School Employees' Retirement System. The records consist primarily of opinions issued by the attorney general from 1927 through 1965 which relate to the implementation of the Public School Employees' Retirement Act. The opinions are numbered consecutively from 2 to 384, although not inclusively. Also included are a summary list of legal opinions, 1918-1945, a log of requests for legal opinions, 1932-1944, and excerpts from board minutes and opinions of the Justice Department, with an index, for the years 1918-1954. Registers contain retirement data on teachers, including African American dating from the early 1900s. Examples include: James Garfield Young, born in 1881, retired in 1947 from the Carlisle School District after forty years of teaching; and Emma Thompson McGowan, born on January 26, 1876, retired on July 1, 1943 after thirty years of teaching.

RG-51. RECORDS OF THE LEGISLATIVE REAPPORTIONMENT COMMISSIONS

The periodic establishment of Legislative Reapportionment Commissions to redistribute the representation in the General Assembly in each year following the federal decennial census is mandated as part of the 1968 constitutional process to amend the state constitution (Section 17, Article 11, approved April 23, 1968). Prior to this amendment, the General Assembly was responsible for apportioning the state into legislative districts.

Records of the 1971-1972 Legislative Reapportionment Commission, 1971-1972. (3 cartons) Arranged chronologically by date of document. Administrative files of the commission chairman of the 1971 Legislative Reapportionment Commission, consisting primarily of minutes, correspondence, reports, hearing transcripts and tapes, census data, maps, news clippings, press releases, court appeals, and the preliminary and final plans for the legislative reapportionment of Pennsylvania after the federal census of 1970. Exceptions and objections to the plans from senatorial districts 1-6 include a December 16, 1971 memo from the New Democratic Coalition citing gerrymandering: "This plan is designed to limit black leadership and is discriminatory in the way districts are created."

Records of the 1981-1982 Legislative Reapportionment Commission, 1981-1982. (4 cartons) Arranged chronologically by date of document. Administrative files of the commission chairman of the 1981 Legislative Reapportionment Commission, consisting primarily of appeals in the courts, census data, commission expenses, correspondence prior to filing the preliminary plan, exceptions to the preliminary plan, computer printouts, maps, minutes, newspaper clippings, public hearing transcripts, and the preliminary and final plans for the legislative reapportionment of Pennsylvania after the federal census of 1980. The files include the following items:

- A letter from Charles Bacas to the Honorable James J. Monderino dated February 26, 1981 addressing the undercount of African Americans who lived in urban areas which were found to exist in censuses prepared and issued by the Census Bureau. An example of a discrimination case is *Young vs. Klutznick* (September 25, 1980, Detroit, Michigan). In that case, a district judge enjoined the Census Bureau from certifying "a population count based on the actual unadjusted head count." *(Other relevant cases that might be cited here include City of Philadelphia vs. Klutznick, City of Chester vs. Klutznick, City of Atlanta vs. Klutznick, Bernard Carey vs. Klutznick, etc.)*

- A *Fortune* magazine article dated February 9, 1981 which discussed the issue of the undercount of minorities in urban areas.

Records of the 1991-1992 Legislative Reapportionment Commission, 1991-1992. (2 cartons) {unprocessed} Files pertaining to the original, preliminary, and final plans for reapportionment of voting districts in Pennsylvania following the 1990 census. Among the materials found are court appeals, census data, public hearing transcripts, preliminary reapportionment plans, computer printouts of voting and population statistics from the Legislative Data Processing Center, maps, minutes, newspaper clippings, and a copy of the final reapportionment plan. Among the appeals is a February 5, 1992 civil action suit in which William Harrison, et al. claimed discrimination by the Pennsylvania Legislative Reapportionment Commission. The case cites specific violations of the Voting Rights Act which was designed to prevent voting blocks and the limitation of opportunities for minority leaders. Included in exceptions and objections to the plan is a letter to the Commission rejecting the plan from the Norristown branch of the National Association for the Advancement of Colored People (NAACP). The letter explains that the plan has "put up a wall thru the black population of Norristown and also thru the whole community of Norristown. You have virtually eliminated Norristown's black, and its white, voice in state legislative elections."

RG-52. Department of Transportation. Commonwealth Media Services. The swearing in of C. DeLores Tucker as secretary of state, I/6/75.

RG-52. RECORDS OF THE DEPARTMENT OF TRANSPORTATION

The Pennsylvania Department of Transportation was created in 1970 as a merger of the Department of Highways, the Pennsylvania Aeronautics Commission, the Bureau of Motor Vehicles, and related agencies. It is the supervising authority of all state highways, airports, and other matters dealing with transportation.

COMMONWEALTH MEDIA SERVICES

Main File, 1970-1976. (12.5 cartons) {unprocessed} This is a continuation of the **Main File of RG 12, RECORDS OF THE**

DEPARTMENT OF HIGHWAYS and numbers over 10,000 black and white and color negatives of varying size with matching contact prints or enlargements. The file, arranged by number, is accompanied by a logbook with numerical entries containing subject, date, photographer, etc. Topics cover activities of the department, publicity, and news events from the administration of Governors Shafer and Shapp. Included are photographs of African Americans. Of special interest is the swearing in of C. Delores Tucker as secretary of state with Judge Genevieve Blatt and Governor Milton Shapp, January 6, 1975. Tucker was the first African American appointed as secretary of state in Pennsylvania, as well as in the United States. A sampling of other photographs include: Governor Shapp signing the Proclamation for Afro-American History Month, February 1976, with the Philadelphia Chapter of the Association for the Study of Afro-American Life and History in attendance; Governor Shapp signing the Proclamation for Dr. Martin Luther King Jr.; Voter Registration Day; a luncheon on April, 17, 1974 featuring Rev. Jesse Jackson; and a photograph of William Young, secretary of Labor and Industry.

RG-54. RECORDS OF THE LOCAL GOVERNMENT COMMISSION

The Local Government Commission was created in 1935 to provide research assistance on local government issues to individual legislators and to the entire General Assembly. The commission, a bipartisan legislative service agency, is composed of five senators and five house members, appointed by the president pro tempore of the senate and speaker of the house, respectively. Administrative duties and functions of the commission are carried out by a professional staff under the direction of an executive director.

Summaries of Legislation, 1974-1983. {unprocessed} Contains summaries to bills signed by the governor which related to African Americans, such as:

- Senate Bill #561, Unfair Insurance Practices Act, July 22, 1974.
- House Bill #1386, Pennsylvania Minority Business Development Authority Act, July 22, 1974.
- Senate Bills #1221, #1222, and #1223, Unemployment Compensation Law, December 5, 1974,
- Senate Bill #738, which authorized municipalities to expend federal general revenue sharing funds or general funds for social services programs for the poor, the disabled, and the aging, and to jointly cooperate in the sponsorship, establishment, administration, maintenance, and operation of such programs, December 10, 1974.
- House Bill #921, which amended the Pennsylvania Human Relations Act.
- Senate Bill #1618, regarding the Pennsylvania Ethnic Heritage Studies Center.
- House Bill #1756, which provided for the observance of January 15 of each year as Martin Luther King Jr. Day.

RG-55. RECORDS OF SCHOOL DISTRICTS

The Pennsylvania Constitution directs the General Assembly to provide for the support of an efficient system of public schools where all children of the Commonwealth above the age of six may be educated. Since 1834, when the first public school law was enacted, the General Assembly has passed legislation to gradually develop the present school system. The laws relating to Pennsylvania schools are consolidated into what is known as the Public School Code, which sets up five classes of school districts according to population. School districts are administered by nine member school boards elected by the people for four year overlapping terms, except in Philadelphia. In Philadelphia, in accordance with the Educational Supplement to the Home Rule Charter, a nine-member board is appointed by the mayor from a list submitted by an education nominating panel. As of January 1998, there were 501 public school districts in the Commonwealth. *(Access may be restricted. Contact the State Archives for more information.)*

CARLISLE AREA SCHOOL DISTRICT (CUMBERLAND COUNTY)

Alumni Registers, 1848-1853, 1856-1900, 1902-1932 and undated. (1 microfilm roll). {unprocessed} Alumni registers for the classes of 1902-1932 provide the name of each alumnus; address; occupation, public or official position; whether a graduate of another institution; and date of death. Cited in the listing for the class of 1929 is Irene F. Calloway from Mount Holly Springs, and William E. Cuff at 409 North West Street, Carlisle, both African Americans. Irene Calloway was a teacher in the Carlisle School District, and one of the directors of the Carlisle African American Community Center. Included also is a document entitled *Teachers Salaries from 1836 to 1860* that reveals the names of teachers.

LINCOLN INTERMEDIATE UNIT (ADAMS, FRANKLIN, AND YORK COUNTIES)

Directories of Teachers and School Directors of York County, 1878-1971. (13 volumes) {unprocessed} These directories give the following information: name, type of certificate, term, salary, school, and address. The directory for 1877-88, for example, lists Malachi Gilson as a principal in a school having fifteen colored and mixed children. Ella J. Robinson later served as assistant in this school from 1888 to 1889 while James Stuart served as principal.

RG-56. RECORDS OF THE STATE ETHICS COMMISSION

The commission was created by Act 170 of 1978 and amended by Act 9 of 1989, to administer and enforce the provisions of the Public Official and Employee Ethics Law. The law provides that public office is a public trust and any effort to realize personal financial gain through public office is a violation of that trust. The act was passed to strengthen the faith and confidence of the people of Pennsylvania in their government.

The Ethics Law provides that the commission shall comprise seven members who are cognizant of the responsibilities and burdens of public service. Three commission members are appointed by the governor, only two of whom may be of the same political party. One member each is appointed by the president pro tempore of the senate, the minority leader of the senate, the speaker of the house, and the minority leader of the house. All are appointed without confirmation. Commission members are eligible to serve two full three-year terms. During the 1989-90 term, Helena G. Hughes, an African American, was chairman of the State Ethics Commission.

Statements of Financial Interest, 1984-1989. (2 cartons)
Grouped by year. Statements of financial interest by elected state officials and appointees to state office between 1984 and 1989 disclose financial ties with private firms or interest groups. A sampling of the 1984 records include: financial interest statements by such African American public officials as Shirley M. Dennis and William R. Davis, Senators H. Craig Lewis and James K. Rhodes, and state house Representatives Harry E. Bowser, Dwight Evans, K. Leroy Irvis, David P. Richardson and James R. Roebuck.

RG-57. RECORDS OF THE PENNSYLVANIA STATE SYSTEM OF HIGHER EDUCATION

Comprising the fourteen publicly owned state universities, the State System of Higher Education (SSHE) was created by Act 188 of 1982. Its twenty-member board of governors includes the governor and the secretary of education (both ex officio), four-teen others appointed by the governor with the consent of the sen-ate (one of whom must be a student), two members of the senate, and two members of the house of representatives. The chancellor, appointed by the board, is the chief executive officer. The board establishes broad fiscal, personnel, and educational policies, as well as procedures. The mission of SSHE is "the provision of in-struction for undergraduate and graduate students to extend be-yond the master's degree in the liberal arts and sciences, and in the applied fields, including the teaching profession."

The beginning of the State System of Higher Education can be traced to the Act of May 21, 1857 which set up a procedure for establishing "normal schools" to provide professional training for common school teachers. The state was originally divided into twelve normal school districts. A thirteenth normal school district was recognized with the creation of Clarion State Normal School in February 1887, but the last of the originally planned twelve districted institutions was Slippery Rock, which was not recog-nized until February 1889. Cheyney State Normal School was the successor to "The Institute for Colored Youth" located in Bristol Township, Philadelphia County, which had been chartered by the state in 1842. In 1904 this institution was moved to Cheyney in Delaware County and began functioning as an industrial normal school. By a decree of the Court of Common Pleas of Delaware County in July 1914, the name was changed to Cheyney Training School for Teachers.

The School Code of 1911 established a method for the state to buy schools through appropriations to be made in succeeding sessions of the legislature. Once the state acquired ownership of a school, the trustees were appointed by the State Board of Education. On July 30, 1913 the state acquired sole ownership of its first normal school, West Chester. On June 24, 1920, Cheyney was acquired, and by 1922 the state had completed its acquisitions with Mansfield. Until 1923, the normal schools were essentially secondary schools with students being admitted without receiving a diploma from a four-year high school. In 1925 the State Council on Education authorized normal schools to confer bachelor of science degrees for particular curricula as soon as the school proved these groups of courses met standards set by the American Association of Teachers' College. As a result, the fourteen schools acquired their first bachelor of science in education certifications in 1926 and all subsequently changed their names to "State Teachers' Colleges." On May 23, 1932, the last of the fourteen, Cheyney, made this change. By an act of January 8, 1960, all state teachers' colleges were reclassified as state colleges. University status was achieved in 1982.

Cheyney University Yearbooks, 1939, 1941, 1943, 1949-53, 1955, 1957-1960, 1962-1972, 1974-1979, 1983-1988. (3 microfilm rolls)
Arranged chronologically by year. As a result of the Historical Records Microfilming Project, master negative copies of records from select state schools were given to the Pennsylvania State Archives. Among those records are microfilm copies of the yearbooks of Cheyney University. These yearbooks provide some valuable information on African American students, the bulk of whom were from Pennsylvania. Cheyney had its beginning in 1837 with the establishment of the Institute for Colored Youth, made possible by a bequest from the estate of Richard Humphreys. Information in the yearbooks includes the graduate's full name, hometown, and occasionally the street address; the history of the college; biographi-

cal information on the president; identification of the administrative staff and faculty; and a pictorial record of activities and campus life. Also included are advertisements from the surrounding area, fraternity and sorority members, and alumni chapters throughout the state and country.

RG-58. RECORDS OF THE DEPARTMENT OF CORRECTIONS

Created in 1984, the Department of Corrections is responsible for the management and supervision of the Commonwealth's adult correctional system. Included are all state correctional institutions and regional facilities, as well as community-oriented prerelease facilities, known as community service centers. In the 1920s, Pennsylvania's major prison facilities were placed under the jurisdiction of the Department of Welfare, along with mental health facilities and juvenile institutions. A legislative investigation into major prison riots at Pittsburgh and Rockview in 1952 led to the establishment of a Bureau of Correction within the Department of Justice to oversee reforms and to operate the system. Governor John S. Fine signed the bill on August 31, 1953. In 1980, the attorney general became an elected rather than an appointed position, and the bureau was transferred from the Justice Department to the newly created Office of General Counsel within the governor's office. Four years later, the bureau was elevated to departmental status through legislation proposed and signed by Gov. Dick Thornburgh. During 1989 through 1990, David S. Owens Jr., an African American, was the commissioner of the Department of Corrections.

PRESS OFFICE

Newspaper Clippings, 1953-1985 (17 cartons) Newspaper articles about the state prison system and its inmates including such

African Americans as William Cook, Mumia Abu Jamal, Phil William Africa, William Hines, and Eugene Lambert. Some of the photographs relating to African Americans in this file depict blind youth Gerald Sheasley, Mohammed Salaihdeen, students laying bricks, chess games, musicians, and the White Hill Industrial School. For earlier information on the penal system, refer to **RG-15, RECORDS OF THE DEPARTMENT OF JUSTICE.**

RG-60. RECORDS OF THE PENNSYLVANIA PUBLIC TELEVISION NETWORK COMMISSION

The Pennsylvania Public Television Network Commission is a twenty-two member commission created in 1968 to operate, on behalf of the Commonwealth, a public television network system interconnecting all noncommercial television stations in the state; to aid in the improvement of broadcast operations, programming and capital facilities; to apply for and distribute federal, state, public, or private funds to insure diversity, freedom, objectivity and initiative in programming; and to prevent misuse of the network for political or other unconstitutional propaganda purposes. In addition to other functions, the commission and the networks provide programming-based educational materials to primary and secondary schools, and a variety of educational services to classrooms and communities statewide.

GENERAL MANAGER

General Correspondence, 1967-1978. (2 cartons) {unprocessed}
Arranged chronologically by date of correspondence. Correspondence, memoranda, and other documents passing between the commission, the Pennsylvania Public Television Network and others. The following programs were produced for local broadcast during 1977-78: "Cultural Affairs Calendar," "US (Ethnic Magazine Pro-

gram)," "Black Horizons," "Equal Justice Under the Law," "Black Perspectives on the News," "Who Cares About Culture?" "Civil Rights, 1968," "Black Journal," "NET Journal," "Talking Black: Special Program following the Death of Dr. Martin Luther King Jr.," and "Black Perspectives on the News."

RG-64. RECORDS OF THE OFFICE OF THE LIEUTENANT GOVERNOR

From 1776, when Pennsylvania became a state, until 1873, the Commonwealth had no lieutenant governor. The office of lieutenant governor was created by the Constitution of 1873, and its functions and duties have changed little since then. The lieutenant governor presides in the state senate, performing duties as set forth in the senate rules, which the president pro tempore of the senate performs in the lieutenant governor's absence. When presiding, the lieutenant governor signs legislation and other formal measures passed by the senate.

BOARD OF PARDONS

All of Pennsylvania's lieutenant governors have served on the Board of Pardons. Since 1923, when the board became a unit within the Department of Justice, the lieutenant governor has held the powers and duty of the chairman of that board. The Commonwealth Attorneys Act of 1980 placed the administrative office of the Board of Pardons in the Office of the Lieutenant Governor. The office is constitutionally within the Executive Department and submits a regular budget request, but is not itself a department. As with the governor's position, the Constitution of 1968 made the lieutenant governor eligible to succeed himself or herself for one additional four-year term.

Each prisoner's file contains the following forms supported by additional documentation consisting of letters and other forms of communication. Each file contains a photograph of the prisoner, thus providing easy identification of African Americans, who are well represented.

Requests for Commutation and Pardons-Denied, 1948-1952. (21 rolls) {unprocessed} Arranged by date of document. Series contains the following sub-series:

Applications for Clemency provide the following information: name, case number and date of session, date of previous application, date and place of birth, aliases, court's sentence, crime, name of institution, date sentence began, court and county of sentencing, term and number of indictment, nature of plea, name of trial judge, name of district attorney, name of defense attorney, nature of appeals, details of crime, a complete Pennsylvania arrest record, justification for requesting pardon, conduct during confinement, whether granted commutation, where and with whom prisoner would reside, possible employment, names and other information on relationship of dependents, new justification for latest application (if previously applied to the Board of Pardons), and name and address of lawyer who will represent prisoner before the Board of Pardons.

Classification Summary Forms provide the following information: date, name, race, age, number, alias, date and place of birth, citizenship status, address at time of arrest, legal residence, religious affiliation, marital status, parents' birth dates, social security number, military service, sex, nature of offense, sentence imposed, date of indictment, judge, county, minimum sentence expiration, maximum sentence expiration, nature of plea, date of sentence, amount of back time, date received, new maximum sentence imposed, where inmate was transferred from, and a record of any detainers. Other information: height, weight, build, complexion, hair and eye color, any distinguishing scars or marks, nature of release (parole, re-parole, commutation) and the date, and a "criminal record" giving information on the date, place, and the nature of the offense and disposition.

Commutation Summary Forms were used by all prisons. However, in the case of Western State Penitentiary, the category "color" was added. Information found includes inmate number, name, alias, age, nationality, citizenship status, intelligence rating, IQ, mental age, and the type of intelligence test used. Under the heading "previous criminal record" is found the number of arrests, convictions, parole violations, and types of crimes. Under the heading "current case" is listed the crime for which the prisoner was most recently convicted, the county wherein the offense occurred, the term of court in which the conviction occurred, the name of the trial judge, the total sentence imposed, the date the sentence was imposed, the date the prisoner was received at the prison, the effective date, the minimum sentence expiration date, the maximum sentence expiration date, the total time served to date in prison, the names of any accomplices, and the final disposition of the case.

Summary of Investigation for the Board of Pardons Forms provide the following information: prisoner's name, date, verification of allegations in application, parole plan (home, employment, and sponsor), and other information such as reputation of applicant, previous parole violations, and comments of the judge and the district attorney.

RG-68. RECORDS OF THE PENNSYLVANIA HERITAGE AFFAIRS COMMISSION

Created by Executive Order in January 1980, the Pennsylvania Heritage Affairs Commission became a statutory agency in 1992. The commission's authorizing legislation addressed a wide range of public policy issues relating to cultural diversity in Pennsylvania. The commission was composed of not less than thirty-seven commissioners, nine at-large members appointed by the governor, and four members of the General Assembly appointed by majority and minority caucuses in the senate and house. These commissioners represented forty-six ethnic communities. The following persons represented the African American community: Dr. Rowena Steward, Dr. Stanley E. Denton, Anita Pernell-Arnold, and Dr. Niara Sudarkasa (the president of Lincoln University). An executive committee, which determined commission policy, was composed of the at-large and legislative members. The lieutenant governor served as chairman. Commissioners served two-year, non-salaried terms. The executive director of the commission, appointed by the governor, developed and implemented policies and programs, and maintained liaison activities with federal, state, and local agencies on matters concerning the impact of cultural diversity on public programs and policies. The Pennsylvania Heritage Affairs Commission was abolished on June 30, 1996.

OFFICE OF FOLKLIFE PROGRAMS

Records of the Pennsylvania Heritage Affairs Commission. {**unprocessed**} The Pennsylvania Heritage Affairs Commission developed public programs to document, present, and conserve ethnic and folk cultural traditions. Staff members provided technical assistance to individuals, organizations and communities which sought to preserve their cultural traditions. Following are examples of programs related to African American culture:

The Green Circle Program, Inc. This program was founded by Gladys Rawlins in 1959 "to change the pattern of prejudice and discrimination and to provide a positive approach to overcoming racial, ethnic, and religious barriers." Included among documents related to this program are letters, surveys, and charts regarding population statistics of African Americans in Pennsylvania in 1990.

Governor's Conference on Ethnicity: A Conference to Explore the Impact of Pennsylvania's Cultural Diversity on Public Policy, June 8-9, 1990. The proceedings of this conference were edited by Shalom Staub and published by the Pennsylvania Heritage Affairs Commission. This conference's sessions addressed many subject areas with specific reference to African Americans. The session on "Inter-Ethnic Relation" included a presentation by George Love from the National Association for the Advancement of Colored People, Harrisburg Chapter. The session on "Multi-Cultural Education" addressed such topics as multi-racial, multi-cultural, and multi-ethnic education. The keynote address was delivered by Lincoln University President Dr. Niara Sudarkasa.

Also included in these records are the following publications and press clippings:

- ***Cultural Diversity in Curriculum, 1991-1992,*** a booklet issued by The Pennsylvania State University. In 1991, Pennsylvania State University implemented a "diversity" requirement to increase awareness of the richness and variety of the racial and ethnic backgrounds which students, faculty, and staff brought to their campuses. As part of this initiative, the university sponsored a seminar/workshop session addressing "diversity" and this booklet was part of the packets of materials that were distributed to students.

- *Older Minorities in Pennsylvania*, published by the Pennsylvania Department of Aging.
- *Pennsylvania: America Starts Here; African American Cultural Guide*, published and distributed by the Pennsylvania Department of Commerce, Office of Travel Marketing.
- *Press Clippings:* "A Celebration by the United Black Business Association (UBBA)," "Dr. Brenda Mitchell-Deputy Secretary for Policy, Planning, and Administration," "Penn Houses Black Culture Data," "Underground Railroad Gets Another Look" (with reference to Charles Blockson), "King's Dream Retold as Speakers Honor Slain Rights Leader," "Trustees OK Nation's First Ph.D. in African American Studies (Dr. Molefi K. Asante)," "First Ph.D. Program in Black History Begins at Temple," and "Self-made Historian Keeps 46 Years of Afro-American History in Basement."

MANUSCRIPT GROUPS

MG-2. BUSINESS RECORDS COLLECTION, 1681-1963.

L edgers, journals, daybooks, and related records of Pennsylvania turnpike, canal, and railroad companies, iron forges and furnaces, etc. The following volumes contain references to African Americans:

ACCOUNTS OF IRON FORGES AND PLANTATIONS, 1681, 1737-1913

Anonymous, 1789-1793

Time and Coal Book, Rents, July 4-June 4, 1793. On page 1, under the heading "Sundry Grains and Threshing," an entry dated July 30, 1791 reads, "threshed by John Epply and Black George." Under "Contra Accounts" appears an entry for September 3, 1790 recording "Cash paid Negro Cyrus, Cash paid-Negro George"; for March 9, 1791, "Cash paid Black George"; for May 26, 1792, Mulatto "George paid him when he went to fair"; and for May 26, 1792: "Nancy Mulatto-paid her."

Cash and Pig Book, 1789, May 7-June 1, 1793. Under the heading "List of Working Hands" for 1793 are listed "Negro George," "Mulatto Nancy," and "Negro Cyrus."

Berkshire Furnace, Berks County

Journals, 1767-1826. The Journal for September-October 1767 contains references to a "Negro Dan," "Negro Perow," "Negro Jack," and "Mulatto Jo."

Berkshire Furnace and Charming Forge

Ledgers. 1748-1898. For 1753 there are accounts for "Black Tom" and "Mulatto Jo," for 1766-67 references to "Negro Cato," "Mulatto David," and "Mulatto Solomon," for 1785-1787 references to "Negro Robin" and "Negro Ish," and for 1789-1791 references to "Negro Robin" and "Negro Ish." One account shows that "Negro Robin and spouse" owed for a pair of shoes.

Elizabeth Furnace and Speedwell Forge, Brickerville,
Lancaster County, 1764, 1829-1839

Day Book, 1764, 1829-1836. Documents store and individual accounts of workmen and slaves employed at Elizabeth Furnace and nearby Speedwell Forge. Among the slaves mentioned are Andrew Jack and Edward Jack. Book also includes mention of "a visit of George Washington, the slave," as well as other furnace and forge workmen and "negro" slaves.

Laurel Furnace, Mount Braddock, Fayette County, 1804-1812

Day Book, 1804-1812. Included in this book is a monthly record of employee reimbursement. Among the names listed are "Black Peter" and "Black Ben."

MG-2. Business Records Collection, 1681-1963. Accounts of Iron Forges and Plantations, 1681, 1737-1913. Robesonia Iron Company. Ledger, 1898-1913.

Robesonia Iron Company, Robesonia, Berks County, 1898-1912

Ledger, 1898-1913. Employee accounts for Hiester Filbert's Store are found for the following African Americans: Matthew Carter, Henry Roberts, Warick Umbel, Charles Walker, Noah Gordon, Adeson Payne, Lewis Rector, and John Walker. The names were verified as being African Americans by a living descendant, Floyd J. Umbles of Reading, in 1996.

MG-4. COUNTY RECORDS COLLECTION, 1767-1918.

Various records of county, township, and municipal governments, including the following with reference to African
Americans:

CUMBERLAND COUNTY

Tax Lists, Assessor's Duplicates: Hopewell Township, 1825. A
list of pauper children in Hopewell Township appears at the end of
the volume. Identified as "colored" are Elizabeth Howard, William Howard, and Mariah Howard.

Tax Lists, Assessor's Duplicates: Mifflin Township, 1825. At
the end of the tax list for Mifflin Township is a single sheet with
the title "Name and ages of children that are at school in the county
of Cumberland." Under the subtitle "Black Children's Names" are
listed: David Wilkinson, ten years old; Palm Denford, eleven years
old; Margaret Denford, nine years old; and David Denford, seven
years old.

DAUPHIN COUNTY

County Commissioners' Records, 1832-1847. The Record Book
of Returns of School Children, 1832-41, contains returns for poor
children residing in Dauphin County. Listed under the subtitle
"Return of Colored Children for Harrisburg, 1833" are: Sarah Ann
Butler, nine; Martha Brown, eleven; James Barr, ten; Mary Barr,
seven; Emely Philip, nine; William Maydon, twelve; George
Maydon, fourteen; Isaac Maydon, eight; John Prise, ten; and Sarah Prise, eight. Under the subtitle "Return of Poor children,
Susquehanna Township, 1832" is listed: Angeline Moore, seven,
"colored."

Tax Records: Assessor's Duplicates and Returns, 1794-1847.
Grouped by township: Antrim, Fannett, Franklin, Greene, Guilford, Hamilton, Letterkenny, Lurgan, Metal, Montgomery, Peters, Quincy, St. Thomas, Southampton, Warren, and Washington. Entries list the name of the taxpayer, township of residence, and property owned (slaves, acres, and livestock), the valuation, and the amount of the tax that was paid. The returns for each township are grouped alphabetically according to taxpayer's surname.

MG-6. DIARIES AND JOURNALS COLLECTION, 1763-1938.

Diaries, travel accounts, memoranda books, weather journals, etc., accessioned as individual items. Among these is **Manuscript Diary of Lydia J. Hunn, 1875.** Hunn, a Quaker, was the wife of retired Philadelphia merchant Ezekiel Hunn. She corresponded with many friends and wrote on many subjects. Included in this diary are references to the passage of the 1875 Civil Rights Bill. An entry dated March 2, 1875 states that President U. S. Grant signed the Civil Rights Bill on March 1, 1875. An entry dated June 12, 1875 tells of Hunn's trip to Easton and her visit to "E. Conigill's colored settlement" where there was a meeting house, school, store, and 250 people.

MG-7. MILITARY MANUSCRIPTS COLLECTION, 1758-1931.

Miscellaneous private papers concerning military service by Pennsylvanians from the French and Indian War through the Vietnam War. Materials from the Pennsylvania Militia and the Pennsylvania National Guard include correspondence, photo-

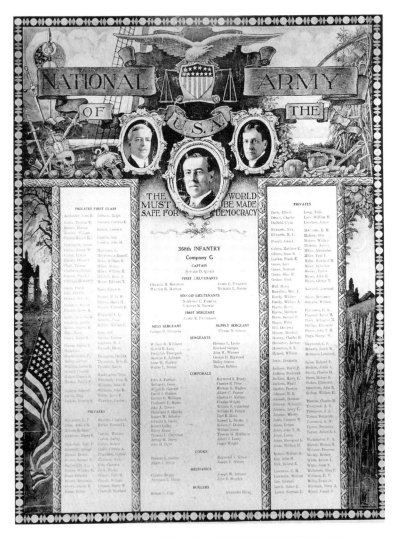

MG-7. Military Manuscripts Collection, 1758-1933. #384, National Army of the U.S.A. of the 368th Infantry, Company G Poster.

graphs, and personnel records. The following materials relate to African Americans:

- **# 69, Wheler Collection, [ca. 1861-1865].** The Wheler Col-

lection consists of one item, an undated letter from Harry A.
Wheler and W. M. Wheler to their sister that contains references to African Americans. Wheler reported an occasion when
he went into "the niggers' houses and [took] their cakes off
the stove . . . [and] apples" hidden under the bed. Harry A.
Wheler wrote a poem about the Civil War, dedicating a portion of it to the "Colored Soldiers belonging to the 54th and
55th Massachusetts."

- **#157, 12th Regiment, "Firemen's Legion," Co. C., Record
  Book of Captain John H. Stewart, 1861-1868.** This volume
  contains pejorative entries about African American workers in
  1861 and 1862.

- **#192, Camp Curtin Ledger, 1863-1864.** The ledger lists African Americans as contraband on August 20, 26, and September 3, 1864.

- **#357, List of the Inducted in the United States Service by
  Local Board of Huntingdon County, Pennsylvania, 1918.**
  This list includes names of African Americans.

- **#358, U.S. Military Personnel (Including Missing and Captured Declared Dead) in the Vietnam War, 1957-1981.** This
  list provides names, rank, place of residence, date of casualty,
  and category of casualty.

- **#359, U.S. Military Personnel Who Died From Hostile Action (Including Missing and Captured) in the Korean War,
  1950-1957.** This list provides name, place of residence, date
  of casualty, and category of casualty.

- **#384, National Army of the U.S.A. of the 368th Infantry,
  Company G Poster.** On November 29, 1917, the War Department authorized the creation of the 92nd Division, the first
  African American Division in the United States Army. The
  368th Infantry Regiment was designated as part of the 92nd
  Division. This poster provides the names of the soldiers in the
  following arrangement: captains, first lieutenants, second lieu-

tenants, first sergeant, mess sergeant, supply sergeant, sergeants, corporals, colonels, mechanics, buglers, privates first class, and privates. The poster was originally exhibited at the Pennsylvania Military Museum, Boalsburg.

MG-8. PENNSYLVANIA COLLECTION (MISCELLANEOUS), 1626-1993.

Spanning the period from the seventeenth to the twentieth century, these miscellaneous papers pertain to legal, political, military, business, medical, educational, social, civic, and religious subjects. Topics covered including Democratic, Know-Nothing, Republican and Whig politics; the French and Indian War, Revolutionary War, War of 1812, and Civil War; the Pennsylvania Railroad Company, Pittsburgh and Western Railroad Company, and Delaware and Hudson Canal Company; various forges and furnaces; colonial land policies; slavery; and the Society of Friends. Items referring to African Americans include:

- **# 33, Broomal, John M., Washington DC, letter to M. Wakeman, Esq., December 19, 1866.** Expresses views on equality for African Americans and reconstruction in the South.
- **# 221, Proud, Robert, Philadelphia, Notebooks, [ca. 1775-1800].** Robert Proud, of Philadelphia, authored *The History of Pennsylvania* (1797-1798). One of three notebooks contains his views on slavery, which he termed "Iniquitous Property," as well as some data on African American mortality rates from 1759-1796.
- **# 281, (Virginia) Assessments, 1778.** A list of people assessed for property holdings, acres of land, slaves, and money.
- **# 344, Will of Andrew Hamilton, Philadelphia. August 2, 1741.** In his will, Hamilton, a slave owner, divides his slaves up among his children.

- **# 417, Tredell, Robert, Return of the Inhabitants of Horsham, Bucks County, 1756 (Incomplete).** Tax list of people from Bucks County showing number of slaves owned.
- **# 433, Bond, of Luke Morris to John Penn (Re: Negro Slave), November 10, 1770.** Legal contract to insure that Morris would remove his slave, Will, accused of burglary, from the province or pay a penalty of $100.
- **# 704, Map of Gettysburg and Adams County Underground Railroad Routes, undated.**
- **# 958, Scrapbook of Peter Richter of Selinsgrove, PA, [ca. 1860-1875].** Contains a newspaper article entitled "Slaves of Rebels Declared Free: a Proclamation."
- **# 1164, Colonel Edward Cook and Other Historical Papers.** Contains a 1992 booklet and curriculum guide entitled "Freedom Community, 19th Century Black Pennsylvania" together with miscellaneous posters and photographs. Among the posters are portraits of Richard Allen, Thomas J. Bowens, Thomas Morris Chester, Fanny Jackson Coppin, William Howard Day, Martin Robinson Delaney, James Forton Sr., Elizabeth Taylor Greenfield, Charlotte Grimke, Frances Ellen Watkins Harper, Francis Johnson, Absalom Jones, Jarena Lee, Gertrude Bustill Massell, Nathan Francis Massell, Christopher James Perry Jr., Robert Purvis, William Still, Benjamin Tucker Tanner, and William Whipper.

MG-9. PENNSYLVANIA WRITERS COLLECTION, 1899-1970.

Notes, manuscripts and related materials pertaining to works of certain Pennsylvania authors, composers, and poets.

HARRY T. BURLEIGH

Harry T. Burleigh (1866-1949), was one of the nation's foremost popular singers and composers through the mid-twentieth century. Born in Erie in 1866, he was the grandchild of a blind ex-slave from Maryland. Burleigh's father passed away while he was still a young boy and he grew up in poverty with his grandfather. By the end of his life, he had composed and arranged over 250 songs, spoke five languages, and had attained international prominence. The Burleigh Collection features four photographs and thirteen compositions.

Songs, 1895-1911. Nine of the compositions are original scores and four are published sheets of music: "Deep River," ca. 1917; "Ethiopia's Paean of Exaltation," ca. 1921; "The Lord's Prayer," ca. 1920; "A Corn Song," ca. 1920; "Go Down, Moses," ca. 1917; "By an' By," ca. 1917; "Oh, Didn't It Rain," ca. 1919, "Balm in Gilead," ca. 1919; "Hard Trials," ca. 1919.

STEPHEN COLLINS FOSTER

Stephen Collins Foster (1826-1864) was born in Lawrenceville, Pennsylvania and was one of American's foremost composers of folksongs in the nineteenth century. Noted for his negro minstrel songs, he wrote and composed many enduring tunes. Included are the following compositions:

Songs, First Editions, c. 1851-1865, 1931.

- "Farewell My Lilly Dear, " pub. by Firth, Pond & Co., ca. 1851.
- "Hard Times Come Again No More, " pub. by Firth, Pond & Co., ca. 1854 No. 28.
- "Old Folks at Home," pub. by Firth, Pond & Co. ca. 1851.

Songs, Later Editions, 1848-1893, n.d.

MG-9. Pennsylvania Writers Collection, 1899-1970. Harry T. Burleigh. Original scores of "Deep River".

- "Camptown Races," pub. by F. D. Benteen, ca. 1850.
- "Farewell My Lilly Dear," pub. by Firth, Pond & Co., ca. 1851.
- "Hard Times Come Again No More," pub. by Wm. A. Pond & Co., ca. 1885; by Mrs. Wiley and Mrs. Marien Foster Welch, 1882.

- "Oh! Susanna," pub. by C. Holt, ca. 1848
- "Old Black Joe," pub. by McKinley Music Co., n.d.
- "Massa's in De Cold Ground," pub. Firth, Pond & Co., ca. 1852 (5th ed.).
- "Uncle Ned," pub. by G. Willig, ca. 1848.
- "Way Down in Ca-i-Ro," pub. by Pond & Co., ca. 1850.
- "Nellie Was A Lady: A Beautiful Ethiopian Melody," pub. Firth, Pond, & Co., ca. 1849 (tenth ed.).
- "Oh Boys, Carry Me Long: A Plantation Melody," pub. by Firth, Pond & Co., ca. 1851 (20th ed.)
- "Songs of the Sable Harmonists: Consisting of the Louisiana Belle, Away Down South, Oh! Susanna, Wake Up Jake or the Old Iron City, and Uncle Ned." pub. O. Willy, ca. 1848.

Photographs, MSS From Notebook, Stephen C. Foster, n.d.

- "Massa's in De Cold Ground," n.d.
- "Old Black Joe," n.d.
- "Poor Uncle Tom Goodnight," n.d.
- "Way Down Upon de Old Plantation," n.d.
- "Hard Times Come Again No More," n.d.

Songs, Compositions and Arrangements (Foster Hall Reproduction), 1933 Set No. 261.

- Down South"
- Better Times Are Coming"
- "De Camptown Races"
- "Commence Ye Darkies All"
- "Don't Bet Yer Money on de Shanghai"
- "Hard times come again no more"
- "Lou'siana Belle"
- "Massa's in de Cold Ground"

- "My Budder Gum"
- "Old Black Joe"
- "Old Folks at Home"
- "Old Uncle Ned"
- "Plantation Jig"
- "Ring de Banjo"
- "A Soldier in de Colored Brigade"
- "Oh! Susanna"
- "We Are Coming Father Abraham"
- "Way Down in Ca-i-ro"
- "The Great Baby Show, or the Abolitionist Show"

CLARENCE AUGUSTUS FAULCON

A History of the Musical Firsts of Pennsylvania Before 1850, Doctoral Thesis, May 1962. A thesis presented to the faculty of the Philadelphia Conservatory of Music, in partial fulfillment of the requirement for doctor of music degree by Clarence Augustus Faulcon, May 1962. Faulcon cites biographical information about Benjamin Carr (1768-1831) who, after arriving from London in 1793, became a noted Philadelphia composer, opera and concert singer, choral conductor, organist, pianist, and music publisher. Faulcon further noted that Carr composed and wrote "perhaps one of the very first Negro songs ever written down; as suggested by an incident in Mungo Parke's Travels." Mungo Parke, the Scottish traveler killed in Africa in 1806, narrated in his journal that Benjamin Carr, almost destitute and exhausted, entered a town on the River Niger and was taken care of by a Negro woman. "They lightened their labor by songs," Parke wrote in his journal, "one of which was composed extempore, for I was myself the subject of it. It was sung by one of the young women, the rest joining in a sort of chorus. The air was sweet and plaintive and the words literally translated were these: 'The winds roared and the rains fell; the poor white man, faint and weary, came and sat under our tree

. . . ' It was versified (rendered into poetic form) by the Duchess of Devonshire, and was composed by Benjamin Carr, etc."

MG-11. MAP COLLECTION, 1681-1973.

More than one thousand historical maps are arranged into seven major sub-groups: (1) Colony and Commonwealth, (2) Counties, (3) Townships, (4) Cities and Boroughs, (5) Boundaries, Topography, Geology, Parks, (6) Transportation (Indian trails, roads and turnpikes, rivers and streams, canals, railroads, and airways), (7) Military and Battlefields (French and Indian War, Revolutionary War, Civil War). Many of the maps also indicate the locations of homes and other buildings, forges and furnaces, coal mines, gristmills, sawmills, lumber camps, etc.

Although not identified as such, these maps can also be used to verify the locations of farms where African Americans lived as slaves or free persons, forges and iron furnaces that employed African Americans, and churches, businesses, schools, and homes owned by African Americans as well as African American graveyards. Map #327-1 *Historical Map Adams County, L.E. Wilt, 1942*, identifies routes of the Underground Railroad.

MG-13. JOHN ADLUM PAPERS, 1794-1816.

John Adlum (1759-1836) was a Pennsylvania surveyor, land speculator and "Father of American Viticulture." One letter, dated February 22, 1820, found in the series **General Correspondence, 1794-1836**, is from Thomas Barker to his son, Luke W. Barker. Luke asked his father if he had heard from a Dr. T—, who was making employment arrangements for "Negro" slaves. Apparently, Dr. T— did not pay for the previous use of Barker's "Negro."

278

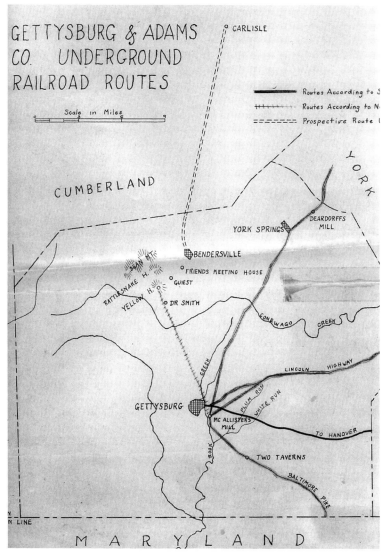

Legend (partial):
- ———— Routes According to S
- ++++++++ Routes According to N
- ======= Prospective Route

MG-8. Pennsylvania Collection (Misc.), 1626-1993. #704, Map of
Gettysburg and Adams County Underground Railroad routes.

279

MG 17. SAMUEL PENNIMAN BATES PAPERS, 1853-1895.

Samuel P. Bates (1827-1902) of Meadville, prominent for many years as an educator, was in 1864 appointed state historian and charged with preparing a history of the Pennsylvania Volunteers. He contributed to the volume of historical studies relating to the Civil War with the *History of Pennsylvania Volunteers* (1869-1871) and *Battle of Chancellorsville* (1883). His papers are mainly research materials and manuscripts for these publications and also include manuscripts for the *History of Crawford County*, *History of Green County*, and *Martial Deeds of Pennsylvania*. Included are a letter book, 1872-73; a letterpress book, 1871-71, containing biographical material on Pennsylvania governors; sermons, 1853-90; and photographs. Also included is a listing of the United States Colored Troops who were trained at Camp William Penn, Chelton Hills, Philadelphia, Pennsylvania. Bates made several references to slavery in his sermons, stating one "should patiently and prayerfully study his word and approach the subject (principles) and bigotry and all those hindrances which hampers and bind us to low . . . thought." In such sermons he frequently refers to the overthrow of slavery and the "sin of slavery."

MG-19. SEQUESTERED BAYNTON, WHARTON, AND MORGAN PAPERS, 1725-1827.

The Baynton, Wharton, and Morgan Papers are the correspondence and business papers of the famous trading house of colonial Philadelphia that began about 1757 as Baynton and Wharton, a partnership of John Baynton and Samuel Wharton. The firm was involved in trade with Europe, the West Indies, other mainland colonies, and settlers in the western regions of the continent. Its papers came into the possession of the Commonwealth during legal proceedings to settle the accounts and land transactions of Peter Baynton, state treasurer, 1791-1801. The documents are rich in information covering the years between the French and Indian War and the American Revolution. There is a particularly heavy focus on the early development of the Illinois country, on the fur trade, and on the supply of provisions for military posts, and they generally shed light on the role played by this firm in western expansion.

PETER BAYNTON PAPERS, 1725-1745

Letter Book, 1729. Includes Peter Baynton's correspondence with James Young, June 28 and July 14, 1729, which refers to various slave transactions, recording both the physical conditions and the deaths of slaves.

BAYNTON, WHARTON, AND MORGAN PAPERS, 1757-1787

General Correspondence, 1758-1787.

Correspondence of Baynton, Wharton, and Morgan, A-Z 1763-1783. Includes many letters pertaining to commercial activities with merchants in South Carolina, Alabama, Jamaica, Martinique, and Lisbon. For instance, correspondence from Thomas Brignall of Port Royal and St. Peters, Martinique from 1761 through 1762 provides information on slavery in the West Indies. Also included are letters concerning plans for Baynton, Wharton, and Morgan to establish a trading house on the island. See: Thomas Brignall to Baynton, Wharton, and Morgan (firm), January 22, 1762; February 16, 1762; March 7, 1762; April 13, 1762; and May 25, 1762.

Miscellaneous Correspondence, A-Z 1759-1799. Includes a

record of "Imports and Exports of Merchandise the Produce of South Carolina, 1760-1766." This record enumerates slave sales transacted by the Baynton, Wharton, and Morgan firm for these years.

Business Accounts, 1746-1776.

Baynton, Wharton, and Morgan Accounts, 1762-1776.

Journals, 1754-1765.

Supplement, Journal A, 1762-1765. Entry for an African American slave named "Negro Martin," owned by John Beck and hired out to sea by Robert Field.

Accounts Current, 1766-1771.

Account with the Plantation (Kaskaskia and Ft. Charters), 1768-1770. Plantation account book contains two entries that list "3 shirts for Negroes" and "Two Negro Men and Negro Boy."

Ledgers, 1766-1771.

Ledger, 1767-1768. Covers sale of "Negroes" at Kaskaskia (in present day Illinois), December 9, 1767 to October 29, 1768, and also contains a list of "negroe bonds" bearing interest at 10 percent from December 9, 1767 to May 6, 1768.

MG-23. Arthur C. Bining Papers, [ca. 1898-1955]. New coke ovens, Short Creek, No. 2.

MG-23. ARTHUR C. BINING PAPERS, [CA. 1898-1955].

Notes, photographs, clippings, and bibliographical references used by Arthur C. Bining in the preparation of his books and articles relating to the development of the iron and steel industry. Manuscripts of some of Bining's writings, such as *Pennsylvania Iron Manufacture in the Eighteenth Century*, are included, as are letters from George W. Schultz and Frank W. Melvin. Included are photographs of numerous forges and furnaces and of various facilities owned by the Bethlehem Steel Company, Carnegie Steel Company, and Robesonia Iron Company, Ltd. Included among the photographs of forges and furnaces are photographs of African American mine workers probably employed by the Robesonia Iron Company. For other information on African Americans at the

Robesonia Iron Company, see the **Coleman Collection** in MG-82, LEBANON COUNTY HISTORICAL SOCIETY DEPOSIT OF MANUSCRIPT COLLECTIONS.

MG-53. REAH FRAZER PAPERS, 1739-1879 (BULK 1821-1856).

Correspondence, legal papers, and accounts of Reah Frazer (1804-1856), prominent attorney and for many years a major political figure in Lancaster County. Also included are business and family papers of his father, William Clark Frazer (1776-1838), who also served as a Lancaster attorney and supreme court judge in the Territory of Wisconsin, 1836-38, and his grandfather, William Frazer (1753-1817), Revolutionary War veteran and justice of the peace in Newcastle County, Delaware. Among the many legal documents, accounts and letters are some that provide evidence of the treatment of fugitive and freed African Americans in the Lancaster County area. The personal papers of the three Frazer men also contain accounts and legal papers relating to individual African Americans, 1775-1831, giving insight into their living conditions.

LEGAL PAPERS OF WILLIAM FRAZER, WILLIAM CLARK FRAZER AND REAH FRAZER

Accounts (Including notes, bills, receipts, judgments), 1774-1818 (Incl. Negro, 1801, 1814). Among these materials are two items concerning African Americans dated 1801 and 1814.

Cases (Including Schuylkill Navigation, 1847). The case papers contain information for the years 1760, 1803, 1804, 1827, 1829 regarding arrests of African Americans, a runaway slave case, and the selling of African American children.

Notes of Arbitration, 1821-1839. This file includes detailed descriptions of both civil and criminal cases, statements of witnesses, references to previous cases, settlements and verdicts. Items relating to African Americans are found in the 1828-1833 and 1838-1839 folders.

Notices to Appear in Court. Writs or summonses to appear before the courts of Lancaster County. Included is a Capias writ issued by the state of Delaware, New Castle County, to Negro William Anderson in 1789 and a court summons issued to John Ingersom (a free Negro) of New Castle County, Delaware in 1815.

MG-54. J. ALEXANDER FULTON PAPERS, 1846-1900 (BULK 1846-1861).

Correspondence of J. Alexander Fulton (b. 1822), a Kittanning lawyer, who became a member of the Pennsylvania House of Representatives in 1853, and was an active figure in state Democratic politics prior to his relocation to Delaware in 1865. Included in the correspondence are letters from John W. Forney, chairman of the Democratic State Central Committee and Governor William Bigler, 1842-55, discussing their opposition to slavery. Also found is a scrapbook covering the years 1861-66 that contains a newspaper article on the American Anti-Slavery Society and its final convention.

MG-59. JOHN S. GOODWIN COLLECTION, 1861-1865.

Letters of John S. Goodwin, Civil War soldier, to his mother and sister in Delaware County relating to service in the 97th Regiment, Pennsylvania Volunteers. In several of his letters, he refers to a "regiment of nigers" and complains that "they have it better than my regiment." One letter refers to the "Black regiment at Port Royal, Hilton Head" and "blacks at Camp Hamilton."

MG-64. HALDEMAN-WRIGHT FAMILY COLLECTION, 1789-1899.

Correspondence, legal papers, accounts, and memorabilia of the Haldeman and Wright families of Cumberland and Dauphin Counties, including the papers of Jacob M. Haldeman, iron manufacturer, investor in real estate, president of the Harrisburg Bank and the Harrisburg Bridge Company, founder of the Harrisburg Car Company, director of the Dauphin Deposit Bank, and founder of Haldemanstown (New Cumberland). References to African Americans are found in the following items:

- Indenture Agreement, October 31, 1808, between Margaret Bayle and a Negro servant Rachel, stating that Rachel wished to voluntarily go to Maryland with Margaret. Rachel's parents also signed the agreement. Furthermore, the agreement states that Rachel must remain a servant until her twenty-eighth year of age.
- Bill of Sale, April 18, 1811, Margaret Bayle sold fourteen-year-old slave to Samuel Jacobs Esq., for the sum of $200.
- Bill of Sale, December 11, 1809, Esther Brisben sold a six-year-old Negro girl named Esther to Jacob Haldeman for $120.
- Certificate of Registry, October 29, 1806, for a male Negro, Abner, submitted by William McClean, a farmer. Abner was born in August, 1781 and was officially registered March 31, 1789.
- Ledger Book, which contains the accounts of three African Americans, John Woodward, George Johnson, and George (no

last name). The monthly wages, and credit for cash or supplies are shown (pages 43, 47, 57).

MG-66. EDWARD HAND PAPERS, 1777-1788.

Lancaster physician Edward Hand (1744-1802) served with distinction in the Revolutionary War. Active in organizing the Lancaster County Associators, he participated in engagements at Long Island, White Plains, Trenton, and Princeton. Promoted in 1777 to the rank of brigadier general, Hand was dispatched to Western Pennsylvania to mobilize the militia against the Indians and Tories. Late in 1778, he assumed command at Albany and aided Sullivan's expedition in 1779. He was elected adjutant general in 1781, served as General Washington's aide at Yorktown in the same year, and in 1783 was named a major general. After the war, Hand resumed his practice of medicine, devoting considerable time to political affairs. The following are letters or communications relating to African Americans:

General Correspondence, 1777-1784. A letter, June 5, 1778 from Thomas Wilson to Mrs. Hand talks about the status of the G.H. Plantation and that "the Negro Bob wants shirt and trousers," asking the person to whom the communication is being sent "if you send linen my wife will make them." A subsequent communication from Jasper Yeates of Lancaster to Thomas Wilson, included with this letter and dated June 6, 1778 reports that "stuff for the boy's shirt and trousers" will be sent and that "Mrs. Wilson can spare a little . . . cloth for that purpose."

MG-72. HIESTER FAMILY PAPERS, 1750-1865.

These papers represent three generations of a Pennsylvania German family descending from the pioneer Daniel Hiester (1713-1795), a family which played an important role in the political life of the Commonwealth and particularly in the counties of Berks and Dauphin. Gabriel Hiester (1749-1824), a well-educated farmer of Bern Township, Berks County, was a member of the Constitutional Convention which framed Pennsylvania's Constitution in 1776. He sat in the General Assembly of Pennsylvania for many terms and served as state senator for Berks and Dauphin Counties, 1795-96, 1805-12.

Gabriel's son, Gabriel Hiester Jr. (1779-1831), was appointed Berks County clerk of courts by Governor Simon Snyder in 1809 and served as prothonotary of Berks County, 1811-1818. As a member of the Pennsylvania Militia, he served in the campaign at Baltimore and Washington during the War of 1812, and he was subsequently appointed surveyor general of Pennsylvania by Governor J. Andrew Shulze.

Augustus O. Hiester (1808-1895), son of Gabriel Hiester Jr., graduated from Dickinson College in 1828 and became a partner in the rolling mills of Hiester and Callender that produced bar iron and boiler plate until 1836. In 1851, Governor William F. Johnston appointed him as associate judge in Dauphin County and he was afterwards twice elected to that office. During the Civil War, on the appointment by Governor Curtin, Hiester became one of three commissioners charged with investigating the damages inflicted by Confederate raids in south central Pennsylvania.

Among these papers is a copy of a declaration of the theft of services of a Negro slave that was filed with the Supreme Court of Pennsylvania, April-June 1769. The case concerned John Lesher and Conrad Reiff of Berks County. John Lesher took a male Negro slave "Joe," who was the property of Conrad Reiff, and illegally employed him for his own personal use from June 1, 1761 until May 1, 1766. Reiff requested a damage payment amounting to sixty pounds.

In a letter dated March 16, 1813, Jacob P. Kershner of Hagerstown, Maryland wrote: "Dear Sir, I shall write you these few lines to inform you that father on his arrival at Readingtown, is the bearer of a letter to you and your father which I expect he will do...about the conveyance of the Negro eunuch . . . These few lines is merely to let you know that he has a letter for you and your father."

An undated broadside entitled "Front Street Circus" includes in the listing of activities: "Comic Negro song . . . by Mr. Boyce, 'Settin on a Rail.'"

MG-73. LILIANE STEVENS HOWARD COLLECTION, 1915-1959.

Reflecting Liliane Stevens Howard's efforts in support of the Philadelphia County Woman Suffrage Society and in support of the woman suffrage movement in Pennsylvania, this collection contains her correspondence with several women's organizations, such as the Pennsylvania Woman Suffrage Association, 1915, the New York State Woman Suffrage Party, 1916, and the Women's Centennial Congress, New York City, 1940.

Howard wrote an autobiographical paper in which she spoke of seeing a "women's building" in Chicago "filled with creations of utility and beauty, ever the handiwork of women. It was a frame . . . holding a group of bust pictures of five persons: a miner, an American Indian, a Negro, a convict and in the center the face of Susan B. Anthony. . . . An accompanying result of this awakening was to make me a student of human relations."

Books and Pamphlets. Contains a book entitled *Woman Suffrage: History, Argument, Results*, edited by Frances M. Bjorkman, 1913.

Equal Rights Amendment, 1943, 1956. Contains information on efforts to pass an Equal Rights Amendment.

Scrapbooks of News Clippings, 1945, 1947-1959. In the 1947-1959 scrapbook of newspaper clippings is an article about Edith S. Sampson of Chicago, Illinois, who was nominated as an alternate to represent the United States at the fifth session of the United Nations General Assembly on September 19, 1950. She was the first African American to serve on the United States delegation to the UN General Assembly. The article includes biographical information about Sampson.

MG-75. JOSEPH M. HUSTON COLLECTION, [CA. 1903-1907].

Consisting of original architect's drawings for the state Capitol building completed in Harrisburg in 1906, these files also include competition drawings, photographic prints, blueprints, and newspaper clippings.

Newspaper Clipping Scrapbook, 1901-1905. Contains an article from the *Philadelphia Press*, December 4, 1904, p. 3, entitled "Splendid Park as a Fitting Setting to Our New State Capitol." The article is accompanied by pictures of the shacks and shanties lining the narrow alleys of an African American neighborhood and also mentions the South Street Colored Church.

MG-76. HORACE A. KEEFER PAPERS, 1881-1934.

Horace A. Keefer, the son of Major John Brua Keefer of Harrisburg, was a clerk at the Paxton Furnaces, Harrisburg. In 1879 he became superintendent of the South Mountain Mining and Iron Company, Pine Grove Furnace, Cumberland County that was owned by Jay Cooke in the 1880s. He also served as president of the K.C.& L. Railway, Wallula, Kansas during the 1890s and was Populist member of the Kansas Legislature from 1896 to 1900. The papers contain incoming and outgoing correspondence relating to political and economic matters and histories of Pine Grove Furnace and the iron industries of Dauphin County. His manuscript, "Recollections Historical and Otherwise Relating to Old Pine Grove Furnace, 1770-1928," mentions that "the forge workers were all negroes, and a finer lot of men I never worked with."

MG-81. McALLISTER FAMILY PAPERS, 1775-1850.

These papers include numerous items from Col. Richard McAllister (1725-1795), founder of Hanover in York County, and his descendants, many of whom were key figures in York, Lancaster, and Dauphin Counties from the Revolutionary War period into the middle of the nineteenth century. References to African Americans include an "Inventory of the Goods and Chattels, Rights and Credits of Richard McAllister, October 9, 1795," that lists Negroes included in McAllister's estate who were bequeathed to his children on his death and notes on their monetary value. Also present is a letter of receipt dated October 15, 1795 by Patrick and Nancy McAllister Hayes for two Negroes (Poll and Jonathon), left to them by Richard McAllister. Other items include a double entry ledger, 1790-1798, of Capt. Archibald McAllister and the

MG-85. J. Horace McFarland Papers, 1859-1866, 1898-1951. Col. George F. McFarland Papers, 1862-1873. Bridgewater School (Colored), Bucks County.

cash book, February 12, 1794-July 28, 1796, which contain entries that document store purchases made by African American workers.

MG-85. J. HORACE McFARLAND PAPERS, 1859-1866, 1898-1951.

Noted for his work in the field of conservation, J. Horace McFarland (1859-1948) for many years conducted campaigns for the preservation of Niagara Falls, for the preservation and development of national parks, and for roadside development. The author of numerous articles and books on roses and horticulture, he edited the "Beautiful America" department of the *Ladies Home Journal* and lectured widely. Chairman of the State Art Commission for many years, he served as secretary of the Municipal League of Harrisburg, 1901-45; as a member of the Harrisburg Park commission, 1905-13; as vice president of the National Municipal League, 1912-28; and as president of the American Civic

Association, 1904-24. In 1935 McFarland was named a member of the National Park Trust Fund Board by President Franklin D. Roosevelt. A master printer, he was president of the Horace McFarland Company and of McFarland Publicity Service.

Lantern Slides, [ca. 1890-1905]. There are several Harrisburg photographs of now demolished buildings including private residences, churches, businesses, the YWCA, and the YMCA that were previously owned and used by African Americans. The property is now part of the state's East Capitol Park complex, ca. 1936. Slide no. H-37 is entitled "How a Poor Colored Woman Cleaned Up."

COL. GEORGE F. McFARLAND PAPERS, 1862-1873

Father of J. Horace McFarland, Col. George McFarland was an educator at the Freeburg Academy who later purchased the McAllister Academy in Juniata county. He served with the 151st Regiment of Pennsylvania Volunteers during the Civil War and upon the organization of the Soldiers' Orphans' Schools, McFarland also transformed the McAllister Academy into such a school. Included in his papers are reports of the superintendent of the Soldiers' Orphans Schools of Pennsylvania which give information about the "Bridgewater School (Colored)," in Bucks County, as well as other schools in which African Americans were allowed to enroll.

MG-90. JOHN R. MILLER COLLECTION OF CUMBERLAND COUNTY GOVERNMENT RECORDS, 1768-1914.

This collection of Cumberland County government records includes election returns, 1808-1912; lists of voters, 1808-89; oaths of office, 1784-1914; assessors oaths, 1768-1882; licenses applied for and granted, 1850-55; letters and papers pertaining to bridges, 1812-43; miscellaneous papers relating to bonds, estates, and tavern licenses, 1769-1837; returns made by owners of slaves, 1780; court proceedings, 1780-1875; lists of grand and reverse juries, 1806-56; papers relating to the education of paupers, educator's bills and receipts, 1807-36; tax returns, 1770-1843; tax duplicates, 1783-98; county commissioners' receipts, 1780-1887; bounty receipts for foxes and wolves, 1774-1844; viewers of road receipts, 1804-25; treasurer's receipts, 1807-49; and military records, 1845-46. Scattered through these are items which pertain to slaveholdings, the administering of family slaves, and slave crimes.

Negro Slave Name and Age Returns, 1780, 1791, 1828. The returns are arranged by the date of the document and usually give the slave's name, sex, age and owner's name. Occasionally, the slave's job is mentioned and quite often the owner's residence and occupation appear as well.

Lists of Pauper Children, 1832-1835. Lists of poor children in Cumberland County. Information given includes the name of the child, age, township, and date of list. Occasionally, children are described as being "col'd." African American children listed for Carlisle, in 1835, are: George Boyer, five; Samuel Clelence, nine; Henry J. Clelence, seven; Ann Campbell, seven; Catherine Diggs, nine; John Green, five; Ann Hawkins, eight; Alfred Hawkins, five; Kisigh Hamilton, six; Andrew Lancaster, five; Samuel Lawson, seven; John Powel, nine; Harriett Sanders, eight; Margaret Smithy, eight; Eliza Amy Watson, seven; Homer Watson, eight; Isaac Whiten, nine; Mary Ann Whiten, eight; Nathan Whiten, six; Elenore Whiten, six; Mary Jane Woods, eight; and David Woods, five.

Election Records, 1779-1914.

Voters' Lists, 1808-1903. These lists provide names of qualified voters by township or city ward. African Americans listed include: Upper Allen Township, 1871: William Claborne; Shippensburg, 1871: Daniel Right, Henry Johnston, Isaac Russ, Robert Gray, and David Baer; Carlisle, 1st Ward, 1888: Robert Lane, Robert Stevenson, William Streets, John Alexander, Eli Anderson, Henry Taylor, Thomas Kohn, Abraham Parker, William Scott, James Anderson, and Ben Lindsey; New Cumberland, 1889: J. W. Johnson; Carlisle, 4th Ward, 1889: James Alexander, Elias Hodge, William Hodge, William J. Jackson, Joseph Jordan, Robert Jordan, John Lane, William Peck, Noah Pinkney, H. C. Whiting, and J. W. Whiting. The 1871 and 1888 lists identify "col[ored]" voters, but the 1889 rolls do not indicate race.

Abstracts of Wills in Will Book "A" (Photostats), 1750-1768. Abstracts of wills of various individuals living in Cumberland County. Included are:

- Robert Dunning: 4/9/1750-7/24/1750, Book A, page 1: "Slaves: Whiteball and Philis."
- John Harris, Peters Township: 5/29/1759, Book A, page 60: "Negro woman, Jean."
- Philip Davis: 5/15/1753-11/6/1760: Book A, page 71: "Negro Mary, Negro George, Negro Dinah, Negro Will, Negro Kitt, Negro Jean."
- James Johnston, Antrius Township: 7/25/1764-3/5/1765: Book A, page 130: "Negro boy, Jeremire."
- Nathaniel Wilson, Letterkenny Township: 8/22/1765-11/25/1765: Book A, page 138: "Negro slave, Warwick."
- James Moore, Middletown Township: 12/31/1766: Book A. page 167: "Gaven McKee (will give freedom if . . . at 21 years)."

- Robert Elliot, Peters Township: 5/23/1768: Book A. page 190: ". . . his Negro woman."

Treasurer's Accounts, 1768-1883, 1904. Warrants signed by the county commissioners for payment of expenses incurred by county operations. Under the heading "Cumberland County: to Thomas Alexander Gasler" is cited "Negro Julius for burglary to subsistence from 25th, December 1788 to 19th, June 1789 both days included makes 177 days at 6 pence for day" and "Negro Harry on suspicion of murder subsistence from 25th, July 1788 until 24th, January 1789 in all 189 days at 6 pence for day." Also part of the series is the following subseries:

> *Court Proceedings, Costs and Fees, 1780-1875.* Documentation of constable fees paid by the county for court proceedings. Under the heading "List of Indictments for Sheriff Cryer" is cited "*Republic vs. Negro Abraham*: Indictment of Larceny, October 1797, tried & convicted," and "*Republic vs. Negro Jack Robison*: Indictment of Larceny, convicted on submission."

MG-92. SEQUESTERED JOHN MITCHELL PAPERS, 1758-1781.

John Mitchell was a Philadelphia merchant and deputy quartermaster general during the American Revolution. The papers of Mitchell, and his brother and business partner, Randall Mitchell, were sequestered by the Commonwealth, ca. 1785, during an investigation of the Mitchells' activities as a contractor with the Pennsylvania Navy. Included are Deputy Quartermaster General Mitchell's letter book, 1780-81; and business letters, 1762-77, pertaining to merchandising, prices, and commodities such as chocolate, feathers, rum, coffee, tea, molasses, paper, and slaves.

Items relevant to African Americans are correspondence of Thomas Hovender, 1774, relating to the sale of his "negroes," and receipts and vouchers, 1736-1770, with entries on African American slaves and workers.

MG-93. MOORE FAMILY PAPERS, 1749-1934 (BULK 1749-1887).

Family correspondence, 1807-82, legal papers, 1749-1887, and miscellaneous items, 1800-1934, primarily concerning members of the Moore and Parker families of Carlisle, Pennsylvania.

Legal Papers. Miscellaneous deeds, wills, and other family legal papers. Included are a slave return from John Moore, a West Pennsboro farmer, and a will of William Moore. The slave return lists Jack, a male Negro slave for life, fifteen years [old]; Joe, a male Negro slave for life, fifteen years; Ann a female Negro, born November, 1785; Tobe; Hannah, a female Negro child, born May 1797; Cosey, born October 31, 1799; and Tom a male Negro slave for life, twenty-one years. The will of William Moore "Bequeath[s] unto my son James My Negro Man Sampson, age about 30 years being a slave for life. (1800)"

MG-98. ORBISON FAMILY PAPERS, 1750-1902.

These papers are primarily the business records of William Orbison (1777-1857), Huntingdon lawyer, founder of Orbisonia, president of the Huntingdon Bank and also of the Huntingdon Academy; of Ellen Matilda Orbison Harris (1816-1902), daughter of William Orbison, wife of Dr. John Harris (d. 1881), and secretary of the Philadelphia Ladies' Aid Society, an organization devoted to the relief of soldiers during the Civil War;

and of William A. Thompson d. [ca. 1805], a Huntingdon attorney associated with William Orbison.

PAPERS OF WILLIAM ORBISON, 1777-1857

Legal Papers. Miscellaneous legal papers relating to land transactions, court dockets, trials, and wills. Included is item 22, an undated memorandum on Scipio Young and other slaves who belonged to a Mr. Garnett.

MG-100. PENNSYLVANIA ASSOCIATION OF WOMEN DEANS, ADMINISTRATORS, AND COUNSELORS PAPERS, 1922-1984.

The Pennsylvania Association of Deans of Women was formed on February 25, 1931. The purpose of this organization was to work for the progress of women in employment in the state of Pennsylvania. The executive committee of this association consisted of three people: one chosen from the universities and colleges, one from the normal schools (now the state universities), and one from the high schools. Each year at the association's annual meeting pertinent topics would be addressed, i.e., those having to do with women's rights and effective changes in all areas of education. In later years, the association expanded its name to the Pennsylvania Association for Women Deans, Administrators, and Counselors. At the 1984 annual conference, they prepared resolutions addressing the Civil Rights Act of 1984 (Senate Bill 3568).

Contained in this collection are president's notebooks, 1922-1938; minutes and reports, 1929, 1936-1970; bulletins, 1938-1950, 1964-1970; handbooks, 1929-1958, 1969; newsletters, 1971-1972; programs of annual meetings, 1939-1966; golden anniversary program, 1970; membership and registration lists, 1938-1949. These records indicate that the organization included African American women as early as 1938-1939, i.e., Helen V. Barton, head of guidance at Coatesville High School; Bertha Turner, dean of girls at William Penn High School, Harrisburg; and Harriet Young, acting dean of women, Cheyney State Teachers College.

Mildred Wheatley, an African American, was president of the association in 1973 and served as president of the executive board in 1977-78; she was executive associate dean of students at East Stroudsburg University. Several other African American women are listed as members and officers. They are Delain Allen, Dorothy R. Griffin, Carol F. Hollis, and Marie Vernon Patricia Dixon.

MG-104. POTTS FAMILY PAPERS, 1704-1853.

Papers of a family prominent in Pennsylvania's early iron industry, containing correspondence, business papers, and legal records relating to Charming Forge, Hopewell Forge, Mount Joy Forge, Colebrook Furnace, and Warwick Furnace. Notable correspondents include Stephen Chambers, Robert Coleman, Curtis Grubb, Edward Lewis, Richard Sheldon, and Jasper Yeates.

General Correspondence, 1772-1852. Letter dated March 30, 1738, from Jasper Yeates, Esquire, to Odwin Burd, Esquire, refers to the "work of slaves to be delivered in May."

Accounts, 1732-1845 and undated. An account page for Mount Joy Forge, dated March 1762, of Thomas Potts and Company, states: "Negros Stephen's Team: 80 lb.; Negros Pomp Hector & Dobb: 300 lbs.; Slaves: 15 lbs."

MG-109. GEORGE W. SCHULTZ COLLECTION, 1875, 1927-1947.

This miscellaneous collection of typed excerpts and transcripts from newspapers and letters pertaining to events of the colonial and Revolutionary War period includes items on the development of furnaces and forges. Included is a paper entitled "Crusades and Crooks of War Times-John Brown" that makes references to African Americans.

MG-113. LEWIS SLIFER SHIMMELL PAPERS, 1873-1931 (BULK 1873-1915).

Dr. Lewis Slifer Shimmell (1852-1914) of Harrisburg was an educator and author. The collection contains correspondence, addresses, photographs and published works. An address of February 12, 1909, "Lincoln's Great and World-Wide Work," tells of Abraham Lincoln's belief and desire that all men should be free and that slavery should be abolished. Another address of December 18, 1911, entitled "Abbey's Pennsylvania As Canvas: Apotheosis of Pennsylvania," discusses Thaddeus Stevens and mentions his support of the African American and the abolition of slavery. Shimmell's book *A Short History of Pennsylvania*, discusses the Friends and their philosophy "that no one should buy slaves except to Free." Also included is information on the Underground Railroad, race riots, and the Convention of 1833, which formed the American Antislavery Society, and the burning of the society's headquarters, Pennsylvania Hall, in 1838.

MG-115. MRS. LAWRENCE M. C. SMITH COLLECTION, 1775-1925 (BULK 1823-1874).

Items pertaining to Pennsylvania's constitutions including summaries, reports, and speeches relating to pending legislation that were collected by Mrs. Lawrence M. C. Smith, a member of the Pennsylvania Historical and Museum Commission, 1955-1963. Included in this collection is a January 10, 1823 issue of the Philadelphia newspaper *The National Gazette & Literary Register*. Among the advertisements in this paper is an advertisement for "Negro cloths and linseys."

MG-117. JOHN SPENCER PAPERS, 1828-1861.

Letters, newspapers, etc., of John Spencer (1801-1884), a native of Huntingdon County who was an itinerant Methodist minister in the Pittsburgh Conference, 1828-1852, and resident of Oregon after 1852. Among his ministerial notes and papers, 1828-1847, are copies of newspapers containing references to African Americans. They are: the *Wellsville Patriot*, July 16, 1861, featuring an article: "Repeal of the Fugitive Slave Law," and an advertisement in the *Pittsburgh Christian*, August 20, 1845, announcing the publication of a book entitled *Minstrel of Zion, A Book of Religious Songs, Accompanied with Appropriate Music*, by W. Hunter and Samuel Wakefield." Also included is an envelope on which the following information is written: "Pittsburgh, Pennsylvania, Subscriptions-1847, to buy & free a slave and her children. Her husband, Mr. J. Hughes, already free, asks for help." The envelope contains a list of individuals who gave John Hughes money and the amount contributed by each one.

MG-121. JOHN STROHM PAPERS, 1816-1874.

Correspondence of John Strohm (1793-1884), a Lancaster teacher and surveyor who served in the Pennsylvania House of Representatives, 1831-1833.

MG-117. John Spencer Papers, 1828-1861. Subscriptioin letter and listing.

Correspondence. Contains a letter dated January 15, 1836 from Columbia lumber merchant and African American abolitionist Stephen Smith denouncing the "commerce in human flesh," and pleading with Strohm to "uphold the rights of man" and to "secure such laws as will aid in securing and protecting the citizens of this commonwealth from those acts of popular violence from which you are aware I am a common sufferer"; a letter from Isaac Strohm, a relative of John Strohm, August 11, 1839, mentioning abolition in Ohio; and a letter from "Passmore," August 4, 1841, containing a poem critical of slavery and territorial expansion.

Memorials/Petitions. These are position papers submitted with a petition for proposing amendments to the Constitution of Pennsylvania. The file contains a "Memorial to the Honorable, the Delegates of the People of Pennsylvania in Convention at Philadelphia Assembled, January 6, 1838, " that was "signed on behalf of the people of color in the city and county of Philadelphia [by] Charles W. Gardner [and] Fredk. A. Hinton." The two signers of this controversial petition were African American abolitionists involved in the Negro Convention Movement and other African American self-help activities. Also contained in this file is a "memorial to the Convention to withhold from Negroes the right of Suffrage, [Wm.] Meredith, January, 1838," and a "Memorial to the Convention on the Subject of Negro Suffrage-Citizens of Philadelphia, [Wm.] Meredith, January, 1838," both of which are anti-African American in their content.

MG-133. WELLES FAMILY PAPERS, 1805-1898.

Correspondence, accounts, etc., of the family of Charles F. Welles (1789-1866), a prominent resident of Wyalusing, Bradford County, from 1822 until his death. The personal correspondence, 1805-98, includes letters written between Charles F. Welles and his wife, Ellen J. Welles. Among them are five items written in 1867 that describe the new Lincoln University at Oxford, Chester County, to which Mrs. Welles had contributed. The correspondence also contains acknowledgments from Thomas McCauley, treasurer of Lincoln University.

MG-137. JASPER YEATES FAMILY PAPERS, 1726-1830 (BULK 1761-1812).

Correspondence, accounts, and legal papers of Jasper Yeates (1745-1817), Lancaster attorney, chairman of Lancaster County Committee of Correspondence, 1775, captain of the Lancaster County Associators, 1776, a commissioner for Indian Affairs, 1776, and associate justice of the Pennsylvania Supreme Court, 1791-1817. Also found are materials relating to Jasper's father, Philadelphia merchant John Yeates.

LEGAL PAPERS

Accounts, 1725-1804, and undated. Included is a document dated July 19, 1774 signed by Calvin Cooper concerning the "trial of capital offenses committed by negroes in the province of Lancaster County" and "of a mulatto slave named Ester who mothered a bastard child."

MG-139. FRANK W. MELVIN PAPERS, 1708-1961 (BULK 1820-1861). 8 CU. FT.

Papers of Frank W. Melvin (1884-1961), a Philadelphia lawyer who held many important legal and historical positions in Pennsylvania. He served on the executive committee of the Pennsylvania 300th Anniversary Commission, 1937-1938, was chairman of the Pennsylvania Historical Commission, 1935-1939 and chairman of the Pennsylvania Historical and Museum Commission, 1956-1961. This collection contains correspondence, reports, minutes, copies of legislation, invitations, programs, newspaper clippings, booklets, pamphlets, photographs, and maps. The following booklets pertain to African Americans:

- *Gustavus Hesselius, 1682-1755*, tells of the life of this Penn-

sylvania artist and craftsman, stating that he built the first pipe
organ in America. It further states that he willed to his daughter Lydia "my Negroe Woman Pegg" and "my Negroe man
Tom." His son, John, married a wealthy widow and spent the
rest of his days on an "extensive plantation 'Bellefield,' on the
Severn River near Annapolis, where he boasted many more
slaves than his father's "Pegg" and "Tom."

* *The Horse-Shoe Trail* identifies the following places that have
  an African American association: Hershey Industrial School,
  Hopewell Park and Hopewell Furnace, Joanna Furnace, Elizabeth Furnace, Cornwall Furnace, Governor Dick Hill, and the
  Swatara Creek area. For additional references to African Americans at these furnaces see MG-2, Business Records Collection.

MG-141. JOHN D. BLACK PAPERS, 1815-1923 (BULK 1861-1923)

John D. Black (d. 1923) was a member of the Erie Regiment,
Pennsylvania Volunteer Infantry, 1861, and of the 145th Regi-
ment of Pennsylvania Volunteers, 1862-65; assistant superinten-
dent of elections, Bureau of Refugees, Freedmen and Abandoned
Lands in North Carolina, 1868; captain in the Dakota National
Guard beginning in 1886; and chief commissary of subsistence,
U.S. volunteers, 1898-99. His papers include the following letter
and news articles referring to African Americans:

* Letter, dated July 10, 1898, to "Friend Johnson: . . . arrived in
  the city of magnificent distances on the 16the of June and after a bath and lunch, went up to Army Headquarters where I
  found Colonel Huggins, formerly attached to General Miles
  staff, but now a newly appointed Colonel of the First Regiment of colored Immunes."

305

- An undated news clipping concerning an African American witness to a murder in 1905.
- An article subtitled "First Mixed Negro-White Panel was Drawn in '65." The article, which appeared in the November 25, 1865 issue of *The Minneapolis Tribune*, referred to the treason trial of Jefferson Davis.

MG-142. JOHN R. HAUDENSHIELD PAPERS, 1901-1962.

Chiefly papers of John R. Haudenshield of Carnegie (1888-1959), member of the Pennsylvania House of Representatives from Allegheny County, 1939-40, 1943-49, and member of the Pennsylvania Historical and Museum Commission, 1951-56. The papers consist of correspondence, genealogical notes, and other manuscript materials; printed items including booklets, brochures, newspaper and magazine articles, and family histories; and a number of photostats and photographs. A portion of the correspondence is with officials of the Pennsylvania Historical and Museum Commission. The papers relate to the history and development of Pittsburgh and surrounding areas of southwestern Pennsylvania; more general aspects of Pennsylvania history; various people and places of interest, both inside and outside the United States; and genealogical matters including lineage and military service. With reference to African Americans, the following items are noted:

- *The Settler, a Quarterly Magazine of History and Biography*, published by Bradford County Historical Society, Towanda, April 1953, included "The Underground Railroad and Its Stations in Bradford County," by Mrs. George A. Dayton.
- The Washington, Pennsylvania *Daily Reporter*, dated September 3, 1932, includes an article entitled "Local Negro is sentenced to workhouse, Shotgun All Right for Hunting, But Not

for Hunting Work" and an announcement of a "Missionary program" at the St. Paul A.M.E. Church.

- *Pittsburgh Post-Gazette*, dated November 26, 1958, includes an article entitled "Home Areas for Negroes Limited," subtitled "Council to Discuss Anti-Discriminatory Ordinance Today."

MG-143. SARAH R. MESEROLL COLLECTION, 1733-1939.

Received from the estate of Sarah R. Meseroll of Washington, D.C., this collection contains papers of the Preston family, chiefly of Buckingham and Plumstead Townships in Bucks County, with a branch located in Stockport in Wayne County. The collection contains correspondence, legal papers, invoices and receipts, essays, poetry, books, lecture notes, and newspapers from several cities. Of interest in this collection are the following anti-slavery newspapers and magazines:

- *New York Tribune*, May 2, 1865, article entitled "End of Truce-Negotiations in Progress - meeting of the Colored People of Raleigh."
- *New York Daily Tribune*, May 5, 1865, article on "Colored Troops in Richmond."
- *Sunday Times-Advertiser*, Trenton, New Jersey, July 25, 1915, article entitled "Crosswicks was once an important station on the 'Underground Railway' through which fugitive slaves were permitted to make their escape."

MG-145. DANIEL H. HASTINGS PAPERS, 1877-1931.

Daniel H. Hastings (1849-1903) served as governor from 1895 to 1899 and adjutant general from 1887 to 1891. These papers include executive correspondence, appointments, invitations, proclamations, speeches, scrapbooks, and material on the new capitol building from his files as governor. Personal papers of Hastings and his wife include correspondence, photographs, speeches, scrapbooks, and printed material. Also found are business correspondence and accounts.

Executive Correspondence, 1894-1899. Contains a letter dated November 18, 1896 from a Rev. G. W. Kincaid to Governor D. H. Hastings which states: "My dear Sir: The colored people of this vicinity are preparing for a monster emancipation celebration January 1, 1897 and are desirous of having you address them on this occasion. . . . Among others, we have invited Hon. Garret A. Hobart, Prof. Booker T. Washington, and the Mayors of Pittsburgh and Allegheny." Also found is a letter to the secretary of the interior, dated April 20, 1898, from J. L. Davenport, acting commissioner of the Bureau of Pensions, which informs the secretary of the "illegal acts in the execution of pension vouchers of one Daniel A. Stubbs," a notary public of Oxford, Chester County, whereby claims of Caroline T. Newell Baldwin, mother of Charles B. Newell, late of Troop B, 7th U.S. Cavalry, Certificate No. 355,769, were not properly executed. Also involved in this case was Edward Jones of Lincoln University who was appointed as Mrs. Baldwin's guardian because he was her brother-in-law.

MG-146. ROSS A. HICKOK PAPERS, 1768-1943.

Ross A. Hickok (1876-1943) was a leader in the civic, social, and cultural life of Harrisburg and influential in educational and business circles. He was a director of the Harrisburg National Bank, an officer of the Brubaker Coal Company, and president of the W. O. Hickok Manufacturing Company. In this collection is a copy of *My Own Song Book: A Well Selected Collection of the Most Popular Sentimental, Patriotic and Humorous Songs* (Harrisburg, Pa.), sold by W. O. Hickok in 1840, which includes songs such as "Jim Brown," "Jim Crow," and other songs written in the African American dialect. Also found is an article from the May 26, 1891 issue of the *Harrisburg Telegraph* reporting a police incident in Steelton involving "Annie Hawkins, a colored woman residing along the Pennsylvania Railroad, charged with disturbing the peace."

MG-153. MARLIN E. OLMSTED PAPERS, 1874-1913.

Scrapbooks of Marlin E. Olmsted (1847-1913), a Harrisburg lawyer who served as a Republican member in the United States House of Representatives, 1897-1912. Included in these scrapbooks are numerous newspaper articles referring to slavery in Pennsylvania.

- *Harrisburg Call*, August 12, 1896, "The Republican Recital a success" (subtitled "Afro-Americans Not In It"). The article summarizes the caucus defeat of African American supporter, John W. Bailer.
- *Harrisburg Patriot*, August 12, 1896, "It was M'Ilhenry's Day, His Slate Went Through the Convention Without a Scratch"

(subtitled "All Nominations Were Made by Acclamation-Colored People Chagrined at the Failure of Bailer to Secure a Place-Threaten to Bolt the Ticket").

- *York Gazette*, August 12, 1896, includes an article in support of candidate J. W. Bailer, editor of the Harrisburg *Sentinel Gazette* and secretary of the Afro-American League of Pennsylvania.
- *The North American*, September 9, 1911, "Christiana Recalls Riot, One of Causes of Civil War" (subtitled "Lancaster County Commemorates Battle of Fugitive Slaves and Masters-Governor Tener Comments on Coatesville Lynching").
- *The North American*, September 12, 1911, "The Christiana Riot and the Treason Trials of 1851, Following the Enactment of the Fugitive Slave Law, commemorated in an Historic Manner at Christiana Saturday."

MG-155. CURTIN IRON WORKS RECORDS, 1810-1941.

Founded in 1807, this Centre County business once covered over six thousand acres, including furnace, forge, and supporting facilities. The firm was later known as the Eagle Iron Works.

Ledgers.

Provisions Book, August 9, 1830-April 1833. Entries for purchasing goods are found for the following African Americans: John Brown, Jerry Cook, John Cornish, Lewis Dorsey, John Gibson, Thomas Green, James Jacobs, George Johnston, Robert Norris, Charles Peters, Daniel Till, and Henry Watkins.

Time and Payroll Books.

Time Book and Miscellaneous Accounts, March 3, 1815-Sep-

tember 1, 1828. This book contains on page 44 an entry reading: "Black man-started Tuesday, September 10, worked 6-1/2 days" and an entry on page 83 reveals "J. Brown, July 5, 1824-July 30, 1824, worked 23 days."

MG-156. EDWARD MARTIN PAPERS, 1866-1967 (BULK 1894-1966).

Edward Martin (1879-1967) served as Governor of Pennsylvania from 1943 to 1947, Pennsylvania auditor general from 1925 to 1929, state treasurer from 1929 to 1933, state adjutant general from 1939 to 1943, and a United States senator, 1947-1958. A member of the Pennsylvania National Guard from 1898, he served in the Philippine Campaign, 1898-99; the Mexican Border Campaign, 1916; and World War I. Named brigadier general in 1922, in 1939 he was promoted to major general in command of the 28th Division and was inducted into federal service as commanding general of the 28th Division of the United States Army in 1941. Martin's Papers are divided into the Governor's Papers, 1943-47; Senator's Papers, 1947-58; Private Papers, 1866-1967; and Correspondence, 1898-1967. References to African Americans have been found most frequently in the gubernatorial files. A smaller collection of Martin's senatorial papers are housed at The Pennsylvania State University, University Park.

GOVERNOR'S PAPERS, 1943-1947

Subject File, 1943-1947. Contains Fair Employment Practices Commission legislation of 1946 together with a questionnaire from the National Association for the Advancement of Colored People used to assist African American voters. This questionnaire contains questions about the Fair Employment Practices legislation, civil rights policy, welfare programs, discrimination in the armed forces, and veterans' benefits.

General Correspondence File, 1943-1946. Contains letters from Herbert Brown, secretary of the Allied Veterans Association, regarding African Americans in the Pennsylvania National Guard; a program for the dedication of a monument at Camp William Penn, a training camp for African American soldiers during the Civil War; telegrams and letters protesting a Philadelphia transportation strike and for establishing an "Inter-racial Committee of South Philadelphia;" correspondence with African American state Representative Homer S. Brown regarding a ship christening; a letter from Mrs. Homer S. Brown accompanied by an article from the May 1, 1945 issue of *Look* magazine concerning racial prejudice in America; a letter from the NAACP regarding discrimination in employment; a letter from African American state Representative Thomas Trent regarding a newspaper article concerning "un-American practices;" and a group of letters from Major Richard Robert Wright, president of the Citizens and Southern Bank and Trust Company of Philadelphia, concerning the first National Freedom Day celebration. Also present are copies of the *Congressional Record* containing resolutions to proclaim February 1, 1943 as National Freedom Day and a booklet entitled *National Freedom Day Album* that contains photographs and biographical information on Major Wright, materials on African American owned businesses, historical articles, and transcripts of addresses delivered at the Philadelphia Academy of Music.

Scrapbooks, 1898-1904. The scrapbooks contain many newspaper articles and photographs pertaining to African Americans who served in the 9th and 10th Cavalry, a photograph labeled "a company street of 9th Cavalry troopers enjoying a game of craps," a photograph showing troopers of the 9th Cavalry waiting for rations; photographs of a "colored soldier at Fort Riley," and an article written by Captain William B. Cochran entitled "On Behalf of Negro Troops."

MG-159. JOHN S. FISHER PAPERS, 1886-1940.

John Stuchell Fisher (1867-1940) served as governor of Pennsylvania from 1927 to 1931, was a Pennsylvania state senator from 1900 to 1904, and Pennsylvania commissioner of banking from 1919 to1922.

OFFICIAL PAPERS, 1907-1910, 1919-1920, 1926-1931
Governor's Papers, 1927-1931.

Reports (Departmental), 1927-1931.

- **Department of Public Instruction, 1925-1931.** Arranged chronologically. Includes reports on Cheyney Training School for Teachers dated June1, 1925-May 31, 1927 and June 1, 1927-May 31, 1927. These reports contain audit and examination books and various account records pertaining to the school. The Shelter for Colored Youth is also documented.

- **Department of Public Welfare, 1925-1931.** Arranged chronologically. Included in these papers is a fourth biennial report of Welfare Secretary E. Grace McCauley for 1927-1928 addressing "children under supervision of child welfare, institutions and agencies" that includes a category of statistical information identified under the heading "Colored." Other reports regarding homes for the aged provide information on the Julia White Priscilla Home for Aged Colored People at LaMott and the Aged Colored Women's Home at Williamsport founded by Mary Slaughter. The largest portion of this document is the report submitted by Maude P. Coleman, field representative of the Interracial

Unit of the Department of Welfare, that provides information on the following African American agencies, institutions, organizations, and people: Association for the Protection of Colored Women, Philadelphia; Convalescent Home for Negro Women and Girls, Philadelphia; Coleman Industrial Home for Negro Boys, Pittsburgh; Davis Temporary Home for Negro Children, Pittsburgh; Downingtown Industrial School; Frederick Douglas Memorial Hospital, Philadelphia; Home for Aged and Infirm Colored Women, Pittsburgh; Home for Aged Colored Women, Williamsport; Laurelton State Village (for Negro girls), Pittsburgh; Lemington Avenue Home for Aged Colored Women, Pittsburgh; Mercy Hospital, Philadelphia; State Federation of Negro Women's Clubs; Philadelphia Association for Colored Women; Pittsburgh Home for Colored Women; Robert Woods Industrial Home for Colored Children, Philadelphia; and Termon Avenue Home for Negro Children, Pittsburgh. The department's general fund appropriations for 1925-1927 were disbursed to the African American and African American-supported agencies cited above as well as to the Colored Women's Relief Association of Western Pennsylvania in Pittsburgh.

Executive Correspondence, 1926-1931.

Pre-Inauguration, 1926-1927. Arranged chronologically. Contains the following brochures and letters relating to African Americans:

- Fisher for Governor," a Colored Campaign Committee letter dated May 1, 1926 that was sent to prospective voters.
- A brochure entitled "John S. Fisher for Governor" issued by the John S. Fisher for Governor Republican Colored

Citizens Campaign Committee for Delaware and Chester Counties.

- Fisher for Governor," a Colored Campaign Committee letter dated October 27, 1926 signed by Secretary George E. Jessup, Manager Samuel D. Brown, and William H. Ridley, director for Delaware and Chester Counties.
- A letter of congratulations from the Colored Citizens Political Club of Clearfield County dated November 8, 1926 and signed by John W. Nipson and William A. Pratt.
- A letter dated December 21, 1926 from Philadelphia lawyer Raymond Pace Alexander to Governor Fisher's son, Robert Miller Fisher, asking him to "consider the trained Negro for high office in state departments."
- A letter dated December 22, 1926 from Raymond Pace Alexander to Governor Fisher asking him to give serious consideration to the letter he had written to his son. Raymond Alexander and Robert Fisher had been roommates at Harvard Law School.
- A letter from the Colored Women's Relief Association of Western Pennsylvania dated December 31, 1926 signed by President and Secretary Addie B. Cole endorsing the work of Welfare Secretary Dr. Ellen Potter.
- A letter from the Armstrong Association of Philadelphia dated December 23, 1926 signed by Executive Secretary Forrester B. Washington and bearing the names of the officers and board members in the letterhead.
- A letter dated December 27, 1926 from Mary Owens of 124 South Penn Street, York.
- A letter from the Hallie Q. Brown Club of New Kensington (affiliated with the Pittsburgh City-County Federation of Negro Women's Clubs) dated December 28, 1926 having a letterhead that identifies all officers and their individual addresses.

- A letter from the Colored Protective Union of McKeesport dated December 30, 1926 signed by President D. N. Nelson, Secretary John N. Walker, Executive Chairman William W. Gittins, and Executive Secretary B. J. Duncan.
- Letter dated January 1, 1927, Principal Thomas J. Anderson of the James A. Adams School in Coatesville on behalf of the Inter-Racial Committee of Coatesville.
- Letter from the Emergency Girls Club of York, Pennsylvania State Federation of Negro Women's Clubs, dated January 1, 1927, signed by President Ida S. Grayson and having the names of federation officers throughout the state printed in the letterhead.
- Letter from President Pearl Foster, Housekeepers Federation Club of Canonsburg dated January 2, 1927 and signed by Pearl Foster, Vice President John Walls, Secretary Mrs. Nathan Clarke, Corresponding Secretary Mrs. George Betts, and Treasurer Mrs. Albert Griffin.
- Letter dated January 3, 1927 from Rev. C. F. Jenkins, pastor of the Second Baptist Church of Harrisburg.
- Letter dated January 5, 1927 from Edith H. Benn, secretary of the Inter-Racial Committee of Coatesville.
- Letter dated January 12, 1927 from President Callie L. Walker of the Semper-Fidelis Club of McKeesport.
- A letter dated May 9, 1929 from Maude Coleman to Governor Fisher inviting him to attend the twenty-sixth Annual Convention of the Pennsylvania State Federation of Negro Women's Clubs held in Harrisburg, July 30-August 2, 1929.

MG-169. HERMAN BLUM COLLECTION, 1681-1971. 2 CU. FT.

H erman Blum (1885-1973), chairman of the Board of Craftex Mills, Inc., of Pennsylvania and a trustee of the Philadelphia College of Textiles and Science was a member of the Pennsylvania Historical and Museum Commission, 1963-1971; Pennsylvania member of the United States Civil War Centennial Commission; and an avid collector of historical books and manuscripts.

C. PRINTED MATERIAL, 1682, 1684, 1757, 1784, 1833, 1850, 1891, 1932

A collection of miscellaneous newspapers and magazine clippings printed in London, England and Philadelphia, Pennsylvania. Included are two advertisements and an article with reference to African Americans. They are:

- October 6, 1784 issue of *The Pennsylvania Journal and the Weekly Advertiser*, contains advertisements and articles referring to slaves.
  - *FOR SALE.* "A Negro woman with a male child." . . . "A Negro boy, excellent for the sea-service, or waiting on a gentleman."
  - *Three Hundred Dollars Reward.* "Negro GEORGE ran away from Elk Forge, near Head of Elk, Cecil County, Maryland, on the 2nd of August, 1784" . . . "Negro CATO ran away from the same place, the 24th of May 1783" . . . "Negro DICK ran away from the same place, the 23rd of April 1781, . . ." [point of contact] THOMAS MAY.
- July 5, 1757 edition of *The London Chronicle: or, Universal Evening Post*, contains an "Extract of a letter from Capt. Baille, to his owners, dated River Bonny in Africa, Jan. 31: We ar-

317

rived here the 6th of December, and found the "Hector" with about 100 slaves on board. . . ."

MG-170. PENNSYLVANIA HISTORICAL ASSOCIATION PAPERS, 1932-1965.

Founded in 1933, the Pennsylvania Historical Association is an organization of professional and amateur historians dedicated to promoting research and teaching of Pennsylvania history.

Correspondence, 1949-1960. This series contains many letters to and from persons who authored articles for various association publications, some of which addressed African American history in Pennsylvania. Representative correspondence includes: a letter from Ernest C. Miller, referring to the publishing of the original letters of John Brown; a letter dated November 30, 1950, from J. Cutler Andrews to Donald H. Kent, associate editor of *Pennsylvania History*, mentioning Thomas E. Drake's *Quakers and Slavery in America*; letters from Ira V. Brown referring to authored articles and books such as "Pennsylvania and the Rights of the Negro, 1865-1887"; a letter of December 14, 1960, to Larry Gara referring to his article on William Still and the Underground Railroad; a letter of December 8, 1960, to Horace Montgomery referring to his article "A Union Officer's Recollections of the Negro as a Soldier: Major John McMurray, Sixth United States Colored Regiment"; and a letter dated June 2, 1959 listing a "Negro Bob, death warrant issued September 22, 1795, offenses not known (probably murder)" and date of execution not known.

MG-171. SAMUEL W. PENNYPACKER PAPERS, 1802-1816, 1851-1916.

Pennsylvania Governor Samuel W. Pennypacker (1843-1916) served on the Board of Public Education in Philadelphia, 1885-1889, as a judge of the Common Pleas Court No. 2 in Philadelphia, and was elected governor in 1903. During his gubernatorial administration, the State Archives was established as an administrative unit within the State Library. He was an active member of the Historical Society of Pennsylvania, a noted genealogist and amateur historian.

GOVERNOR'S PAPERS, 1902-1907.

Executive Correspondence, 1902-1907. Includes a letter dated November 5, 1902 from Robert J. Nelson of Reading, president of the Afro-American Republican League of Pennsylvania, congratulating Pennypacker for his gubernatorial victory "on behalf of 55,000 colored voters in Pennsylvania."

Applications for Miscellaneous Positions, 1902-1907. This series contains letters to and from Governor Pennypacker re garding applications for positions in state government. Included are the following letters relating to African Americans:

- A resolution from the Afro-American Republican League of Pennsylvania dated August, 1903 supporting the governor's appointment of Robert J. Nelson to the Department of Mines.
- A resolution dated January 21, 1903 to United States Senator M. S. Quay and United States Senator Boise Penrose from F. L. Jefferson, secretary of the Afro-American Republican League of Pennsylvania.

- A letter dated January 22, 1903 to Governor Pennypacker from Afro-American League President Robert J. Nelson applying for a clerical position with the state.
- A letter and a resolution dated January 23, 1903 to Governor Pennypacker from P. S. Blackwell, a state organizer of the Afro-American Republic League of Pennsylvania.
- A letter dated February 3, 1903, to Governor Pennypacker from Cyrus T. Fox of Reading, president of the Pennsylvania State Editorial Association.
- A letter dated February 4, 1903, to Governor Pennypacker from Solomon Hood, pastor of the Campbell A.M.E. Church of Reading.
- A letter dated February 9, 1903 to Governor Pennypacker from B. F. Hunsicker of the Reading School District.
- A letter dated March 27, 1903 to Barclay Wharton from Robert J. Nelson.
- A letter dated March 31, 1903 to Governor Pennypacker from P. S. Blackwell.

Resolutions of Conventions and Associations, 1903-1906.

- **Afro-American Republican League** file contains a letter dated August 13, 1903 and signed by F. L. Jefferson together with a copy of a resolution adopted by the league's Ninth Annual State Convention. The resolution endorses the election of Samuel W. Pennypacker and is signed by League President Robert J. Nelson and Secretary F. L. Jefferson. Also present is a letter dated June 17, 1905 and a resolution adopted at the league's Eleventh Annual State Convention, also signed by Nelson and Jefferson.
- **Frederick Douglass Memorial Exposition, 1905** file contains two letters from the organization's president, Chicago attorney John G. Jones, dated May 9, 1905 and July

14, 1905, informing Governor Pennypacker about the Frederick Douglass Exposition of North America. The letters state that the exposition would open in Washington, D.C. in May 1906, and asked Governor Pennypacker to send a Black Pennsylvanian to represent Pennsylvania on the organization's board of directors.

Legislation, 1903-1906. The Appropriations 1905 file contains the following letters to Governor Pennypacker which were received from churches, schools, and other organizations seeking state funding:

- Avery College Trade School. March 29, 1905, from Robert Boggs; March 31, 1905, from "a citizen of the 3rd Ward;" April 3, 1905, from Joseph L. Mahony, secretary and treasurer of Avery.
- Berean Manual Training and Industrial School. April 12, 1905, from Matthew Anderson; April 12, 1905, from Clarkson Clothier; April 14, 1905, from John F. Rayburn; April 14, 1905, from Matthew Anderson; April 17, 1905, from John H. Converse; and April 25, 1905, from E. W. Clark. Also present are two copies of *The Berean Record*, for November 1904 and March 1905 and an article entitled "Berean Manual Training School" that appeared in the January 19, 1905 issue of the *Philadelphia Press.*
- A letter dated April 8, 1905 from the Rev. Dr. D. S. Scott representing the Western Colored Industrial School for Farming and Domestic Science in Lawrence County.
- A letter dated April 11, 1905 from James A. Wakefield requesting funds for the Home of the Good Shepherd in Allegheny County.
- A letter dated April 12, 1905 from the Rev. E. E. Bland in support of the State Normal Industrial School for Colored

Persons in Philadelphia.

- A letter dated April 14, 1905 from Thomas J. Gatewood (a former slave of Judge Pennypacker in old Virginia) in support of the Home for the Aged and Infirm Colored Women of Pittsburgh.
- A letter dated April 14, 1905 from attorney Harry W. Bass requesting funds for the Normal and Industrial School for Colored Persons in Philadelphia.
- Charter, constitution, and by-laws of the Philadelphia Protectory for Boys in Montgomery County dated March 13, 1899. Under Article II "no boy shall be excluded from the institution, nor shall any inmate thereof."

MG-172. HARRY SHAPIRO COLLECTION, 1911-1939, 1956-1959.

Records of Harry Shapiro of Philadelphia, a Republican senator in the Pennsylvania legislature, 1933-1944, secretary of Pennsylvania's Department of Welfare, 1955-1958, and secretary of the Commonwealth's Department of Public Welfare, 1958-1959. Included are materials concerning the Department of Welfare (reports and recommendations, 1956; legislative bills, 1911-1939; press releases, 1956; legal papers 1956-1957) and materials concerning the Department of Public Welfare (reports and recommendations, 1959; legislative bills, 1959; press releases, 1959; statistics, 1959; and legal papers, 1958-1959). Minutes and reports of the Commonwealth's Mental Health Center, Philadelphia Region, include references to the nursing home and boarding-out program. Recorded was a "discussion . . . relative to the topics of . . . segregation in participating homes . . ." stating that the "homes" did . . . not have a policy of segregation," and suggesting ". . . a nonsegregation clause be included in future contracts." Also included in the files are monthly statistical reports that give information on African American patients and residents. **Record Group 23, RECORDS OF THE DEPARTMENT OF PUBLIC WELFARE,** OFFICE OF PUBLIC ASSISTANCE, provides statistical information on African Americans and **the Record Group 15, RECORDS OF THE DEPARTMENT OF JUSTICE**, provides census reports on the inmates incarcerated in Pennsylvania's prisons.

MG-175. PINE GROVE FURNACE COLLECTION, 1785-1914.

Records of the Pine Grove Furnace, Cumberland County, as well as records of business concerns connected with the operation of the furnace, covering the period 1785 through 1914. The furnace was originally built by George Stevenson, Robert Thornburgh and Joseph Thornburgh in 1782. By the early nineteenth century, Michael Ege became sole owner of the furnace, which continued to be operated by members of the Ege family until 1838. In that year it was sold to C. B. Penrose and Frederick Watts and operated successfully under the management of William M. Watts from 1845 until 1864, when it was sold to William G. Moorehead, who in turn deeded the furnace to the newly organized South Mountain Iron Company. In 1877, the iron company folded and the Pine Grove property was purchased by Jackson C. Fuller, who in the same year transferred the property to South Mountain Mining and Iron Company, whose major stockholders included John M. Butler, Jay Cooke, Edward J. Williams, Barclay J. Woodward, and William H. Woodward. In 1891 several tracts of Pine Grove land in Adams and Cumberland Counties were conveyed to the Fuller Brick and Slate Company, Ltd., which manufactured bricks up to around 1913. In about 1895, the Pine Grove Furnace ceased operations. The following is a sample list of volumes which have entries pertaining to African Americans:

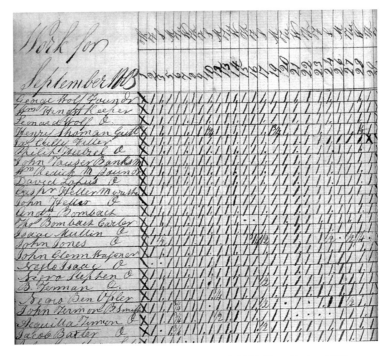

MG-175. Pine Grove Furnace Collection, 1785-1914. Time Books, 1803-1914. Time sheet for September 1803 showing the "Negroes" employed.

Day Books, 1790-1882. Volumes used in bookkeeping that contain daily records of receipts and expenditures in the order of their occurrence. The following are typical entries on African Americans: "December 24, 1779: Sundries Debited to Peter Coleman: Negro Ben for soling 1 pair shoes own leather"; "Furnace Debited to Sundries: To Negro Ben for 12 mon work at 37/6."

Journals, 1789-1911. Daily records of financial transactions of the Pine Grove Furnace. Journal entries are in order of their occurrence. Typical entries for African Americans are: "Jan. 19, 1799: Sundries Debited to Store: Negro Jonathan for 3 1/2 yards Dowlas [and] 1 pair Shoes"; "Feb. 9, 1799: Sundries Debited to Cash: Negro Ben paid Fistle"; "Feb. 23, 1799: Sundries Debited to Cash: Ne-

324

gro Ben paid for Sundrie$" ; "Feb. 23, 1799: Sundries Debited to Store: Negro Jonathan for 2 Twists Tobacco"; "April 20, 1799: Sundries to Debited to Store: Negro Bob for 1 pair Shoes."

Provision Books, 1811-1848. Volumes used to record provisions purchased by workers on credit at the company store. African Americas documented in the entries are: "Negro Stephen, Negro Sampson, and Negro Lewis."

Time Books, 1803-1914. Registers used to record the days worked by individuals at Pine Grove Furnace. Information includes the name of the employee, the type of work (in some cases), and whether he or she worked on a particular day. African Americans whose workdays are documented are: "Negro Isaac, Negro Stephen, Negro Ben, Negro Lewis, and Negro Venis."

MG-180. MILLICENT BARTON REX COLLECTION, 1762-1949 (BULK 1814-1880).

Papers used by Millicent Barton Rex, historian, in preparing lectures, essays, and articles on the life and career of James White (1802-1873), a physician in Hartstown, Crawford County. The collection contains correspondence, commissions, licenses to practice medicine, legal papers, land papers, photographs, etc., and accounts of James White, correspondence and photographs of A. McLeon White, and miscellaneous White family materials. Also included are letters of inquiry, notes, and manuscripts of essays and articles, 1942-49, by Millicent Barton Rex.

JAMES WHITE

General Correspondence, 1814, 1823, 1833-1859, 1880. A letter to Wilson King from C. Canning Smith of Memphis, Tennessee, dated August 27, 1864, describing a Confederate raid on Memphis, reporting that "one of the rebels caught a young Negro boy and had him pinned to the earth by driving a bayonet through each eye; another boy (black), seven years old, was shot dead by another rebel soldier." Observing that Confederate soldiers killed several blacks, Smith questioned the commanding general's failure to restrain his troops.

MILLICENT BARTON REX

Notes. *Western Pennsylvania County Histories* contains a reference to Samuel Marshall, one of the first settlers of Butler County, whose home was an asylum for the needy and oppressed and a prominent station on the Underground Railroad. Marshall opposed the United States Constitution because he felt it sanctioned and protected slavery.

MG-181. WILLIAM A. STONE PAPERS, 1898-1903.

William Alexis Stone (1846-1920) was governor of Pennsylvania from 1899 to 1903. He also served as a soldier in the Civil War, a district attorney in Tioga County, a United States district attorney for the Western District of Pennsylvania, and a member of the Fifty-second, Fifty-third, and Fifty-fifth Congresses.

Executive Correspondence, 1898-1903.

Legislation, 1899-1902. Files are arranged alphabetically by subject and then chronologically by year. The appropriations file for 1899-1920 contains lists of appropriations to state-aided institutions that represented or supported African Americans, such as Frederick Douglass Memorial Hospital and Nursing School, Home for Aged and Infirm Colored Women in Pittsburgh, the Home for Colored Children in Allegheny County, the Home for the Aged in Philadelphia, and the Pennsylvania Soldiers' and Sailors' Homes.

Public Instruction, Superintendent of, 1901-1902. File contains the *Annual Report of the Pennsylvania Commission of Soldiers' Orphan Schools for the year ending May 31, 1902.* The enrollment statistics for the Soldier's Orphans School at Scotland that enumerated African American children are given as 159 boys and 139 girls.

MG-182. LEBANON COUNTY HISTORICAL SOCIETY DEPOSIT OF MANUSCRIPT COLLECTIONS, 1757-1951.

Consists primarily of business records of the iron furnaces and ore hills operated by the members of the Coleman family of Lebanon and Lancaster Counties, which figured prominently in the iron industry during the eighteenth and nineteenth centuries. The first Coleman to become involved in the iron industry was Robert Coleman, 1748-1825, who came to Pennsylvania from Ireland around 1764. He was employed by Peter Grubb at Hopewell Forge and James Old at Speedwell Forge and Reading Furnace. In 1773 he married James Old's daughter, Anne, and for the next three years they rented Salford Forge near Norristown. In 1776 he rented Elizabeth Furnace, where he lived until his retirement in 1809, after which he moved to Lancaster. In his will Robert Coleman left considerable property holdings to his four sons William, Edward, Thomas Burd, and James, including his dominant interests in the Cornwall Ore Hills, Colebrook Furnace, Cornwall Furnace, Elizabeth Furnace, and Hopewell, Martick, and Speedwell Forges.

ROBERT H. COLEMAN, 1850-1900
Reports, 1889-1890.

Jackson, Tampa, and Key West Railroad Reports, 1889-1890.
Includes a letter dated January 9, 1890 from Robert H. Coleman
to C. O. Parker, assistant manager of the Jackson, Tampa, and
Key West Railroad. Enclosed is an application for a fireman
position in which Coleman refers to the applicant as "one of
our old negro firemen, . . . 'Black Diamond.'" He further writes
that "unless our engines improve in appearance within a very
short time, I will advocate the discharge of all the white firemen on our road who will attend to their business, and substitute in their place the negro firemen whom we have heretofore
had, and who have always kept their engines up well. If it
should be necessary to make this change, you must not forget
Black Diamond, otherwise known as Mr. Key."

MG-185. HARMONY SOCIETY PAPERS, 1742-1951.

Founded by George Rapp, the leader of a group of German
Separatists who had emigrated from Württemberg, Germany,
1803-1904, the Harmony Society was formally established as a
"Christian communist" community at Harmony, Butler County,
Pennsylvania in 1805. Following the War of 1812, Rapp and his
followers moved to a site near the mouth of the Wabash River in the
Territory of Indiana where they constructed a new town, which also
was called Harmony. In 1824-25, the Indiana property was sold to
the Scottish reformer, Robert Owen, who renamed it New Harmony,
and the Harmonists returned to Pennsylvania where they established
the most lasting of their communities, the town of Economy, Beaver County, about twenty miles north of Pittsburgh. The death of
George Rapp in 1847, the coming of the Industrial Revolution, and

rather strict adherence to the practice of celibacy were factors involved in the decline in the association's fortunes and membership in the latter half of the nineteenth century. In 1905, on its one hundredth anniversary, the Harmony Society was dissolved.

LEGAL FILE

Indentures, 1809-1889. Included in the records is an indenture dated May 18, 1807, which states that a "Negro woman of the age of sixteen years being a slave named Henny belonging to John Waller and by him brought into this territory from the State of . . . shall serve him for a period of seventy years." The agreement was signed and dated October 2, 1817 in Knox County, Indiana.

MG-186. FRANCIS A. PITKIN PAPERS, 1933-1966.

After holding engineering positions in Pittsburgh and Philadelphia, and a brief stint with the Civil Works Administration, Francis A. Pitkin joined the staff of the State Planning Board in October 1934. He was promoted to executive director of the Planning Board in 1936, and remained in that position until 1964, except for the period 1955-1959 when he served as director of the Bureau of Community Development in the Department of Commerce. Included in this collection is a report of the activities of the Social Surveys Section of the Department of Research and Statistics, Pennsylvania State Emergency Relief Board, entitled *One Year of Social Surveys, December 15, 1933 to December 15, 1934*. This report provides statistics on African American employment and housing, referring to a bulletin, *Report on the Negro Worker, Job No. 805*.

MG-188. WOODS FAMILY COLLECTION, 1794-1952 (BULK 1861-1866).

Papers of the Woods family, Centre County, including Civil War letters, 1861-1865, of John F. Woods, and letters of various family members, 1849-1895. One such letter is dated October 11, 1861 from John F. Woods to his sister. Stationed at Prospect Hill, Virginia, he explained that his regiment, the 49th Pennsylvania Volunteer Infantry, had just moved from their earlier location to merge with another unit and notes that "some of the Negro cooks started with us to march and he [the commanding officer] sent them back and told them and us that he did not associate niggers with his men."

MG-190. JAMES H. DUFF PAPERS, 1943-1951.

James Henderson Duff (1899-1969) served as governor of Pennsylvania from 1947-1951. A graduate of the University of Pittsburgh Law School in 1907, Duff served as a delegate to the Republican National Conventions in 1932, 1936, 1940, and 1948 and he was Pennsylvania's attorney general from 1943 to 1947 and a United States senator from 1951to1957. The State Archives only retains papers relating to Duff's service as attorney general and as governor. References to African Americans have most frequently been found in the gubernatorial papers.

General Correspondence File, 1947-1951.

- *Joseph Baker, Chief of the Division of Negro Research and Planning of the Department of Labor and Industry.* Regards prejudicial treatment towards him from state officials with regard to supporting and approving staffing for his office. Also includes his response to having to move his office, requests for additional personnel, information on African American employment under Governor Duff; and letters from the Republican National Committee requesting employment information and listing the duties of the division.

- **Civil Rights Congress.** Contains copies of materials sent to President Truman and all of the governors requesting that steps be taken to halt injustices to African Americans, and urging them not to extradite African Americans to southern states due to the discriminatory and unfair practices that prevailed there.
- **Girard College.** File contains numerous requests for a proclamation for a Stephen Girard Day or a Girard College Centennial Day. One letter addressed to President Truman from the Philadelphia Federation of Teachers concerns investigations by a committee into allegations of discriminatory practices at the college, especially the exclusion of African Americans from enrollment.
- **Lincoln University.** File contains various budget requests, aid for building maintenance and surplus property, and an invitation to the forty-second Lincoln-Howard football game between the nation's oldest African American college and the largest African American university.
- **Carl Murphy, president of the Afro-American Newspapers.** File contains a letter requesting the establishment of a Reserve Officer Training Corps at Lincoln University.
- **NAACP Correspondence.** File contains letters regarding a case in which a university professor was dismissed for opposing discriminatory housing practices and for involvement with the school's NAACP chapter, letters urging Governor Duff to encourage civil rights legislation, and complaints concerning discriminatory hiring practices.
- **National Negro Business League.** File includes a letter thanking Governor Duff for proclaiming Civil Rights Day and a

letter from the commissioner of the State Police concerning an investigation into the activities of the director of the National Negro Council, who was cited as being an "inter-racial agitator."

Subject File, 1947-1951. Arranged alphabetically by subject.

Appointments and Recommendations, 1947-1951. Also arranged alphabetically by subject.

Pennsylvania, 1947-1951.

- **Commission on Interracial Cooperation.** Contains a description of the commission detailing its composition, functions, and relationship with state government.
- **Fair Employment Practices Commission (FEPC).** Includes correspondence urging the passage of fair employment legislation, reports detailing unfair employment practices in Philadelphia, news releases announcing the appointments of field representatives to the Philadelphia Fair Employment Practices Commission, a letter from Governor Duff commending the Philadelphia FEPC, FEPC annual reports, information on Fair Employment Week, correspondence on establishing a Committee on Civil Rights, from the Erie City Council urging a fair employment legislation, recommendations for members to serve on a statewide organization to improve interracial relations and documents expressing disappointment at the failure of the state legislature to enact fair employment legislation.
- **Lincoln University's Report on Racial Discrimination, 1950.** Contains letters complaining about the treatment of African American students from Lincoln University by Oxford businesses, a statement issued by the university's

president, and letters urging Governor Duff to enforce civil rights laws and to investigate the acquittal of Oxford businessmen accused of violating civil rights laws. Also present is a resolution asking Governor Duff to make clear his position on civil rights, a brief history of segregation in Oxford, and petitions signed by students at Lincoln University.

State Colleges, 1947-1950.

- *Cheyney State Teachers,* 1947, 1949. Contains letters of recommendation for appointments of members of the board of trustees of Cheyney State Teachers College. In 1947 Samuel L. Smedley and Dr. Frederick D. Stubbs left the board. Maude B. Coleman, a representative of the Educational Equality League and the Baptist Ministers' Conference of Philadelphia, submitted the names of Rev. William J. Harvey and Magistrate Hobson Richardson for consideration in filling these vacancies, while William Morris Maier and Dr. Alfred H. Williams submitted the names of James G. Vail and Verona Beckett. The latter two individuals were selected to serve on the board.

MG-191. DAVID L. LAWRENCE PAPERS, 1959-1966.

Governor of Pennsylvania from 1959 to 1963, David Leo Lawrence (1889-1966) also served as the secretary of the Commonwealth from 1935 to 1963, was chairman of President Johnson's Committee on Equal Opportunity in Housing, 1963-1966, and was elected to an unprecedented four terms as mayor of his native Pittsburgh. The papers are arranged into the following series: Appointment Files, 1959-1963; Subject File, 1959-1963;

Legislative File, 1959-1963; Speeches, 1963-1966; General Correspondence, 1963-1966; and Photographs, 1963. Within each series, files are arranged alphabetically by subjects or names of persons or organizations. Within each file, papers are arranged chronologically. The following series contain information on African Americans:

GOVERNOR'S PAPERS, 1959-1963.

Appointments File, 1959-1963.

Statutory Appointments, 1959-1963. These records are divided into three categories labeled the Live File, the O.K. File, and the Dead File that provide information on candidates considered for appointment to various posts. In the live files may be found information on candidates seeking appointments at Cheyney State Teachers College, the State Advisory Committee on Civil Rights, and the Human Relations Commission. The O. K. files provide additional materials relating to appointments at Cheyney State Teachers College and the Human Relations Commission as well as information on Migratory Labor Camps. The dead file contains appointment materials relating to the Scotland School for Veterans' Children.

General File, 1959-1963. The following files contain information on African Americans:

- *African Methodist Episcopal Church of Philadelphia (Bethel), 1959-1961.* Contains a copy of the autobiography of the founder, Rev. Richard Allen, and materials relating to the history of the church and its bicentennial celebration.
- *Andrew M. Bradley, 1959-1962.* Bradley was Pennsylvania's first African American secretary of Property and Supplies. This

file contains materials relating to Emancipation Proclamation Day, civil rights legislation, educational opportunities for African Americans, housing discrimination, the Human Relations Commission, the NAACP, Leon Higgenbotham Jr., and the Freedom Jubilee in Pittsburgh, and also contains an *Ebony* magazine article about Bradley.

- *Catholic Interracial Council of Pittsburgh, 1960-1962.* Contains a newsletter with information on African Americans.
- *Civil Rights File, 1959-1961.* Contains correspondence concerning the governor's Civil Rights Conference, news releases, and summaries of legislative hearings.
- *Commission on Human Relations, 1959-1962.* Contains copies of the *Pittsburgh Human Relations Review.*
- *Cheyney State Teachers College, 1959-1962.* Contains a news release dated March 2, 1959 that provides information on budget authorizations for 1957-59 and 1959-61 and a February 17, 1960 letter to Governor Lawrence from Cheyney President James H. Duckrey informing him of the death of former Cheyney President Dr. Leslie P. Hill. Also present is a letter dated January 19, 1962 addressed to Superintendent of Public Instruction Charles H. Boehm and signed by Cheyney staff and faculty that objects to comments made by Boehm concerning a proposal to merge Cheyney with West Chester State College. Finally, in a letter dated April 3, 1962, Harry E. Brumbaugh writes "that the sanctuary of Cheyney College should be rededicated to the purpose of graduate study in the humanities."
- *Congo Youth Project, 1961.* Contains materials relating to Pittsburgh YMCA fellowship program between the United States and the Republic of Congo.
- *Alice M. Cookman, President, Security Civic League of Pittsburgh.* In a letter dated May 1962 Cookman complains to Governor Lawrence about abusive and racist language the Demo-

cratic ward chairman had directed toward her and other voting poll workers in Pittsburgh's Seventh Ward.

- ***Emancipation Proclamation, 1963.*** Contains speeches, letters, and news releases pertaining to the centennial of the Emancipation Proclamation.
- ***Greater Zion Baptist Church.*** Contains an invitation to Governor Lawrence to attend a 1962 concert in Harrisburg.
- ***Judge A. Leon Higgenbotham, 1959-1962.*** Contains materials relating to the NAACP, civil rights legislation, and desegregation.
- ***Hill City Youth Municipality, 1959-1962.*** This was a community service bureau that provided consultation and guidance to the African American residents of the Hill District and the Homewood community in Pittsburgh who were experiencing either community or family conflicts. The file contains a progress report for 1959, minutes dated March 28, 1959, a newsletter dated March 25, 1960, a list of nominees dated 1959, and an undated amendment to the bylaws. Board members included Rev. Charles H. Foggie, Mrs. Robert L. Vann, and Daisy Lampkin.
- ***Dr. Alma Johnson Illery.*** Contains correspondence addressed to Governor Lawrence concerning the George Washington Carver Day celebration.
- ***K. Leroy Irvis, State Representative.*** Contains materials relating to an article entitled "Negro Voters on the Fence" that is contained in the 1962 Democratic Campaign file.
- ***Frances Jones.*** Contains materials relating to Jones election as a state representative, and a newspaper article, transcripts of speeches, and tributes to Dr. Martin Luther King Jr.
- ***Lincoln University, 1959-1962.*** Contains a history of the school, invitations to commencements, and an honorary degree conferred on Governor Lawrence.
- ***Mercy Hospital, 1960-1962.*** Among the items in this file are

an "Adjudication and Order in the Matter of the Application of Mercy Hospital of Pittsburgh for Registration and Permit to Conduct Pharmacy" and letters concerning the application and problems involved in establishing a pharmacy at Mercy. Other materials include a grant proposal for installing a closed circuit television and computer system, an application to the Hill Barton Fund to fund building improvements, a letter concerning the admission of the governor's wife as a patient at the hospital, and an undated letter from a Mercy Hospital employee to the local bus company complaining of the impact of a bus company strike.

- *National Association for the Advancement of Colored People (NAACP), 1959-1962.* Contains materials relating to discrimination and civil rights protests. These focus on Governor Lawrence's record on civil rights, NAACP protests of a 1959 Memorial Day service honoring the Confederate flag, a 1960 protest of segregation in national Civil War commemoration ceremonies, unfair housing practices in Harrisburg in 1961, inadequate youth programs in Chester in 1961, the harassment of African American Pennsylvanians by Delaware State Police in 1962, and remarks by Governor Lawrence to the Annual Pennsylvania State Conferences of the NAACP held at Philadelphia on July 10, 1961 and at Harrisburg on October 26, 1962.

- *Negroes.* Contains letters concerning racial discrimination, the Association for the Study of Negro Life and History, Negro History Week, and National Negro Newspaper Week.

- *Norristown High School, 1960.* Contains material concerning the robbery of a gas station by two African Americans on October 31, 1960 and how the Norristown police subsequently entered the Norristown High School where they lined up approximately a hundred African American students and examined their shoes for evidence of blood.

- *United Negro College Fund, 1959-1963.* Contains correspondence concerning fund drives and sponsors.

Subject File, 1959-1963. Includes the following subjects:

- *"Below the Belt" Correspondence, 1959-1963.* Contains two derogatory letters dated August 28, 1961 and November 16, 1962 criticizing Lawrence's stand on civil rights.
- *Capital Cases, 1959.* A record of eleven capital cases including that of defendant Isaiah Greene, an African American convicted for the murder of an elderly white shopkeeper.
- *Citations and Recommendations, 1959-1963.* Includes a letter recommending Dr. Harold F. Grim of Lincoln University for consideration as a positive role model for African Americans.
- *Governors' Conference on Civil Rights, 1959-1960.* Letters and proceedings relating to the Third Annual Conference of Governors on Civil Rights held March 3-4, 1960.
- *Housing File, 1959-1962.* Covers cases of discrimination in housing.
- *Human Relations Commission File, 1959-1962.* Contains letters, complaints, and reports concerning discrimination in housing, employment, and communities.
- *Migratory Labor File, 1959-1960.* Contains letters proposing the construction of Negro Glade Lake in Somerset County, 1960-61.
- *Presidential Campaign of 1960.* Contains copies of the fiftieth anniversary edition of the *Pittsburgh Courier* and materials relating to African American voting patterns in the 1960 presidential campaign.
- *Segregation File, 1962.* Contains materials on discrimination in schools, the Educational Equality League, civil rights cases, the NAACP, prison riots, and John F. Kennedy press releases.

Photographs, 1963. A photograph album entitled "Football's Greatest Weekend" contains a collection of photographs taken at the dedication of the National Professional Football Hall of Fame in Canton, Ohio, September 7-8, 1963. One of the photographs shows Ohio Governor James A. Rhodes tossing a coin at the opening of the Hall of Fame football game in Fawcett Stadium. The honorary captains were Justice Byron S. (Whizzer) White of the United States Supreme Court, a former Pittsburgh Steeler, and Marion Motley, a former Cleveland Browns back.

Finally, the **Correspondence** and **Speeches** series contains a variety of materials relating to the Presidential Committee on Equal Opportunity in Housing, 1963-1966.

MG-192. DR. PAUL A. W. WALLACE PAPERS, 1931-1967.

Paul A. W. Wallace (1891-1967), for many years chairman of the Department of English at Lebanon Valley College, was editor of *Pennsylvania History*, the quarterly journal of the Pennsylvania Historical Association, 1951-1957; consultant to the Pennsylvania Historical and Museum Commission, 1951-1957; and historian on the staff of the commission, 1957-1965.

A. AUTHOR'S MANUSCRIPTS, 1945-1967

Books, [ca. 1945, 1951-1965]. Included are drafts of Paul A. W. Wallace's manuscript *Pennsylvania Seed of a Nation*, [ca. 1962] containing chapters such as no. 23 "Underground Railroad" and no. 24 "Lincoln," with handwritten notes and references.

B. STAFF HISTORIAN, 1931-1966 AND UNDATED.

General Correspondence, 1957-1965. Correspondence to and from Dr. Wallace during his tenure as historian at the Pennsylva-

Commemorative Exercises

of the

Lebanon County Historical Society

and the

Mt. Gretna Heights Association

at the

Unveiling of Tablet

ENCLOSED SPRINGHEAD, 50 YARDS IN REAR, IS THE PROBABLE SITE OF CABIN OF "GOVERNOR DICK", NEGRO SLAVE CHARCOAL BURNER OF GRUBB'S CORNWALL FURNACE, WHO LIVED AT BASE OF "GOVERNOR DICK'S HILL" FROM ABOUT 1776 TO 1800.

CORNWALL FURNACE RECORDS

Sunday, May 17, 1959
2:30 P.M.

MOUNT GRETNA HEIGHTS
AT THE
BASE OF GOVERNOR DICK
Lebanon County, Pennsylvania

MG-192. Dr. Paul A. W. Wallace Papers, 1931-1967. Staff Historian's Correspondence, 1957-1965. Unveiling of tablet in honor a slave called "Governor Dick".

nia Historic and Museum Commission. Included is a phone transcript regarding the slave "Governor Dick." According to Dr. Herbert H. Beck, the slave "Governor Dick" lived at the base of "Governor Dick's Hill" and was a charcoal burner at Grubb's Furnace. The Mt. Gretna Heights Association and Lebanon County Historical Society honored him in 1959 with a marker placed at the base of the hill.

MG-196. HORACE M. ENGLE COLLECTION, 1971-1973.

Born near Marietta, Pennsylvania, Horace M. Engle was an inventor and master photographer. Active in mineral exploration and land and water power development at Roanoke, Virginia and Ontario, Canada, among other places, he served as an alternate delegate to the 1888 National Convention of the Prohibition Party held in Indianapolis, Indiana. Included in this collection is a July 2, 1862 issue of the *Philadelphia Inquirer* containing articles entitled "Great Meeting in New York," "Protest Against Negro Agitation," "Our Fortress Monroe Letter," "The Proceedings of Congress," etc., all of which address "negro freedom" and the Civil War.

MG-197. ALLEGHENY COUNTY WORK HOUSE RECORDS, 1866-1971.

In response to a petition from the Board of Prison Inspectors of Allegheny County, who were concerned with the rising costs of maintaining prisoners at the county jail in increasingly crowded conditions, the state legislature in 1866 authorized the construction of a workhouse in Allegheny County. The Allegheny County Work House and Inebriate Asylum at Claremont (Blawnox) admitted its first inmates in 1869, two years before the buildings and wall were completed. The Work House was officially closed in 1971.

POPULATION RECORDS

Discharge Descriptive Dockets, 1873-1971. A record of prisoners discharged from the Allegheny County Work House. Information includes the prisoner's name, number and dates received and discharged; age; race (white, mulatto, or black), and gender; date sentenced, crime committed, how discharged (expiration of sentence, commutation, order of the court, escaped, paroled, or died); time served, occupation and amount earned in prison; and remarks. The records are arranged by discharge number.

Escaped Prisoners Books, 1882-1971. A record of prisoners who escaped from the Allegheny County Work House generally providing escapee's name, time in prison, and offense. For the years 1921-1946 information given also includes prisoner's age, complexion, color (Negro, white, or black), hair and eye color, height and weight; occupation; marital status; sentence, term and offense; time served in prison; and date escaped. The records are indexed alphabetically by surname of prisoner.

Register to Include All Prisoners Tried and Sentenced to Hard Labor Books, 1869-1971. A documentation of prisoners who were tried by the courts and sentenced to hard labor at the Allegheny County Work House. Information provided includes each prisoner's name; date received at the prison; age, race, complexion, color of hair and eyes, and height; marital status; parental relations (both parents living or dead at age sixteen or mother or father living or dead at age sixteen); education (whether able to read or write); type of schools attended (public or private); age on leaving school, never went to school, whether attended Sunday school; whether apprenticed; occupation before conviction and during prison term;

habits (abstinent, moderate drinker, occasionally intemperate, or intemperate); military service; term of sentence; court and county where tried; number or convictions; how discharged; and remarks.

PRINTED BOOKS AND MANUSCRIPTS

Reports, 1873, 1879-99, 1924. Annual reports of the Allegheny County Work House. Information includes the manager's report; superintendent's report, and financial and statistical tables. One of the tables shows the number of colored males and females admitted to the workhouse for the year.

MG-199. RAILROAD MUSEUM OF PENN-SYLVANIA COLLECTIONS, [CA. 1830-1974].

Minutes, reports, photographs, maps, drawings, timetables, accounts, and other records of or chiefly relating to the former Pennsylvania Railroad, together with records of other railroads which have operated or are operating in Pennsylvania. Also included are materials of a general character relative to the administrative and operational history of the railroad industry, nationally and internationally.

GEORGE E. HASSEN COLLECTION

Assembled by George Hassen, a forty-year employee in the Dining Car Department of the Pennsylvania Railroad and Penn Central Railroad Companies, it is a collection of photographs, press releases, pamphlets, etc., relating to the "Congressional" and "Senator" trains. Of particular interest are photographs bearing the following captions: new Congressional bar lounge, new Congressional dining car, new Congressional coffee shop, new Congressional and Senator drawing room, new Congressional and Senator observation car, and the new Congressional and Senator parlor cars. In these photographs African Americans appear working as bartenders, waiters, cooks, attendants, and redcaps (luggage handlers).

MG-200. POSTER COLLECTION, 1854-1971 AND UNDATED.

Nearly five hundred posters, most relating to political issues such as campaigns and elections, or to the Civil War, World War I, or World War II. Included in this collection are:

- No. 8. Political-Freedman's Bureau (anti), "Geary for Climer opposed," ca. 1863.
- No. 9. Political-Lincoln (anti), "Elect Lincoln and the Black Republic Ticket," undated.
- No. 12. Political-McClellan Campaign, "Defeat Negro Equality," ca. 1864.
- No. 15. Political-Stevens, Thaddeus (anti), Mass Convention, Lebanon, Pa., Oct. 6, 1866, "Anti-Negro Suffrage," 1866.
- No. 38. Freedom-"The World Cannot Live Half Slave Half Free" (quotes of Pres. Wilson and the Kaiser), State Council of Defense, undated.
- No. 275. WW I-Freedom, Office of Facts and Figures, "This World Cannot Exist Half Slave and Half Free," Artist: John Falter, 1942.
- No. 515. Pennsylvania Historical and Museum Commission Conference on Black History posters, 1981-1995.

MG-201. GERTRUDE HOWARD NAUMAN PAPERS, 1780-1972.

The collection consists of political, civic, and personal papers of Gertrude Howard Nauman (1901-1973) as well as civic and personal papers of Gertrude Howard Olmsted McCormick (1874-1953), the mother of Gertrude Howard Nauman. Mrs.

McCormick was one of the organizers of the Harrisburg Symphony and the Harrisburg Art Association. Also included in the collection are three pieces of sheet music composed by African Americans: "Carry Me Back to Old Virginny," by James A. Bland; "W. C. Handy's Collection of Blues," and "It Ain't Gonna Rain No Mo," by Wendell W. Hall.

MG-203. CORNWALL FURNACE COLLECTION, 1768-1940.

Erected by Peter Grubb in 1742, Cornwall Furnace came under the control of Robert Coleman in 1798 and ownership remained in the Coleman family until 1932 when the property was donated to the Commonwealth. The collection consists primarily of account books, 1768-1892, pertaining to Cornwall Furnace and several other furnaces and forges, including Charming Forge, Colebrook Furnace, Hellem (Helmstead) Forge, Hopewell Forge, Speedwell Forge, and Spring Forge. A number of these volumes include references to African American slaves and workers. Placed inside the account books are loose pages of typed notes on the African American slaves and workers written by the late historian of Pennsylvania's early iron industry, Herbert S. Beck [ca. 1940].

Account Books, 1768-1892.

Coal (Cole) Books, 1768, Hopewell Forge. According to Herbert S. Beck, contains credits to colliers (charcoal burners) from April 25 to December 8, 1768 that include an entry reading, "Three credits go to Negro Bob, a slave."

Individual Accounts, 1779-1780, Hopewell Forge. Accounts are shown for the following: Molatta Abb for July and December 1779 and February and April 1780 and for Molatta

Sue in September, October, November, and December 1779 and February through September 1780.

Account Book, April 12-July 19, 1790. Notes by Herbert Beck state: "In account book dated April 12-July 19, 1790, the 'Negro accounts' at store include negro Jack, Negro Harry, Negro Cato, Negro Tommy, Negro Oston, Negro Samson and Gov. Dick. The account of May 30 is this: 'Negro acct pr shows Govr Dick.' This shows that the collier, [who] prior to 1780 [was] a slave, was called Governor Dick in 1790. It is the first documentary mention of this man for whose cabin located, at its base, Governor Dick's Hill was named."

Miscellaneous Accounts, 1791, Pallas Stewart. Herbert Beck writes: "this book, which curiously found its way to the Cornwall Furnace, is a smart boy's schooling book on legal forms, book-keeping accounts, etc." It contains a passage entitled "Liberation of a Slave" dated 1782, that Beck has described as "a superb sample of Spencerian handwriting."

Cash Book, 1795, Union Forge. Beck's notes state: "Cornwall Furnace purchased 2 ton, 2 cwt of anconies, which, curiously enough, were made by 'Cato.'" Cato was often listed as working at both Cornwall Furnace and Hopewell Forge. In an entry dated Jan. 13, 1795, Negro Bob is listed as receiving a number of gallons of liquor for the use of the slaves. Beck goes on to state that "The Union Forge was built in 1782 by Curtis Grubb and these slaves were owned by Grubb . . . The slaves working there were Grubb's Dec. 25, 1794. Negro account page . . . Bob, Toney, Diana, Jack-Christmas . . . apparently these were Christmas presents." Beck also gives further information on Governor Dick and Governor Dick's Hill.

MG-204. STATE YMCA OF PENNSYLVANIA RECORDS, 1869-1969.

Minutes, reports local studies, proceedings of annual conventions, legal papers, photographs, manuals, and related materials of the Pennsylvania Young Men's Christian Association. Founded in 1869, these records reflect the wide range of YMCA activities with African Americans and among immigrants in the anthracite and bituminous coal fields. During the early 1900s separate African American branches of the YMCA emerged in Pennsylvania's metropolitan areas. Between 1910 and 1920, African American branches were established in Philadelphia, Pittsburgh, and Sewickley and by 1925 branches were also opened in Germantown and Harrisburg, and by the late 1930s, in Wilkes-Barre. These provided both recreational opportunities and welfare-related programs to their respective African American communities.

YMCA (National) Yearbooks and Official Rosters, 1902-1960. Provide information on size of membership, property, activities, and financing for the "Colored Men's Associations." The names of the top officers of each association are frequently given and the information is arranged by state, county, and educational institution. Before World War II the African American branches were designated as "Colored."

Pennsylvania State YMCA, Special Committees Meetings: 1926-1930, Minutes. Includes the minutes of the State Committee of Colored Work, 1927 and 1928 and the report of the Pennsylvania Employed Officers Conference, 1928. Also present is a subcommittee report on "Colored Work" at Harrisburg dated October 8, 1927. The subcommittee convened at the Broad Street Branch of the YMCA with Chairman C. Sylvester Jackson presiding and the following members present: James H. Irvin, Boyd L. Proctor, John C. Robinson, Rev. C. F. Jenkins, W. F. Burden, State Secretary P. C. Dix, and J. H. Dalrymple who was "responsible for the promotion of work among the Colored race." One of the main items of discussion was the Phalanx Movement of the Conference of Colored Boys and the concern was that there were only twenty-one such associations in Pennsylvania.

Pennsylvania State Centennial Committee of the State YMCA Scrapbook, Being a Collection of Materials Produced by YMCAs of Pennsylvania During the Centennial, 1944, Harrisburg, PA (1944). Includes a program of the Christian Street YMCA of Philadelphia which contains many photographs and lists of African American supporters.

Pennsylvania Hi-Y News, 1937-1947. Some issues in the post-World War II years make occasional references to notable African Americans connected with the YMCA.

MG-206. JOHN S. FINE PAPERS, 1951-1955.

John Sidney Fine (1893-1978) served as Republican governor of Pennsylvania, 1951 to 1955. A native of Nanticoke, Luzerne County, he graduated from Dickinson Law School in 1914, completed his post-graduate work at Trinity College, Dublin, Ireland in 1919 and was admitted to the Luzerne County Bar in 1915. He later served as Republican district chairman for Luzerne County and was long a secretary for the Luzerne County Republican Committee. Fine was elected as a judge of the Superior Court, 1947-50. before he became governor.

APPOINTMENTS, 1951-1955

General and Specific Appointments, 1951-1955.

Letters of Application and Recommendation, Special, 1951-1955.
A file containing letters submitted to Governor Fine by applicants
seeking state appointments and letters recommending candidates
for such appointments. Among the items present are:

- **Cheyney Training School-President, 1951**. Letters of recommendation and approval for Dr. James Henry Duckrey
  to become president of the Cheyney Training School for
  Teachers upon the retirement of Dr. Leslie Pinckney Hill
  after the 1950-51 school term.
- **Public Assistance-Instruction—Scotland School Superintendent, 1952.** Letters of recommendation and approval
  for the appointment of Dr. Willard Montgomery Stevens
  to replace Mr. J. C. Allen as superintendent of the Scotland School in June 1952.

Boards and Commissions, 1951-1955.

"O.K." Files, 1951-1955. This file contains both letters of recommendation and letters of approval for individuals appointed to various State boards and commissions by Governor Fine. Among items
of interest are:

- **Migratory Labor, Governor's Committee on, 1952-
  1953.** Includes letter announcing the creation of this committee and appointing David M. Walker as chairman. Also
  contains a list of the names of the committee members.
- **Industrial Race Relations Committee, 1952-1954.** Contains letters of recommendation and appointment for members to serve on this committee. The following African
  Americans were appointed: The Honorable Homer S.
  Brown, Dr. James Duckrey, and Mrs. Robert S. Vann. Also
  included is a committee brochure listing William H. Gray

Jr., an African American, as its executive director.

- **Cosmetology, State Board of, 1952-1954.** Contains a letter from Governor Fine to Arianna Preston appointing her to the State Board of Cosmetology. Also includes Arianna Preston's letter to Governor Fine expressing her appreciation for being the "the first Negro woman" appointed to the board.
- **Scotland School for Veterans' Children, 1952-1953.** Contains letters of recommendation and appointment for Lillian W. Stevenson to the board of directors of the Scotland School.

Justices of the Peace Files.

Duncan C. McCallum's File, 1951-1955. A World War I veteran, Duncan C. McCallum was long employed by the United States Steel Corporation, in the real estate business, and in automobile sales. After the war, McCallum served five electoral terms with the American Legion. He was appointed secretary of personnel to the governor in 1931 and reappointed secretary to the governor in 1951 during Fine's administration.

Letters of Application and Recommendation, 1951-1955. A file containing letters submitted by applicants for state appointments to various boards and commissions and letters recommending candidates for such appointments. Files containing documents relating to African American candidates are listed below:

Boards and Commissions (Individual), 1951-1955.
- **Cheyney State Teachers College, 1952-1953.** Contains letters of recommendation for the appointment of Mrs.

Morris E. Leeds to the board of trustees of Cheyney State Teachers College, and a list of the names of the members of the school's board of trustees. Another African American, Verona Beckett of Philadelphia, was also appointed to serve on the board from January 12, 1950 until the third Tuesday of January 1955.

- **F.E.P.C. (Fair Employment Practice Commission), 1953 Session.** Contains letters to Governor Fine from Dr. John P. Turner, an African American physician, requesting an appointment to this commission.

- **Industrial Race Relations Committee, 1952-1959.** Contains letters recommending that the Reverend J. Pius Barbour and Dr. William H. Gray Jr. be appointed committee members. There is also a complete list of the names of committee members showing Dr. Gray as executive director. Among written documents issued by the committee are: "A Directive of Purpose for the Governor's Commission on Industrial Race Relations," "Proposed Steps in the Creation of the Governor's Committee on Industrial Race Relations," and "A State Commission on Industrial Race Relations."

- **Children and Youth, Governor's Committee on, 1952-1954.** Contains a listing of the committee's officers, representatives and members. Included on the listing is Alberta J. Braxton, president of the Pennsylvania State Federation of Negro Women's Clubs, Inc.

- **Migratory Labor Committee, 1953.** Contains a note directing the secretary of Labor and Industry to prepare letters for the governor to begin the formation of the Committee on Migratory Labor.

- **Cosmetology, Pennsylvania State Boards of, 1951-1954.** Letters of recommendation for the following African Americans to be appointed to the State Board of

Cosmetology: Arianna Preston, recommended by Carolyn Dismond, president of the Pennsylvania State Association of Modern Beauticians and Cosmetologists, Inc., and Nathaniel B. Donaldson, recommended by E. Washington Rhodes of the *Philadelphia Tribune*. Also includes a letter from Cordelia Greene Johnson, President of the National Beauty Culturists' League, Inc., to Governor Fine urging the appointment of an African American to serve on this board.

- **Scotland School for Veterans' Children, 1951-1953.** Contains letters recommending nominations for the following persons to serve on the school's board of trustees: Howard C. Bradley, Robert S. Ogilvie, and Lillian W. Stevenson. Lillian Stevenson of Wilkinsburg was appointed to serve from May 5, 1950 until the third Tuesday of January 1953 and until her successor shall have been appointed and qualified.

Also included in this file is a listing of "statutory appointments" which would expire December 22, 1951. African Americans cited are Verona Beckett of Philadelphia appointed to the board of the Cheyney Training School for Teachers and Lillian W. Stevenson of Wilkinsburg appointed to the board of the Scotland School.

GENERAL FILE, 1951-1955

This file is arranged alphabetically by surname of correspondent and documents the following subjects relating to African Americans:

- Letters to Governor Fine from Dr. Horace M. Bond, president of Lincoln University, and H. F. Grim, dean of Lincoln University, congratulating him as governor and welcoming him to the board of trustees. Also present are letters dated 1954 to Governor Fine from the university's President Frazier S. Taylor, regarding support for the Varsity Club. Other letters concern the university's commencement exercises for the years 1951-54; a Lincoln-Howard football game, 1951; Founder's Day Dinner, 1952; note sent to Governor Fine from President Horace M. Bond regarding the book *Higher Education Is Serious Business*, undated; and a telegram to Governor Fine, October 4, 1952, from Fred D. Hawkins regarding the Civil Rights Matinee to be held in Chicago, October 9, 1952. This event was part of a national effort to end segregation at the state level.

- Letters from Dr. Erma Johnson Illery, president of the National Achievement Clubs, Inc., to Governor Fine urging him to sign a proclamation recognizing January 5 as George Washington Carver Day as established by Act of Congress and proclamation of President Harry S. Truman. Also present are copies of such state proclamations signed by Governor James H. Duff in 1951 and by Governor Fine in 1954.

Scattered through the file are correspondence, income statements, and invitations to banquets including an invitation to Governor Fine to attend the opening of a "Negro" Housing Project and an order form for a new publication entitled "The Negro Newsletter."

FILES OF PLANNING AND RESEARCH CONSULTANT ROBERT J. O'DONNELL, 1953-1954

Robert J. O'Donnell was the planning and research consultant in the Governor's Office during Governor Fine's administration. The file contains a variety of miscellaneous research materials used to assist the Governor's Office in strategic planning.

Research Materials, 1953-1954.

Pennsylvania Exposition, 1954. Though this sub-series is labeled Pennsylvania Exposition, it actually consists of various issues of the *Philadelphia Afro-American*, an African American newspaper, that contain references to that exposition. Included in these materials is the June 5, 1954 issue of the *Philadelphia Afro-American* that contains the following articles:

- "Bethel's Members Appeal for Return of Minister," describing Bethel African American Episcopal Church of Bryn Mawr's intention to appeal the transfer of their pastor, Rev. William P. Stevenson, to the New York Conference.
- "Commencement Calendar" for twenty-one historically African American colleges and universities, including Lincoln University in Pennsylvania. Information provided for each institution includes the number of graduates, date of commencement, name of commencement speaker, and the names of all recipients of honorary degrees.
- "Morgan to Give Degrees to 197 on June 6, 6 Honorary Degrees." The eleven students from Pennsylvania who received degrees were: Dorothy Haysel, Chester; Frances Williams, Pennlyn; Jacqueline Epps, Inez Jackson, Alice Monroe, Wesley Wilson, and Barbara Wood, all of Philadelphia; Gwendolyn Graham, Pittsburgh; and George Jefferson, West Chester.
- "Betty Chapman Wins Oratorical Contest." Chapman, an eleventh grade student at William Penn High School in York, was awarded first place prize of $50 in an oratorical contest sponsored by the Central Pennsylvania Baptist Association.
- "Carrier Explosion Takes Heavy Toll, Total of 26 Dead

Identified by the Navy as Colored Member of the Crew." The explosion occurred on the aircraft carrier U.S.S. *Bennington* while at sea near Quonset, Rhode Island. Included in the article are the name and rank of each deceased member of the crew together with the names and addresses of their parents.

- "86 Graduated from Cheyney College." United States Appeals Court Judge William H. Hastie was the guest speaker at the commencement exercises. Of the eighty-six graduates, eighty were from Pennsylvania. Information provided includes the names of the graduates and the hometowns of each.
- "Downingtown to Hold Commencement June 6." This article provides the name and hometown of each graduate at the forty-ninth annual commencement held at the predominantly African American Downingtown Industrial School.
- Photograph of John T. Brown, an elevator operator at the Gimbel Brothers' store for forty-five years.

FILES OF PUBLIC RELATIONS SPECIALIST WILLIAM W. WHEATON, 1951-1955.

William W. Wheaton was a public relations specialist in the Governor's Office during Governor Fine's administration, 1951-55. The file contains miscellaneous research materials originally used for preparing press releases for the Governor's Office.

Research Materials, 1951-1955.

Fair Employment Practices Commission, 1952-1953. This file contains news releases, statements, newsletters, and reports pertaining to the Fair Employment Practice Commission, many of which demonstrate Governor Fine's commitment to end discrimination in the state's military forces and the State Police.

Lincoln's Birthday Celebrations, 1953. Includes four speeches given by Major General Edward Martin, 1942-43, and four undated speeches that appear to have been written by Governor Fine. These speeches note Lincoln's stand on freedom and slavery.

Speech Material, 1951-1952. Includes a speech delivered by Governor Fine at the Seventeenth Annual Convention of the National Negro Funeral Directors Association in Philadelphia, August 9, 1954.

Publications, 1951-1952. Includes the following items: *Broadening Our Horizons for Correctional Service*, by Dr. William H. Gray Jr., 1952; *FEPC and the Minority Machine: The Conquest of American Cities*, by Robert H. Williams, undated; *Report of the Governor's Committee on Industrial Race Relations: Employment Practices in Pennsylvania*, January 1953; *Statement of Presentation of Governor Fine of Commission's Study of Employment Practices in Pennsylvania*, by Samuel H. Daroff, n.d.; and *Survey of Discrimination: Employment Practices in Pennsylvania, November-December 1952*, February 1953.

SUBJECT FILE, 1951-1955

Advisory Boards, 1951-1953.

Capital Cases Completed, 1951-1954. Lists the races of victims and defendants in capital punishment cases. Contains revised higher court decisions giving life imprisonment to Jasper Johnson and James Harris Johnson, both African Americans.

Commendable Letters, 1951-1954. After segregation was officially abolished in Pennsylvania in 1952, John R. Dudley of Wilkes-Barre became Pennsylvania's first African American State Policeman. The file contains eighty-five letters and telegrams addressing the abolition of discrimination toward African Americans in the Pennsylvania National Guard and the Pennsylvania State Police. Representative of some of the correspondents are: Greater Philadelphia Branch, American Civil Liberties Union; NAACP Branches in Bryn Mawr and Philadelphia in Pennsylvania, as well as in Delaware and New Jersey; the Rev. Franklin L. Henley; the Fair Employment Committee; the Pennsylvania Fair Employment Practice Commission; the New York State Commission Against Discrimination; and the *Philadelphia Tribune*.

Fair Employment Practice Commission (Industrial Relations Committee), 1951-1954. Contains newsletters, reports, and correspondence dealing with the Fair Employment Practice Commission and the Industrial Relations Commission.

Invitations Accepted, 1951-1955. File Includes several letters to Governor Fine from Dr. Horace M. Bond, president of Lincoln University, and others, concerning the governor's receiving an honorary degree of doctor of law at the university's commencement exercises, June 2, 1953.

Invitations Regretted, 1951-1954. Some of the invitations declined were from: Mrs. Harriet Wright Lemon, 1950, National Freedom Day; Emanuel C. Wright, 1953, National Freedom Day; Dr. Burrell K. Johnson, 1953, National Association for the Advancement of Colored People.

National Freedom Day Association, 1953-1954. Includes correspondence to Governor Fine from Emanuel E. Wright, president of the National Freedom Day Association concerning National Freedom Day celebrations on February 1, 1952, 1953, and 1954; letters of invitation and response to and from the Honorable Homer S. Brown and Dr. Horace M. Bond, 1953; schedule of events for National Freedom Day, February 1, 1953; news releases, 1953; and proclamations for National Freedom Day for February 1, 1953 issued by Governor Fine and Philadelphia Mayor Joseph S. Clark Jr.

Scotland School Closing, 1952-1953. Contains over two hundred letters opposing proposals to close the school. The school was being reviewed as a financial burden, and serious legislative discussion centered on closing of the veterans' school. The arguments in defense of keeping the school open prevailed and it is still in operation today.

Also present are an income statement of the general fund for year ending December 31, 1951 referencing the National Association for the Advancement of Colored People; a letter dated April 4, 1952 concerning a conference at Bucknell University; and a letter dated September 3, 1952 referencing African Americans Robert J. O'Donnell and Dr. Burrell K. Johnson.

MG-207. GEORGE M. LEADER PAPERS, 1955-1959.

George Michael Leader (b.1918) served as governor of Pennsylvania from 1955 to 1959. A native of York County, before his election, Leader served as chairman of the York County Democratic Committee and as a member of the Pennsylvania Senate. The papers are divided into subject, general, legislative, appointments, releases, and miscellaneous files.

Appointments (Statutory-Live File), 1955-1959.

Cheyney State Teachers College, 1956-1957. This folder contains the following items regarding members of the board of trustees:

- Letter from Albert L. Baily Jr., West Chester, to Governor Leader stating that he would like to serve on Cheyney's board of trustees. Albert Baily's grandfather, Joshua L. Baily of Philadelphia, had been the director of the Institute for Colored Youth (the predecessor of Cheyney), an active member of the board, and had assumed the costs of building the dormitory named Baily Hall.
- Letter from William J. Green to Genevieve Blatt recommending Adolphus W. Anderson Sr. be added to Cheyney's board of trustees.
- Letter from David V. Randall to Andrew M. Bradley reminding him to send his appointment report to Cheyney.
- An up-to-date listing of the members of the board of trustees of Cheyney.
- Correspondence of the Governor's Committee on Children and Youth (letterhead includes names of its board).
- Program of the Governor's Conference on Today's Opportunities and Responsibilities, September 27, 1958.
- A listing of statewide and regional organizations represented on the Governor's Committee on Children and Youth.

Civil Rights, State Advisory Committee on, 1958. Contains letters recommending the following persons to serve on the State's Advisory Committee on Civil Rights: Andrew M. Bradley, secretary of Property and Supplies; Lewis J. Carter, ex ecutive director of the Urban League in Philadelphia; Rev. James B. Cayce, pastor of the Ebenezer Baptist Church in Philadelphia; James D. Reber, general secretary of the Pennsylvania Council of Churches; and Rev. Leon H. Sullivan, pastor of the Zion Baptist Church of Philadelphia and founder of Opportunities Industrialization Centers.

Children and Youth, Governor's Committee, 1955-1959. Includes a complimentary letter from the committee to the governor dated January 17, 1959. The letterhead letter contains the names of all the officers and members including Mrs. Homer Brown, wife of Judge Homer Brown of Allegheny County, as a delegate-at-large.

Fair Employment Practice Commission, 1955-1956. Contains letters recommending the following persons to serve on the Fair Employment Practices Commission, 1955-1956: Attorney Sadie T. M. Alexander, Philadelphia Commission on Human Relations; Thomas E. Barton; William Block, publisher of the *Pittsburgh Post-Gazette*; Dr. Richard Brown; W. Beverly Carter, publisher of the *Pittsburgh Courier*; Rev. Charles H. Foggie; Judge Charles E. Kenworthy; Robert Allen Klein; Aaron Levinson, president of Levinson Steel Company; Frederick McKee, National Casket Company; Attorney Henry R. Smith Jr.; Ewell Sykes, president of the Yellow Cab Company in Philadelphia; and Boyd L. Wilson, United Steel Workers of America.

Funeral Directors, State Board of, 1955-1957. This file has letters requesting that William F. Frederick from Braddock and Mrs. Millicent Hooper of Harrisburg be given consideration for membership on the State Board of Funeral Directors. The letters state that there should be some "colored representation" on the board. Also are letters from: the Keystone State Funeral Directors Association, signed by Leon K. Prout; the Democratic National Committee, signed by David L. Lawrence; and the Independent Funeral Directors Association, signed by Albert J. Charles.

Migratory Labor, Interdepartmental Committee on, 1958. Contains a status report on the committee's achievements and plans.

Appointments (Statutory-O.K. Files), 1954-1959.

Cheyney State Teachers College, 1956-1957. File includes letters and news releases of the newly appointed board of trustees of Cheyney University: Albert L. Baily Jr., Verona E. Beckett, James M. Brittan, Paul Comly French, William M. Maier, C. Milbourne Smith, Dr. Orville R. Walls, and Dr. Alfred H. Williams.

Fair Employment Practice Commission, 1956-1957. Includes several letters recommending the following African Americans be appointed to the Fair Employment Practice Commission: Thomas Barton, Rev. Charles H. Foggie, and Henry R. Smith. There is also a letter of recommendation for Robert A. Klein and a booklet *The Negro Market*, issued by WDAS, an African American radio station in the Philadelphia area managed by Klein.

Judges, 1955-1959. Includes letters relating to the governor's appointment of the Honorable Homer S. Brown as judge of the Court of Common Pleas of the Fifth Judicial District of Pennsylvania, Allegheny County. Included also is a biographical sketch of Brown.

***Labor Camps, Advisory Board on Revision of Regulations,
1957.*** Includes a news release issued by the governor on May
15, 1957 charging the board that "they will see to it that Pennsylvania protects the rights of the migrant farm workers," and
a letter dated February 26, 1958 to Henry R. Smith, president
of the Pittsburgh NAACP, asking for the organization's support of the activities of the Committee on Migratory Labor.

General File, 1955-1959. Arranged alphabetically by subject.

***African Methodist Episcopal Zion Church, Pittsburgh, Pa.,
1956.*** A letter of regret from the governor, April 6, 1956, declining an invitation to attend the eighty-third General Conference of the A.M.E.Z. Church, May 4, 1956, in Pittsburgh.

Raymond Pace Alexander, 1955-1958. Correspondence in-
viting the governor to attend a civic night celebration at the
Zion Baptist Church in Philadelphia; to the Philadelphia
Tribune's Charities Dinner; the wedding of Raymond
Alexander's daughter; a YMCA program in Downingtown; and
the forty-first annual testimonial dinner of the Phi Beta Sigma
Fraternity honoring Joseph S. Clark Jr. and Richardson
Dilworth. Other correspondence addresses the following sub-
jects: Educational Equality League and the problems of de-
segregation; the Supreme Court's decision on integration in
Pennsylvania; and a statement issued by the governor on a
racial incident that occurred in Levittown.

Sarah A. Anderson, 1958. Letter to the secretary to the governor of August 7, 1958, requesting financial assistance to research and study teenage delinquency and to implement possible solutions to the problem. Other correspondence deals with

deletion of racial terms on applications for state military veterans.

Armstrong Association of Philadelphia, 1957. The association was a United Way community-service agency which studied problems confronting the "Negro" community in the Delaware Valley, proposed concrete constructive action, and enlisted the support of concerned leadership. File includes a letter dated January 7, 1957 requesting the governor's presence at the fiftieth anniversary celebration, the governor's acceptance letter of January 14, 1957, and a program of the annual celebration. The program notes that Marian Anderson was honored and that Dr. Horace Mann Bond, president of Lincoln University, and Theodore W. Kheel, president of the National Urban League, were the keynote speakers.

George Washington Carver Day, January 5, 1956-1959. Includes letters dated October 13, 1955, October 1, 1956 and September 4, 1957 from Dr. Alma Johnson Illery requesting the governor proclaim George Washington Carver Day, on January 5, 1956, 1957, and 1958. There is also a letter dated December 15, 1958 from Robert D. Holiday, president of the George Washington Carver Memorial Institute, requesting the governor to proclaim January 5, 1959 as George Washington Carver Day. The letterhead contains the names of all officers and members of the institute.

Cheyney State Teachers College, 1955-1958. Includes a letter to Governor Leader from Milton M. James, chairman of Cheyney's Alumni Association dated December 20, 1958 stating that the association would be establishing an archives collection and requesting the original will of Richard Humphreys. Humphrey designated $10,000 in his will to establish a school for children of African descendants and this bequest represents the beginning of what became Cheyney University. The file also includes communications referring to a boycott in the dining hall during the fall of 1958, a faculty award service on February 15, 1957, and a January 7, 1959 letter from the governor to Cheyney President Dr. James H. Duckrey.

Citizens' Committee of Philadelphia, 1956. Requested the governor to proclaim a "Roy Campanella Day" for February 2, 1956.

T. E. Harper and L. G. Carr, 1958. Contains a letter dated June 12, 1958 to Attorney General Thomas McBride from Rev. T. E. Harper, pastor of St. Matthew A.M.E. Church and Rev. L. G. Carr, pastor of Vine Memorial Baptist Church, of Philadelphia, informing Governor Leader of an unprovoked attack on a group of African Americans at Forrest Park in Chalfont, Pennsylvania that occurred on May 30, 1958. The letter contains several signatures. Other supporting letters are included.

Citizens' Committee on Housing, 1956. Press Release No. 7792, October 5, 1956, announcing Governor Leader's appointment of the Citizens' Committee on Housing. This committee was directed to survey the state's part in promoting home construction, slum clearance, and urban redevelopment in Pennsylvania, including housing for African Americans.

Color Magazine, 1956. Letter to the governor referring to a special issue of an African American magazine entitled *Color Magazine* that would focus on the Democratic Party and "the sure way to win the Negro vote."

Committee on Discrimination in Housing, 1958. File includes a memo dated December 15, 1958 recommending legislation to terminate discrimination in housing.

Hugh Francisco, 1958. Letter to Governor Leader dated March 13, 1958 requesting that women be assigned as beauty parlor inspectors and citing an African American woman who reported illegal operations as an example of this approach.

Fraternal Order of Eagles, 1957-1958. Contains letters from November 10, 1957-September 4, 1958, addressing the "Jobs After 40" campaign created by the National Fraternal Order of Eagles to end job discrimination based on age. The letters also request Governor Leader's support of the campaign, a copy of *the Pennsylvania State Law on Age Discrimination*, and letters thanking him for his support and participation.

Lincoln University, 1955-1959. Contains undated announcement by Dr. Horace M. Bond, president of Lincoln University, to the university's board of trustees informing them of an unrestricted grant of $1,000 from the International Nickel Company. There is also a memorandum from Dr. Seiffert to the board of trustees informing them that Lincoln University has an independent charter giving the board the responsibility of selecting a president for the university. A letter also states that Governor Leader is considering recommendations to the board of trustees. Representative of some dated letters: May 29 1955, Governor Leader accepts invitation to Lincoln's commencement on June 4, 1955; January 26, 1956, invitation sent to the governor requesting him to deliver the commencement address at Lincoln University on June 4, 1956; an April 27, 1956 letter from H. F. Grim, secretary of the board of trustees stating that the General Education Board was now in a position to transfer up to $250,000 from the endowment to the building fund; a

November 6, 1958 letter to Mrs. George M. Leader from Mary M. Mackae, the wife of a board member, stating her opposition to the recent decision that Lincoln would begin admitting female students; a January 12, 1959 letter to Governor Leader declaring his nomination to the board of trustees (including a listing of all other nominated trustees); a recommendation for appointment of a Dr. Brice as president of Lincoln University; President Nkrumah's visit to Lincoln: governor's meeting the Lincoln School of Chester while at the State Capitol, May 26, 1955.

National Achievement Clubs, Inc., 1958. Letter dated March 26, 1958 from Dr. Alma Johnson Illery, founder of the National Achievement Clubs, Inc., requesting state funds to assist in maintaining summer camps sponsored by the Philadelphia branch. The letterhead contains the names of the members and officers of the Philadelphia branch.

National Dental Association, 1958. The National Dental Association was an organization founded by African Americans in 1913. The file contains letters dated July through September 1958, and a program brochure referring to the August 1958 association meeting held in Pittsburgh, Pennsylvania. Also included are letters from and to the following: Governor Leader; Mrs. R. Q. (Ethyl Horton) Venson, president of the association's ladies auxiliary; and Mrs. S. P. Harris, public relations director of the auxiliary. The letterheads contain the names of all the organization's officers.

National Freedom Day, 1955-1958. Correspondence and proclamations in this file refer to National Freedom Day observances, February 1, 1955-58. Former President Harry S. Truman signed the National Freedom Day Bill on June 30, 1948, which reads as follows: "RESOLVED that the President of the United States is authorized to issue a proclamation designating the first day of February of each year as National Freedom Day for the purpose of commemorating the signing by President Abraham Lincoln on February 1, 1865, of the joint resolution adopted by the Senate and the House of Representatives of the United States of America." Under Pennsylvania's senate concurrent resolution approved February 6, 1945, the governor issued a proclamation for the observance of National Freedom Day on February 1st of each year in Pennsylvania.

Negro Alliance of America, Inc., 1957. Contains an invitation asking Governor Leader to address the National Interracial Mass Meeting of the alliance held in Chicago on August 6-9, 1957. The governor sent his regrets stating he would be unable to attend the meeting.

Negro Democratic Association, 1955. James G. McKee, president of the association, wrote to the governor on August 10, 1955, and to the commissioner on August 23, 1955, in support of complaints made by Rev. Peter Foster regarding racial abuse from his neighbor, Arthur L. Stern. Included is other correspondence giving accounts of the incidents.

Negro, Miscellaneous, 1955-1958. Correspondence includes a letter dated March 2, 1955 from Earl Chud concerned with the employment of African Americans as toll collectors at the Delaware River Bridge; a December 14, 1955 letter with accompanying photographs of African American toll collectors on the Pennsylvania Turnpike; a 1956-57 annual report of the National Scholarship Service and Fund for Negro Students; an August 20, 1957 letter from John E. Whitted stating his personal views on civil rights; an April 22, 1958 letter to Governor Leader requesting assistance in eliminating discrimination in prom dances at Steelton High School; a November 3, 1958 letter from James Itchko regarding an incident of refusal to serve African Americans in a restaurant; a November 17, 1958 letter from Walter M. Petty discussing employment of African Americans by the Pennsylvania Game Commission, Pennsylvania Fish Commission, and the Pennsylvania Department of Forests and Waters. Also included is a copy of a magazine entitled *The Negro in Civil Service* that was published by Color, Inc.

New England Baptist Missionary Convention, 1958. Includes letters referencing the eighty-fourth annual convention in Boston, Massachusetts during June 10-13, 1958. Letter of May 28, 1958, from Rev. William J. Shaw, pastor of the White Rock Baptist Church, Philadelphia, requests Governor Leader to prepare a letter to the 1958 convention in Boston, extending an invitation to the convention to hold the 1959 New England Baptist Missionary Convention in Philadelphia. Also includes a letter from Governor Leader expressing his regret in not being able to attend the 1958 convention.

Pennsylvania Equal Rights Council, 1958. File contains a letter stating that Andrew Bradley would represent Governor Leader at a meeting of the Pennsylvania Equal Rights Council held at the Harrisburg YWCA on February 4, 1958. The purpose of the meeting was to discuss the creation of a state study commission on discrimination in housing.

Pennsylvania Railroad Company, 1957-1958. This file contains a May 3, 1957 letter addressing a decision in the case of the *Pennsylvania Railroad Company vs. Individuals* (Brotherhood of Railroad Trainmen) and a letter dated May 2, 1958 referencing racial notations on Pennsylvania Railroad passes.

Pennsylvania Turnpike Commission, 1955. Contains a newspaper release announcing the appointment of the first three African Americans to serve as Pennsylvania Turnpike toll collectors: Albert Tucker, Dawson Gant, and Horace Whalen.

Walter M. Pettey, 1956, 1958. Includes letters of March 31, 1956 and October 15, 1958, from Walter M. Petty to Governor Leader stating that no African Americans are employed by the Pennsylvania Game Commission, Pennsylvania Fish Commission, or the Pennsylvania Department of Forest and Waters. A letter of April 21, 1956 to Pettey from the governor provides pertinent information from the heads of the three agencies regarding the status of African American employment in their respective agencies.

Pittsburgh Courier, 1956. File contains correspondence between Governor Leader and Mrs. Jessie M. (Robert L.) Vann, president and treasurer of the *Pittsburgh Courier*, referencing the creation of the new African nation of Ghana. In addition Budget Director Andrew M. Bradley sent letters to the *Pittsburgh Courier*, *Philadelphia Afro-American*, *Philadelphia Independent*, and the *Philadelphia Tribune* containing a statement by the governor with reference to Ghana.

Press Releases and Membership Card Indexes, 1955-1959. The following citations are taken from index cards giving press release information on appointments, organizational memberships, numbering of press releases, proclamations, speeches and statements representing the African American presence during Leader's governorship.

- **Appointments, 1955-1957.** Arranged chronologically. #270, 7/18/57: Andrew Bradley, secretary of Property and Supplies.
- **Organizations-Governor Membership, 1955-1958.** Arranged alphabetically. Amen Corner, January 1, 1955; Hampton Institute, October 24, 1957, a member of the board of trustees and a Life Member of the Alumni Association; Lincoln University, June 4, 1957, an honorary member of the board of trustees.
- **Press Releases, 1955-1959.** Arranged chronologically and numerically. Represents all news releases cited in this manuscript group.
- **Proclamations, 1955-1959.** Arranged chronologically. Representative press releases concerning proclamations relating to African Americans are as follows: press release #836, 12/2/56, George Washington Carver Day, January 5, 1957; press release A58, 4/10/57, Afro-American Day, April 14, 1957; press release A296, 8/28/57, Red Cap Month, September 1957; press release A501, 1/22/58, Freedom Day, February 1958.
- **Speeches, 1954-1959.** Representative press releases concerning speeches relative to African Americans are: press release #565, 3/28/56, on the dedication of Mercy-Douglass Hospital, Philadelphia; speech at the Democratic State Committee, "Civil Rights and the Campaign," at Convention Hall, Philadelphia; 6/6/58; speech at banquet honoring Andrew M. Bradley, given by Masons at Mechanicsburg.
- **Statements, 1955-1959.** A sample of press releases in this sub-series relating to African Americans are: press release #560, 3/28/56, regarding Booker T. Washington and the postage stamp honoring him; press release A58, 4/10/57, Afro-American Day, April 14, 1957; press release A969,

370

1/16/59, Report by Public Instruction on Racial Integration in the Public Schools.

Subject File, 1955-1959.

Biographies. Includes a biographical sketch of Homer S. Brown who was appointed judge of the Court of Common Pleas for Allegheny County on May 16, 1956.

Boxing Investigation, 1955-1956. Includes letters, press releases, adjudication papers and orders issued by the State Athletic Commission, with regard to the suspension or relocation of the boxing license of Harold Johnson due to suspected betting. Johnson was represented by Raymond Pace Alexander and G. Wesley Allen of the Philadelphia Bar. Also found is information on a private hearing regarding the illness of Frederick Terry, a Philadelphia boxer.

Camps for Underprivileged Boys, 1957-1958. On October 8, 1957 Governor Leader appointed a five-member committee to formalize a plan whereby Pennsylvania inactive military installations could be used as summer recreational centers for teenage boys. A letter dated October 27, 1957 from Rev. William L. Brown, pastor of Bible Way Church, Harrisburg, inquired concerning the possible state assistance to provide wholesome recreation for young boys at some of the inactive military installations.

Capital Cases, 1951-1956. Cited here is information taken from dated capital case criminal information sheets concerning criminals identified as "colored." The following African Americans were charged with committing murder on the following dates: William Durant Cole, Pittsburgh, May 29, 1954;

Theodore Elliott, Philadelphia, December 30, 1949; Alphonso La Rue, Philadelphia, July 30, 1952; William Maxwell, Philadelphia, February 27, 1954; Benjamin Robinson, Chester, May 5, 1954; and Elijah Thompson Jr., Aliquippa, October 25, 1954.

Fair Employment Practice Commission, 1955-1958. The Pennsylvania Fair Employment Practices Act established and declared that "there shall be no discrimination in employment because of race, color, religious creed, ancestry, age or national origin." The act further provided for a nine member commission appointed by the governor and approved by two-thirds of the senate, to administer the law. The following agencies and people are represented in correspondence, articles, and brochures included in this file: *ABC's of the Commission*, Albert Simmons, Allegheny County Council on Civil Rights; *Appraisal Inventory of Pennsylvania FEPC Goals and Accomplishments for the First Fiscal Year of Operation ending June 1, 1957*; Central Democratic Club; *Fair Employment; Employment Practices in Pennsylvania*; Human Relations Council of Bucks County; Pennsylvania Railroad Company; *People's National Gas Company vs. Earl E. Palmer*; *Pittsburgh Press*; Jack Reynolds; Rhode Island Commission Against Discrimination; State Convention of Pennsylvania FEPC; Third Annual Report on Governmental Contracts; Transport Workers Union; United Auto Workers of Pennsylvania; Virginia State College; and *You and Civil Rights in Pennsylvania*.

Invitations, Accepted (Governor), 1955-1958. This file includes the following letters of acceptance:

• **Interdependence Council.** This council sponsored a "Declaration of the Interdependence" at Independence Hall on January 18, 1956. The file contains copies of letters of invitation to the governor, and the governor's remarks. Noted on the letterhead as a member of the executive committee is Dr. Leslie Pinckney Hill, a president emeritus of Cheyney State Teachers College. Dr. Hill wrote an "interdependence hymn" for the event and delivered dedication remarks.

- **Mercy-Douglass Hospital, 1956.** Includes a letter dated February 24, 1956 to Governor Leader from Secretary of Welfare Harry Shapiro announcing the opening of the 110 bed psychiatric unit at the hospital and inviting Shapiro to be present. Also present is a letter of regret dated March 7, 1956 from the governor declining an invitation to March 18 opening ceremony, a letter dated March 20, 1956 from board of directors President Herbert E. Millen inviting the governor to speak at the hospital dedication on March 28, 1956, and a copy of the "Remarks of Welfare Secretary Harry Shapiro," March 28, 1956.

- **National Association for the Advancement of Colored People, 1958.** *Pennsylvania Institute of Certified Public Accountants, 1957.* A seating list for the sixtieth anniversary banquet includes the following African Americans: the Honorable Andrew M. Bradley, secretary of Property and Supplies; Matt S. Anderson, representative, Allegheny County, 1st District; Samuel Floyd, representative, Philadelphia, 6th District; Susie Monroe, representative, Philadelphia, 11th District; and Jesse J. Shields, representative, Philadelphia, 10th District.

- **Scotland School for Veterans Children, 1958.** Includes letters inviting Governor Leader to be the commencement speaker on Saturday, May 31, 1958 and a commencement program. Other correspondence gives historical and statistical information. A letter to Superintendent Dr. Willard M. Stevens from the Governor's Office reveals the school's budget appropriation for 1951-1953 and 1953-1955.

- **State Council for a Pennsylvania FEPC (Fair Employment Practices Commission) 1955.** A letter dated May 13, 1955 provides information about the conference. Both letter and the conference program contain a listing of affiliated organizations, to include the National Association for the Advancement of Colored People and the Urban League.

Invitations, Regretted (Governor), 1955-1958. The following are organizations who invited Governor Leader to speak or attend various meetings and occasions and received letters of regret: First African Presbyterian Church, Philadelphia; National Association for the Advancement of Colored People, from the following Branches-Dauphin County, Philadelphia, and York; National Negro Newspaper Publishers; Negro Alliance of America, Inc.; New England Baptist Missionary Convention; Philadelphia Federation of Negro Women's' Clubs; and the *Philadelphia Tribune* Charities. Several of the letters include a list of the names of officers.

Job Files Correspondence, 1957-1958.

- **Federal State Action Committee, 1957-1958.** File contains five folders of correspondence between Governor Leader, the Governor's Secretary David V. Randall, Secretary of Labor and Industry William L. Batt Jr., Secretary of Agriculture William L. Henning, and other state department heads as well as Meyer Kastenbaum, special assistant to the president, concerning the interstate living and working conditions of migratory workers. As a result of a Conference of Atlantic Seaboard States which looked into the problems of migratory farm labor, certain congressional and state legislation was recommended to correct some of the inequities confronting migratory farm workers. The conference was hosted by Pennsylvania, November 21-22, 1957.

- **Juvenile Delinquency Correspondence, 1956-1957.** Contains correspondence, news releases, and other material relating to youth programs such as the Youth Forestry Camps.
- **Laurelton State Village Investigation, 1955.** Contains seven volumes of miscellaneous hearings and several letters giving the background of abusive treatment to the female patients there. One letter to Governor Leader dated February 19, 1955 describes abusive treatment of an African American girl.
- **Levittown State Police Action, Correspondence, A-Z, 1957.** Consists of two large folders with over two hundred pieces of correspondence addressing positive and negative reactions to Daisy and William Myers, an African American couple who moved into Levittown, a totally white community.

Mercy-Douglass Hospital of Philadelphia, 1955-1957. This file contains several letters and articles addressing the financial needs of Philadelphia's Mercy-Douglass Hospital. The hospital was created in 1948 from the merger of two formerly African American hospitals, Mercy Hospital and the Douglass Hospital. The hospital was remodeled and reopened as a new mental health facility. The governor's dedication remarks on March 28, 1956 are included. In 1957 several people wrote the governor requesting financial support for the hospital that resulted in provisional funding.

National Conference for Human Rights, 1958. This conference was sponsored by Governor Leader and David J. McDonald, president of the United Steelworkers of America, in Philadelphia. The premiere showing of the film *Burden of Truth* opened the conference. Produced as a project of the United Steelworkers of America Committee on Civil Rights, it graphically depicted the tragic effects of discrimination against "Negroes." Included in this file are programs and photographs of the following African American cast members: Hari Rhodes, Shirley Shawn, and Robert de Coy.

Segregation and Integration, 1955-1959.

- **Educational Equality League, 1955-1959.** This file contains over eighty pieces of correspondence, newsletters and other printed material. Some of the correspondence is from or to Charles H. Boehm, director of public instruction; Floyd L. Logan; Otis B. Morse; David V. Randall, secretary to the governor; Sarah Anderson; Harry E. Seyler, senator; Herbert B. Cohen, attorney general; and others.
- **General Correspondence, 1955-1959.** This file consists of seven folders totaling over three hundred pieces of correspondence representing views for and against racial integration. Many letters opposed to integration came from the South. Some of the following African Americans are represented in this file: Raymond Pace Alexander and Sarah A. Anderson; Thomas J. Anderson, president of the Coatesville NAACP; Rev. H. B. Barkley, pastor Bethel A.M.E. Church, Harrisburg; Mr. Julius Foster, Prince Hall Grand Lodge F. and A.M. of New Jersey; Charles A. Shorter, executive director, Philadelphia; Henry R. Smith, NAACP of Pittsburgh; Rose Denny, S.E. District of the Pennsylvania State Federation of Negro Women's Clubs, West Chester; Bernard Scott and Raymond Hopson, Centre Avenue YMCA, Pittsburgh; Dr. Lancelot Tynes, president, Cheyney Alumni Association; Thomas McBride, attorney general. Representative of some of the pamphlets found in the file

are: *Bible Passages Support Segregation*, T. V. Huggins; *A Christian View on Segregation*, by Rev. G. T. Gillespie; *Integration-Is It Right or Wrong?* by Robert Dane Cook; *Jesus: Master Segregationist*, by Lawrence W. Neff; *Non-Segregation for Education in the South*, by Walter Scott McNutt; *Integration-Is It Right or Wrong?* by Robert Dane Cook; *Segregation and Integration*, by Georgia Hodges; *Segregation Is Constitutional But Compulsory Integration Is Unconstitutional*, by W. Eason; *Thou Shalt Not Bear False Witness*, by the NAACP; and many others.

MG-208. WILLIAM W. SCRANTON PAPERS, 1963-1967.

William Warren Scranton (b.1917) was governor of Pennsylvania from 1963 to 1967. Prior to that, he was special assistant to the United States secretary of state, and was elected a member of the Eighty-seventh Congress from the 10th Congressional District of Pennsylvania in 1960. Scranton was also an unsuccessful candidate for president of the United States in 1964. The papers are arranged in the following series: General File, 1963-1966; Subject File, 1963-1967; Legislative File, 1963-1966; Boards and Commissions File, 1963-1966 (appointments: letters of application and recommendations); Releases, 1962-1967; End of Administration File, 1967; James Reichley, legislative secretary, 1962-1966; William D. Johnson, executive assistant, 1963-1966; William G. Murphy, Secretary, 1963-1967; Jack L. Conmy, press secretary, 1963-1966; Robert C. McCormick, public information specialist, 1963-1966. Within each series, folders are arranged alphabetically by subjects or names of persons or organizations. Within each folder, papers are arranged chronologically. The following series contains information on African Americans.

General File, 1963-1966. This series contains information on the following topics:

African Descendants Pioneering Association. Advocated the return of Americans of African descent to Africa.

African Students. Studying at Penn State University.

Afro-American Advancement Association for Human Dignity. Correspondence about discrimination and related subjects.

Edward W. Brooke (then attorney general of Massachusetts). Correspondence to and from Governor Scranton with reference to Brooke's senatorial campaign and preparation of a position paper on "Creative Federalism."

Cheyney State College, 1963-1966. Letters relating to appointment of a new president during 1965, the appointment of Hobson R. Reynolds as a board member in 1963, construction of new athletic field and physical education plant in 1964, installation of directional highway signs in 1964, a pay freeze and salary increments during 1963, invitations sent to the governor during 1963-66, negative *Philadelphia Inquirer* articles about Cheyney during fall 1964.

Civil Rights, 1963-1966. Materials on Pennsylvania's Civil Rights Act and the Civil Rights Task Force, discrimination, Civil Rights Day, and speeches delivered by Scranton on these subjects.

Human Relations. Materials concerning the Human Relations Commission and Human Relations Week.

Dr. Alma Johnson Illery. Letters reference the annual celebration of National George Washington Carter Day and activities of the National Achievement Clubs.

Institute on Local Government Responsibility in Racial and Community Tension. Information on "Brotherhood Week" related conferences.

Lincoln University. Correspondence and material relating to the university's budget, the dedication of new buildings, commencements, and the Founder's Day ceremony during which Scranton received an honorary doctorate of civil law degree.

Migratory Labor Program. Annual reports for 1964 and 1965 and accompanying letters and information on Family Day Care for Migrant Children, Head Start programs, and Neighborhood Youth Corps, 1965-66.

National Association for the Advancement of Colored People, 1963-1966. Complaints of excessive violence towards African Americans by the Pennsylvania State Police, discrimination in housing and against nursing home employees, discrimination in housing, the lack of representation in the military, invitations to NAACP dinners, the integration of Girard College, the NAACP National Convention, Emancipation Proclamation Day, and the NAACP Rules for Public Demonstration.

"Negroes." Materials relating to efforts by the National Negro Century of Progress Committee to create special fifty cent pieces commemorating the progress of the American Negro, references to the *Negro in America* television series, a book entitled *the Negro American*, the Association for the Study of

Negro Life and History, an exhibition of contemporary Negro art, the Negro Educational Emergency Drive, the Conference on Negro Employment, Negro History Week, a list of Pennsylvania newspapers, political activities, the Negro Republican Assembly and Republican State Council, the Negro Women's Community League, African American attitudes toward Governor Scranton's administration, and general research on Blacks in Pennsylvania divided under the headings doctors, teachers, veterans, and voters.

Opportunities Industrialization Centers (OIC). Over twenty letters referencing Governor Scranton's designation of the months of April and May 1966 as OIC Months in Pennsylvania. Contains letters to Governor Scranton from Rev. Leon H. Sullivan, founder and president of OIC, invitation letters to the governor from OIC to attend dedication ceremonies for two new Philadelphia OIC centers in May and November 1965, a letter from William J. Devlin, president of the Republican Central Campaign Committee, giving the governor "a complete background of Rev. Sullivan's tremendous work in developing the Opportunity Industrialization Center," April 1965, a letter concerning a complaint of state non-support of OIC, a letter from the Department of Commerce documenting state support, and letter of congratulations from the governor to Dr. Sullivan on receiving the Philadelphia Award.

Philadelphia Tribune, 1963-1966. Subscription statement to the governor's office, letter to the governor requesting him to serve as honorary chairman for the twelfth annual Philadelphia Tribune Charities, Inc. Dinner on May 7, 1964, a letter from the governor accepting the chairmanship, a printed program of the twelfth annual dinner that is illustrated with photographs of those receiving awards: Mr. Roy Campanella, Attorney William T. Coleman, and Mrs. Albert M. Greenfield (awards were presented by Honorable William H. Hastie, Mr. Joe Black, Mr. E. Washington Rhodes and address was given by Honorable A. Leon Higginbotham), a program listing all members of the dinner committees, a letter of invitation to attend the dedication of a new building on September 13, 1964, a request to the governor to contribute to the *Tribune*'s special edition tribute to organized labor, an invitation to the governor to be speaker at the Philadelphia Tribune Charities fourteenth annual dinner on April 28, 1966, and a copy of Governor Scranton's address given at this dinner.

Urban Leagues of Lancaster County and of Philadelphia. Letter from the executive director of Lancaster's Urban League, Edward W. Allen, asking Governor Scranton to use his power to prevent the KKK from "becoming entrenched in Lancaster County and in Pennsylvania" and letters from the executive director of Philadelphia's Urban League thanking the governor for appointing an African American to the Philadelphia office of the Bureau of Employment Security and for his support of public assistance and a year-end report for 1964.

Young Men's Christian Association. Information regarding Harrisburg's Forster Street YMCA and a congratulatory greeting to the YMCA in recognition of the dedication of the new Camp Curtin YMCA building at Sixth and Woodbine Streets, Harrisburg October 2, 1966.

Subject File, 1963-1967. The following subjects relevant to African Americans are documented:

Economic Opportunity Act of 1964. Information on programs that resulted from legislation such as the Anti-Poverty Program, 1964; Community Action Program (CAP), 1966; Neighborhood Youth Corps, 1965-66; and Project Head Start.

Human Relations Commission, 1963-1967. Press releases, civil rights bills, investigations into racial conflict in Chester, annual reports, propaganda and newsletters, the integration of Girard College, newsletters of Harrisburg's Human Relations Council, a formal statement by Scranton on the situation in Selma, Alabama, sessions of "Government Responsibility in Racial and Community Tension," letters concerning a bi-racial tutorial project in Philadelphia, information about rioting in Folcroft, Pennsylvania, essays against civil rights by the "Rhyming Martian," and references to the Philadelphia riots of 1964.

Boards and Commission and Files-Appointments, 1963-1966.

Letters of Application and Recommendation (OK), 1963-1966. This file contains correspondence and news releases concerning applicants nominated or rejected to serve on boards of the following: Cheyney State Teachers College, 1963-66; the Human Relations Commission, 1963-66; Governor's Committee on Migratory Labor, 1963-64; and Scotland School for Veterans Children, 1963 and 1965.

James Reichley, Legislative Secretary, 1962-1966.

Departmental Legislation, 1964-1965. Included is a folder on Civil Rights, 1964-1965, with information on anti-discrimination legislation in twenty-two states and legislative proposals to amend Pennsylvania's Human Relations Act.

Subject File, 1962-1966. Under the subject "Negroes, 1962," there is information on the sixth annual report on the Pennsylvania Human Relations Commission; the *Negro Press Digest* (June 23-July 28, 1962); Scranton's statement on "Campaigning and Better Understanding the Needs of Minorities, Especially Negroes"; and Scranton's statement before the Republican Party Platform Committee concerning his stand on the civil rights issue.

William D. Johnson, Assistant Secretary to the Governor.

Letters of Application and Recommendation, 1963-1966. Included is correspondence relating to applicants to serve on boards of the following: Commission on Racial Demonstration of Chester, 1964; Cheyney State College, 1963, 1964; Human Relations Commission, 1963-65; Lincoln University, 1963-1966, with information on gubernatorial scholarships to the university, and a university publication dealing with civil rights; Governor's Committee on Migratory Labor, 1965; and Scotland School for Veterans Children, 1963-66.

Jack L. Conmy, Press Secretary, Governor's Office, 1963-1966.

Category File, 1963-1966. This file contains information on the following topics: Civil Rights, 1963-1966, news releases and articles concerning demonstrations, segregation and integration, interviews with Scranton, and a Chronology of Civil Rights in Pennsylvania; Girard College, 1965, news editorials and articles dealing with integration efforts and information on court proceedings; copies of several newspaper articles concerning "Human Relations," 1966; and "Racial," 1963-1966, with news releases, articles, and editorials dealing with discrimination in housing, racism in politics, segregation/integration, riots in Chester and Folcroft, Pennsylvania, and the situation in Selma, Alabama, the NAACP, rallies and demonstrations, etc.

Robert C. McCormick, Public Information Specialist, 1963-1966.

General File, 1963-1996. Includes information on the following subjects: Anti-poverty, 1965, a press release announcing the governor's approval of an anti-poverty program for Chester and the Summary of the Proposed Greater Chester Movement Title II Program; a folder labeled "Child Welfare Services, 1966," a press release announcing funding for state Child Welfare Services; a folder labeled "Public Welfare, 1964-65," a press release announcing the allocation of funds to subsidize juvenile probation services, police service to youth, medical assistance for the elderly, and child welfare programs; a folder labeled "Student Loans, 1964", and copy of a "Status Plan for Guaranty Loan Plan for 1964" that contains a chart showing Cheyney University receiving $25,503 in student loan money for forty-one students and Lincoln University receiving $2,000 for two students.

MG-209. RAYMOND P. SHAFER PAPERS, 1967-1971.

Raymond Philip Shafer (b.1917) was Republican governor of Pennsylvania from 1967-1971 and lieutenant governor under his predecessor, William Scranton, 1963-1967. Twice elected president of the Crawford County Bar Association, Shafer also served two terms as district attorney of Crawford County and was elected to the Pennsylvania State Senate in 1958. The papers are arranged in the following series: General File, 1967-1970; Subject File, 1966-1971; Press Conference and Audio Tape Recordings, 1967-1970; Boards and Commissions File, 1965-1971; Press Releases, 1965-1970; Legislative File, 1967-1968; Press Room File, 1968-1971; News Clippings, 1967-1970; and Scholarship File, 1967-1970. Within each series, files are arranged alphabetically by subjects or names of persons or organizations. Within each file, papers are arranged chronologically. The following series includes information on African Americans.

General File, 1967-1970. Contains information on the following topics:

Sarah Anderson. Letter concerning the proclamation of Negro History Week.

Cheyney State College, 1967-1970. Over 140 documents including a "Report of Audit of Cheyney State College" prepared by the state's secretary of administration and the budget secretary of Cheyney's Student Government Cooperative Association on June 1968, Governor's Shafer's announcement of the election of Dr. Wade Wilson as president of Cheyney, letters inquiring about student unrest that occurred during the fall 1968 semester, and letters concerned with enlarging the college's dining room and constructing an industrial arts building.

Congress of Racial Equality (CORE). This file deals with unfair employment practices in the Delaware River Port Authority and contains a news release on Governor Shafer's address at the annual convention of the Improved Benevolent Protective Order of Elks of the World on August 26, 1970, where Shafer called for the cooperation of all citizens "including responsible leaders of the Black Community in continuing efforts to bring the Negro into the mainstream of American life."

Foundation for Freedom and Democracy in Community Life. The foundation's resolution in support of Freedom of Residence Program, proclamations for Freedom of Residence Days for Connecticut, Rhode Island, Vermont, and Pennsylvania that were issued during the last week in March 1967, and a brochure for the Second International Conference on Freedom of Residence held in Milwaukee during March and April 1967 which carried the theme "The Pursuit of House and Happiness."

Greater Philadelphia Chamber of Commerce. News, June 1, 1967, features the following articles concerning African Americans: "Over 1,000 Pay Tribute to Reverend Sullivan," "National Figures Laud Selection of Reverend Sullivan" (as the Chamber's eighteenth William Penn Award winner), "Help Find Ways for Negroes to Enjoy Economic Benefits . . . ," "Equal Employment Seminar to Meet June 8 at Sheraton," and "Meet the Press" featuring Reverend Sullivan among others.

Harrisburg, Pa. Announcement of the appearance of John Howard Griffin, author of *Black Like Me*, at the Forum Building in Harrisburg and correspondence regarding mistreatment of daughters of African Americans by militants at Camp Curtin Junior High School and racial imbalance existing in the Harrisburg School District.

National Assembly on Progress in Equality of Opportunity in Housing. Assembly's brochure dated March 18-20, 1965 featuring forty-five names as well as photographs of panelists, resource leaders, and participants, at least twenty of whom were African Americans. Also present is an invitation from A. Leon Higginbotham Jr. to attend a convention of the American Foundation for Negro Affairs.

Human Relations Commission, 1967-1970. News releases and records of commission appointments and resignations.

Martin Luther King Jr. Approximately ninety items including booklets, brochures, correspondence, cross-reference sheets, news releases, pamphlets, and telegrams covering such varied subjects of King's funeral, the creation of Martin Luther King Jr. Day as a state holiday, celebrations connected with the Martin Luther King Jr. holiday, appellations of King's name to various buildings and streets, and the text of Governor Shafer's Martin Luther King Jr. Proclamation of April 8, 1958.

Lincoln University File, 1966-1968. A list of new faculty and staff, invitations to dinners, and Shafer's speech at the 1968 commencement exercises.

Mercy Hospital. Bulletins dated March and May 1967 provide information on improvements made to the hospital and its services.

Montgomery County Negro Republican Council Newsletter, 1968. Features William D. C. Dennis of Willow Grove who was chosen by Governor Shafer as his special assistant during the 1968 gubernatorial campaign.

National Association for the Advancement of Colored People, 1966-1970. This file contains over a hundred pieces of correspondence including a letter dated October 1, 1970 to Governor Shafer from Barton A. Fields, president of the Harrisburg NAACP, requesting employment and training information on African Americans employed by the Commonwealth. This data was to be used to prepare for the thirty-sixth Annual NAACP Conference held in Pennsylvania during October 1970. Also contains a letter dated October 1, 1970 concerning an investigation into charges that the Juvenile Division of the Erie Police Department engaged in conduct detrimental to juveniles. A letter dated July 11, 1967 to Roy Wilkins, executive director of the NAACP, from William J. Hart, secretary of Labor and Industry, delineates the "equal opportunity policy" then practiced in Pennsylvania in awarding state contracts and was written in response to an earlier letter Wilkins wrote to Governor Shafer requesting him to withhold contracts for state construction until "Negroes" were given an opportunity for employment. Other letters in this file relate to migrant farm labor practices and include a letter reporting that Marcella Hilbert was charged with not having a license to operate a farm labor camp in Berks County and a letter drawing attention to the small numbers of African Americans enlisted in the National Guard or employed by the State Police and by the Commonwealth. Finally there are invitations for the governor to attend various NAACP heritage and achievement programs and a copy of the publication, *Honor Guard*, which lists the names of life-members of the NAACP.

"Negro," 1967-1970. Information on African American State Police officers and officers in the armed services; an article entitled "The Negro Trouble in America," information on the American Foundation for Negro Affairs, materials on a Negro Public Officials Conference, materials on Negro History Week, materials on the Association for the Study of Negro Life and History, reports on African American voter registration, and the number of African Americans employed by the Commonwealth, items relating to the Negro Republican State Council, and proposals, newsletters, voting information, and opinions on Shafer's budget and tax proposals.

Opportunities Industrialization Center (OIC). The quarterly progress report of the OIC of Dauphin County for August-October 1967, a letter dated August 1, 1968 stating "OIC of Dauphin County has met all the criteria for approval for veterans education under the provisions of Title 38, U.S. code, Section 1776," and letters requesting proclamation of April as OIC month in 1969 and 1970. Also present are invitations to the governor to attend OIC banquets and dedication ceremonies in Philadelphia, Erie, and Harrisburg, as well as a May 1969 issue of the *Harrisburg OIC News*, which includes OIC news of the Carlisle OIC Center that contains an article on Mildred B. Jones, who was trained in Carlisle's first keypunch class, in the February issue and pictures of Rev. W. W. Bowden, Mildred Neal, and Toby Young from Harrisburg. Finally, there is a letter dated May 22, 1969 signed by F. L. Henley giving statistics on enrollment, graduations and employment, and several letters dated November-December 1970 opposing the closing of the Ramos Antonini Center in Philadelphia.

Pennsylvania Council of Churches. "Religious Affiliation of Elected State Officials Commonwealth of Pennsylvania," a list including Herbert Arlene, an African American senator from Philadelphia, and Robert N. C. Nix Sr., an African American congressman from Philadelphia.

Pennsylvania State Police. *State Police Demonstrations Incidents, 1967-70*, which reports on various public demonstrations to which the State Police responded.

The Philadelphia Police. A publication by Peter H. Binzen, featuring an article entitled "Ghetto Negroes Fear Bluecoats as Their Army of Occupation."

Philadelphia School District. The board of education sent a letter addressed to "Friend of Public Education" dated May 9, 1968. Also present is an article entitled "Salute to Schools" which appeared the *Philadelphia Sunday Bulletin,* April 21, 1968 and which recognized the one hundred fiftieth anniversary of public education in Philadelphia.

Subject File, 1966-1971. Contains information on the following subjects:

Governor's Conference on Minority Employment, 1967. News releases, annual reports, pamphlets, newsletters, books, texts of speeches, and correspondence relating to segregation in education and housing, discrimination in the workplace and in admission to cemeteries; a survey of non-white employment in state government; materials on the American Foundation for Negro Affairs; materials on the Governor's Code of Fair Practices; investigative reports and recommendations for reducing racial tension; copies of civil rights and affirmative action legislation; and materials relating to implementing affirmative action procedures at Girard College, the Governor's Conference on Minority Employment and Human Relations, the Poor People's Campaign, and the United States Commission on Civil Rights.

Housing, 1967-1970. A large file of statements and news releases by Governor Shafer's office relating to educational opportunities and housing and job discrimination. From July 27, 1967 to November 10. 1967, Governor Shafer's new Housing Task Force was charged with making it possible for every family in Pennsylvania to have an adequate and decent home regardless of its economic status.

Human Relations Commission, 1966-1971. Correspondence, news releases, and telegrams expressing concern with developing implementation legislation for the Civil Rights Act of 1968, program information on the Governor's Conference to Examine the Effects of Prejudice in State Government held on September 11-13, 1968, and other governor's conferences addressing racial equality. Also present are several letters dated from 1966 through 1968 that discuss the will of Stephen Girard, which had limited admission to Girard College to "white orphan boys."

Racial Imbalance in Education, 1967-1970. News releases and correspondence dealing with desegregation efforts by state colleges and resistance to integrating elementary schools through bussing.

Rioting, undated. A large file containing reports, correspondence, and newsletters dealing with race riots and the fear of race riots, the role of local police, State Police, and the National Guard during such riots, public reaction to race riots (specifically white concern over black militancy, anarchy and communism, and black concern over oppression, racism, and social injustices), and contingency plans for possible riots. There are materials specifically concerned with committees on civil disorder, NAACP concerns over use of chemical mace in riots, the National Association for the Advancement of White People which opposed civil rights legislation, and efforts by the African American community to end discrimination in employment, schools, and housing.

Boards and Commissions File, 1965-1971. Contains three files for the Human Relations Commission. One of these is dated 1963-69 and contains a survey of non-white employees in state government, annual reports, newsletters, progress reports, and correspondence dealing with discrimination, reorganization of the commission, desegregation of racially unbalanced schools, and picketing at Girard College. Two files covering the period 1967-70 contain correspondence and newsletters providing information on recommendations and appointments to the commission as well as actions taken by the commission.

Press Room File, 1968-1971. Includes news releases concerning civil rights legislation.

News Clippings of Bette Little, 1967-1970. Contains newspaper articles concerning civil rights legislation, Stephen Girard's will, the Human Relations Commission, the Negro Employment Conference, and various race riots.

Scholarship File, 1967-1970. Included are requests and awards of scholarships at Lincoln University.

MG-214. WARREN J. HARDER COLLECTION, [CA. 1828-1968].

Warren John Harder (1905-1968), a lifelong resident of Harrisburg, was a news correspondent, commercial photographer, and amateur local historian. His collection includes correspondence, notes, newspaper clippings, photographs, and lantern slides. Among the items found in the series labeled **Various Negatives** and the sub-series labeled *Civil War* are photographic negatives which depict scenes from the antebellum era. These include scenes labeled "Slave Auction Room," "'Contraband' (African Americans) Coming North for Protection of Union Lines," "Capture of Slave Ship by British War Vessels, 1860," "'Sunny North,' 702 Negroes Aboard," and "Congress Passes Resolution to Abolish Slavery." Among the series labeled **Lantern Slides** are a group of lantern slides labeled "Southern Scenes" that were taken around the turn of the century in the deep South. Other pertinent slides are a scene of a slave ship at Mozambique Channel, Africa, and of a slave auction.

A number of photographs in the series **Subject File** document Harrisburg's African American community and city life in general throughout the twentieth century. Of particular interest are Friendship Fire House (1905), Second Baptist Church (1922), Matthew Wilson's hotel, Mt. Olivet Baptist Church (Colored), and the Jackson Lick apartment building, among others. One picture shows a 1925 Ku Klux Klan parade in Harrisburg. Reference is also made in the subject file index to the "Colored School, Cherry alley, S. W., John Wolf, teacher," and "North Ward (colored) school, West alley, near East State Street, William J. Lawrence, principal."

Among the sub-series entitled *Newspaper Clippings* in the series **Reference Materials** are an advertisement dated July 19, 1828 for a runaway slave named Jenny McClintock of Carlisle and an undated advertisement announcing "A magnificent and original production of Uncle Tom's Cabin, a $20,000 production . . . 2 brass bands . . . white and colored band, and Colored Lady Bugle and Drum Corps." The collection contains some photocopy pages of George H. Morgan's *Annals of Harrisburg*, written around 1858 and revised in 1906.

MG-215. ETHNIC STUDIES COLLECTIONS, 1789-1975.

This manuscript group contains ethnic newspapers, oral history materials, and photographs of immigrant workers and families. They provide information on ethnic and religious organizations, church anniversary histories, and information on ethnic groups obtained under the Pennsylvania Ethnic Studies Program sponsored

1873   1973
100th Anniversary
"Hitherto hath the Lord Blessed us"
1 Samuel - 7:12

CAMBRIA A. M. E. ZION CHURCH
Johnstown, Pennsylvania
Allegheny Annual Conference

Rt. Rev. Charles Herbert Foggie, Bishop
Rev. Arizona Nicholson, Presiding Elder
Rev. Joseph Harris Jones, Sr., Minister

"There remaineth yet very much land to be possessed." *Joshua 13:1*

MG-215. Ethnic Studies Collections, 1789-1975. Church Anniversary Histories.

by the Pennsylvania Historical and Museum Commission.

Church Anniversary Histories. Nearly two hundred church anniversary publications representing numerous Pennsylvania ethnic and racial groups have been collected and placed in the Ethnic Studies Collections. These booklets offer valuable historical and biographical information as well as photographs. Examples of the

African American church anniversary booklets include the following:

- *Jerusalem Baptist Church,* Duquesne (Allegheny County), *75 Anniversary, 1897-1972.*
- *Morning Star Baptist Church,* Clairton (Allegheny County), *50th Anniversary, 1919-1969.*
- *Mt. Ararat Baptist Church,* Pittsburgh (Allegheny County), *64th Anniversary, 1906-70.*
- *St. Paul A.M.E. Church,* McKeesport (Allegheny County), *106th Anniversary.* (1997)
- *Cambria A.M.E. Zion Church,* Johnstown (Cambria County), *100th Anniversary, 1873-1973.*
- *Shiloh Baptist Church,* Johnstown (Cambria County), *Golden Anniversary, 1917-1967.*
- *Shiloh Baptist Church,* Carlisle (Cumberland County), *100th Anniversary, 1868-1968.*
- *West Street African Methodist Episcopal Zion Church,* Carlisle (Cumberland County), *120th Anniversary Celebration, 1863-1983.*
- *Second Baptist Church,* Harrisburg (Dauphin County), *75th Anniversary, 1869-1944,* and *The Centennial Celebration, 1869-1969.*
- *St. Paul Missionary Baptist Church,* Harrisburg (Dauphin County), *106 Years of Service, 1997.*
- *Shiloh Baptist Church,* Williamsport (Lycoming County), *One Hundred Years, 1879-1979.*
- *Second Baptist Church,* Philadelphia (Philadelphia County), *Centennial, 1869-1969.*
- *African Methodist Episcopal Zion Church,* York (York County), *133rd Anniversary, 1811-1944.*
- *Small Memorial A.M.E. Zion Church,* York (York County) *History in the Making,* 1968.

MG-216. CARLISLE INDIAN SCHOOL COL-LECTION, 1878-1969.

The United States Department of the Interior's Bureau of Indian Affairs operated a school for Native American children at Carlisle Barracks, Carlisle, Pennsylvania from 1878 to 1918. This small collection of items from the school contains documents, photographs, programs, catalogues, and miscellaneous publications including the school newspapers. One of these newspapers, *The Indian Helper*, contains various references to African Americans:

- Volume 5, number 38 (May 23, 1890), page 3, mentions a convention of the African Methodist Episcopal Church held in Carlisle.

- Volume 5, number 39 (May 30, 1890), page 2, column 2, cites a report by student Charlie Moneravie, previously a student at Hampton Institute, who described a trip to the Carlisle Indian School in which he observed that "the Indians and Negroes are in distinct apartments and quite as separate as though there were two schools. In the higher grades the Indians mingle with the Negroes in class."

MG-217. HARRISBURG HOME STAR COL-LECTION, 1895-1971 (BULK 1962-1971).

Photographic files of the *Harrisburg Home Star*, a weekly newspaper published in Harrisburg by Paul Walker from 1948 to 1971. The paper had various titles over time: *Harrisburg Guide*, *Harrisburg Home News*, and *Harrisburg Home Star*. The collection contains photographs of local, state, and national politicians, businessmen, civic leaders, pastors, military personnel, members of various clubs and civic organizations, local establishments, and entertainers.

MG-217. Harrisburg Home Star Collection, ca. 1948-1971. Photographs. OIC (Opportunities Industry Corporation), Harrisburg, Rev. Franklin L. Henley and others.

Photographs (Prints): The following African Americans and related images are depicted: Samuel L. Adams, 6/10/70; Howard A. Achenbach, 3/25/65; Samuel L. Adams, 6/10/70; Count Basie, undated; Bethesda Mission, n.d.; Rev. W. W. Bowden, 3/25/65; William D. Boswell, undated.; Camp Curtain United Methodist Church, 1964 (now Camp Curtin Mitchell Memorial United Methodist Church); Central High School Building, Forster and Cap[ital] Streets. 9/16/68; William S. Clark, 6/30/95; Edison Junior High School football team, n.d.; Elk's Home, undated; Barton Fields, undated; Dr. Thomas W. Georges Jr., undated; ground breaking at

Camp William Penn, Training Camp for Colored Troops Enlisted into the United States Army, located in Cheltenham Township, Montgomery County, Pennsylvania, 1863

MG-218. Photograph Collections, [ca. 1853-ongoing). VII. Military B. Civil War. Camp William Penn, 1863.

Central Pennsylvania Business School; Hall Manor Junior Tenant's Association, undated;, Lionel Hampton, 11/15/67; Harlem Globetrotters, 1962 (Bobby Joe Mason, Tom Long, and Meadowlark Lemon); Harrisburg Area Schools; John Harris High School football team, 11/17/65; Harrisburg Community Theater and Danny Williams, n.d.; Harrisburg Gas Company, undated; Twila Howard, undated; Ink Spots, 1/26/66; Byron M. Jackson, 3/2/66; Beau Jenkins (trumpet player) for the Policemen's Ball, undated; Stanley Lawson, 5/14/69; Johnny Mathis, undated; William McBride, undated; Julius McCoy, undated; Clarence C. Morrison, undated; OIC (Opportunities Industry Corporation) and Rev. Franklin L. Henley, 5/18/66; William Penn High School football team, 11/17/65; Karin Pierce, undated; Jackie Robinson, undated; Wilbert F. Singleton; Up With People, 1970; Barbara Tyson, undated; William Willie Williams (Virginia Union University), undated; YMCA (Camp

Curtin), undated; and George "Toby" Young, Duke Ellington, and Stanley Larson. Included under the category "Harrisburg Area Schools" is a published booklet entitled *Education in Harrisburg as Seen 100 Years Ago* that includes photographs of the DeWitt Building, Melrose Building, and African American children.

MG-218. PHOTOGRAPH COLLECTIONS, [CA. 1853-ONGOING].

Collections of photographs, generally arranged by counties, pertaining to Pennsylvania's forges and furnaces, iron and steel companies, coal and other mines, gristmills, sawmills, covered bridges, transportation systems (canals, roads and turnpikes, railroads, etc.), and county courthouses. The collections also hold photographs of or pertaining to Pennsylvania's capital buildings, military history, governors and other political leaders, political campaigns and elections, and the Commonwealth's civic, religious, and business leaders. Photograph #36 in the **Political** sub-group depicting members of the state senate in the Senate Chamber at the end of World War II (approximately April or May 1945) includes a few African American men.

MG-219. PHILADELPHIA COMMERCIAL MUSEUM PHOTOGRAPH COLLECTION, [CA. 1840-1954].

Dedicated in 1897 by President William McKinley, the Philadelphia Commercial Museum promoted American and foreign commerce and industry through a series of changing exhibits. Located at 34th and Vintage Streets, Philadelphia, the museum is today called the Museum of the Philadelphia Civic Center. In 1961 over six thousand prints of varying sizes were given to the Pennsylvania State Archives by the Commercial Museum. Used

MG-219. Philadelphia Commercial Museum Photographic Collection, [ca. 1840-1954]. "Shucking Oysters in South Jersey, 1934".

to illustrate commerce, trade, business, and industry in the United States and the world, most of the images were gathered from Pennsylvania and the Philadelphia area. Included in the collection are photographs of workers in Philadelphia's major industries, including African Americans.

MG-227. SOLOMON FOX COLLECTION, 1862-1879.

Civil War letters and miscellaneous items relating to Solomon Fox, a native of Berks County who served as a private in Company G, 93rd Regiment Pennsylvania Volunteers. This collection includes a letter Fox wrote to his wife on March 16, 1862, from Camp Edward, Virginia, telling of African Americans coming in large numbers to seek the protection of the "Yanky" soldiers.

MG-233. THEODORE GREGG COLLECTION, 1851-1874.

Letters, commissions, service records, etc., of Theodore Gregg, a native of Centre County, who served on the United States schooner *Van Buren* during the Seminole War, during which he took part in an expedition in the Everglades. Also contains materials relating to Gregg's service as a sergeant in Company A of the 4th U.S. Infantry, 1st Division, United States Regulars during the Mexican War and as a brevet colonel in the 45th Pennsylvania Volunteer Infantry during the Civil War. Included is a forty-one page manuscript by Richard C. Brown, entitled "Theodore Gregg: An American," which describes Gregg's participation in the battle of Vicksburg as the commander of the 45th Regiment that was assisted by a "Negro Brigade." Also included is Gregg's letter of August 9, 1864 to Colonel Z. R. Bliss, which provides further details about the battle.

MG-247. ALGERNON SYDNEY LOGAN AND ROBERT RESTALRIG LOGAN PAPERS, [CA. 1680-1945].

This collection consists of manuscript and printed material pertaining to the Logan family including James Logan, first provincial secretary of William Penn, his father Patrick Logan, and descendents Algernon Sydney Logan (1849-1925) and Robert Restalrig Logan. Included are three volumes of printed and manuscript copies of Indian treaties and other material relating to Indian affairs covering the period 1722-1762, copies of John Dickinson correspondence, 1753-76, and one volume of minutes and related items of the Indiana Company, 1776-89.

B. JAMES LOGAN ITEMS, 1722-1762

Contains printed and hand written copies of treaties made with the Indians. Of particular interest is a treaty made with the Indians of the five nations: "Maquose, Oneida, Onnondages, Cayouges, and Simmekaes." Included in a collection are handwritten copies; this treaty was signed in September 1722 by Virginia Governor Alexander Spotswood and contained a provision requesting the aid of the five nations in seizing runaway slaves. Governor Spotswood promised the Indians "one good gun and a blanket" for the capture and return of each runaway slave. For their part, the Indians of the five nations avowed to the governor that "if any runaway Negroe or Slave shall happen to fall into our hands we will carry them to Col. Mason's on the Potowmach River for the reward promised."

C. ALGERNON SYDNEY LOGAN ITEMS, 1776-1934

Contains a handwritten transcript entitled "Records of the Families of Logan and Norris" (1815) by Deborah Norris Logan. The book contains genealogical information, obituary notices, personal accounts, a copied manuscript entitled "An historical account of the ancient and honorable Family of Logan of Edinburgh," poems, sonnets, and a copy of an article that appeared in the *American Magazine* for 1790. The article describes an incident that occurred on the island of Jamaica in 1692 when an earthquake destroyed Port Royal and also killed a slave attempting to rescue his master, a merchant from Philadelphia. Later, "a cradle was seen floating on the water with a female Negro child alive, and a large silver dirk the property of the merchant. Upon examination, the child appeared to be the daughter of the Negro man who had lost his life in attempting to save his master. Both the child and the dirk were sent to the elder son of the merchant who lived in Philadelphia." The master was Thomas Norris and the dirk belonged to the Norris family.

Portraits and Photographs, 1865-1922. Photographs and portraits of, or taken by, the Logan-Norris family. Photographs taken by A. Sydney Logan, 1877-1913, include: A scene showing John Freeman mowing grass and being followed on foot by Charly Freeman, labeled "Field A, Delaware, June 1887"; a scene labeled "Brookdale Farm, Jones' Heck, Delaware, circa. 1883," showing five African American men making hay; a scene showing three African American men thinning corn labeled "Field C, Delaware, June 1887," and a scene taken at Brookdale Farm depicting blacks and whites threshing wheat together.

MG-250. HARRISBURG COMMUNITY THEATRE RECORDS, 1925-1975.

Correspondence, photographs, scrapbooks, business records, and related materials covering the history of the Harrisburg Community Theater from the time of its formation in 1925.

Pictures (by Season), 1930-1973, and undated. Photographs from various plays produced by the Harrisburg Community Theater. African Americans appear in photographs of scenes from various plays such as:

- *Gypsy* (1971), with Danny Williams, Marilyn Patcher, Tawnya Phillips, Kristen Krathwohl.
- *A Raisin in the Sun* (1976), with Lalla Mills, Carol Lynn Carter, Samuel Johnson, William F. Peterson.
- *NEAT* (n.d.) at Downey Elementary School, with Wanda Pierce, Barbara Jackson, William Peterson, and Barbara Crabb.
- *The Roar of the Greasepaint* (1978), with Edward E. Randleman Jr., and Michele Ray.
- *Something's Afloat* (1978), with Anthony Alexander as producer. Mr. Alexander also served as co-chairman of HCT's

Production Center as well as a member of its board of directors (1978).

- *The Miracle Worker* (1980), with Michelle Hinton and Vann Culpepper.
- *Pippin* (1982), with Linda Newkirk Barber.
- *Boys in the Band* (1984), with A. Cedric Alexander as Bernard.
- *Man of La Mancha* (1984), with Nicole Millicent Austin as Maria, the innkeeper's wife.
- *You Can't Take It With You* (1985), with Marcia P. Haymon and Bob Hubbard.
- *Baby* (1986), with Robin Fulton and Judith Blair Brown in the chorus.
- *The Crucible* (1986), with Margaretta L. Daniels.
- *A Funny Thing Happened on the Way to the Forum* (1986), with Karla Pierce.

The files also contain photographs of actors Darryl Barbee, Madella Artis, Ralph Crabb, and Charles Lloyd.

Scrapbooks, 1926-1971. Unbound scrapbooks containing news clippings of various theater productions. Several articles feature musical director J. Leonard Oxley, who appeared on several occasions at the Harrisburg Community Theater in such musicals as *Oh Kay!* and *Oklahoma*.

MG-252. STEPHEN GIRARD COLLECTION, 1786-1856 (BULK 1828-1842).

Stephen Girard was a Philadelphia merchant, financier, and philanthropist, who engaged in foreign trade and owned eighteen seagoing vessels. He also became involved in real estate, insurance, and banking. His will, a copy of which is included in the

MG-250. Harrisburg Community Theatre Records, 1925-1975. Pictures, 1930-1973. *A Raisin in the Sun,* 1976, with Lalla Mills and others.

collection, stipulated large sums of money for charities and for the establishment of Girard College. Though challenged by the heirs, the will was upheld by the United States Supreme Court in the landmark case of *Vidal et al. v. the City of Philadelphia*, a classic in American legal history in clarifying the laws regarding charities. The will contains several references to African Americans, including mention of his "black woman" Hannah, to whom he gave an annual sum of two hundred dollars for the remainder of her life. He also specified that part of his real and personal estate near Washita, Louisiana, including thirty slaves, be given to his friend Judge Henry Bree.

MG-253. JACOB J. BIERER PAPERS, [1795-1907].

Jacob J. Bierer, a native of Westmoreland County, served in the Civil War as a captain of Company C, 11th Regiment, Pennsylvania Volunteers from November 1861 to April 1864. He subsequently served several terms as school director of Latrobe Borough and was chief burgess of Latrobe in 1869, 1862 and 1882. He was elected to the Pennsylvania House of Representatives as a Democrat in 1883 and again in 1891 and was commissioned as a notary public in 1886 and 1910. The collection includes correspondence, legal papers, photographs, and other items pertaining primarily to Bierer's Civil War service.

Two letters in the **Correspondence** folder contain unfavorable opinions of slavery, the Freedmen's Bureau and "Negroes." These are a letter from Michael Schall Jr. to Michael Schall Sr. dated February 21, 1831 and a letter from John Bachman of Charleston, North Carolina, to J. J. Bierer dated February 12, 1862.

Also found in the collection are several **Newspapers** that provide information about slavery and situations involving African Americans. Some of these are: *The Greensburgh Gazette* dated May 31, 1822 that contains a reward advertisement for a servant mulatto boy named Frank, *Greensburgh Democrat* dated February 7, 1863 containing articles entitled "Negroes in Fort Lafayette," "The Effect of the Proclamation," "Niggers to be Made Soldiers," "Kentucky and Emancipation," "The Negro Tax," "Treaty with Liberia," and a copy of the *Republican & Democrat* dated November 30, 1864, containing an article entitled "A Hill in Labor," that discusses slavery as the cause of Civil War and an item headed "Election news," that states that the Abolition candidates received 255,081 votes against the Democratic candidates who garnered 242,123 votes.

MG-254. AUDIO-VISUAL COLLECTION, [CA. 1920-ONGOING].

Miscellaneous acquisitions of motion picture films, videotapes and sound recordings. Included is a 1926 one-reel film on Wyoming, Pennsylvania featuring various ethnic parades and a recording entitled *Francis Johnson: American Cotillions*. Francis Johnson was an African American who is described on the label as "one of those men who, by his own unaided exertions, has won his way from the lowest to the topmost round of the ladder of fame without fear of contradiction, that as a composer or a musician, he stands without rival in the States." (*Detroit Daily Free Press*, September 19, 1839).

MG-262. GENERAL MICROFILM COLLECTION, [CA. 1620-1975].

This collection consists of rolls of microfilm copies of Pennsylvania records and manuscripts primarily held by other institutions. Over the last fifty years the State Archives created this collection by making special arrangements with individual donors to microfilm letters, diaries, business records, etc. Because of its diverse sources and themes, this collection complements many of the State Archives' own manuscripts and records. The majority of this material was gathered by the Division of Research and Publications, now called the Division of History, as source materials for conducting research and writing books and articles on Pennsylvania history. Through such special arrangements, letters, diaries, and business records relating to Pennsylvania were microfilmed from materials deposited at other institutions in the Commonwealth and throughout the nation. In April 1977, the administration and preservation of microfilm holdings were transferred from the Division of History to the Division of Archives and Manuscripts within the Bureau of Archives and History. [For a more detailed description of this collection a copy of the *Guide to the Microfilm Collections in the Pennsylvania State Archives* by Roland M. Baumann and Diane S. Wallace may be consulted. Though this volume is no longer in print, a copy is available at the Archives and at the State Library.]

NEWSPAPER COLLECTIONS

The State Archives has a small collection of microfilmed newspapers that includes commemorative editions and daily and weekly editions from eight counties, German language editions, and other ethnic newspapers. Newspaper editions that include articles on African Americans are:

Bedford County

Bedford Gazette. The June 10, 1864 edition of the Bedford Gazette cites names of new Civil War draftees from Snake Spring and Cumberland Valley Townships (Bedford County). Those who served in the United States Colored Troops were: Andrew Dean, James Leach, Benjamin Plowden, John Plowden, Jacob Plowden, George Ramsey, Lewis Reed, Jacob Ritchey, R. M. Skillington, Nimrod Warren.

Juniata County

Juniata Journal. The September 1, 1835 issue of the Juniata Journal contains the following articles: "The Abolitionists," "Religion versus Abolition," "The Burnt Papers," "Another Slave Atrocity," and an untitled article that states, "we understand that a gentleman of this city, received yesterday from New York, a large box containing . . . pictures of slaves being whipped." The article, "The Burnt Papers," was reprinted from the Emancipator, an Abolitionist's newspaper.

Cumberland County

Americana Volunteer. The October 22, 1902 issue of the *Americana Volunteer* printed an article on the death of J. N. Choate, one of Carlisle's successful photographers. The funeral announcement gave the names of the active and honorary pallbearers. Among the active pallbearers were African Americans Charles Whiting, Amos Johnson, William Chapman, and Diston Barnes.

Abstracts of Obituaries in the Carlisle Evening Sentinel, 1906-1915 compiled by John C. Fralish). By 1906, the Carlisle *Evening Sentinel* appears to have instituted a policy of collecting obituary information relating to the inhabitants of Cumberland County. Some examples of African Americans for which such obituaries are available are: Agy, William, "Colonel," a Dickinson College janitor, February 2, 1911, aged about fifty, local preacher. Funeral, February 3, 1911; Arter, Fannie, Mrs., in Shippensburg, March 17, 1908, widow of J. Hugh Arter, was born a slave in Jefferson County, Virginia; Bell, Daniel, Underground Railroad figure, was born in Carlisle, February 14, 1832, moved at age thirty-nine to Harrisburg, date of death there not given, widower about two and a half years, daughters named; Brown, Jucetta, Mechanicsburg, March 11, 1907, age not given but lived there all her life, interment in Garret Cemetery; Butler, Mrs., of Newville, December 26, 1910, interment in Newville Cemetery; McCard, Maria Randolph, Mrs., Carlisle, January 11, 1913, aged ninety-five, formerly Mrs. Randolph, mother of Rev. John Philip McCard, pastor of Shiloh Baptist Church Rev. McCard, other children named; Taylor, Elizabeth Beals, Mrs., in Chicago, formerly of Carlisle, September 14, 1909, aged thirty-four, daughter of Isaac Beals, no mention of children, burial in Union Cemetery.

BUSINESS RECORDS

Cornwall Furnace and Hopewell Forge Journals and Ledgers, 1752-1766. The volumes give reference to African American employees, namely: "Negro Jack," "Negro John," "Negro Tom," and "Negro Will." The accounts give status of purchases made as well as wages and work performed.

Hopewell Village National Historic Site Deposit, 1802-1876. Ledger pages from Hopewell Furnace reference known African American employees. Cited are members of the Cole family who worked at the furnace and, in 1856, helped to establish Mount Frisby African Methodist Episcopal Church that was located on the northern boundary of Hopewell Furnace.

CHURCH RECORDS

Cumberland County

First Presbyterian Church of Carlisle, Pa. Records, 1761-1920. A minute book (1816-1834), pew records (1828-1841), and miscellaneous papers consisting of building plans and warrants, membership lists, financial records, church registers, copies of the act of incorporation and the charter, minutes of deacons and trustees, and other items. Included in the marriage records are the following:

- October 9, 1798-Adam Simonton (Black) to [illegible] Orr, a mulatto woman.
- December 6, 1806-"Francis Lewis to Peggy Standsburry, black persons-the man belonging to Mrs. M. Laird-the woman to

Mrs. Campbell."

- December 23, 1806-"John Brown to Betsy Finley-these were black people."

Dauphin County

Harrisburg Monthly Meeting of Religious Society of Friends Records, 1909-1965. The records contain minute books for 1928-1965 (five volumes) and a treasurer's book, 1909-1960 (one volume). The organization was very supportive of activities and causes that improved the needs and conditions of the African American community in Harrisburg. The minutes refer to a conference featuring Maude Coleman of the Department of Welfare. Discussion centered on the housing condition of an African American community in Harrisburg where sixty persons were without housing due to a fire and the construction of the Capitol Park extension. The Religious Society of Friends was generous in financial support of several organizations including the Phyllis Wheatley Young Women's Christian Association (the African American YWCA). The Religious Society of Friends had a Friends Race Relations Committee that became involved with racial problems in the city.

HISTORICAL RECORDS

Simon Cameron Papers, 1824-ca. 1919. A prominent Harrisburg financier, Simon Cameron also served as a United States senator and subsequently as the first secretary of war under Abraham Lincoln. The collection consists of correspondence and business papers in the possession of the Dauphin County Historical Society that include thirteen letters or drafts written by Mr. Cameron. Among these is a letter dated April 23, 1862 to Mr. Cameron from Thomas Morris Chester, an African American native of Harrisburg who served as a Civil War correspondent and became friends with Simon Cameron. T. Morris Chester writes "that the thought of sending slaves in the District of Columbia back to Liberia is not a good idea." He states, "it would be unwise and inhumane in the government at Washington to send them to Liberia. I desire them to be immigrants to our adopted country. . . ."

Sol Feinstone Collection of the American Revolution, 1739-1859. Originally assembled by Sol Feinstone, a businessman and collector, this collection includes 1,742 letters and documents relating to the American Revolution. Among these items are the following documents relating to the institution of slavery:

- A document dated August 5, 1776 signed by Cornell Stevenson of Burlington County, New Jersey, setting his Negro slave Pompey free.
- Receipt dated January 10, 1737 to John Fisher from Ebenezer Stearns for the purchase of a Negro named Jack for eighty pounds.
- Receipt dated January 7, 1716 to John Fisher from John Howe, for the purchase of a Negro boy in Boston named Prince for forty-two pounds.
- A document dated September 21, 1791 at Accomack County, Virginia and signed by John Custer and Tully Wise stating that Tomthy, a Negro man, had forged a document claiming that he was free.

Albert Gallatin Papers, 1761-1849. Albert Gallatin served as a member of the Pennsylvania Legislature and the United States Congress, as a foreign diplomat, and as United States secretary of the treasury. The papers include genealogical and biographical items, political papers, correspondence, pamphlets, and miscellaneous family papers. Included is a copy of Albert Gallatin's membership certificate in the Pennsylvania Abolition Society.

Graeme Park Collection, 1743-1918. Graeme Park, the only surviving residence of a colonial Pennsylvania governor, is a historic site operated by the Pennsylvania Historical and Museum Commission. The buildings of Graeme Park were constructed by William Keith, who served as deputy governor 1721-1722, and were originally intended as a distillery before the property was sold to Dr. Thomas Graeme in 1739, who renovated the mansion to serve as his country estate. Elizabeth Graeme Ferguson, Graeme's only surviving child, inherited the estate and subsequently divided the property into lots. In 1920, Mr. and Mrs. Welsh Strawbridge acquired the land upon which the main house stands and restored the mansion to its original condition. In 1958, the Strawbridges gave the property to the Commonwealth of Pennsylvania. The collection contains two issues of the *Pennsylvania Packet or, the General Advertiser* containing advertisements for the sale and return of runaway slaves. The issue dated August 29, 1787 has an advertisement for the sale of a "negro man," and the December 7, 1782 issue has an advertisement placed by Benjamin Rittenhouse seeking the return of a runaway "Mulatto Wench named Chloe."

Hershey Family Papers. Papers of a prominent Lancaster County family and their descendants including correspondence (1832-1853) relating to economic events, political conditions and religious trends in both Erie and Lancaster Counties, account books, a family history, pamphlets, and an incomplete newspaper file (1851-1863) of the *Conneautville Courier* of Crawford County. Included are the following materials related to slavery, abolition, and the Civil War.

- The text of a February 5, 1851 lecture on slavery delivered by a Professor Williams of the Methodist Church.
- Several articles on the Fugitive Slave Law dated February 19, 1851 are present including "The Great Compromise Measure,"

that presents the story of a "colored" woman known by the name of Tamar Williams who resided at the corner of Fifth Street and Germantown Road. It was alleged that her real name was Mahala and that she was a fugitive slave belonging to William T. Parnell of Worcester County, Maryland. The story relates that she had escaped from a southern plantation in the year 1820 and subsequently married and bore five children. Mahala's husband also had been arrested as a fugitive slave and there is also an article on an Indiana fugitive slave case.

- A February 26, 1851 issue of the *Courier* contains an article on the Fugitive Slave Act of 1850 and an article on a fugitive slave named Frederick Williams that states, "A mob of 300 negroes stormed the Court Room (in Boston), and in despite of the officers, carried off the fugitive in triumph. The fugitive's whereabouts is not yet known, but it is supposed he is on his way to Canada via Burlington."

- An April 2, 1851 article entitled "Selling Slaves in Pennsylvania" addresses the issue of the Fugitive Slave Law and the possible development of a new market in slaves captured by slave agents in Pennsylvania for return to the South.

- The May 7, 1851 article "Virginny Neber Tires" refers to man who was a member of one of the first families in Virginia who entered "Douglas's" shop for a shave. "As the gentlemen was being lathered, a Bostonian, a warm free-soiler, asked Douglas, what would you do if your old master attempted to carry you back into slavery? Shoot him down, was Douglas's reply. The Virginian jumped into the middle of the floor with lather, towel and all, . . ."

- A January 4, 1854 article entitled "Verdict Against Mrs. Stowe" recounts the case of *Harriet Beecher Stowe vs. F.W. Thomas*, a German book publisher in Philadelphia. Stowe charged F. W. Thomas with "an infringement of the plaintiff's copyright of *Uncle Tom's Cabin*, by publishing a German translation.

Pennsylvania Abolitionist Society Papers, 1775-1916. This collection, owned by the Historical Society of Pennsylvania, includes minutes and manuscripts of *The Society for the Relief of Free Negroes Unlawfully Kept in Bondage*. Organized one year before the War of Independence, the society was lead by Quakers, Presbyterians, Episcopalians, and Jews. Temporarily suspended during the war, it was vigorously reactivated in 1787 and adopted the title of "The Pennsylvania Society for Promoting the Abolition of Slavery and the Relief of Free Negroes Unlawfully held in Bondage." This was the first formal abolitionist society founded in the United States of America.

Pennsylvania History, General, Papers Relating to Pennsylvania, 1681-1913. Papers include accounts, correspondence, deeds, legal papers, military records, minutes, printed items and other materials relating to business matters, military affairs, politics, and many other subjects. Items relevant to African Americans are: the case of "Negro Cato," the slave of Matthias Slough of the Borough of Lancaster, who was no longer in good health; an indictment for larceny of "Negro Isaac," a slave owned by Matthias Slough, who was taken to the public whipping post to receive twenty-one lashes on his bare back and paid a fine of twenty pounds; a lading bill for a negro boy valued at thirty pounds; an act addressing the trials of "negroes" who committed murder, manslaughter, rape, burglary and any other illegal acts as specified by William Penn's *Laws of the Province of Pennsylvania* published by the Order of the General Assembly, which includes "an Act for the better regulating of Negroes in this Province."

Thaddeus Stevens Papers, 1814-1868. These papers consist of the private and public correspondence, speeches, legal and business papers, and congressional records of United States Congressman Thaddeus Stevens, an outspoken advocate for the abolition of slavery. The originals are scattered across the United States and this microfilm edition is composed of the following four series:

General Correspondence and Miscellaneous Documents. Includes information on the following persons or subjects: Abolition Society of Pennsylvania, American Anti-Slavery Society, Frederick Douglass, Ku Klux Klan, Lucretia Mott, New York Tribune, Pennsylvania Equal Rights League, John Peck, Thaddeus Stevens, Thaddeus Stevens Jr., Lucy Stone; Charles Sumner.

Speeches and Resolutions. The following subject are included in this segment: copies of the Thirteenth and Fourteenth Amendments, materials on various abolition societies, Black cavalry units and Black military history, African Americans in Pennsylvania, Black railroad passengers, Black refugee aid, Black soldiers, Black suffrage in Pennsylvania, Black apprenticeships, court testimony by African Americans, African American migration to Pennsylvania, the legacy of John Brown, the Brownsville Female Academy, the Christiana Riot trial, civil rights and trial by jury, civil service, Civil War veterans, emancipation, equal rights legislation, freed slaves, Freedman's Bureau, fugitive slave arrests, Pennsylvania's fugitive slave laws, the federal Fugitive Slave Law, African Americans and higher education in Pennsylvania, Indian slaveholding, military hospitals, "Negro" soldiers, readmission of states, the rights of seceded states, secret societies, and the questions of abolition, extension of slavery, protection of slavery, and restrictions on slavery in Washington, D.C., in the territories, and in Utah.

Legal Arguments and Legal and Business Papers. Included on this reel are summaries from a few cases argued by Stevens dealing with slavery and slave ownership. They are: *Butler and others vs. Delaplaine*; *Scott vs. Waugh*; and *Kauffman vs. Oliver*. Also included is the summation of John M. Read of the 1851 Christiana trial (*United States vs. Hanway*), in which Stevens and three other lawyers successfully defended Caster Hanway, two other whites, and thirty-eight African Americans from charges of treason for helping fugitive slaves escape.

Congressional Committee Minutes. In Benjamin J. Kendrick's *The Journal of the Joint Committee of Fifteen on Reconstruction, 39th Congress, 1865-1867,* (New York, 1914), is the full text of resolutions and bills that the committee considered.

MILITARY RELATED RECORDS

The Negro in the Military Service of the United States, 1639-1886. Microfilm copy of eight bound volumes of records compiled for publication by the Colored Troops Division of the Adjutant General's Office (AGO). This compilation was created under the leadership of Elon A. Woodard, chief of the Colored Troops Division along with several clerks during 1885-1888. Included are documents copied from published and unpublished primary sources. Also, there are copies from a few original documents and extracts of material from secondary sources that were intended to cover periods of history for which primary sources were not readily available, such as correspondence, telegrams, endorsement books, and general and special orders. The volumes are part of Record Group 94, the Records of the Adjutant General's Office, 1780's-1917. Some of the items included are letters from and to Simon Cameron, who was the first secretary of war during the Civil War, as well as many letters from military and governmental officers with reference to African Americans becoming part of the army. Included are various statistical and census reports on African Americans. Microfilm Publication M858, National Archives.

Revolutionary War Rolls, 1775-1789. Revolutionary War records for Pennsylvania, 1775-1789, consisting of correspondence, lists of officers, muster and pay rolls, returns, etc., that include names of African American soldiers. Information includes names of officers and enlisted men, commission or enlistment dates and military units. Also included are payroll books "A" and "B," ca. 1781-1789 and pay rolls (Pierce's certificates) of officers and enlisted men from Pennsylvania who served during the Revolutionary War. The two volumes are certified copies made by the auditor general of Pennsylvania in 1818, and include approximately 10,300 names. Microfilm produced by National Archives.

PRINTED MATERIALS

Prison Society Journals, 1845-1920.

Pennsylvania Journal of Prison Discipline, **July 1845**, contains information on African Americans under the following article headings: "Mortality Among the Colored Population of Philadelphia," "Table of Diseases and Deaths in the County Prison of Philadelphia," and "The Sixteenth Annual Report of the Inspectors of the Eastern State Penitentiary of Pennsylvania."

Pennsylvania Journal of Prison Discipline, **October 1845**, contains information with reference to African Americans in Article VII, "Report of the Inspectors of the Western Penitentiary of Pennsylvania, for the year 1844." Information is cited according to date, inmate number, color, age, and disease. Other statistical information is listed according to sex and color.

Pennsylvania Journal of Prison Discipline and Philanthropy, **April 1846**, specifies race with reference to the specific trades, i.e., white and colored weavers, white and colored shoemakers, colored bobbin-winders, etc. Also included is a "Tabular View of the Fatal Cases in the Eastern Penitentiary of Pennsylvania, from the opening of the Institution (October 25, 1829) to December 31, 1845." This chart gives the following information: year, prisoner number, color, sex, age, nativity, occupation (before conviction, in prison), when admitted, state of health on admission, offenses, sentence, time of death, nature of fatal disease, time in prison, number of convictions, personal habits, social state, and time spent in county prison.

The Pennsylvania Journal of Prison Discipline and Philanthropy, **January 1849**, under "Alleviation of Miseries of Public Opinion," is an article entitled "Philadelphia House of Refuge for Colored Juvenile Delinquents." The facility was built to accommodate 300 inmates, 206 males and 94 females.

The Pennsylvania Journal of Prison Discipline and Philanthropy, **January 1850**, discusses the "separate system" of racial segregation in Pennsylvania's prison system, and the health of African American inmates.

THESES AND DISSERTATIONS

The Evolution of the Constitution of Pennsylvania, 1683-1838, with Special Emphasis Upon the Constitution of 1838, by Russell Henry Kistler (Lehigh University, 1943). This thesis discusses Pennsylvania politics, the state constitution that defined the status of the "negro" and the philosophy of abolitionist congressman Thaddeus Stevens. According to Kistler, the African American population of Bucks County had increased to a point that "elections in that county were generally closely contested and the blacks had enough votes to 'swing' the election, therefore, the legitimate voters were . . . defeated by NEGRO SLAVES."

The Triumph of Militant Republicanism: A Study of Pennsylvania and Presidential Politics, 1860-1872, by Erwin S. Bradley. Discusses the Kansas-Nebraska Act, Missouri Compromise, Dred Scott Decision, Lancaster and the Christiana Riot, Pennsylvania Anti-Slavery Society, Negro suffrage/Negro voting, and many of the Pennsylvania politicians during this time period: Henry D. Foster, John C. Fremont, Thomas L. Kane, Thaddeus Stevens, Simon Cameron, David Wilmot, Andrew Curtain.

MG-264. INTERNATIONAL UTILITIES POLITICAL MEMORABILIA COLLECTION, 1789-1972.

The International Utilities (I.U.) of Philadelphia is a business conglomerate with diversified services in distribution, agriculture, utilities, and other areas. The memorabilia relate to successful and unsuccessful United States presidential candidates, their vice-presidential running mates, and their election campaigns. Also included are materials pertaining to such national political issues as the tariff, sectionalism, slavery, the Civil War, reconstruction, western expansion, progressivism, and civil rights.

Campaign Literature, 1861-1972.

> *George Wallace, 1964, 1968.* Pamphlets, bumper stickers, and leaflets relating to George Wallace's run for the presidency. Governor of state of Alabama, George Wallace actively opposed such legislation as the Civil Rights Act of 1963, federal interference into state and local administration of public schools, and the activities of National Association for the Advancement of Colored Peoples (NAACP).

Cartoons, 1860-1884, 1972.

Miscellaneous, 1860-1972. A small collection of political cartoons from various presidential campaigns. Items pertaining to African Americans from the Lincoln campaign are "The True Issue or 'That's What's The Matter,'" (quote from cartoon "No peace without abolition") and "The Rail Candidate" (quote from cartoon "Dis Nigger strong and willin but its awful hard work to carry Old Massa Abe on nothing but dis ere rail!"). Items from the Grant campaign are "The Irrepressible Conflict or The Republican Barge in Danger," "The Man of Words, the Man of Deeds, Which Do You Think the County Needs" (the cartoon shows a Negro man being lynched in front of a building titled "Colored Orphan Asylum"), "Re-Construction, or 'A White Man's Government,'" "Freedom of Suffrage to the Blacks Means Freedom of Suffrage to the Whites."

Newspapers, 1836-1968.

Bedford Gazette, **October 7, 1836**, contains several articles regarding the "poll tax" that was implemented to prevent the poor, the uneducated, and non-land owners from voting. Also, this issue contains a brief piece entitled "Negroism."

Bedford Gazette, **December 2, 1836**, contains two advertisements for runaway slaves. The first advertisement offers six cents reward for an eight-year-old child and the other is a six hundred dollar reward for four Negroes who escaped from jail.

The Boston Evening Atlas, **November 7, 1860**, provides the results of Abraham Lincoln's election as president in 1860. Also present is a brief excerpt entitled "The Negro Suffrage Movement."

Christian Science Monitor, November 25, 1963, contains a

retrospective on President Kennedy's political achievements, together with commentary from the African American and Asian American communities. Topics include:

- A chronology of Kennedy's political achievements, 1961-1963.
- An article entitled "Chicago Ponders U.S. Directions" provides three different views on civil from an African American, a white veteran and a white business man.
- An article entitled "Afro-Asians: He Was First" provides an international perspective on Kennedy's foreign policy.
- An article entitled "Assessment, Historic Imprint of a Brief Term" gives an overall assessment of Kennedy's policies and in the process makes important references to the African American community.

The Los Angeles Herald Examiner, July 18, 1940, contains a transcription and discussion of the July 17, 1940 address Franklin D. Roosevelt delivered at the Chicago convention that gives special attention to African Americans in the armed forces.

The Los Angeles Herald Examiner, August 23, 1956, has a display advertisement for the May Company featuring blues singer Dinah Washington.

The Lost Angeles Herald Examiner, article entitled "Watts Safe for Festival Visit" that discusses recovery from the Watts riots.

The Los Angeles Times, August 8, 1968. An article entitled "Angered Negros Rampage in Miami" refers to a riot started by Negro youths who objected to the appearance of police at a black rally. The riot took place ten miles from Miami Beach, the site of the Republican National Convention. An article entitled "Negro Testifies He Saw Newton Fire at Officer" recounts the case of a Negro bus driver who testified that he saw Black Panther leader Huey P. Newton shoot an Oakland, California police officer. An article entitled "Chamberlain to Aid Nixon's Slum Program" cites Los Angeles basketball star Wilt Chamberlain's willingness to back President Nixon's economic plan for inner city slums.

The New York Herald, November 13, 1864, contains an article entitled "The Next Congress-The Vote on the Constitutional Amendment Abolishing Slavery," that predicted the downfall of the amendment and explains why it was unlikely to pass..

The New York Tribune, October 22, 1860, contains numerous articles that discuss the issue of slavery. They are: "The question of Slavery in the Territories," "Who opposed the Compromise and Why?" "What do we mean by the Slave Power?" and "The extinction of Popular Sovereignty."

The San Francisco Examiner, November 6, 1968, contains an article entitled "All Time High-Nine Negroes in the House" that lists the following African Americans as being members of the United States House of Representatives: Adam Clayton Powell, Shirley Chisholm, Louis Stokes, and William Clay. Other articles are "Brown Wins, Going Away" and "Black Student Strike in S.F. State."

The Washington Post, January 21, 1965, contains an article entitled "School Boycott Leader Arrested at New York," that describes the arrest of the Rev. Milton A. Galamison, who was protesting the inferiority of education available in those schools serving mostly Negro and Puerto Rican children.

The Washington Post, November 7, 1968 contains an article entitled "N.Y. School Crisis is Mayor's Biggest" that discusses the dismissal of eighty three union teachers by the local school board of an experimental school district in Brooklyn's largely black and Hispanic neighborhood.

Pamphlets, 1796-1912 and [ca. 1932]. Pamphlets from various presidential campaigns for both Democratic and Republican Parties. Topics covered include the Missouri Compromise of 1850, the Kansas-Nebraska Act, free labor, sectionalism, and slavery. Items are unarranged.

1856 Democratic Party

- The Democratic Party as It Was and as It Is!" A Speech of the Hon. Timothy C. Day, of Ohio, delivered in the House of Representatives on April 23, 1856.
- Hon. James Buchanan. Remarks of Hon. J. Glancy Jones, of Pennsylvania, delivered in the House of Representatives," May 13, 1856.
- A pamphlet comparing the positions of John C. Fremont and James Buchanan on issues of sectionalism and the Constitution in 1856

1856 Republican Party

- "Speech of Hon. John M. Read in favor of Free Kansas, Free White Labor, and of Fremont and Dayton, at the Eighth Ward Mass Meeting, Held in the Assembly Buildings, on Tuesday Evening, Sept. 30, 1865," Philadelphia, 1856.
- "The Dangers of Extending Slavery," and "The Content and the Crisis," two speeches delivered by William H. Seward, Washington, D.C., 1856.

- Immigrant White Free Labor, or Imported Black African Salve Labor," a speech delivered by William H. Seward, at Oswego, New York on November 3, 1856, Washington D.C., 1856.
- "Important Facts drawn From Authentic Sources, Proving Beyond a Doubt That The Approaching Presidential Election Is Forever To Decide The Question Between Freedom and Slavery," 1856.
- "Southern Slavery Reduces Northern Wages," 1856.

1860 Democratic Party

- "Union or Disunion, Speech of the Hon. John M. Botts, at Holcombe Hall in Lynchburg, Virginia, on Thursday Evening, October 18."
- Non-Interference by Congress with Slavery in the Territories. Speech of Hon. S. A. Douglas, in the Senate, May 15 and 16, 1860."

1860 Republican Party

- "Free Homes For Free Men," a speech delivered by the Hon. G. A. Grow of Pennsylvania. in the House of Representatives, February 29, 1860.
- "The Issues: The Dred Scott Decision: The parties," a speech delivered by the Hon. Israel Washburn Jr., of Maine, in the House of Representatives, May 19, 1860.
- "Freedom v. Slavery," a speech delivered by John Hutchins of Ohio in the United States. House of Representatives, May 2, 1860.
- "Political Record of Stephen A. Douglas on the Slavery Question," a tract issued by the Illinois Republican State Central Committee.

MG-269. STATE MUSEUM OF PENNSYLVANIA COLLECTION, 1827-1965.

Originally called the Decorative Arts Collection, this collection contains miscellaneous ephemeral memorabilia transferred to the Archives by The State Museum. In the past, when The State Museum received a collection that included papers as well as artifacts, often the papers were given to the Archives. Included in the collection are many postcards.

Postcards, 1896-1917. The postcards are filed under various subheadings such as art, birds, Halloween, and leather. Those cards that feature African Americans show them in satirical situations or portray stereotypical blackface. Included are:

> ***Halloween-Humorous:*** *Watermelon Jake*; Leather-*There are some good openings here!* (man in blackface falling into the mouth of an alligator).

> ***Leather:*** *I've no time to monkey* (man in blackface falling into the mouth of an alligator).

> ***Miscellaneous:*** *A Bluff in Chicago* (group of men playing cards with a Negro butler); *A Raise in the South* (group of Negroes playing cards with exaggerated facial features).

Trade cards, 1879-1911. Trade cards are also filed under various subheadings such as antiques, baking powder, boots and shoes, cement, drug and druggists, and dry goods. Many trade cards feature African Americans promoting products in various satirical situations or with exaggerated facial features. Included are:

> ***Baking Powder:*** J. Monroe Taylor's Gold Medal Soda & Bak-

ing Powder (Negro male cook baking on a ship).

Cement: Van Stan's Stratena *Ten who shall dare to chide him for sticking to the Old Arm-Chair* (Negro man in silhouette falling out of rocking chair) and *Cement-Van Stan's Stratena* (two Negro boys in silhouette stuck together).

Drug & Druggists: *Ayer's Cathartic Pills* (Negro grandfather with two children on his knee).

Soaps, Cleaning Powders: *What Dreydoppel's Soap Did* (pictured is a small Negro boy washing an elephant).

Stoves and Stove Polish: *Rising Sun Stove Polish.* "Come In, Ephraim! Ise not mad with you dis time, case yer sent me de genuine RISING SUN STOVE BLACKING, an' It shines de stove in good shape. An' here's yer dinner all ready. Somethin' again yer no, deed I have't ; yer think Ise an anjul to get along without good Stove Polish?" (Negro man and woman with exaggerated facial and body features); *Stoves & Stove Polish-Rising Sun Stove Polish* "NO DINNER? Ise een rubbin on dat stoye all day" (Negro man and women with exaggerated facial and body features); *Stoves & Stove Polish-Dixon's Carburet of Iron Stove Polish* "What Uncle Obadiah says about Dixon's Stove Polish" (Negro grandfather and grandchildren all with exaggerated facial and body features).

Miscellaneous: *J. B. Shannon & Sons Ready Mixed Paint* (Negro boy poorly dressed with exaggerated facial features).

MG-271. FRANCES TOBY SCHWARTZ COLLECTION, 1838-1972.

Originally accompanying a donation of artifacts made to The State Museum in 1976, this collection contains almanacs, published books, greeting cards, postcards, photographs, and other ephemera. Among the **Postcards, 1903-1954 and undated**, are two trade cards from J. B. Shannon & Sons, 1020 Market Street, Philadelphia, for "Atlas Ready-Mixed Paint" featuring a colorfully dressed African American man and a similarly attired African American woman carrying a basket on each arm.

MG-272. PENNSYLVANIA MILITARY MUSEUM COLLECTIONS, 1789, 1856-1970, AND UNDATED.

A collection of papers removed from various artifact collections donated to the Pennsylvania Military Museum, Boalsburg. These items document the military experiences of Pennsylvanians and Pennsylvania military units from the era of the Revolutionary War to the Vietnam War. Found in the collection are such items as commissions, letters, diaries, and photographs. The GENERAL COLLECTIONS include the **28th Division History Collection** having folders labeled "Photographs, 491st Eng. Bri., Annual Unit Training, IGMR 1957. (Capt. Paul Friend)" Among these are five photographs of parade scenes which include African Americans. The INDIVIDUAL COLLECTIONS include several folders of material from individual donors whose names appear on the folders. Files with information on African Americans are as follows:

Edward H. Lightner Collection, 1917-1918, 1928-1931, 1952-1953, and undated. Contains several pages from the November

11, 1918 issue of the *Pittsburgh Chronicle Telegraph* having advertisements recruiting either white and/or "colored" workers.

Fletcher McKnight Collection, 1906, 1912-1920 and undated. Fletcher McKnight of Fruitville, California was a Sergeant in the 28th Division who enlisted in the United States Army on May 10, 1917. Among the postcards in his collection is one from the Salvation Army entitled "At Work in the Slums" depicting two members of the Salvation Army entering a building outside of which are two African American boys and two white boys.

Jeremiah Seiders Collection, 1859-1907 and undated. Seiders was a Civil War solider from the Harrisburg area who is also identified as Jeremiah Siders in the catalog of Pennsylvania Volunteers. Recruited in Newport, Perry County, and mustered in on December 10, 1863, his collection contains two diaries, some loose papers, and a large ledger. Included in the ledger is a story written in dialect and refers to "de darkies." It is unclear what the story is based on or to what it refers. The page is dated July 16, 1865 and inscribed Charleston, South Carolina.

MG-274. LEHIGH VALLEY RAILROAD COMPANY RECORDS, 1849-1962 AND UNDATED.

The Lehigh Valley Railroad Company was originally incorporated under the name of the Delaware, Lehigh, Schuylkill, and Susquehanna Railroad Company by an act of the Assembly passed on April 21, 1846. The name of the company was changed to Lehigh Valley Railroad Company in 1853 and, although the railroad carried passengers, the company depended primarily on the transportation of coal. After ten years of financial difficulties occasioned by the decline of the anthracite coal industry, the railroad was taken over by the Pennsylvania Railroad in 1960. The collection contains several boxes of employee records and **Applications for Employment, 1937-1969**, including two applications for employment completed by African Americans. They provide considerable personal information such as the applicant's name, address, age, height, weight, hair and eye color, race and nationality, as well as information on parents, spouse, and children. Information concerning education and previous work experience are also found. Most applications document a physical examination record of the prospective employee.

MG-275. MISCELLANEOUS MANUSCRIPTS OF THE REVOLUTIONARY WAR ERA, 1771-1791 AND UNDATED.

A rranged chronologically, this collection was created by the State Archives from miscellaneous correspondence, extracts, receipts, petitions and certificates pertaining to the Revolutionary War era. Included among the manuscripts is a decree from the Admiralty Court of Pennsylvania between George Geddin of Pennsylvania and the sloop *Sall* concerning "Five Negroes," October, 16 1779. After being captured by the brigantine of war *Holken* the Admiralty Court decreed that the *Sall* was to free five Negroes from its cargo and surrender its tackle, furnishings, and cargo to the *Holken*.

MG-280. ARTHUR D. BRANSKY COLLECTION OF CHARLES ROSS PHOTOGRAPHS, 1905-1906.

C harles E. Ross, a professional photographer from Stroudsburg, Pennsylvania, traveled with his wife, Linnie, through towns in eastern central Pennsylvania during the autumn of 1905 and the winter of 1906, photographing commercial sites. This collection

MG-280. Arthur Bransky Collection of Charles Ross Photographs, 1897-1900. Barbershop in Williamsport, Pa., ca. 1906.

of more than a thousand Ross glass plate negatives came into the possession Arthur D. Bransky of Breinigsville, Pennsylvania who in 1979 and 1980 sold to the Pennsylvania State Archives 227 contact prints over which he holds the copyright indefinitely. Categorized alphabetically by town, the photographs frequently show people conducting various business activities. Marked "Nov. 1906," a Pottsville scene includes an African American boy standing behind the bar of a saloon. An African American worker appears in a 1906 photograph of the Stony Point Granite Works in Temple, Pennsylvania and three 1906 pictures of Williamsport depict African Americans among their subjects: A print labeled "Barber Shop, Winter 1906" shows a black man dressed in a suit standing beside a shoeshine chair along with seven white barbers; a print labeled "Hotel Kitchen" shows three African American cooks; and a print labeled "Saloon" shows an African American man dressed in a suit and hat standing at a bar.

MG-281. SAMUEL W. KUHNERT PAPERS, [CA. 1915-1992].

Samuel Wilhelm Kuhnert (1890-1978) was born in Steelton and raised on a farm near Halifax. He ran a photography processing business from his home in Camp Hill and later in Harrisburg. Having a special interest in aviation, he began experimenting in 1919 with aerial photography. Over the following two decades he made and sold aerial views of communities throughout central Pennsylvania. The collection consists of over six thousand photographic prints and negatives, motion picture films, miscellaneous newspaper clippings, and personal and business records. The photographs are arranged alphabetically by subject and grouped into the following categories: aerial views, aircraft, pilots, and miscellaneous (including train, airplane, and automobile accidents and other disasters documented for insurance companies; funerals; a 1936 flood in Harrisburg; a 1932 snowstorm in Camp Hill; and various family portraits). For a more detailed description see the *Guide to Photographs at the Pennsylvania State Archives* by Linda Ries.

MISCELLANEOUS

Disasters and Accidents File. Includes many photographs showing African Americans, but most are unidentified. Several African Americans are shown in photographs appearing in a folder labeled "Plane crash."

- One undated photograph shows an African American man dressed in civilian clothing examining the wreckage of an airplane.
- A folder labeled "Single Car Accidents, Unidentified, ca. 1930" contains a photograph showing two African American men and seven African American children among a group of on-

lookers viewing an overturned car in a creek.

- A folder labeled "Miscellaneous Auto Wrecks" contains a photograph of a newspaper article from *[The] Evening [News]* dated July 30, 1958. A photograph in the article shows an African American man in a crowd.
- In the folder entitled "Dr. Marshall Murder Prints" there are two photographs of police in a morgue in Media, Pennsylvania, one whom appears to be an African American detective.
- A folder labeled "Executions, Murders, Spooks" contains photographs from El Paso, Texas stamped with the name W. H. Horne, copyright, and the date. One of these is labeled "Bodies of three men lying as they fell after being executed," showing three African Americans or possibly Mexicans. The date of the photograph is Aug. 16, 1919. Another photograph in this folder is of what appears to be a soldier shot in the head, bears the partial label ". . . after the battle" and is dated Aug. 10, 1919.
  Pilots File. Includes photographs of Hubert Julian, an African American pilot known as "the Black Eagle."

- There is one picture of Julian standing alone, and a second picture of Julian shaking hands with an unidentified man who is welcoming him to Harrisburg. There are also two pictures of Julian's plane at an airport in Harrisburg with a crowd of people who came to welcome his arrival. Julian was once the head of the Ethiopian Air Corps with the rank of colonel, Colonel Huberto Juliano.

Building and Structures, Portraits and People File. Contains many photographs of Kuhnert's family and friends.

- A folder entitled "Photography-Miscellaneous" contains three photographs of what appears to be a baptism ceremony. Two pictures clearly show two African Americans entering a river,

MG-281. Samuel W. Kuhnert Papers, [ca. 1915-1992]. Pilots File.
Huberto Juliano and an unidentified man.

believed to be the Susquehanna, and the actual baptism ritual. The third photograph shows the crowd of onlookers that appears to be composed of mixed races.

MG-283. GENEVIEVE BLATT PAPERS, 1934-1992.

Genevieve Blatt, known as the "first lady" of Pennsylvania politics, was the first woman elected to a statewide office and the first woman to sit as a Pennsylvania appellate judge. Born in East Brady, Pennsylvania, Blatt attended the University of Pittsburgh where she earned a B.A. in 1933 and an M.A. in 1934. In 1937 she obtained a law degree from the University of Pittsburgh's Law School. She was elected state secretary of internal affairs in 1954, was a Democratic nominee for the United States Senate in 1964, and served on the Commonwealth Court from 1971 to 1993. During her tenure on the bench, Blatt ordered that Pennsylvania high school sports teams could no longer discriminate on the basis of sex. From 1964 through 1968, she was a member of President Johnson's Consumer Advisory Council. In 1956, she was honored as a Distinguished Daughter of Pennsylvania and subsequently received three medals from various popes recognizing her contributions both to the Catholic Church and to society. The papers include correspondence, court opinions, campaign files, subject files, photographs, scrapbooks publicity materials, and memorabilia. Among items relating to African Americans are the following:

Filed Opinions, 1970-1984. Opinions relating to numerous appeals of unemployment compensation cases, some of which involved African Americans. Cases also concerned such types of matters as appeals filed by the Chester City firefighters (1976), Philadelphia City Board of Assistance (1976), and the labor relations case of the Altoona School Board (1975). Such opinions are likely to provide a rich source of material for scholars researching legal precedents involving labor relations, public assistance, and employment concerns of African Americans in Pennsylvania.

General Correspondence, 1966-1992. Grouped chronologically by year and arranged thereunder alphabetically by surname of correspondent. African American correspondents can therefore be easily located when the surname is known.

Internal Affairs File, 1955-1966. Contains extensive materials on Board of Pardons investigations, some of which relate to incarcerated African Americans seeking pardons.

Photographs, 1932-1989. Included are a number of photographs that have been reproduced in this book.

Publicity File, 1934-1976. Material dealing indirectly with African Americans is found in this file such as a number of letters dating from August to December of 1975 addressed to Judge Blatt from parents expressing their concerns over mandated bussing of school students in Philadelphia.

Subject Files, 1976-1977.

> *Education, 1976-1977.* Included is a file entitled "Irvis Report" that documents a number of issues of "The Irvis Report: A Periodic Report to the People on Legislative Activities" authored by state House Majority Leader K. Leroy Irvis. Among the topics covered are Irvis's analysis of the Supreme Court decision in the Allan Bakke reverse discrimination case, the text of Irvis's June 4, 1977 address to the House of Representatives concerning fair housing issues and citing the pres-

ence of African Americans at Valley Forge in 1777, and the text of Irvis's October 17, 1977 address to the Lancaster County Democratic Committee. Interleaved with the reports are letters exchanged between Irvis and Genevieve Blatt concerning topics raised in the reports.

Reference Literature, 1934-1964. Contains "Bigotry" by Dr. Maria J. Falco, a study of the 1964 senatorial campaign and ethnic politics. It was this race that Blatt lost to Republican Senator Hugh Scott. Also present are copies of Democratic Party platforms from 1934 to 1954 and of the *Pennsylvania Democratic News*, 1954-1963.

MG-284. LEROY HORLACHER PAPERS, 1918-1925 AND UNDATED.

Leroy Horlacher was a noted Socialist and member of the Industrial Workers of the World, was incarcerated during World War I as a conscientious objector at Camp Meade, Maryland; on Alcatraz Island, California, and at Fort Leavenworth, Kansas. The papers include correspondence exchanged between Horlacher and various family members and friends, photographs of prison scenes and union gatherings, and miscellaneous materials relating to the Industrial Workers of the World. The folder of photographs entitled **Pictures, [ca. 1918-1920]** includes six views of prison barracks, probably at Camp Meade, in which African Americans appear. An African American also appears in a print of a picnic sponsored by the IWW.

MG-286. PENN CENTRAL RAILROAD COL-LECTION, [CA. 1835-1968].

The Penn Central Railroad Company was created in 1968 by a merger of the Pennsylvania Railroad and the New York Central Railroad and survived until 1970 when it filed for bankruptcy. Many of its rail lines are today owned by Amtrak and by the Consolidated Rail Corporation and its successors. The bulk of this collection consists of records of the Pennsylvania Railroad Company, [ca. 1847-1968]. Incorporated on April 13, 1846, by the turn of the century the Pennsylvania Railroad Company had become the largest single employer of men and women in the United States. In addition to the Pennsylvania Railroad Company records, this collection also contains selected materials from the New York Central Railroad, Penn Central Corporation, Penn Central Transportation Company, Lehigh Valley Railroad, Erie Railroad, Erie-Lackawanna Railway, and their subsidiary companies. Only a small sampling of Pennsylvania Railroad Records have been consulted in preparing this guide.

Included among the Pennsylvania Railroad Company materials are administrative and financial records of the president, board of directors, secretary, comptroller, and treasurer; legal files, motive power and equipment records, and engineering drawings and blueprints that illustrate the construction details of locomotives, cars, bridges, and track routes. Numerous records and photographs in this collection document the African American experience. The photographs are arranged in three series. The Pennsylvania Railroad Library Photograph File includes a historical reference file of P.R.R. photographs [ca. 1850-1960]. The Conrail Mechanical Engineering Department Photograph File contains nearly two thousand prints, c. 1930, showing construction details and interior views of locomotives and rolling stock. The Penn Central Auction Pho-

438

tograph Albums depict P.R.R. locomotives, views of snow and ice conditions along the rail lines, various suburban landscapes, and a number of views of the devastation wrought by the 1889 Johnstown Flood.

PENNSYLVANIA RAILROAD COMPANY

Presidents Frank Thomson (1897-1899),
A. J. Cassatt (1899-1906), and James McCrea (1907-1913)

Presidential Correspondence, [ca 1899-1913]. Included is correspondence between A. J. Cassatt, Pennsylvania Railroad General Solicitor James A. Logan, F. T. D. Myers, and a Committee of Alexandria County Colored People (Virginia) concerning passage of the "Jim Crow" bill and incidents connected with the bill. One such incident was the arrest of the daughter of General Robert E. Lee for violating the Virginia "Jim Crow" law by refusing to move to the White section of the car. There is also a letter to Mr. Cassatt from Jerry M. Newman, a bellman from Hot Springs, Virginia, requesting a job either as a messenger at Broad Street Station or as a porter on a Pullman car. Also included are photographs of workmen in the Pennsylvania Railroad tunnels under the North and East Rivers, 1913-14.

President M. W. Clement (1935-1949)

Presidential Correspondence, 1935-1949. Includes the following items:

- Letters between Clement and C. M. Davis, President of the Atlantic Coast Line Railroad Company, requesting the Pennsylvania Railroad's permission to photograph P.R.R. coach #4292 in connection with an American Civil Liberties Union suit alleging racial discrimination (June 1949), a suit brought by an African American clergymen for denying equal accommodations on a train in Chicago (January 1943).

- An invitation to Clement to attend the premiere of a Firestone Tire & Rubber Company film entitled "Liberia, Africa's Only Republic," which portrayed the social, economic and political life of "this little-known nation founded by American Negroes which is celebrating its 100th anniversary." (November 1947)
- Letters from Clement to others concerning possible recruitment of redcaps "from other sources" (July 1943).
- Letter from Clement to Theodore W. High in response to "action of certain members of train crews in violating privacy of colored women employees in rest room at Pennsylvania Station (30th Street), Philadelphia (April 28, 1943)."

Presidents J. M. Symes (1954-1959), A. J. Greenough (1960-1962), and Chairman of the Board S. T. Saunders (1963-1967)

Correspondence, 1954-1967. The correspondence dated October, 1961 includes a letter to A. J. Greenough, president of the Pennsylvania Railroad from Eric Johnston, chairman of the African-American Trade and Development Association, requesting that the Pennsylvania Railroad become a member of the organization. The purpose of the association was to improve relations between American business firms and companies and the countries of tropical Africa. Greenough's letter to Johnson regretfully declined the invitation.

Secretary's Office

Board Files: BF Series, [ca. 1847-1906]. Included are the following two items:

- Letter from headquarters, Supervisory Committee on Colored

Enlistments, No. 1910 Chestnut Street, June 27, 1863, to the Pennsylvania Railroad requesting financial contributions to raise and maintain "colored troops" in Pennsylvania. After they were mustered into service by the governor at Camp William Penn in the Chelten Hills, all expenses of recruitment, subsistence, and transportation were to be provided by the public. In his reply to S. T. Bodine dated September 3, 1863, Pennsylvania Railroad Secretary Edmund Smith stated that the request had been referred by the board to a special committee. However on back of letter appears the notation: "Res. that it is inexpedient for this company to interfere by donating or otherwise with the organization of U.S. forces."

- Letter from W. A. Rice, Financial Agent for the Colored Industrial School in Bordertown, New Jersey, requesting that the railroad donate $250 in order to purchase additional property across the street from the school. Included is a drawing showing the three lots already owned by the school and the Leed's lot which was then for sale. Also present is a copy of the Act of the General Assembly No. 451 from the state of New Jersey, a brochure entitled *The Colored Industrial Educational Association of New Jersey*, and an announcement card for the Rev. W. A. Rice to appear as a soloist.

Minute Books of the Board of Directors, 1847-1956. Under the topical heading of "Black Recruits," the index reveals that the transport of black recruits was discussed at the April 1, 1863 meeting; aid towards the formation of black troops was requested at the February 3, 1864 meeting; and on April 6 and 20, 1864, the board discussed a letter from Thomas Webster of Philadelphia requesting a donation of $2,000 to aid in recruiting a "colored regiment."

Secretary's Office: Pennsylvania Railroad Company Library

Pamphlet files, 1846-1964. Includes a copy of the centennial issue, *The Brown Railroader*, a 1946 pamphlet providing coverage of "Negro Railroaders' activities." It consists of eighteen pages and contains articles that provide a history of African Americans on the railroad, including stories about family members of railroad employees, complimentary and congratulatory letters from African American passengers, contemporary recipes used on the trains, biographies, and a wide variety of illustrations.

Photograph File, [ca. 1830-1963]. Only a sampling of boxes was examined in preparation for this guide. Examples of photographs found showing African Americans are listed below.

Box 1: *Allegheny Portage Railroad—Canals*

- Folder 2.2 Construction of the South Street Bridge, Philadelphia, 1922-23. A photograph entitled "Caisson #3 ready to Launch" shows two African American men. Another photograph shows a group of men, one of whom appears to be an African American smoking a cigarette. The last photograph in this folder is of the middle pilings being formed. The man on the far left below the crane appears to be African American.
- Folder 3.1 Bus Service associated with the Pennsylvania Railroad. A photograph of the Pennsylvania Railroad station in Harrisburg includes a young boy and a porter who are African American. On the back the following inscription is found: "Pennsylvania General Transit Company (P.R.R.) bus leaving Pennsylvania Railroad Station at Harrisburg, Pa., for the trip to Wilkes-Barre. These Buses make one round trip daily between Harrisburg and Wilkes-

Barre." Another photograph in this folder shows an African American porter at Penn Station in New York City. The inscription on the back reads: "Motor coach for Bayville and Oyster Bay departing from the Pennsylvania Motor Coach terminal NYC."

Box 1a: *Penn Central Auction Photograph Albums*

- The box is marked "Copy 8x10 prints of Photo Album. "Photographic views of line on Pa. Schyul. Vlly RR., West of Port Clinton, PA." Owned by J. N. Dubarry, 1884-1887." There are two photographs that appear to depict African Americans, one showing men outside a tunnel laying down track, and the other showing men excavating a canal or tunnel.

Box 5: *Conrail Public Affairs Office Photographs: Monuments-Individual Portraits*

- Folder 17.1b People: Photograph album showing PRR employees in their offices around the turn of the century. African American subjects include three men wearing some type of a uniform, a photograph labeled "Pat Cole" of a seated man holding a porter's hat, an office scene labeled "Washington" showing an African American among a group of ten men, and other similar photographs showing one or more African Americans among groups of white men.

- Folder 16 Passenger Service. Many of the labeled photographs from this folder show African Americans employed in dining cars. Examples include "Photo by William M. Rittase, 243 S. 15th Street, Philadelphia" showing two

African American waiters, "Broadway Limited, 1927" also showing an African American waiter, "New P.R.R. Dining Car in Fiesta Decor" and "A Restaurant on Wheels," both from the 1950s. Other photographs portray African Americans working in dining cars during the 1920s and 1930s.

Box 10: *Stations—Trains*

- Folder 27.4c Stations: Other Philadelphia Stations. African Americans appear in photographs labeled: "Front-Passenger Station Chambersburg, 1884," "Haddon Avenue Station, Camden HS," "Loveland, Ohio, station," a 1949 view of Philadelphia Station, and a 1948 view of Wayne Station.

Box 12: *Oversized Photographs*

- One folder in the box is marked "Equipment-Dining Cars-Kitchens & Cooks." Within is a photograph of an African American man named Dennis McCloud oiling an axle, another showing two African Americans among six men working tracks, and a series of ten photographs dated 1925 depicting African American cooks.

- Folder 5. Cartoons, Drawings, and Posters. Included in the folder is a copy of *Modern Railroad*, November, 1958. One article in the magazine includes two photographs showing African Americans moving crates from a station.

- In another folder marked "2 sided prints of mixed categories: bridges, grain elevators, stations, scenery," there are two photographs of African Americans labeled "Slip Rock looking West, P-13" and "Sherman's Creek Bridge" respectively.

Vice-President of Operations
Chief of Motive Power, Mechanical Engineer

Mechanical Engineering Drawings, [ca. 1875-1960]. Included are drawings of passenger car classes #P70A and PB70A, which were used as "Jim Crow" cars for the "colored race."

Vice-President of Public Affairs
Advertising Agent

Wartime Advertising Scrapbooks, 1942-1945. These scrapbooks contain many newspaper advertisements having pictures of African Americans. The scrapbooks also contain folders, leaflets, and brochures. The pictures usually tell a story of a family and their combined years of service with the Pennsylvania Railroad and depict African Americans performing various duties as waiters, porters, redcaps, brakemen, car repairmen, crane operators, and machinists.

Vice-President of Purchases, Stores and Insurance

Photographs and Specifications for Employee Uniforms, 1945-1948. There are photographs of an African American woman wearing an employee uniform for female station and car cleaners and an African American man wearing a porter's uniform.

Voluntary Relief Department

Enrollment Cards, [ca.1865-1968]. Enrollment cards of the Voluntary Relief Department's insurance program for Pennsylvania

Railroad employees. Each card includes such information as the employee's name, date and place of birth; name of wife, mother and father; employee certificate number; dates of service; division, department, and class; occupation and rate of pay; injuries; retirement and pension date; date of death; and other related personnel information. Some of the cards have "Negro" written on them; e.g., Lamb, Samuel . . . , Negro, or "(Colored)"; e.g., Exum, Marone Wilson . . . , (Colored). Access to information on these cards is restricted for twenty-five years after the death of the individual unless permission of the donor is obtained.

MG-292. SALEM UNITED CHURCH OF CHRIST DEPOSIT OF GERMAN RE-FORMED SALEM CHURCH OF HARRIS-BURG RECORDS, 1787-1916.

The German Reformed Salem Church of Harrisburg was founded in 1787. Its records were deposited by its successor, the Salem United Church of Christ, the sanctuary of which currently stands at the corner of Chestnut and Third Streets in Harrisburg, Pa.

CHURCH RECORDS, 1787-1916

Charters, 1818, 1858, 1870. Various charters related to the German Reformed Salem Church. Included is a printed copy of the *Articles of Association*. Listed in Article III is a breakdown of property owned by the Church. "They also own and have in fee simple, in common with the Evangelical Lutheran Zion Church of Harrisburg, all that certain property or Real Estate, late a burying ground, situated in the said borough of Harrisburg, and bounded by Fourth street; lot of A. L. Roumfort; Chestnut street; lot of E. Byers; Colored burying ground; Meadow Lane; property of Presbyterian Church, and Blackberry alley."

Deeds, 1807, 1857-1872. Four deeds of the German Reformed Salem Church. Included is a deed entitled "Lots sold by Lutheran Congregation of Harrisburg, May 23, 1859," in which the "colored grave yard" is mentioned as a contiguous tract. The deed states: "Whereas the said three several and contiguous pieces or lots of ground have, by the direction of a majority of each of the vestries of said Churches, been divided into fifteen several lots or pieces of ground, numbered respectively from One (1) to fifteen (15) inclusive, Beginning at blackberry Alley next the Lutheran Church on Fourth Street, and running down Fourth Street to Chestnut thence down Chestnut to the African grave yard, thence along Meadow Lane to the Presbyterian grave yard."

Minute Books, 1813-1887. Minutes of the German Reformed Salem Church consist of handwritten notes that show the date, the location of the meeting, and the names of those who presided at the meeting. Topics include raising funds for the construction of the new church, policies and procedures, and the hiring of new pastors. Also documented is a record of a church proceeding against Ms. Fanny Jones accused of displaying an "immoral and unchristian like manner." Dated May 10 and 13, 1843, many members of the church congregation testified that Ms. Jones had "carried on" with married men and entertained people of questionable character in her home at different hours of the day. In testimony given by a witness, Fanny Jones "seemed equally familiar in talking both to blacks and whites." Other entries mentioning African Americans include: April 12, 1857, a notice on a lecture that was delivered by Reverend Brown on the Aspects of the Missionary cause of Africa and a March 28, 1859 entry mentioning "the colored graveyard" in relationship to the German Reformed Church lots. On the following page is a rough map of the lots at the Harrisburg cemetery that shows the location of the African Graveyard in relation to the German Reformed and Lutheran lots.

MG-296. THOMAS KRAMER COLLECTION, 1780-1889 (BULK 1835-1882).

Thomas Kramer was a justice of the peace in Palmyra, Lebanon County, from 1844 to 1880. The collection consists primarily of legal papers as well as some genealogical materials pertaining to the Kramer and Segner families. Included in the collection is a handwritten manuscript entitled "A History of Pennsylvania From Its First Settlements by the Swedes and the Dutch Down to the Year 1872" by John F. Wolfinger of Milton, Pennsylvania. This manuscript contains several references to African Americans. In an appendix to chapter 3, the "rebellion of blacks" in the West Indies, Haiti, and St. Dominique is noted. Chapter 10 mentions William Penn's "black servant." References to "blacks" as a group of people among the general population are found in chapters 13, 21, 22, and 24. Chapter 30 discusses the role of Pennsylvania in the Civil War as well as slavery, the Missouri Compromise, and the Kansas-Nebraska Act.

MG-297. MARY SACHS COLLECTION, 1928-1970.

Mary Sachs (1888-1960), an owner of successful retail stores in Harrisburg and Lancaster, was a Harrisburg philanthropist and a founder of the Albert Einstein College of Medicine at Yeshiva University. She was active in Jewish organizations such as the United Jewish Appeal and the Israel Bond Campaign. This collection consists of correspondence, writings, photographs, newspaper clippings, scrapbooks, philanthropic memorabilia, business records, and personal papers, including letters from President Franklin Roosevelt and his wife Eleanor.

A. PERSONAL, 1928-1960

Pictures, 1928-1960. Includes an unidentified and undated photograph of Dwight D. Eisenhower at a dinner with an African American waiter standing in the background.

B. "MERCHANT PRINCESS," 1932-1960

Pictures, 1932 and undated. Includes three photographs depicting African American staff and clerks in the Sachs Department Stores.

D. MARY SACHS, INC., 1960-1970

Pictures, 1962. One photograph shows an African American who may be a caterer at a company party and another shows an African American woman seated at the head of a table.

Miscellaneous—Photographs, 1960. Depicts African Americans at a dinner banquet.

MG-299. COMMONWEALTH ASSOCIATION OF STUDENTS RECORDS, 1973-1979.

The Commonwealth Association of Students was founded in 1973 by students of the state colleges belonging to the Pennsylvania State System of Higher Education as a student lobbying organization to combat rising tuition costs and budget cutbacks that threatened the quality of college programs. In 1983 the dues from the tuition check off program that funded the association were eliminated and it ceased functioning in 1986. Donated to the State Archives in 1980 by the executive director of the organization, the collection includes administrative files and minutes.

Administrative File, 1973-1979.

Affirmative Action and Desegregation, 1975. Memos, essays, and reports related to affirmative action and desegregation in Pennsylvania's state colleges. Included is a report on the "Status of Edinboro State College in Terms of the Affirmative Action Proposals Adopted by the Commonwealth Association of Students," a memo from the "Black Student Movement of East Stroudsburg State College" on ways to improve minority problems, a report from the Commonwealth Association of Students entitled "Affirmative Action: The Role of Students and Student Governments of the Pennsylvania State Colleges and University," and a list of nineteen objectives endorsed by the Commonwealth Association of Students that relate to desegregation.

Appropriations, 1974-1978. Press releases concerning budget appropriations, prepared speeches on the increasing costs of higher education, a copy of Governor Shapp's speech on the budget, letters to the members of the general assembly, and statistics on budget appropriations to state funded universities. Included is a 1974-78 state-related appropriations sheet listing statistical information for Lincoln University and Cheyney University, a fact-file sheet listing state tax funds for higher education in Pennsylvania provides information on Lincoln University, and a copy of the list of state colleges and university deficits contains information on the cost of desegregation programs at Cheyney University. Also present is a membership form for the American Civil Liberties Union and a copy of the study "Patterns of Appropriations for Institutions of Higher Education" prepared by the General Assembly of Pennsylvania in 1955-56, in which Lincoln University and Cheyney University are featured.

Coordinators' Reports and Correspondence, 1976-1977. Memoranda, letters, and general correspondence from members of the Commonwealth Association of Students. Several items deal with affirmative action and the need to get Black organizations on state college campuses involved in CAS activities. Also present is a copy of the *Affirmative Action Register* (AAR), a paper used to direct "help wanted" ads to minorities.

MG-301. JOHN CRAIN KUNKEL COLLECTION, 1798-1873, 1936-1966.

Born in Harrisburg on July 21, 1898, John Crain Kunkel served a total of nine terms as a United States representative from Pennsylvania, 1938-1950 and 1961-1967. During his congressional career, Kunkel held posts on the Banking and Currency Committee, Revision of the Laws Committee, and Select Committee on Foreign Aid. A prominent Harrisburg attorney and businessman, he also served as a Dauphin County commissioner from 1952 to 1956 and on the boards of Wilson College, St. Stephen's Episcopal Church, the Harrisburg Boys Club, and the Lions Club. Both his grandfather and great-grandfather were also members of Congress. The collection contains business, congressional, county commissioner, personal, and political files that include correspondence, pamphlets, news clippings, tape recordings, and videotapes.

CONGRESSIONAL RECORDS (87ᵀᴴ - 89ᵀᴴ)

Administrative File, 1961-1966. Contains information on legislation authored, sponsored, or lobbied for by Kunkel. Several items that refer to African Americans are included in the following subseries:

General File, 1964. Provides information on such varied subjects as the armed forces, the Atomic Energy Commission, the 1964 Civil Rights Act, funding for Housing and Urban Development programs, rationing, banking, immigration, price fixing, communism, flood control, farming, and labor. Also present are two audio tapes of a program broadcast on WHP, Harrisburg, on January 23, 1964 and February 2, 1964, respectively, in which Kunkel discusses civil rights along with other national and world affairs.

General File, **A-Z, 1966.** Includes a copy of the itinerary of the 1966 Candidates' Conference at which J. Earl Dearing and William D. Johnson delivered a speech on "The Negro Vote." Also included are typed telephone messages relating to the African Methodist Episcopal Church in Harrisburg dated September 29, 1965 concerning a church banquet scheduled for October 15, 1965 and one on May 24, 1965 requesting a flag for Cub Pack #239 of Wesley Zion African Methodist Episcopal Church. Also present are numerous political campaign pamphlets from the 1964-65 campaign season and a "Special Release" concerning the accomplishments and failures of the 89th Congress. In the "Did Not Do" category, regret is expressed over failure of the legislature to strengthen Title VII of the 1964 Civil Rights Act, a ten-page news release issued by the Republican National Committee on the subject of housing and urban development programs, and a booklet issued for the Republican congressional campaign that provided source material for campaign speeches on such issues as voting rights.

MG-304. POLITICAL MEMORABILIA COLLECTION, 1900, 1918, 1964-1990.

This artificial collection of Pennsylvania and national campaign materials grew from a variety of donations from both individuals and archival institutions, and contains brochures, flyers, newsletters, newspaper clippings, bumper stickers, posters, stationery, petitions, voter registration forms, sound recordings, and motion picture film. Several items in the collection pertain to African Americans:

- **1968.** A 16mm motion picture film promoting the presidential candidacy of Richard Nixon, on which Senator Edward Brooke of Massachusetts provides a testimonial.
- **1978 General Election.** Includes a flyer directed at "Black Voters" in support of the gubernatorial campaign of Dick Thornburgh.
- **Miscellaneous, 1976-1790.** Includes a flyer printed by the "Voice of Liberty." The "Voice of Liberty" opposed the presidential bid of Jimmy Carter because he favored the Civil Rights Act, forced busing and had an aide, Morris Dees, who raised funds to defend Jo Ann Little, "the black revolutionist who was charged with murdering her white jailer."

MG-306. ERNEST P. KLINE PAPERS, 1965-1978.

Ernest Paul Kline (b.1929), was elected to the senate from the 47th District in 1965 and re-elected in 1966 and 1968; was Democratic floor leader from 1967 to 1969; and was elected as lieutenant governor to Governor Milton Shapp in 1970. He was re-elected with Shapp in 1974. His papers consist mainly of the correspondence and general files covering Kline's tenure as a state senator and lieutenant governor.

LIEUTENANT GOVERNOR'S PAPERS, 1971-1972

Departmental File, 1971-1975. The following topics relate to African American issues:

- *Governor's Office: Terry Dellmuth-Special Assistant for Human Services, 1971.* Includes NAACP items concerning Shapp's Task Force to Combat Discrimination.
- *Human Relations, 1971.* Includes correspondence dealing with desegregation problems in the Aliquippa and Chester School Districts, statistics on state government employees, and lists of African Americans and women currently in Pennsylvania state government positions.
- *Governor's Office (General), 1972.* Among the items present are materials relating to charges from the NAACP alleging discriminatory hiring practices by the Capitol Police, and correspondence noting the creation of an Affirmative Action Council with Kline as chairman.
- *Human Relations Commission, 1972.* Provides statistics on desegregation-induced bussing, correspondence, recommendations and appointments to the commission, information on the contract compliance regulations created to insure non-discrimination and equal employment opportunities, and discrimination complaints.
- *Governor's Office: Terry Dellmuth-Special Assistant for Human Services, 1973.* Contains information on affirmative action, the desegregation of juvenile offender homes, African American enrollment in state-supported colleges, and changes in the employment practices of the state.
- *Human Relations Commission, 1973.* Includes a letter by Ida Belle Minnie of the Commonwealth Association of Student

Government protesting the possible abolishment of the Human Relations Commission, correspondence dealing with the discriminatory height requirements for applicants to the State Police, and the legislative recommendations of the Pennsylvania Human Relations Commission.

- *Governor's Office: Terry Dellmuth-Special Assistant for Human Services, 1974.* Includes correspondence dealing with contract compliance.
- *Human Relations Commission, 1974.* Includes a resolution from the Erie NAACP supporting affirmative action, a plan to change the lack of minority employment in New Castle, community attitudes towards forced racial quota systems, a petition from the Harrisburg Jaycees protesting Senate Bill 653 and 1306 which would weaken the commission, information on contract Compliance, and observations of the commission on Senate Bill 1400 regarding the assignments of students.
- *Affirmative Action Council, 1975.* Contains the affirmative action plans and progress reports filed by various counties, information concerning reorganization of the council, performance evaluations, meetings and minutes, information on contract compliance, concern over summer employment for minority students, and information on the Bureau of Minority Business Development that was concerned with the need to encourage state procurement of services by minority-owned business, and the need for state assistance in community development programs.
- *Human Relations Commission, 1975.* Contains materials relating to the twentieth anniversary of the Fair Employment Practice Act (now known as the Pennsylvania Human Relations Act).
- *Affirmative Action, 1976.* Provides information about the appointment of the director of the council, the creation of an advisory council, and meetings; and an annual report of the

Human Relations Commission.

Subject File, 1972-1976. The following subject files are relevant:

- *Affirmative Action Council, 1972.* Contains newspaper articles detailing discriminatory employment practices, appointments and recommendations, training seminars, minutes of meetings, statements by Shapp about the council, progress reports and council objectives, affirmative action plans accepted by the council, correspondence about discriminatory hiring practices by the State Police and the Department of Military Affairs, and correspondence with C. DeLores Tucker about the employment of African American women.

- *Task Force on Equal Rights, 1972.* Provides historical background and list of accomplishments, memoranda from meetings, information concerning discrimination within the task force itself and physical altercations at a task force workshop, and information on workshop on recruitment practices.

- *Affirmative Action Council, 1973.* Correspondence, minutes, agendas, recommendations, statistics, progress reports, training programs, grievance procedures, directives, reports, information on the Congress for Affirmative Action, and reports on minorities hired by the State Police; and *Project Equality,* concerning equal employment opportunities, and containing a directory of minority contractors, tradesmen, and related professionals.

- *Affirmative Action Council, 1974.* Meeting agendas, requests for assistance, complaints, statistics, training session materials, management guides, and correspondence relating to the council's budget, minority business contractors, affirmative action in higher education and labor and industry, and hiring practices of the Department of Education; *Affirmative Action-Vacancy,* concerning the appointment of Leonard Black

456

as executive director of the Affirmative Action Council, applications and resumes for the position, and interviewing processes; and the *Bureau of Minority Business Development*, including requests for the *Directory of Minority Businesses in Pennsylvania*, and support for House Bill 1386 which would support minority businesses.

- **Bureau of Minority Business Development, 1976.** Includes copies of legislation from California dealing with small businesses and amendments to the Pennsylvania Minority Business Development Act.

Roy Hansard, Staff Assistant to the Lt. Gov. Files. Files exist on the following topics.

- *Affirmative Action, 1974-77.* Includes a budget proposal, job description, structural organization of the Philadelphia Office of Minority Affairs, articles about minority contractors, and information on NAACP discontent that women and Hispanics seemed to be getting more attention than African Americans. Also present are meeting minutes, material relating to training sessions, statistical information about racial discrimination, and articles about affirmative action and the Equal Opportunity Employment Office.
- *Black Bicentennial Steering Committee, 1975.* Includes a letter of thanks to a participant from K. Leroy Irvis, and plans to publish and discuss the meeting at a conference of Black elected officials.
- *Civil Tension Task Force, 1976.* Includes plans for outbreak of civil tension, an outline of services, a list of members of the task force, and "move-in" procedures.
- *Human Relations Commission, 1976.* Includes a guide for complaints, a letter from the commission defending its progress, individual complaints, hearings of particular cases,

pamphlets of laws introduced by the Human Relations Commission, and annual reports.

- *Minority Contractors, 1976.* Includes materials relating to a program to expand the volume of state-solicited minority contracts, and a list of qualified minority contractors.
- *United Negro College Fund, 1976.* Pamphlets, fact booklets, and information on the Pennsylvania State Employees' United Negro College Fund Campaign.
- *Urban League of Pittsburgh, 1976.* A report of a Housing Counseling Service Program which details clients' race (over 50 percent African Americans).

MG-307. ALBERT F. HEESS CORRESPONDENCE, 1899, 1901-1945.

This correspondence is chiefly copies of letters sent by Albert F. Heess, a member of the law firm of Thomson and Heess of Dushore, 1903-1907. Also present are a Republican poll book, 1899, and correspondence and naturalization papers dating from Albert Heess's tenure as Sullivan County prothonotary, register, recorder, and clerk of court from 1908 to 1932 and as district attorney from 1938 to 1944.

Correspondence (Alphabetical), B-W. In Folder C (May 29, 1901-Oct. 19, 1906) is a clipping from *The Philadelphia Inquirer* about robbery suspect Robert Morris who is identified as "Negro." Though undated, the article is believed to have been published on October 25, 1906, and it appears to be incomplete in the file.

Correspondence (Chronological), 1901-1945. In folder marked "Dec. 4, 1922-Dec. 29, 1922" is a letter from the Department of Commerce, Bureau of Census, Washington, D.C. dated December

15, 1922, requesting that a census of prisoners be taken. The census was to provide for each prisoner: "Name, sex, age (exact or approximate), offense, sentence and fine (if any), race (whether White, Negro, Indian, Chinese, or Japanese), and, if foreign born, country of birth and native language."

MG-308. THOMAS W. POMEROY JR. PAPERS, 1969-1979.

Thomas Wilson Pomeroy Jr. (b. 1908) was a Pennsylvania Supreme Court justice from 1968-1979. Originally a lawyer from the Pittsburgh area, he was admitted to the Pennsylvania Bar in 1933, practiced law in Pittsburgh, and subsequently was a partner in the firm of Kirkpatrick, Pomeroy, Lockhart and Johnson, 1948-1968. These papers are chiefly legal opinion files relating to cases heard by the Pennsylvania Supreme Court. Although many of the cases are simply appeals from lower courts regarding contractual obligations, criminality, personal injury, equity, guardianship, estates, and damage awards, some cases deal with such topics as discrimination, collective bargaining, eminent domain, affirmative action, environmental controls, and desegregation. Two concurring opinions relate to cases involving African Americans.

- An equity case appealed from the Philadelphia County Court of Common Pleas to the Eastern District of the Pennsylvania Supreme Court, *New Mount Calvary Baptist Church v. Willie Drayton* (January Term, 1971), involved a review of a chancellor's decree directing that Willie Drayton, pastor of the church and trustee of its property, to convey title to the church property and to deliver the keys to six new officers named as successor trustees by the church.
- In a 1975 appeal from the Allegheny County Court of Common Pleas to the Western District of the Supreme Court of

Pennsylvania, *Jones v. New Pittsburgh Courier Publishing Company*, Richard F. Jones, receiver of the Pittsburgh Liquidating Corporation, took legal action against the New Pittsburgh Courier Publishing Company, an African American newspaper publisher. Other legal opinions on cases involving the Pennsylvania Human Relations Commission are also found in the files.

MG-309. MILTON J. SHAPP PAPERS, 1971-1979.

A pioneer in the cable television industry, Milton Jerrold Shapp (b.1912) was elected governor of Pennsylvania in 1970 and 1974. He graduated from Case Institute of Technology (now Case-Western Reserve University) in 1933 with a B.S. in electrical engineering. During the Second World War he served as a captain in the Army Signal Corps in North Africa, Italy, and Austria and subsequently founded Jerrold Electronics Corporation. During his tenure as governor, Shapp negotiated the settlement of a strike by independent truckers in February, 1974, and implemented a program of fiscal responsibility for state government and financial disclosure requirements for public officials.

Boards and Commissions, 1971-1975. Includes correspondence from Representative Sarah Anderson dealing with the commemoration of Dr. Martin Luther King's birthday, Equal Rights Day, and a request for a proclamation for Negro History Week. Also present is a letter from African American state Representative James Barber inviting Governor Shapp to a dinner held by the Pennsylvania Black Legislative Caucus and also discussing the possibility of the Rev. Jesse Jackson speaking before the House of Representatives.

Recommendations. A record of appointments or nominations made by Governor Shapp to various boards and commissions. Each file generally contains press releases, notification letters from the governor, letters of acknowledgment from appointees, nomination letters to the senate, and sometimes State Police background reports and senate confirmation letters signed by the chief clerk. The recommendation files also generally contain letters of support for appointees. Recommendations for the following categories were found to relate to African Americans:

- Abortion Law Commission, 1972. Includes recommendations for the following African Americans as board members: Dr. Amanda Blount, Mrs. Jesse Clark, and Helen Wright.
- Human Relations Commission, 1971-1972. The following African Americans were recommended to serve on the board: Keith A. Bodden, Alma Speed Fox, Elizabeth Scott, and Nettie W. Taylor.
- Labor Relations Board, 1971. Charles Long, chairman of the A. Philip Randolph Institute of Pittsburgh, was appointed to the board in 1971.
- Governor's Committee on Migratory Labor, 1972. Membership list includes Dr. F. L. Vaughn, president of the NAACP, and NAACP representative John B. Canpbell.
- Pennsylvania Board of Probation and Parole, 1972. Includes a letter dated October 2, 1972 from Rev. Robert Johnson Smith of Salem Baptist Church of Jenkintown recommending the reappointment of John H. Jefferson as a board member.
- State Board of Cosmetology, 1971. Janice E. Williams and Serena B. Patterson were recommended as board members by C. Delores Tucker.

- State Board of Funeral Directors, 1971. Major H. Winfield was recommended as a board member by funeral director Jacob Franklin and Secretary C. Delores Tucker.
- Cheyney State College, 1971-1974. Recommendations and appointments for the board of trustees are: Rev. Jacob L. Chatman (1971); Laverne Coleman, Marjerie Duckery, Bessie Jones, James H. Jones, Edward Lee, Theresa Ruffin, and Paul E. Waters (1973), and Carl O. Dickerson and Donald Wilson (1974).
- Lincoln University, 1973. Recommendations for Mary Baltimore, James Bodine, Fletcher L. Byron, Marjerie Duckery, Elizabeth Greenfield, Charles L. Huston III, Herbert Hutton, Alfred H. Hunt, James H. Jones, Aaron Martin, Mrs. Herbert May, Bishop Roy Nichols, Dr. Leroy Patrick, Benjamin J. Reynolds, James Rowland Sr., Richard Mellon Scaife, Judge Harvey Schmidt, the Honorable William Scranton, Richard B. Tucker, and Paul Waters.

O.K. File. A record of appointments made by Governor Shapp to various boards and commissions. Each file generally contains press releases, notification letters from the governor, letters of acknowledgment from appointees, nomination letters to the senate, and sometimes State Police background reports and senate confirmation letters signed by the chief clerk.

- Department Heads-Correspondence, 1970-1971. Includes a letter dated December 18, 1970 to Secretary of State C. Delores Tucker regarding amendments to the Solicitation of Charitable Funds Act, a letter dated January 14, 1971 from Judge A. Leon Higgenbotham expressing his pleasure at the appointment of C. Delores Tucker as secretary of state, and a letter of response from Governor Shapp. Also present is a letter dated February 16, 1971 appointing Dr. J. Finton Speller as secretary of health together with a letter of acknowledgment from Dr. Speller, and letters of congratulating Dr. Speller on his appointment.

- Task Force to Eliminate Discrimination Against Women and Minority Groups in Government, 1971. Contains Executive Directive No. 2, September 2, 1971, for the Implementation of the Commitment Toward Equal Rights and a news release dated October 1, 1971 in which Governor Shapp announced the creation of this cabinet-level task force.

- Pennsylvania Abortion Law Commission, 1972. The following African American women were recommended for the board: Dr. Amanda C. Blount, Lucille F. Clark, and Helen J. Wright.

- Pennsylvania Affirmative Action Council, 1971-1972. Governor Shapp appointed Lieutenant Governor Ernest P. Kline as chairman of the Council and the members were Secretary of the Commonwealth C. Delores Tucker, Secretary of Administration Ronald G. Lench, Executive Director of the Human Relations Commission Homer G. Floyd, Executive Director of the Governor's Council on Equal Opportunity for the Spanish-speaking Bolivar Rivera, Executive Director of the Commission on the Status of Women Arlene Lotman, representative of Affirmative Action Officers Calvin C. Edmonds, and Pat Quann and Terry Dellmuth, special assistants to the governor.

- Mercy-Douglass Hospital Task Force, 1973. After closing this Philadelphia hospital which had served the community for thirty years, a task force was created by Governor Shapp to explore ways the former hospital facility could be remodeled and reopened.

- Governor's Committee on Migratory Labor, 1971-1972. In 1970 it was estimated that 72 percent of Pennsylvania's migrant population consisted of African Americans who came from southern states. Names of African Americans recommended for this committee were F. L. Vaughn (1971) and John B. Campbell (1972), both members of the NAACP.

- Pennsylvania Labor Relations Board, 1974. Governor Shapp appointed James H. Jones, president of the Negro Trade Union Leadership Council, to the Labor Relations Board.
- Cheyney State College, 1974-1975. Includes letter of resignation from board of trustees member Hobson R. Reynolds, July 9, 1974; an acknowledgment from board President Wade Wilson, July 23, 1974; a letter of recommendation for Edward S. Lee from Robert N. C. Nix, September 9, 1974; and listings for the following Board members: Rev. Jacob L. Chatman (1972-74), Lois G. Peterson (1972-74), Arthur Thomas (1972-74), Edward S. Lee (1973-74), and Philip Lichtenberg (1974). Governor Shapp nominated Charles M. Porter to the board in 1975.
- Industrialized Housing Advisory Commission, 1974. Mrs. Shirley Dennis was re-appointed to the board on December 18, 1974.
- Lincoln University. Dr. Leroy Patrick and George Branch were appointed to the board of trustees and Edward B. Lee recommended the following individuals: Charles Hannah, Robert Hannah, Leo S. Holmes, and Jesse Woods.
- Pennsylvania State University, 1974. The Honorable Joseph Rhodes Jr. was appointed to the board on January 6, 1974.
- Scotland School for Veterans' Children, 1974-1977. List of board members: Berkely R. Fogelsanger, Clay F. Henninger, Crawford M. Mackley, Abe Ruben, Eugene R. Manfrey, Marlin O. Walter, Joseph Shain, Honorable

William Rayhauser, and Dr. Ruth Miller Steese.

- State College and University Directors, 1971. Percy D. Mitchell was reappointed to serve on the board on December 31, 1971.
- Temple University, 1974. Honorable William H. Hastie was reappointed on January 6, 1974 but resigned from the board on July 5, 1974. Several letters concern Hastie's resignation.
- West Chester State College. Charles M. Porter was re-appointed to the board of directors on January 2, 1975.

End of Administration Files, 1979. Records of the final days of the administration containing both general and subject correspondence, citations, nominations sent to the Senate, and letters of recommendation for Governor's Office employees.

General Correspondence, 1979. Includes a letter dated December 2, 1978, together with a resume, from Sylvia Dykes requesting state government employment; a letter dated January 10, 1979 from Sallie Mae Hunt of Tennessee requesting information on her son who was incarcerated in the Camp Hill Penitentiary; and a copy of the *Pittsburgh Courier* dated December 30, 1978 featuring an article entitled "Grandmother of the Year" honoring Dorothy Johnson at the Miller Elementary School in Pittsburgh.

Subject Correspondence, 1979. Contains a letter of acceptance dated December 8, 1978 to Stanley A. Culbreth, president of the Philadelphia Chapter of the Southern Christian Leadership Conference, confirming Governor Shapp's attendance at a mock bill signing for House Bill 163, which created Martin Luther King Jr. Day as a state holiday. Also present is a letter dated December 15, 1978 inviting Governor Shapp to attend the Third Birthday Celebration on January 3, 1979 sponsored by Operation PUSH/Philadelphia, a letter dated September 18, 1978 from Alfred L. Morris, president of the *Philadelphia Tribune*, and other correspondence regarding George Washington Carver Day, January 5, 1979, and a letter from Barton A. Fields dated January 6, 1979 submitting his resignation as secretary of the Commonwealth.

Files of the Special Assistant of Human Services, 1971-1979. Arranged alphabetically by subject. Correspondence, reports, and minutes of the special assistant to the governor for human services. The following represent a sampling of the files relevant to African Americans:

Affirmative Action Council, 1971-1977. Contains Executive Order for the Affirmative Action Plan, membership list, minutes of meetings, and a December 1974 position paper on affirmative action authored by Terry Dellmuth. Materials are also present on the topics of labor and industry, insurance, Civil Service Commission, State Police, and the Departments of Trans[portation] and Welfare.

Cheyney State College, 1977-78. Including letters opposing state budget cuts for Cheyney from: Pamela Rainey Lawler, Cheyney-Temple Cluster Industry representative; William M. McCormick, vice president of the Franklin Mint; Andrea D. Sullivan, director of Crime Prevention Project of the National Urban League; Thomas Cooper, vice president of Girard Bank; and a petition from the Friends of Cheyney College containing over one hundred signatures. Also present is a letter dated December 1, 1977 from E. Sonny Harris containing a resolution passed by the faculty executive committee of Cheyney asking for a right to have a voice in the selection of a new college president.

Human Relations Commission. Contains correspondence to and from the NAACP concerning the deteriorating authority of the commission and repeated attempts by Senator Nolan to abolish or weaken the commission through House Bills 653 and 1306. A memo entitled "Desegregation of Schools" concerns Superintendent Dr. David H. Porter of the Harrisburg School District and Superintendent Harry R. Faulk of the McKeesport School District, who gave testimony concerning school segregation and a report issued by the commission entitled *Problems and Progress of Blacks, Hispanics, and Females in Pennsylvania Higher Education*. The file also contains appointments to the commission and the Pennsylvania Association of Realtors to ensure fair housing practices, invitations to commission luncheons and banquets, a summary of the commission's response to general complaints, correspondence with Representative K. Leroy Irvis, reports on sickle cell anemia, Irvis's case of discrimination against a Moose Lodge in Harrisburg, and Irvis's difficulty in finding depositors for an African American owned and operated savings and loan company in Pittsburgh.

Human Service Integration Project, 1974-1975. Contains information on this national project that was funded by the United States Department of Health, Education, and Welfare, whereby many agencies providing human services would consolidate to better integrate delivery of services. Present is a letter from Governor Shapp thanking Regional 3 Director Gorham L. Black Jr. of the Pennsylvania Department of Health, Education and Welfare for his efforts in preparing the Partnership Grant for the Human Services Integration Project.

Lincoln University, 1977-1978. Contains population data on higher education in Pennsylvania including college enrollments by racial and ethnic categories and materials relating to problems arising at Lincoln University among faculty and students during the presidency of Dr. Herman Branson.

Files of Larry Hochendoner, Special Assistant to the Governor, 1977. Arranged alphabetically by subject, these consist of correspondence, minutes, and reports of the governor's special assistant for planning and economic development.

> ***Bethune-Douglass, Williamsport, 1977.*** Included is a letter dated July 13, 1977 from Hochendoner to Bertha P. Fischer regarding omission of Bethune's project to the Commonwealth.

> ***Chester Group, 1977.*** Contains "Progress Report No. 6" dated July 15, 1977 addressing the goals of the Chester Group's progress in economic development for both the public and private sectors. The Chester Group was created in 1976 with the goal of retaining and expanding businesses and creating a more positive business climate in the Chester area.

General File. Arranged alphabetically by name of person or organization, subject, or title. Within each category the papers are arranged chronologically. The following items pertain to African Americans:

> ***First Term, 1971-1975.***

> - Correspondence from Representative Sarah Anderson concerning commemoration of Dr. Martin Luther King Jr.'s birthday, Equal Rights Day, and a request for proclamation of a Negro History Day.
> - Letter from Representative James Barber inviting Governor Shapp to a banquet at the Pennsylvania Black Legis-

lative Caucus and the possibility of the Rev. Jesse Jackson addressing the House of Representatives.

- A file labeled "Black" contains extensive materials on the closing of the Black Action Drug Center in Pittsburgh, a Black American Film Festival, Black applicants to the Altoona Bureau of Employment Security, a Black Artist Exhibit, the Black Athletes' Foundation for Research in Sickle-Cell Disease, the Pennsylvania Conference on Black Basic Education, the Black Businessmen's Association of Harrisburg, the Black Christian Fellowship, efforts to develop a Black Cowboy Museum, an open house at the Black Cultural Center in Erie, the status of Black employees at the State Bureau of Investigation, Black History Month, Black History Week Proclamation, and similar items relating to the African American experience in Pennsylvania.

- A folder labeled "Gorham L. Black Jr." contains over thirty items dealing with management problems encountered by the Shapp campaign in Philadelphia's African American community and includes a letter from Representative Lucien Blackwell.

- H. A. Bledsoe, an African American, wrote a letter concerning the arrest of his son in Cumberland County for a speeding violation on June 11, 1972.

- Cheyney State College correspondence concerning a project called "Overcome the Odds-1970-1971," including requests by Cheyney President Wilson Wade for Governor Shapp to attend his first press conference at Cheyney in 1970, and to deliver the Cheyney commencement address in 1972, and materials concerning increasing SEPTA service to Cheyney from Philadelphia.

- Christian Charities Inc. Contains letters to Governor Shapp from President-Director Rev. Horace W. Gillison Jr. requesting a proclamation of a day of prayer for the repentance and forgiveness of former President Richard M. Nixon with regard to the Watergate affair. Governor Shapp did not honor the request.

- Human Relations Commission. Correspondence addressed to Governor Shapp concerning legislative efforts to abolish or reduce the power of the commission.
- K. Leroy Irvis. Correspondence and other documentation concerning the closing of a state store located at 1718 Fifth Avenue in Pittsburgh within one block of a school in an African American community. Also legislative recommendations for the Human Relations Commission, reports on Sickle-Cell Disease, Irvis's discrimination suit against a Harrisburg Moose Lodge, and periodic legislative reports issued by Irvis's office.
- Rev. Jesse Jackson. Contains an article entitled "Jackson Demands Black Action" that appeared in the *Pittsburgh Press* on May 5, 1972, in which Jackson urged his audience at the Civic Arena to "grow into a more powerful socio-economic force by expanding their minds."
- Lincoln University, 1971-74. Includes announcement of a vote by the board of trustees on August 19, 1972 that the name of the institution be changed to Lincoln University of the Commonwealth System of Higher Education, an invitation to the inauguration of Dr. Herman Branson as president, and a 1974 report of the auditing team of the adjutant general.
- National Association for the Advancement of Colored People. Contains letter congratulating Governor Shapp on his election and for appointing C. Delores Tucker as secretary of state.
- "Negro" file, 1971-72. Includes citations for achievement in the field of aviation for the Negro Airman International

organization, and for the Negro Civic Organization, the Negro Cultural Center, Negro History Week, and the Negro Trade Union Leadership Council.

- Representative Joseph Rhodes, 1971-73. Correspondence from Representative Rhodes concerning the World Hunger Coalition, Rhodes's support of Shapp's position on the death penalty, Rhodes's involvement in the Youth Treatment Centers, and a proposed drug program for the state.
- C. Delores Tucker. News releases concerning Tucker's appointment as secretary of the Commonwealth, a letter from a "Tired Taxpayer" requesting that her office be investigated, and Tucker's addresses to various seminars, the NAACP, the Organization of Concerned Youth, and the National Catholic Conference on Interracial Justice. Also present are materials relating to Tucker's investigations of charitable organizations, correspondence concerning the Black Political Pageant, a speech on "Black Capitalism" and Black economic development, her participation in Martin Luther King Jr. International Freedom Games, and letters of respect and gratitude from a Pennsylvania NAACP branch.
- United Negro College Fund. Letter dated May 2, 1972 from Philadelphia Chairman Charles K. Cox requesting the governor to sponsor the fall campaign in Philadelphia and a January 15, 1874 memo from C. Delores Tucker informing Governor Shapp that Clarence M. Payne was requesting the governor's support in the statewide campaign.
- United Neighborhood Services of Lackawanna County. Letters to Pennsylvania Department of Health dated March 12, 1974 offering their facility as a sickle-cell anemia testing center.

Second Term, 1975-1979.

- Contains correspondence from Representative James Barber, including a survey on African American employment, various invitations to Governor Shapp, and a letter thanking Governor Shapp for appointing Barber to the board of trustees of Lincoln University.
- A file marked "Black" contains invitations to a Black Arts Festival, a proclamation for the Black Athletes' Foundation, a charity request from the Black Athletes' Hall of Fame, an invitation to a meeting of the Black Coalition on Human Rights, an invitation to the Black College Presidents Workshop luncheon, an invitation to the Black Conference on Higher Education, correspondence from the Black Construction Coalition concerned with problems facing minority contractors, a list of African American employees serving under Governor Shapp in management positions, citations for outstanding achievements in Black Enterprise, materials relating to the Black Heritage Exhibit at the William Penn Memorial Museum, an invitation to the dedication of Black History Month, transcripts of interviews from the television program "Black Perspective on the News," an invitation to a dinner held by the Black Political Forum, a history on "The Black Press in America" and a request for a proclamation to honor the press's one hundred fiftieth anniversary, a charity request for the Black Solidarity Fair, a proclamation for Black Solidarity Week, a request for a proclamation for a Black Veterans Day, a request from the Black Women's Association for a citation honoring Dr. Selma H. Burke, materials relating to the Black Women's Caucus of Harrisburg, a citation for an award winner of Black Youth of the Year, and materials relating to the "Blacks in the Revo-

lution" Contest for the Bicentennial Celebration.

- A file on the Human Relations Commission contains letters of appointment, letters of recommendation, minutes, news releases, annual reports, transcripts of speeches, and pamphlets relating to African Americans. Also includes materials on equal employment opportunity, letters from Representative K. Leroy Irvis concerned with the Black Construction Coalition, the Governor's Justice Commission, summer employment opportunities for minorities, the Pennsylvania Black Democratic Committee, and the Miss African Heritage Competition. A letter from Muhammad Kenyatta requests Governor Shapp's support in Kenyatta's candidacy for mayor of Philadelphia in 1975.
- A file on Lincoln University contains correspondence, newsletters, reports, invitations, and a history of the university.
- A file on the National Association of Colored Women's Clubs, Inc. contains information concerning African American business and professional women's activities and the Negro Trade Union Leadership Council, invitations, grant and proclamation requests, monthly and annual reports, and transcripts of speeches concerning the Opportunities Industrialization Center. There are also letters from Joseph Rhodes dealing with his role on the Subcommittee on Crime and Corrections of the House Judiciary Committee, Rhodes's campaign for auditor general, and materials relating to the controversy concerning the use of "dum-dum" bullets. Also present are letters from Representative David Richardson concerning Richardson's appointment to the Tuskegee Alumni Association and on the subjects of prison and child abuse.
- C. Delores Tucker correspondence with the NAACP concerning the position of African Americans in Pennsylva-

nia politics, the controversy surrounding Tucker's dismissal, African American reaction to Tucker's dismissal, and materials relation to public support for Tucker.

- K. Leroy Irvis file contains materials relating to the Black Construction Coalition, the Governor's Justice Commission, summer employment for minorities, the Pennsylvania Black Democratic Committee, and the Miss African Heritage Competition.
- The file on Secretary of Health Milton Berkes, 1975-79, contains materials on the Human Relations Commission including complaints, reports, and amendments to the Human Relations Act. Also present are reports on minorities in higher education, racially imbalanced local governing units, school desegregation, transcripts of discrimination case hearings, materials relating to the reorganization of the Human Relations Commission, news releases, news articles, and materials concerning the possible absorption of the Commission into the Civil Rights Commission.

Legislative File, 1973-1979. The following pieces of legislation relate to African Americans:

First Term, 1971-1975.

- 1971-72 Session (Inactive): H.B. 796, Lincoln University; H.B. 965, Welfare Reform; H.B. 969, PHEAA Scholarships; H.B. 980, Unemployment Compensation Benefits; H.B. 1029, Mentally Retarded Children; H.B. 1446, Charitable Solicitation; H.B. 1464, 1473, 1494, 1499, 1501, 1514, 1517, 1520, Landlord Act; H.B. 2160, Senior Citizen Property Tax Assistance Act; H.B. 2373, 2422, 2447, Civil Disturbances

- First Special Session of 1972: Senate Bills 4 and 10, Civil Disturbances; Senate Resolution Number 2, Bussing; Senate Bill 253, Low Income Housing; Senate Bill 498, Personal Property Tax; Senate Bill 943, School Bussing; Senate Bill 1236, Judicial Procedure; Senate Bill 1370, 1379, Equal Rights Amendment; Senate Bill 1407, Pennsylvania Housing Agency; Senate Bill 1669, Exceptional Children; H.B. 23, 26, 27, Senior Citizen Day; H.B. 86, Drug Cases; H.B. 96, Pennsylvania Human Relations Act; H.B. 924, Senior Citizen Property Tax Assistance Act; H.B. 1302 (and others), Landlord Tenant Act.

Second Term, 1975-1979.

- 1975-1976 Session (Inactive): H.B. 116, Nursing Home Medical Payments; H.B. 496, Anti-bussing; H.B. 163, Martin Luther King Day; Act 148, Child Care Facilities, 1976.
- 1977-1978 Session (Inactive): General correspondence from the following: C. Delores Tucker, secretary of state; James N. Wade, secretary of administration; Representatives James D. Barber, Lucien E. Blackwell, Aljia Dumas, K. Leroy Irvis, Joel J. Johnson, Joseph Rhodes Jr., David P. Richardson, and John F. White Jr.; and Senators Herbert Arlene, Freeman Hankins, and Paul McKinney.

Subject File, 1971-1979.

First Term, 1971-1975.

- Abortion Law Commission. Letter of recommendation from C. Delores Tucker dated November 1, 1977 containing names for appointment to the commission and a letter dated June 29, 1971 from Charles F. Mebus recommending Eleanor Duffan Adams to the commission.

- Biography-Cynthia Delores Tucker. A biography written before Tucker's appointment as secretary of state.
- Charity Requests, 1971. Includes requests from Aliquippa, Lancaster, Philadelphia, Pittsburgh, and York, with a special emphasis on Darby where gasoline incendiary bombs were thrown against the Bunting Friendship House, an African American community center, in 1971. There are also materials on Monessen where a white tavern owner firebombed the Monessen Junior High School.
- Education-Racial Imbalance, 1970-1971. Contains several letters from the Department of Education concerning racial unrest in various school districts across the state.
- Mansion Function-Martin Luther King Luncheon, March 25, 1974. Includes an announcement for the function, a proclamation, and letters of thanks for the invitations.
- Mansion Function-Jesse L. Jackson Luncheon, April 16, 1974. In addition to letters of invitation and acknowledgments, there is also a letter from James D. Barber, chairman of the Black Caucus, thanking Governor Shapp for his contributions to the country.

Second Term, 1975-1979.

- Education-Cheyney, 1979. Contains copy of a formal complaint filed by the student body on February 19, 1977 entitled "Assembly Resolution to Cite College Administration and State of the Charges." In letter responding to the complaints, Governor Shapp asserted that "improvements in the functioning of the governing system is the responsibility of the student body."
- Lincoln University, 1977. Contains a letter dated May 4,

1977 from Argentine Deigh (Green) Robinson from
Jefferson Medical College to Governor Shapp regarding a
"crisis at Lincoln University." She recommended that a
team of qualified, impartial educators be appointed to investigate.

- Personnel-Dismissal, C. Delores Tucker, 1977. A large file
  containing letters, memoranda, news releases, newspaper
  articles, and telegrams concerning the dismissal of C.
  Delores Tucker by Governor Shapp on September 20,
  1977. Some of the African Americans who sent letters include: Representatives James D. Barber and Henry M.
  Kearney; Gary, Indiana Mayor Richard G. Hatcher; Black
  Political Forum President Wilson Goode; George W. Sellers of the NAACP; Pennsylvania Baptist State Convention President Rev. Dr. William J. Shaw; NAACP Executive Director Gloster B. Currant; and Evelyn Brooks of
  the Negro Women's Clubs.

MG-310. JOHN DUSS PAPERS, 1882-1951.

John Samuel Duss (1860-1951) served as the last trustee of the
Harmony Society from 1890 to 1903. Founded by Johann
Georg Rapp in 1805, the Harmony Society was a religious community which exerted a major influence on the economic development of western Pennsylvania. Duss was born in Cincinnati, Ohio,
and after his father was conscripted into the Confederate Army in
1862 his mother, Sarah Duss, took her son to the Harmonist community of Economy, Pennsylvania. Duss lived with the society at
various times throughout his life, was made a co-trustee in 1890,
and wrote a book about his experience there entitled *The
Harmonists: A Personal History* (Harrisburg, 1943). Duss was also
a musician and a band leader (1883-1950) who conducted the
Economy Band which merged with the Great Western Band of

Pittsburgh in 1900 to form the Duss Concert Band and Metropolitan Opera House Orchestra. The collection includes correspondence relating to Duss's Band, a manuscript of Duss's book on the Harmonists, as well as other personal memorabilia. References to African Americans were found in two series.

Correspondence File, 1905-1950. The bulk of the correspondence pertains to the restoration of Old Economy Village in Ambridge, Pennsylvania, a portion of the last community founded by the Harmonists, which is now operated as a historic site by the Pennsylvania Historical and Museum Commission. In a 1914 letter, George Kallitz, a young composer, asked Duss for his opinion on a project in which Kallitz planned to reintroduce the songs of Stephen Foster. He planned to "write a selection called 'Old Favorite Songs' and mention all the names of the songs . . . and Foster." Songs Kallitz wished to include were "Massa's in the cold, cold ground," "Old black Joe," and "My old Kentucky home."

Manuscript File, [ca. 1940]. This file consists of handwritten and typed drafts for Duss's book *The Harmonists: A Personal History*. Duss told of his experience as a teacher in the Kansas State Reform School, mentioning "little Jimmie Williams (one of my negroes)" and "Big Bill Reynolds (a negro)." Other references are made to these same boys in this chapter.

MG-311. LEHIGH COAL AND NAVIGATION COMPANY RECORDS, [CA. 1792-1970].

The Lehigh Navigation Company was formed in 1798 and the Lehigh Coal Company in 1792. They merged on April 21, 1820 and were incorporated as the Lehigh Coal and Navigation Company in 1822. As of 1978 the company no longer operated as a carrier or a coal producer. The records consist of Minutes, 1821-

1931, Administrative Files, 1801-1950; and Accounts, 1818-1947 of the Lehigh Coal and Navigation Company and its ninety-six affiliates including the Lehigh Coal Mine Company, Panther Valley Water Company, Lehigh and New England Railroad Company; B & M Oil Company; Delaware Division Canal Company, Alliance Coal Mining Company, Automatic Coal Burner Company, B.M. Liquidating Corporation, Wilkes-Barre and Scranton Railroad Company, Split Rock Skeet and Trapshooting Association, Inc., Nanticoke Railroad Company; and the Eureka Furnace Cleaning Company, among others.

Although this is quite a large collection, only a small portion of it deals with employees and few African American workers are clearly identified. References to African Americans are found, however, in the **Inactive Employment Record Cards.** These cards provide such information as name, address, birth date, marital status, employment record, salary, and reason of departure from service.

MG-317. MARY BARNUM BUSH HAUCK PAPERS, 1931-1979.

Mary B. B. Hauck was the Pennsylvania state supervisor of music under the Emergency Education Program of the Works Progress Administration, 1937-42, and organizer of the Dauphin County Folk Festival, 1935-61. She also served as director of USO program services at Fort Indiantown Gap, 1943-46. The collection includes correspondence, memoranda, lecture notes, music books, posters, news clippings, photographs, and other materials acquired by Hauck during her career. While some specific references to African Americans are cited below, also scattered through the collection are photographs of various festivals and programs featuring many races and nationalities.

A. PERSONAL, 1935-1961

Biographies and Photographs, 1935-1961. This file contains biographical information portraying Hauck's involvement with people of many races during her tenure as the Works Progress Administration state supervisor of the Music and the Emergency Education Program, the director of the USO Program Services of Fort Indiantown Gap, and founder and director of the Dauphin County Folk Festival.

B.W.P.A. STATE SUPERVISOR OF MUSIC, EMERGENCY EDUCATION PROGRAM, F.E.R.A., 1937-1942

This subgroup contains both newspaper articles and printed programs pertaining to the summer and winter musical activities in 1934 and 1935. One example is an article that appeared in the *Evening News*, July 21, 1934, entitled "Registration for Free music classes to open." This was a part of the Educational and Recreational Relief Project in music, sponsored by federal, state, and county relief agencies. Instructors were Mary Bush Hauck and John A. Isele. The weekly schedule included "colored people in separate classes on Tuesday and Thursday." Several newspaper articles refer to "mass singing for white and colored groups." Other materials present include:

Folk Festivals (Dauphin County), 1935-1942. A file containing a listing of nationalities that were involved in the "Americans All" pageant that was part of the Dauphin County Folk Festival, 1935-1942. Included is the description "Negroes." The folder titled "Work Manual I" contains several programs from the festival. The file for the Fifth Annual Festival has a list of committee members identified as Negro including Dr. A. Leslie Marshall and Miss Ella Frasier. The program for this festival mentions that on Wednesday evening a Negro "Cake-Walk" was scheduled and provides some background detail on the dance. The file on the sixth annual festival contains a list of the names of committee members, including Dr. Albert Thompson in addition to the two names previously cited. The "Negro" portion of the festival for this year included "Spiritual and Jubilee Scenes" in which Dr. Thompson led the Cosmopolitan Chorus. The folder also contains data on county populations broken down by nationality or race, revealing that more than 200,000 "Negroes" then lived in Philadelphia County. A Christmas Music Bulletin found in this folder acknowledged the contributions of Negroes to Christmas, such as the American Negro carol "Go, Tell It on the Mountain," describing the contributions of African Americans to the origins of some Christmas customs and carols. In the Minutes of the Music Specialists Group, four Negro spirituals were presented. Other references to African American music in this subseries includes a program from the Wall of Fame of the American Common World's Fair of 1940 in New York, which lists prominent African Americans in law, music, and literature.

C. DIRECTOR, U.S.O. PROGRAM SERVICES, INDIANTOWN GAP AREA, 1943-1946

Folk Festivals (Dauphin County), 1943-1946.

Publicity for USO Program Services-Indiantown Gap Area, 1943-1944. Includes several articles that mention Negro service men in the Harrisburg area. Harrisburg's *Patriot* dated November 24, 1943, for example, discusses constructing or converting a building for use as a USO club for Negro servicemen. Another article from Harrisburg's *Evening News*, dated July 28, 1943, contains a call for more cots for African Americans in the city. Also present are various photographs that depict African American soldiers as subjects.

"Americans All," Dauphin County Folk Council, Dauphin County War Finance Committee, 7th War Loan Drive and Department of Public Instruction, June 13 (10), 1945. Contains photographs and publicity materials including a photograph of two African American soldiers labeled on the back with the name of each and other background information. One of the men performing in this photograph was formerly Louis Armstrong's feature singer. The folder also contains a copy of *The Tomahawk*, the Indiantown Gap military reserve newspaper, which makes two references to African Americans on the base.

MG-320. EDWARD STOVER PAPERS, 1857-1935.

Edward Stover was a Middletown lumber merchant who built the Memorial United Brethren Church in Hummelstown, Pennsylvania, which was dedicated in 1872 in memory of the premature death of his son, Edward Stover Jr. Most of the papers consist of business records such as agreements, bonds, insurance policies, leases, mortgages, a deed, and a release for property he owned near Hummelstown. Information found includes the nationalities and races of his workers, and a record of wages paid for planting trees, setting posts, moving rocks, digging ditches, threshing grain, and sawing, hauling and carving wood on the Stoverdale Farms in Dauphin County.

A. ACCOUNTS, 1857-1935

In several of the account books, banking books, and ledgers there are references to "Darkeys" and "Collored" persons employed by Stover. Among these is an 1857 list of names of "4 Darkeys" and the number of hours they worked. A bank book that is dated April 24, 1879 and inscribed "Harrisburg" lists "one collored laborer;

one day taring [sic] off plaster 1.50." There are several entries identifying "collored" laborers giving the number of hours worked and how much they were paid.

C. PRIVATE PAPERS, 1870, 1912-1935

Amongst the papers is a pamphlet entitled *Forest Leaves*, which contains an ad for ten cent books including a Joke Book that has Negro, as well as Irish, German, Yankee, and Hebrew jokes and funny sayings.

MG-321. CHARLES T. DOUDS PAPERS, 1920-1978.

Charles Douds (b. 1898-d. 1982) was a nationally recognized labor arbitrator with state and local governments. Born in Plumville, Indiana County, Douds served as secretary of the YMCA at the University of Rochester in New York between 1922 and 1929 and commenced his labor career as executive secretary of the League for Social Justice in 1932 and as a labor compliance officer with the National Recovery Administration (NRA) in Pittsburgh in 1933. Douds was also involved with the Pennsylvania Security League that was dedicated to improving the industrial security of industrial workers and farmers. He became a Detroit field examiner for the National Labor Relations Board (NLRB) from 1937-1958; was appointed director of the Pennsylvania Bureau of Mediation by Governor George Leader, 1958-1969; and served as president of the Association of Labor Mediation Agencies of the United States and Canada, 1958-1959. The papers consist primarily of business correspondence, reports, publications, newspaper articles, brochures, and other documentation relating to the University of Rochester YMCA, Industrial Relations League, Pennsylvania Security League, League for Social Justice, Pennsylvania State Mediation Board, and the Committee on Labor

Management Relations and General Welfare. Also present are biographical materials, personal and professional correspondence, diaries, photographs from National Labor Relations Board conferences, and two papers authored by Douds. Much of this material has a bearing upon understanding the plight of African American workers in Pennsylvania. Other noteworthy items include:

PERSONAL PAPERS

YMCA File, 1923-1931. Contain several programs and pamphlets for a mid-winter conference on the Dynamic of Christian Living held under the auspices of the Middle Atlantic Field Council of the Student Young Men's Christian Association. Pictured in the program is Howard Thurman, who presided over the worship exercises. Another pamphlet is entitled "A Million Students" and is dedicated to the million college men and women in America. On the cover is a photograph of a group of college students, probably committee members for the paper, and below is a caption "'Northfield,' 1928." Included are several African American men from member colleges such as the City College of New York. The back page also has a photograph of the National Council of Student Associations that includes several African American men. A single photograph of Benjamin E. Mays appears under the heading of "Secretaries of three specially significant aspects of the Movement's work." Mays is identified as the leader of the Negro Colleges who later became the president of Morehouse College in Atlanta, Georgia. Inside the paper are two articles that relate to African American students. One folder contains a history of the League for Social Justice (LSJ) of Pittsburgh, Pennsylvania, 1932-33, that was written by Douds in 1978. This contains an entry about a speech presented January 23 [1933], by Mr. William Pickens, field secretary of the National Association for the Advancement of Colored People, on "Trends in the Labor Movement."

Magazines (Items from), 1932-1935. Included are articles on "The Race Issue at Detroit" and "Race Issue Rocks Detroit Conference" from *The Christian Century* dated January 14, 1931.

Miscellaneous Items, 1933-1936. Includes a chart titled "A Survey of the Parties-1932" which was a special supplement of *The World Tomorrow*, September 28, 1932. The chart lists all the parties sponsoring candidates for office, a brief history of each, and their political positions on selected issues including race relations and civil liberties. Also present is a program for the Community Forum of Pittsburgh, 1935-1936. The topic for discussion on December 16 was "Our Own Race Problem" by Dr. Mordecai Johnson, president of Howard University. A copy of *The Penn Stater* dated March/April 1982, page 14, contains a photographs of Larry Atwell, coordinator of the Lion Ambassadors (Penn State Student Alumni Corps), and a photograph labeled "Planning military maneuvers with King Juan Carlos of Spain in 1981" depicting "Alumni Major General William E. Brown, Class of 1949."

MG-324. OLD MILL VILLAGE COLLECTION, 1845-1847, 1857-1870, 1883-1897, 1907-1915, 1932-1937 AND UNDATED.

Old Mill Village recreates early farm life in Pennsylvania near New Milford, Pennsylvania. This living and working museum was under the direction of the Pennsylvania Historical Museum Commission, in cooperation with the Associate Members of Old Mill Village Museum. The collection contains account books, portrait photographs and stereoscopic views of the Civil War, Europe, Africa, and Texas. Among the Civil War views are pictures of African American soldiers: "Colored Army Teamsters, Cobb Hill, Va.," "Sacramentos Kroo Boys Taken by Lt. Bartles at Loanda, March 1st 1867," and "Colored Pickets on duty near Dutch Gap."

MG-324. Old Mill Village Collection, 1845-1937. Stereoscopic view "Colored Army Teamsters, Cobb Hill, Va.

A greeting card album contains two cards with cartoons of African American children.

MG-325. THE PINE STREET PRESBYTE-RIAN CHURCH SLIDE COLLECTION, [CA. 1895-1925].

This collection consists of 176 black and white and color slides of Harrisburg and its environs taken by an unknown photographer. The slides are fitted on 2" x 2" cardboard mounts, and are film copies of glass originals. Slide no. 116 shows the aviation field in Harrisburg during the 1920s. It was used by Pilot William McDonald Felton to teach flying when he operated his Auto and Aeroplane Mechanical School at 25 North Cameron Street. The aviation field was commonly known as the Felton Airfield. Felton was one of America's first African American aviators, having taught hundreds of African Americans to fly. His school in Harrisburg

486

was known nationally and he had students from all over the United States

MG-329. IVAN L. CARTER PHOTOGRAPHS, [CA. 1922-1938].

A lifetime resident of Carlisle, Ivan L. Carter (1894-1971) was a druggist and amateur photographer occasionally hired to record community events. The State Archives received his negatives in 1980 from Donald Garlin of Palmyra, who obtained them at an estate auction. Over four thousand glass plate and film negatives, dating between 1920 and 1938, depict Carlisle and south central Pennsylvania, particularly Dickinson College and the Medical Field Service School (Carlisle Barracks). African Americans appear in a number of the photographs:

Contact Prints.

*   Photo #105-African American twins from Carlisle, 1933.
*   Photo #104-Both white and African American twins from Carlisle, 1933.
*   Photo #334-Carlisle High School football squad, 1933.
*   Photo #348-Carlisle High School vs. Mechanicsburg High School, one member was an African American, 1933.
*   Photo #385-Dickinson College doll show. The dolls, at least three of which were African American, were sent to children of prisoners in New York City, 1933.
*   Photo #389-Civilian Conservation Corps boxing at the Medical Field Service School. Pietro Camp 51 (white) won the decision against Elliot Camp M.P. 2 (African American), 1933.
*   Photo #391-Civilian Conservation Corps boxing at the Medical Field Service School, 1933.
*   Photo #392-Civilian Conservation Corps boxing at the Medi-

MG-329. Ivan L. Carter Photographs, [ca. 1922-1938]. Photo #105 – African American twins from Carlisle, 1933. Standing, Clinton and Albert Thompson; Carl and Carolyn Washington; Seated, Elizabeth and Jacob Hodge; Alice and Mildred Jackson.

cal Field Service School, 1933.

- Photo #393-Civilian Conservation Corps boxing at the Medical Field Service School, 1933.
- Photo #397-A community organization event. Girl Scouts Christmas party for Children's Fund. Girls gathered around Christmas tree. There is one African American girl, 1933.
- Photo #404-Mechanicsburg High School basketball team, one member is African American, 1933.
- Photo #425-Carlisle High School basketball game vs. Newport High School, one player is African American, 1934.
- Photo #493-Fire at Gehring's Jewelry Store, 36 S. Hanover St., [Carlisle], at least one pedestrian is African American, 1934.

MG-332. Henry Mohn Family Collection, [ca. 1844-1960]. Miss Mohn's Class, Leetsdale.

- Photo #1306-a partial shed is identified as being the "end of the Underground Railway on Woods Farm," undated.

MG-332. HENRY MOHN FAMILY COLLECTION, [CA. 1844-1960].

Henry Mohn, son of Albert and Melina Faucht Mohn, was born on December 8, 1902. Melina was a daughter of Henry Faucht, a member of the Harmony Society and blacksmith in Leetsdale, Allegheny County. The collection primarily concerns the Fauchts of Leetsdale, with some Mohn family items acquired after Albert married Melina Faucht in 1898. Correspondence and receipts (1844-1958) are mainly between members of the Faucht family and to Mrs. Mohn, including letters written by Melina's sister Emilia on her tour of Europe in 1901. The other large group is photographs of family, friends, homes, and other buildings in Leetsdale, including several class school pictures that depict African American children and one photograph of a KKK rally.

MG-333. GEORGE WASHINGTON FENN PAPERS, 1829, 1861-1929 AND UNDATED.

Born in Litchfield, Connecticut, George Washington Fenn (1845-1866) was a long time Harrisburg resident and a partner in publishing the *Upper Dauphin Register*. In 1862 he enlisted as a private in Company A, 127th Regiment of the Pennsylvania Volunteers, later served as a second lieutenant in Company I, 181st Regiment, and was eventually promoted to the rank of captain in Company C, 201st Regiment, Pennsylvania Volunteers. He saw action at Manassas Gap, Virginia, among other places, served as a judge advocate for military court martial cases, was captured in 1865 and later escaped. Fenn's military papers include commissions, general and special orders, a journal of court martial cases, soldiers' memorials, pension applications, and correspondence with his wife, Anna Rober Fenn. Also present are genealogical materials, a diary kept by Samuel K. Dietrich, 1862-1864, and photographs of various members of the Fenn family.

A. MILITARY PAPERS, 1864-1866

Orders, Special and General, Oct. 1864-June, 1865. Contains a copy of General Order No. 108 from General U. S. Grant that makes a general reference to slavery.

Journal of Courts Martial Cases, Alexandria, Va., November 18, 1864-February 27, 1865 (Fenn, Judge Advocate). Provides the names of soldiers who were court martialed, the date the case commenced, the date finished, and the date the result was sent to headquarters. Other information provided includes descriptions of the charges brought against each soldier and the decision of the court. Among those court martialed were several soldiers identified as "colored substitute," "colored recruit," or belonging to the United States Colored Troops (USCT). African Americans named include George Taylor, John W. Jacobs, George Austin, James Smith, and Henry Harris. The following men were also listed as members of the USCT but are not otherwise specifically designated as being African Americans: George White, Henry Dickson, George Batty, John Adams, and Sylvester Hill.

B. PERSONAL AND FAMILY PAPERS,
1829, 1862-1927

Correspondence, G. W. Fenn to wife, 1863-1865. In a letter dated October 16, 1864 from Manassas Gap Railroad, Virginia, Fenn wrote that he was "now in command of over 2000 niggers and whites."

C. NEWSPAPERS, 1861-1866

Upper Dauphin Register, **Aug. 17- Oct. 12, 1865.** Contains several articles on African Americans including the following:

- August 17-"A Convention of the Colored Men of Tennessee Is Being Held."
- August 24--"(A) Number of White Laborers Seeking Employment in the South." "Betsy Wilder, a colored woman, who was present at Yorktown when Cornwallis surrendered, died recently in Richmond, Va., at the age of 108."
- "A colored man named Curry returned to Raleigh, N.C. . . . was violently attacked . . ."
- The position of ex-Senator A. O. P. Nicholson of Columbia, Tennessee on the right of Negroes to vote.
- A summary of a speech by General Thomas Francis Meagher before an Irish society in support of Negro suffrage.
- August 31-"Suffrage in Rhode Island" that deals with Rhode Island's liberal suffrage laws with regard to African Americans.
- September 14-"Indictment against the Democratic Party" in

which the unnamed author cites reasons Pennsylvania voters should turn against the Democratic Party, including the party's opposition to "the enlistment of Negroes."

- September 21-A poem entitled "Laus Deo" pays tribute to the passing of the constitutional amendment abolishing slavery.
- An article on the condition of Mt. Vernon after the war mentions Washington's slaves.
- A notice of Robert Orrick becoming the first "colored man" to be awarded the position of mail carrier.
- September 28-"Honor to the Brave" mentions Negro suffrage as a factor in voter turnout at the election.
- October 5 - Article describes how the Copperheads put "an independent Negro-suffrage man on track" to defeat General Harry White in the senatorial district of Cambria County and Jefferson County, Indiana.
- October 12-Among the editorial news items is an announcement for "The Colored Odd Fellows" holding a parade in Baltimore. Another item concerns the First District Columbia Colored Regiment arriving in Washington, D.C. and in Havre de Grace, Maryland.

MG-339. CORNWALL ORE BANK COMPANY RECORDS, 1802-1935, 1954.

The Cornwall Ore Bank Company was formed in 1864 by Robert W. Coleman, Robert H. Coleman, Anne Coleman, Robert Coleman, George Dawson Coleman, Edward B. Grubb, and Clement B. Grubb to manage mining operations at the Cornwall Ore Banks in Lebanon and Lancaster Counties. This land had provided iron ore to various furnaces since the eighteenth century and under a reservation contained in the deed of Peter Grubb Jr. dated May 9, 1786 the owners of Robesonia Furnace were entitled to continue to take enough ore from the banks to supply their furnace. The new arrangement stood until the Bethlehem Steel Company purchased most of the ore rights held by the Coleman and Grubb heirs by 1920. The records are divided into Business Records, 1862-1924, Legal Papers 1859-1929, and Accounts, 1802-1935. These sub-series include such diverse material as minutes, letter books, and telegrams, 1862-1924; articles of association and agreement, 1854-1864; agreements, deeds, leases, powers of attorney, and releases, 1859-1929; cash books, 1802-1921; construction ledger sheets, 1907-1912; day books, 1824-1921; iron books, 1828-1880; records of iron ore shipments, 1864-1919; journals, 1805-1924, ledgers, 1802-1922; ore books, 1854-1864; powder reports, 1886-1911; and sales receipts, settlement papers, records of shipments, and time books, 1823-1935. Also included are eighteen rolls of 35mm microfilm produced in 1954 that contain blueprints, tracings, and drawings of open pit cross sections, buildings, and structures, and mine and railroad maps; underground and surface survey calculation books; and diagrams of mining equipment such as electrical shovels, magnetic separators, scrapters, and hoisters. Only a small sample of the records were inspected and the following African American references were found:

A. BUSINESS RECORDS, 1862-1924

Letter Books (Received), 1864-1886. On page 232 of the book covering September, 1876-Dec. 7, 1881 is an entry that reads "1 car of Negro strads(?) and oblgr(?)" Lebanon, Pa., March 15, 1878, Ephraim Light. A similar entry is made on page 30 of the same book dated Oct. 10, 1877.

C. ACCOUNTS, 1802-1924

Day Books, 1824-1921.

Day Book, 1850-1862 (Mt. Vernon). Contains several scattered listings for a John Eisenhour (black) who appears to have been part of the work crew in the Blue Mountain Coal Depot. The earliest mention of his name appears in an entry dated Sept. 19, 1850.

MG-342. GEORGE H. EARLE PAPERS, 1932-1939, 1949, 1966 AND UNDATED.

Born in Devon, Chester County, George Howard Earle III was Democratic governor of Pennsylvania from 1935 to 1939. He served in the Second Pennsylvania Infantry during the 1916 Mexican Border Campaign and in the U.S. Navy during World War I. He distinguished himself in a number of businesses in Philadelphia, including the Flamingo Sugar Mills and the Pennsylvania Sugar Company. During the 1930s, he entered politics, supporting Franklin Roosevelt in the 1932 presidential election. He was appointed as U.S. Minister Plenipotentiary to the Republic of Austria in 1932, which post he resigned to run for governor of Pennsylvania in 1934. During his gubernatorial term, Earle secured passage of the 1935 Equal Rights Act, which prohibited racial discrimination in hotels, restaurants, and places of amusement. After an unsuccessful bid for the U.S. Senate in 1938, he served as U.S. minister to Bulgaria in 1940 and assistant naval attaché to Turkey and assistant governor of Samoa from 1940 to 1945. He returned to private life in 1945 and died on December 3, 1974. The collection consists of Earle's official gubernatorial files and of personal papers belonging to him and his wife.

OFFICIAL PAPERS

Subject File, Campaign Data 1938. Includes an "Itinerary for George H. Earle-Thomas A. Logue" (Thursday, September 22, 1938, to Saturday, September 24, 1938) which lists a scheduled appearance at the "Regional Colored Picnic" to be held at Mt. Gretna Park.

Speeches File. Contains the "Address of George H. Earle, Governor of Pennsylvania, at Olympic Celebration, Friday Evening, September 6, 1935, 8 P.M. (DST) at Philadelphia Municipal Stadium." In this address Governor Earle made several general comments about the racial prejudices of Hitler's Nazi government and suggested that the United States ought to consider boycotting the games.

MG-343. CARL W. GATTER ARCHITEC- TURAL RESEARCH BOOKS, 1981.

Carl W. Gatter was an architect who conducted research for a possible reconstruction of the Slate Roof House, William Penn's Philadelphia residence from 1700-1701. Erected between 1698 and 1700 by Samuel Carpenter, it was the first example of an H-Plan house in America. The birthplace of William Penn's son, John, in 1700, it was here that William Penn granted Pennsylvanians the Charter of Privileges in 1701. The seat of Pennsylvania government from 1701 to 1704, the home was long occupied by William Penn's secretary, James Logan, and was also owned and occupied by William Trent, the founder of Trenton, New Jersey, from 1704 to1709 when it was sold to Isaac Norris. Thereafter, the ownership remained in the Norris family until 1869. A Mrs. Graydon leased the building for use as a boarding house during much of the eighteenth century. Her boarders included George Washington, Benedict Arnold, Baron von Steuben, Silas Deane, and John Adams. The house also served as the headquarters of British General Sir Henry Clinton during the British occupation of Philadelphia, 1777-78. The papers comprise sectional drawings and photographs of exterior and interior elevations of the building, and of drawings and photographs showing hearths, tiles, furnishings, and walks; maps; archaeological reports; and historical background on the home's various owners and occupants. Also present are newspaper clippings concerning possible reconstruction of the house as a historic shrine and plans for erecting a marker. The information on African Americans found in this collection is described below:

Workbooks: Slate Roof House, 1700-1701, by Carl W. Gatter, 1981.

Book III—Isaac Norris. In an unidentified biography of Isaac Norris there is a published letter from John Dickinson in which he refers to selling slaves and "taking care to get them good masters." A little further in the letter, Dickinson "expects seventy or eighty pounds at least for women and children on an average." Only a brief excerpt from the letter is provided by Mr. Gatter and the location of the original is unknown. Also present are letters copied from something called the "North Carolina Papers" concerning the ratification of the Constitution in which slavery is discussed. These copies bear the stamp of the Historical Society of Pennsylvania.

Book III—James Logan. In a paragraph dealing with the pending French and Indian War, the author notes that Logan found shipping Delaware tobacco at this time "the greatest cheat as well as slavery in trade." The origin of the quotation is not cited in the collection.

Book III—William Penn. A biography of William Penn provides a great deal of information on Hannah Penn. In a description of their summer move to Pennsbury Manor, the author lists a "negress" among the household staff. Later in the same book, a letter to James [Logan] is included which describes how Hannah was coping with living in Pennsylvania, mentioning a "black Jack" and suggests he help with the fleet in Philadelphia. Again, the original sources are not cited.

Book III—Benjamin Rush. In a letter to John Adams, Rush expressed his opinions on the issue of slavery, quoting Lord Howe on the slavery of mankind. It is unknown were the pages are from.

Book III—R. T. Paine. In a letter to Thomas Lynch Jr. from Thomas Lynch, a reference is made to "Negro Houses" in a discussion of liquor. The letter is dated Dec. 28, 1775 but there is no other information provided as to where this letter came from.

Book III—John Penn. In a biography of John Penn is a copy of several pages from the *Philadelphia Directory and Register* for 1821, one of which is entitled "Directions to the Reader." According to these directions, a person of "colour" is denoted with a cross (x). Several African American men and women are listed along with their names, addresses, and occupations.

Book VI—History. In a copy of *Philadelphia As It Is, in 1852,* is a brief history of the public buildings, places of amusement, and maps of Philadelphia and surrounding area. The "Old London Coffee-House" described as once being used as an auction house where "negro men, women, and children were bought and sold as slaves." A copy of several pages from the *Encyclopedia of Philadelphia* is also in this section. The beginning paragraph of "Slaves and Slavery in Philadelphia" is on the same page as some information on the Slate Roof House and so was included in the collection.

MG-346. CORNWALL FURNACE AND HOPEWELL FORGE ACCOUNT BOOKS, 1752-1966.

Peter Grubb developed Cornwall Furnace and Hopewell Forge several miles apart on Hammer Creek in Lebanon County, Pennsylvania. Around 1739, construction began at Cornwall, which was to supply the Hopewell Forge with pig iron. Cornwall Furnace was a large blast furnace and had a monopoly on the smelting of iron ore in the area for its first fifty years of operation. By 1790, both facilities were under the control of iron magnate Robert Coleman, who spent twelve years purchasing the works from Grubb's heirs, giving him full ownership in 1803. Cornwall Furnace remained in operation until disbanded in 1883; the site was donated to the Commonwealth of Pennsylvania in 1932. The journals and ledgers in this collection date from the era of Peter Grubb's ownership.

HOPEWELL FORGE

Journals, 1753-1764.

- Journal, 1757, includes several entries for "Negro John." (October 15, 1757: items charged were 10 buttons, tape, 1 yd. flannel).
- Journal, 1759, in the Sundry Accounts is listed "the purchase of 1 Negro Man, 80.00 and 1 Negro Woman, 50.00.
- Journal, 1762, mentions a credit to "Negroe Jack (Barbados)" and "Negroe Tom" for overcharging on washing, April 10, 1762.

MG-347. JEAN F. GERDES COLLECTION OF JAMES H. DUFF PHOTOGRAPHS, [CA. 1925-1958].

The collection consists of photographs of Governor James H. Duff (1947-1950) during his career as state auditor general, governor, and United States senator. The photographs were collected by his wife, Jean T. Duff, and were donated to the State Archives in 1981 by his grandniece, Jean F. Gerdes. Most photographs show Duff with a variety of people including his family, entertainers, as well as state and nationally known politicians. Included are photographs of various African Americans at different political events, such as the National Republican Women's Conference, May 9, 1955; the Republican Convention, July 1952; and the Senate Hearings on Teamster Corruption, 1958.

MG-348. MARTIN G. BRUMBAUGH PAPERS, 1879-1919.

Martin Grove Brumbaugh was Republican governor of Pennsylvania from 1915 to 1919. He served as superintendent of schools for Huntingdon County, 1884-1890; president of Juniata College in 1895 and 1926; superintendent of public schools of Philadelphia, 1906-1915; and was appointed the first commissioner of education in Puerto Rico from 1900 to 1902. Author of *A History of the German Baptist Brethren in Europe and America*, he is the only member of the Church of the Brethren to have held the Commonwealth's highest executive office.

Executive Correspondence, 1915-19. Correspondence to and from Governor Brumbaugh. Included are several telegrams from Washington, D.C. concerning draft boards. The April 5th, 1918 telegram requests colored men for general military service. Also included is a copy of a procession order for an unidentified military parade. Dated Oct. 7, 1916, from "Philadelphia, Headquarters, Chief Marshall, Military Parade, 408 City Hall," the order affirms the inclusion of Company B of the First Colored Regiment in the parade.

Personal Papers, 1879-1915. Contained in this series are invitations to different events, programs of the Huntingdon County Teachers' Institute programs, and copies of three newspapers. *The Daily Local News*, July 22, 1887, contains three articles about African Americans. The first article, from Atlanta, Georgia, concerns "colored teachers from all parts of the state refusing to attend the Peabody Normal Institute." The second article from Chicago is about a group of African Americans who were refused service in a saloon. Two men had the saloon keeper arrested and taken to court were he was held for violating the rights of "all citizens in their civil and legal rights." The last article from Summitville, Indiana, reports the stabbing death of an African American woman with a ten-inch butcher knife.

MG-350. AMERICAN ASSOCIATION OF UNIVERSITY WOMEN, PENNSYLVANIA DIVISION RECORDS, 1942-1981.

The American Association of University Women-Pennsylvania Division (AAUW-PA) was organized on October 26, 1924 to promote the advancement of women and encourage their intellectual growth and commitment to social responsibility. Most records document club activities and major networking projects.

DIVISION RECORD

Division Board Member Portfolios.

President, 1961-1974. Contains a copy of the Women in History Project publication *Our Hidden Heritage: Pennsylvania Women in History*, edited by Janice H. McElroy, that features fifteen women including abolitionists Lucretia Coffin Mott, Hannah Longshore, Anna Dickenson, Angelina and Sara Grimke, and Hannah Gibbons. Also mentioned is Martha Schofield, who moved into the South after the Civil War to help feed, clothe, and educate freed slaves. Some of the African American women featured are Marian Anderson, Anna Lucille Carter, Fanny Marion Jackson Coppin, Ella Frazier, Ida Jones, and the Rev. Bessie S. Wheeler.

Division Standing Committee Records.

Legislative Program, 1965-1977. Includes reports of the Citizen Task Force on Regional Community Treatment Centers for Women which contain a breakdown by race of "Women and Girl Offenders by Human Service Areas, Percentage Distribution, 1966-1975." There is also a report on the Muncy Women's Facility that includes a statistical breakdown on African American inmates.

DIVISION PROJECTS

Status of Women, 1961-1963. The booklet entitled *Status of Women, 1961-1963*, is a survey of opportunities of continuing education for mature women that includes materials on female migrant workers in Pennsylvania.

MG-352. MACLAY FAMILY PAPERS, 1788-1933.

The Maclay Family Collection contains material that spans five generations of the descendants of Charles Maclay (1703-1953), who along with his brother John (1707-1758) sailed from Belfast, Ireland on May 30, 1734 and settled in Chester County, Pennsylvania. Charles Maclay moved his family to Lurgan Township, Franklin County in 1742 and his offspring played important roles in the development of Pennsylvania as a province and a state. Two of his sons, William (1730-1804) and Samuel (1741-1811), held numerous state offices and served in both the state and national legislatures. His son John (1734-1804) served as a member of the Provincial Conference held at Carpenter's Hall in June, 1776, and three terms in the Pennsylvania legislature. Almost all of the material in this collection deals with John Maclay's descendants. The collection consists of family correspondence, 1788-1933; legal papers, 1794-1914; genealogical materials, 1824, undated; account books, 1812-1887; political memorabilia, [ca. 1800-ca. 1930]; and miscellaneous material, 1788-ca. 1910. The bulk of the correspondence pertains to David Maclay (1762-1839) and his son Charles Templeton Maclay (1812-1888). Likewise, all but two volumes of the account books belonged to David and Charles Templeton Maclay. Also included are materials relating to the Pomeroy family who became affiliated with the Maclay family through the marriage of Charles Templeton Maclay's son, David Maclay, M.D. (1852-1908), to Mary Pomeroy in 1878.

CHARLES TEMPLETON MACLAY, 1812-1888

Question Book (Sunday School Attendance Book), 1861-1880.
For June 19, 1864 there is an entry for a "Male Colored class" with 1 student, and a "Female Colored class" also with 1 student.

Political Memorabilia, [ca. 1800-1930].

Speeches, Addresses. Printed copy of a speech by William Maclay delivered at the constitutional reform convention of Pennsylvania on January 17, 1838, in opposition to excluding "Colored Men" from the right of suffrage.

MG-354. OLD ECONOMY VILLAGE COLLECTION [CA. 1813-1953].

Old Economy Village is the restored nineteenth-century home of the Harmonists, a utopian Christian community known for both its piety that also operated numerous industrial enterprises in western Pennsylvania. The Harmony Society was founded by George Rapp, a German Pietist who sought a return to what he perceived to be the greater purity in the practice of the Christian faith. Gathering a group of followers, Rapp left Württemberg, Germany to come to America in 1803 and first established a community at present-day Ambridge in Butler County, Pennsylvania, in 1805. In 1814, the group moved to Harmony, Indiana, hoping to further their industrial growth with the advantage of river transportation. In 1825, the Harmony Society returned to Pennsylvania, establishing their third and final home in Economy, Pennsylvania. George Rapp died in 1847 and eventually the society was dissolved in 1905. In 1919, Old Economy Village became a historic site operated by the Pennsylvania Historical and Museum Commission.

Historical Photographs, [ca.. 1866-1950]. Photographic prints, postcards, news clippings, engravings, and similar items collected by the staff of Old Economy Village. Each item is numbered and arranged numerically. Photographs that depict African Americans are:

- No. 74-"Cider Press," several African American men standing outside of a large building.
- No. 312-"Mercer Street, Harmony, Pa.," two African American girls standing on the sidewalk.
- No. 689-"Bee Yard," an African American man holding a hose.
- No. 706-"Unknown Harmony," appears to contain some African Americans.
- No. 758-"Typical Dwelling," a young African American girl in front of a large house with other people.

MG-356. DANIEL B. STRICKLER COLLECTION, 1916-1919, 1943-1957, 1967 AND UNDATED. {UNPROCESSED}

Pennsylvania lieutenant governor from 1947-1951, Major General Daniel Bursk Strickler was born on May 17, 1897 in Columbia, Pennsylvania, the son of Harriet Bursk and Calvin Ruby Strickler. At the age of eighteen he enlisted as a private in Company C, 4th Pennsylvania Infantry, Pennsylvania National Guard on January 31,1916. He participated in the Mexican Border Campaign on April 8, 1916, distinguished himself as an officer in the First World War and during World War II he commanded the 109th Infantry, 28th Division and saw action in France and Germany. He subsequently served as a major general of the Pennsylvania National Guard until he was elected lieutenant governor. Among items in the photographic albums of the collection are three photographs of African Americans. One of these depicts a black soldier serving in the "Chow Line, Indiantown Gap Military Reservation, August 1947," the second depicts an African American woman observing a "Group attending ceremonies 'Laying away of the colors,' State museum, Harrisburg, Pa., Oct. 1949," and the third shows two African American ministers at the "Installation of Judge Millen as Elder in Presbyterian Church, 1947."

MG-357. PENNSYLVANIA WOMEN'S LEGIS-LATIVE EXCHANGE COLLECTION, 1968-1981.

The Pennsylvania Women's Legislative Exchange (PWLE) was created in 1968 to act as a conduit for information regarding legislative actions pertaining to women in the Commonwealth. The PWLE is composed of representatives from more than twenty-five member organizations interested in legislative issues. The collection contains correspondence, publicity notices, programs, and brochures from member organizations and newspaper clippings, expense statements, workshop summaries, and evaluations of PWLE conferences. In addition, there are lists of organizational members, 1972-1978; a description of the guidelines and organization of the PWLE; and the minutes of the monthly exchange meetings, 1972-1978. African American members included Velma M. Strode, director of the Equal Employment Opportunity Commission for the United States Department of Labor, 1971 (featured on the cover of *Jet* magazine, April 1964 and in a photograph of the sixth conference of PWLE in March 1974). The 1974 *Legislative Conference* book provides information on HB#1061 that was concerned with incentive grants for school desegregation, human relations, and training and HB#1783, a House Education Committee school desegregation plan.

MG-358. MRS. JAMES LEWIS HOOK AUTO-GRAPH COLLECTION, 1752-1810.

Mrs. James Lewis Hook was a collector of autographs of signers of the Declaration of Independence. The collection contains letters, accounts, legal papers, and other documents acquired for their autograph value. Item #15 is a letter dated May 20, 1782 from George Reade to the Prothonotary of Bedford County, Virginia, regarding the return of "Negro Hamble."

MG-359. 104TH CAVALRY PENNSYLVANIA NATIONAL GUARD VETERANS' ASSOCIATION COLLECTION, [CA. 1914-1975]. {UNPROCESSED}

The 104th Cavalry, Pennsylvania National Guard, was originally constituted in 1874 with the designation as the 8th Infantry Regiment, Pennsylvania National Guard. After undergoing several reorganizations and re-designations, the unit was consolidated in 1921 to include four troops from the 1st Cavalry (one of which was known as the Governor's Troop) and was re-designated as the 104th Cavalry. Thereafter, the entire 104th Cavalry was commonly referred to as the Governor's Troop. The unit was mustered into federal service during the Spanish-American War and also saw overseas action during both the First and Second World War. The 104th Veterans Association that was founded in 1966 donated this collection to the Pennsylvania State Archives in 1983. Among the collection are a number of photographs that show African Americans, none of which are dated or marked in any way. One is of a baseball game among army personnel in which the umpire is an African American. Other photographs portray African Americans in various group scenes.

MG-360. PENNSYLVANIA STATE POLICE MEMORABILIA COLLECTION, 1910-1920 {UNPROCESSED}

The Department of State Police was created in 1905 to help preserve law and order throughout the Commonwealth and to cooperate with and assist local law enforcement officers in the apprehension of criminals. When the State Highway Patrol that was originally established to enforce motor vehicle laws was merged with the department in 1937 and the name of the agency was changed to the Pennsylvania State Police in 1943. This collection contains memorabilia donated by various individuals. A seventy-fifth State Police anniversary booklet published in 1980 includes a photograph of African American secretaries among various employee group portraits. A clipping taken from *The Washington Reporter*, Washington, Pennsylvania, dated July, 1937 contains a report from Topeka, Kansas concerning two women who were allegedly attacked by three "negroes." One section of the paper entitled "Afro-American Notes" carried information about the local community and various African American church groups.

MG-362. DENISE WEBER PHOTOGRAPHS, 1906. {UNPROCESSED}

The Vinton Colliery Company operated bituminous coal mines near Vintondale, Cambria County from the summer of 1906 when it opened No. 6 mine and constructed coke works and other support facilities. The operations were observed by John Huth, a Vintondale resident who was a mining engineer and labor assistant superintendent for the company. Huth either took or acquired these photographs of the work in progress consisting of thirty-three 5"x 7" and two 4"x 5" glass plate negatives. No original prints are present. Housed in one loose-leaf binder, the Pennsylvania State Archives contact reference prints were made in December 1983. The captions were supplied by the donors, Huth's granddaughter Denise Weber of Indiana, Pennsylvania and his daughter Aileen Michelbacher of Vintondale. Photograph 34 shows African Americans building footers for the coke ovens, but the names of the laborers are unknown.

MG-363. WILLIAM K. SOWERS COLLECTION, 1917-1957.

William K. Sowers was a native of Harrisburg, Pennsylvania who graduated from the Pennsylvania State College in 1926 and served four years as an Infantry Reserve Officer in the Civilian Conservation Corps. This collection contains information on the Civilian Conservation Corps (CCC) Camps and includes official files, 1935-40; a scrapbook, 1933-35; newspaper clippings, 1936; and issues of *Happy Days*, the authorized weekly newspaper of the Civilian Conservation Corps, November 16, 1935-May 9, 1936, and December 4, 1937. At the beginning of the Civilian Conservation Corps scrapbook are three articles referring to the CCC boxing championship tourney in Carlisle Barracks' gymnasium. Participating in this tournament was Camp MP-2, an African American CCC camp. An article in the February 1, 1936 issue of *Happy Days* states that a CCC Camp located in Mineral, Virginia and known as Company 2359 was built on an abandoned "Negro Graveyard." See also the Ivan L. Carter Collection (MG-329) for similar photographs of CCC Camps depicting African Americans who lived in many of the 125 CCC camps, such as a depiction of Elliot Camp MP 2 (Colored) at the boxing tourney at Carlisle Barracks in 1933.

MG-368. GENERAL ASSEMBLY COLLECTIONS, 1798-1996.

ANNE BRANCATO WOOD PAPERS, 1928-1972

Anne Brancato Wood (1903-1972) was the first Democratic woman to be elected to the Pennsylvania House of Representatives and the only woman ever elected as speaker pro tempore. When not serving in office, Wood operated a telephone answering service, and was a real estate and insurance broker. She remained politically active and involved herself in civic organizations in the Philadelphia area until her death. Wood introduced or sponsored legislation of particular concern to African Americans, including the Pawnbrokers' Act, the Hasty Marriage Act, the Mothers' Assistance Fund Law, the Minimum Wage and Hour Law for Women, and supported the creation of more playgrounds in the congested districts of Philadelphia, an Anti-Eviction Bill, and a bill to protect the property rights of women.

BLACK LEGISLATORS IN PENNSYLVANIA, 1911-1974

In February 1974, the Pennsylvania Historical and Museum Commission sponsored an exhibit entitled the "History of Black Legislators in Pennsylvania's General Assembly," which contained photographs and brief biographical sketches of Black legislators who had served in Harrisburg since W. Harry Bass became Pennsylvania's first "Negro" representative in 1911. The legislators cited are: Scholley Pace Alexander, William Allmond, Matt S. Anderson, Sarah Anderson, Herbert Arlene, John C. Asbury, Harry W. Bass, James Barber, Lucien E. Blackwell, John H. Brigerman, Homer S. Brown, Junius Emerson, Crystal Byrd Fauset, Samuel Floyd, William Harvey Fuller, William Gray, Charles P. Hammock, Freeman Hankins, Garfield B. Harris, John W. Harris, Samuel B. Hart, Howard M.

Henry, Dennie W. Hoggard, Samuel D. Holmes, Herbert Holt, K. Leroy Irvis, Walker K. Jackson, Ralph T. Jefferson, Joel Johnson, Theodore Johnson, Frances P. Jones, Paul F. Jones, Paul M. Lawson, Mitchell W. Melton, Lewis M. Mintess, Susie Monroe, Lee Myhan, Frank L. Oliver, J. Thompson Pettigrew, Hobson R. Reynolds, E. Washington Rhodes, Joseph Rhodes, David P. Richardson Jr., Hampton Riley, Ulysses Shelton, Marshall Shepard, Jesse J. Shields, Andrew F. Stevens, Thomas P. Trent, Edwin F. Thompson, William A. Upshur, Earl Vann, Hardy William, and Edward C. Young.

MG-373. RICHARD A. SNYDER PAPERS, [CA. 1962-1984].

Richard A. Snyder (1910-1992), a graduate of Temple University Law School, enlisted in the U.S. Army from 1942 to 45, was Republican chair of Lancaster County from 1958-64, served in the state senate beginning in 1962, and was reelected to six successive terms.

Subject File, 1963-1984. The files are arranged alphabetically by subject and contain the following materials relating to African Americans:

- *Blacks—Reagan Administration, 1984:* Includes news clippings on such topics as unemployment among African Americans and the status of African American political leadership.
- *Bussing, 1975-1983:* Contains correspondence and pamphlets on the issue of forced bussing and the tensions caused by it.
- *Capital Punishment, 1983-1984:* Contains a January 5, 1984 article in the *New York Times* linking the victims' race to the unjust demand of the death penalty and an editorial for a Philadelphia TV station protesting the death penalty as discriminatory towards African Americans.

- *Civil Rights, 1973-1984:* Contains a *US News and World Report* article about the American Civil Liberties Union representing such groups as the Ku Klux Klan, to an African American repeatedly detained by police in white neighborhoods.
- *Civil Rights, 1973-1984:* Provides news articles and newsletters concerning an anti-civil rights bill, affirmative action hiring of minorities and women, opposition to discriminatory airport search policies, school integration, the censorship of books by non-white authors, an article about Representative K. Leroy Irvis' discrimination suit against a Harrisburg Moose Lodge, protests against House Bill 1717 and Senate Bill 1265 which would remove civil rights powers from the Human Relations Commission, and the ACLU's involvement in Black Panther cases.
- *College-Cheyney State, 1977-1982:* Includes news articles and correspondence concerning Cheyney State University. Among the items present is a letter from the president of Cheyney calling for the resignation of Pennsylvania's secretary of education because of his insensitivity to African Americans in education, letters concerning funding problems at African American institutions, letters requesting that a white professor at Cheyney not be dismissed for the purpose of achieving racial balance, information concerning a commencement speech by Coretta Scott King, pleas for an increase in state appropriations to Cheyney, and a letter inviting Senator Snyder to attend a commencement at which President Carter was the guest speaker.
- *College-Lincoln University, 1980-1984:* Contains a letter of recommendation for Herman Branson, a former professor and then president of Lincoln University, to receive the National Medal of Science. Also present is a holiday season address from the president of Lincoln University, a speech on the impact of the recession on minority workers, fundraising letters

to alumni and friends of the University, a letter of gratitude to Senator Snyder for his assistance with the budget, and a *Wall Street Journal* article entitled "An Alienated Generation of Black Students?"

- ***Ethnics, 1976-1983:*** Includes newsletters and correspondence relating to Pennsylvania's rich ethnic heritage, the Pennsylvania Heritage Affairs Commission's list of ethnic publications and exhibits, and materials on Dr. Ralph Proctor, the African American Commissioner for the Governor's Heritage Affairs Commission. Also present is an article on the cultural contributions African Americans have made to Pennsylvania and a *Directory of Ethnic Resources of Philadelphia and the Delaware Valley* which lists African American religious, fraternal, charitable, and welfare organizations, performing groups, political groups, and social, cultural, and educational organizations.

- ***Human Relations, 1980-1983:*** Contains annual reports, a list of programs, information on state support for human services, and a newspaper article protesting the efforts to create a national holiday honoring Dr. Martin Luther King in 1983.

- ***MOVE, 1978:*** Includes newspaper and journal articles relating the history of MOVE and accounts of the demonstrations of MOVE members.

- ***Racism, 1971-1975:*** Contains articles on modern immigration trends, research materials relating to the effects of racism in education and employment, articles on interracial marriages and child custody issues and on forced busing. There is also an invitation to Senator Snyder from state Representative K. Leroy Irvis to attend the Conference of State Governments and an article about Irvis's consultation work for a law firm lobbying for South Africa.

- ***Department of Education, 1983-1984:*** Contains materials on Lincoln University for 1984. Among the items present is a notice of budget hearings, various appropriations requests, and statistics providing racial and income information, life expectancy, death rates, infant mortality, abortions, etc. There are also letters containing arguments from the president of Lincoln University stating that Lincoln must be supported in an effort to lower African American unemployment.

MG-374. AMERICAN CIVIL LIBERTIES UNION, HARRISBURG CHAPTER RECORDS, 1955-1957, 1969-1971, 1974-1983.

The Harrisburg Chapter of the American Civil Liberties Union is a local part of the state ACLU chapter. As a national organization, the American Civil Liberties Union champions the rights set forth in the Bill of Rights of the United States Constitution, including freedom of speech, press, assembly, and religion. The ACLU is a strong proponent of due process of law and fair trial and equality before the law regardless of race, color, sexual orientation, national origin, political opinion, or religious belief. ACLU activities include litigation, advocacy, and public education. The records include correspondence, business records, minutes, membership data, copies of papers filed with the court, and materials pertaining to various issues of interest to the Harrisburg Chapter of the American Civil Liberties Union. Included in the **Minutes** are an October 8, 1980 account of a discussion concerning Ku Klux Klan membership among the Harrisburg police and the activities of white policemen which aggravated racial tensions in the city. Also present is a February 13, 1980 report by an ACLU member on the Society of Friends' resolution condemning the KKK

MG-379. Records of the State Fencibles, [ca. 1813-1964]. Civil War Unit.
The Old Guard of the State Fencibles.

killings in Greenville, North Carolina, and a copy of a resolution condemning Klan-Nazi terrorism by the Harrisburg Area Concerned Organizations and providing information on a rally in Harrisburg. The **Newsletters** include copies of *Civil Liberties*, the national ACLU newsletter, containing articles on desegregation in schools and discriminatory harassment, and copies of the newsletters of the Harrisburg Chapter. The **Complaints File** contains a letter addressed to the mayor of Harrisburg concerning investigations of officers in the city police force suspected of belonging to the KKK and accusations of discriminatory behavior of policemen while on duty. There were also allegations that minority groups were receiving less effective police protection; a letter from the Cumberland Valley Human Rights Organization to a local newspaper cites what the author perceived to be a misleading photographic portrayal of an African American.

MG-379. STATE FENCIBLES COLLECTION, 1813-1885, 1891, 1898, 1911-1981.

The Old Guard State Fencibles, 1813-1981, was a military organization raised in Philadelphia in 1813 as part of the Pennsylvania militia and continued as a unit in the National Guard until independent battalions were abolished around 1900. The unit then was chartered as a Philadelphia City quasi-military unit and continued as a social club.

Scrapbooks, 1813-1926. Included are several newspaper articles on the Civil War and Philadelphia. The scrapbooks contain such articles as "The Panic of September 1873," "Richmond! Babylon Is Fallen: Philadelphia Colored Troops the First to Enter," "Weitzel's Negroes Extinguish the Flames-The Colored People," and "History of Philadelphia" that includes a paragraph labeled "In February there was presented to the House a petition from Philadelphia stating that the number of people of color was 9,672 on record and four thousand runaways not on the record, who were becoming nuisances." Also found is a broadside for a performance of *Uncle Tom's Cabin*, 1856.

MG-389. JAMES A. BEAVER COLLECTION, 1790-1915 AND UNDATED.

James Addams Beaver served as Governor of Pennsylvania from 1887 to 1891. Born in 1837 in Millerstown, Perry County, Beaver served as a Second Lieutenant in Company H of the Second Regiment of Pennsylvania Volunteers during the Civil War and rose to the rank of Brigadier General by 1864. He served as Major General of the Pennsylvania National Guard from 1871-1887 when he was elected Governor. As Governor, Beaver was an advocate of upgrading housing conditions for the poor and orphans.

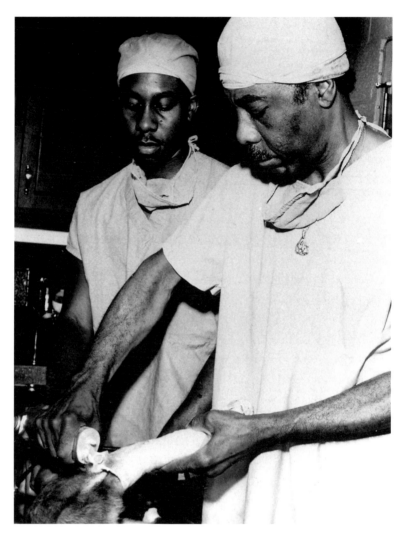

MG-391. Pennsylvania Veterinary Medical Association, 1914-1985. History Book Research Material. Dr. Hodges and a student in a laboratory setting.

Among the items in the collection is a manuscript entitled "Reminiscences from Memory of Events and Incidents on Scouts and Marches with Troops of the U.S. Army before the Civil War in 1861, in Arizona and New Mexico Territories," that was sent to Governor Beaver from, J.C. McKee, a Surgeon and a Lieutenant Colonel. In the paper, McKee refers to his "colored" servant. Also, *Union County Star and Lewisburg Chronicle* dated September 24, 1862 includes a citation that a "General B. F. Butler has freed more slaves than all the Abolitionists in the land as a 'military measure.'" The same issue also contains an article entitled "Proclamation of the President," reporting President Abraham Lincoln's recommendation to congress with regard to slavery.

MG-391. PENNSYLVANIA VETERINARY MEDICAL ASSOCIATION COLLECTION, 1914-1983.

Dedicated to the care and welfare of domesticated animals in Pennsylvania, the Pennsylvania Veterinary Medical Association was established in Philadelphia in 1883. The collection includes minutes, newsletters, and annual meeting records of the association as well as some material pertaining to the United States Veterinary Medical Association and related subjects. Among the photographs, 1905-1982, in the series labeled *History Book Research Materials*, is a picture of two African Americans performing surgery on animals, one of whom is identified as "Doctor Hodges."

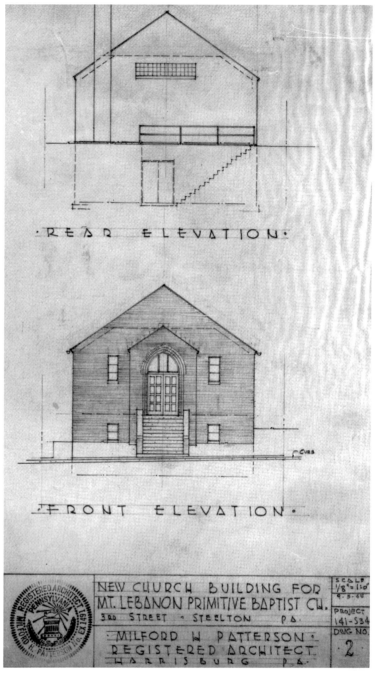

·REAR ELEVATION·

·FRONT ELEVATION·

NEW CHURCH BUILDING FOR
MT. LEBANON PRIMITIVE BAPTIST CH.
3RD STREET · STEELTON P A·

MILFORD H PATTERSON
REGISTERED ARCHITECT.
HARRISBURG P A·

SCALE
1/8"=1'0"
4-5-48

PROJECT
141-534

DWG NO.
2

MG-396. Milford H. Patterson Architectural Designs, [ca. 1940-1980]. Project
#604—Mt. Olive Baptist Church, 14th and Magnolia Streets.

MG-393. PULLMAN STANDARD CAR MANUFACTURING COMPANY OF BUTLER, PENNSYLVANIA RECORDS, [CA. 1902-1970].

Pullman Standard Car Manufacturing Company was a manufacturing branch of Pullman Incorporated of Chicago that resulted from merger between the Pullman Car and Manufacturing Corporation and the Standard Steel Car Company. During the nineteenth and twentieth centuries, Pullman systematized railroad car construction, revolutionized rail travel, and had a significant impact upon the economies of the cities where it operated shops and yards. Like many industries, it fell victim to the increasing competition occasioned by the rise of air and automotive travel after World War II. The records primarily consist of specification books, tracings and mechanical drawings of railroad freight cars and equipment, including "Jim Crow Cars." Other files include Business Correspondence, 1924-1925, 1938-1954; Employee Record Cards (giving the employee name, race, sex, and address as well as information about previous employment and work history), 1909-1945; visual materials such as photographs and motion picture films, showing scenes from World War II, peace time production lines, and such employee social activities as picnics and retirement parties; and audio tapes [ca. 1942-1970],. Materials concerning African American employees may be found in these files.

MG-396. MILFORD H. PATTERSON ARCHITECTURAL DESIGNS, [CA. 1940-1980].

Milford H. Patterson (1910-1983), a registered Pennsylvania architect, graduated from the University of Pennsylvania Architectural School in 1932, was a charter member of the Pennsylvania Society of Water Color Painters, and a member of the American Institute of Architects. Patterson specialized in the design of churches, small businesses, apartment buildings, and private residences, as well as in making alterations and additions to existing structures. The collection consists primarily of blueprints, drawings, and tracings of Patterson's proposed or completed projects in south central Pennsylvania, especially the Harrisburg area, and related business correspondence, ca. 1940-1980. Architectural drawings are arranged by job number, and related correspondence, specifications, and accounts for architectural projects designed by Patterson are arranged alphabetically by customer name. Included are drawings for some of the African American churches in Harrisburg such as: Project #141 First Baptist Church, Steelton; Project #739 Second Baptist Church, Forster Street (tower alteration); Project #403 Hillside Seventh Day Adventist Church, 13th and Herr Streets; and Project #604-Mt. Olive Baptist Church, 14th and Magnolia Streets.

MG-402. PHADRIG CAHILL'S UNITED PRESS INTERNATIONAL PHOTOGRAPHS, 1954-1975.

Phadrig "Pat" Cahill of Camp Hill, Pennsylvania, was a photographer for United Press International's central Pennsylvania region, 1954-1975. His prints were sent by UPI telephoto to appropriate newspapers throughout the state and country. The photographs consist of over six thousand 7" x 9" and 8' x 10" prints, each bearing UPI's code, date, and an extended typewritten caption by Cahill. The reverse often provides additional information. The prints are arranged chronologically by year, and thereunder alphabetically by subject. The original negatives were retained by UPI and use of these prints is subject to United States copyright law. Included are the following photographs featuring African Americans: **1954-Football**: Dean Maas #55, Minnesota's center bringing down Pittsburgh's Henry Ford on his own forty-five yard line after a five yard gain; **1955-Baseball:** Williamsport Little League Series, Pennsylvania vs. New Jersey, shows winning pitcher Wilbur Robinson and a scene in which Henry Singleton, also from New Jersey, was mobbed by his teammates after his home run. Other photographs in this folder show Bruce Gilmore in a Penn State football game with a Boston University in 1956 and a sit-in at the governor's office in Harrisburg by members of the Chester County Committee for Freedom Now.

MG-406. THE CASEY FAMILY COLLEC-TION, 1940-1987.

Though he was born in Jackson Heights, New York, in 1932, Pennsylvania Governor Robert P. Casey grew up in Scranton, Pennsylvania. He graduated from Holy Cross College in Worcester, Massachusetts with a B.A. in English in 1953, and received his J.D. in 1956 from the George Washington University Law School. After working for two years as an associate with the law firm of Covington & Burling in Washington D.C., he returned to Scranton where he opened his own law practice. Elected to the Pennsylvania state senate in 1962, he distinguished himself by authoring environmental legislation and was subsequently elected to two terms as Pennsylvania auditor general, 1969-1977. In 1978 he joined to law firm of Dilworth, Paxson, Kalish, & Kaufmann where he quickly became a senior partner and continued to remain active in Scranton civic affairs as well as state and national politics. He was elected governor of Pennsylvania in 1986 and again in 1990. Included in the collection are several newspapers with references to African Americans: The *Philadelphia Daily News*, Sunday, May 1978, "Blacks Give Nod to Casey," refers to the endorsement of Robert P. Casey by leaders of the African American community and quotes Dr. Leroy Patrick, chairman of the Black

Democratic Committee of Pennsylvania, on the political failures of the incumbent; an article from the *Philadelphia Daily News,* May 1978, displayed a photograph of Joe Frazier with Robert Casey at the Jefferson-Jackson Dinner; an article in the *Scrantonian,* Sunday, May 8, 1940, displayed a photograph of ten city draftees for the military among whom was Willie Williams, an African American player for the Scranton Miners' baseball team; and an article in the *Scrantonian,* March 13, 1949, " Dream Games Lineup," that lists several outstanding players from local teams including African American Clarence Floyd who played forward in St. Michaels in the Catholic League.

MG-407. JOSEPH RHODES JR. PAPERS, 1973-1980.

Pennsylvania state Representative Joseph Rhodes Jr., an African American, was born on August 14, 1947 in Pittsburgh, Pennsylvania, attended Pittsburgh public schools and California Institute of Technology, where he received his B.S. in history in 1969 and Harvard University as a junior fellow in intellectual history, 1969-1972. After completing work at Harvard, Rhodes held a number of teaching positions at the University of Massachusetts, California State College, and the University of Pittsburgh and was also employed at the Jet Propulsion Laboratory, 1967; was involved with the Caltech Student Research Project, 1968; was a staff researcher for the Ford Foundation, 1969-1970; and was consultant for the University of Massachusetts, 1973. Rhodes served in the House of Representatives from the 24th Legislative District for Allegheny County, 1973 to 1980, where he held important positions on the Finance, Judiciary, and Education Committees, including chairman of the Judiciary Subcommittee on Crime and Correction and chairman of the House Investigating Subcommittee on Lottery and Statewide Gambling. In addition, he was a member of the governor's Justice Commission and the Pennsylvania Commission on Crime and Delinquency. A great deal of the material relating to African Americans is found in the following series:

Subject Files, 1973-1980. The following subject files relate to African Americans: Affirmative Action, 1979; American Civil Liberties Union, 1974-79; American Ethnicity, 1975; Bail Reform, 1977; Black Action Center, Pittsburgh, 1974; Black Aged, Black Bus Drivers, 1973-75; Black Caucus, 1973-80; Black Community Affairs, 1973-76; Black Lawyers, 1979; Black Voice, 1973-75; Child Abuse, 1975-76; Child Care, 1974-75; Civil Rights, 1974; Criminal Justice; Desegregation of Schools, Discriminatory Cases, 1995; Black Higher Education: Cheyney College, 1975-76, Equal Opportunity Plan, 1971-74, Lincoln University, 1973-75, Pennsylvania Higher Education Assistance Agency, 1973-80, Temple University, 1975-76, Equal Rights Amendment; Housing, Urban, Jackson State University; Juvenile Justice, Labor, 1975; Landlord and Tenant Act, Minimum Housing Standards, 1975; Minority Business, Bureau of, 1977; Minority Employment, 1977; National Association for the Advancement of Colored People, 1975-79; and files on State Welfare Programs.

Public Hearing Transcripts, 1971-1978. The bulk of these hearings are of the House Subcommittee on Corrections and Rehabilitation, House Special Committee to Investigate the Administration of Justice in Pennsylvania, and the House Judiciary Committee's Subcommittee on Crime and Corrections.

Records Relating to the Investigation of the Lottery and Statewide Gambling, 1971-1978. Provide information on African American involvement in these operations.

Records Relating to the Subcommittee on Crime and Correc-

tions of the Judiciary Committee of the House of Representatives, 1973-1979. A source of information concerning African American criminal activities.

Governor's Justice Commission and Pennsylvania Commission on Crime and Delinquency Records, 1974-1980. A source of information concerning juvenile delinquency and criminal activity among African Americans.

Calendar Documents, 1975-1979. Includes invitations declined and accepted from a variety of African American organizations.

Records Relating to Investigation of Organized Crime, 1977-1979. A record of organized criminal activities including those conducted by African Americans.

Miscellaneous, 1973-1980. These files contain several items related to African Americans including nomination petitions for C. Delores Tucker, 1980; an article on Philadelphia's Samuel Evans entitled "The Gray Eminence of Black Politics," by David Gelsanliter (*The Philadelphia Magazine*, October 19, 1980); and several annual reports of the Pennsylvania Crime Commission.

MG-409. ORAL HISTORY COLLECTION.

Tapes in the Oral History Collection are divided into twenty projects of interviewing carried out in various Pennsylvania cities by staff members of the Pennsylvania Historical and Museum Commission. These interviews shed light on the daily lives of African Americans, European immigrants, Hispanics, and Jews in the Commonwealth. Indexes of the contents as well as transcripts are available for many of these tapes.

Three of the projects focus exclusively on the lives of African

Americans. These are the Harrisburg, Chester, and West Chester projects. In the Harrisburg project, the thirty interviews focus on the lives of Black women who migrated from the South and lived in an uptown neighborhood. Collateral material includes a booklet, *Glimpses Into Our Lives: Memories of Harrisburg's Black Senior Citizens*, written at the Harrisburg Uptown Senior Citizen Center, and two half-hour videotapes. The thirty West Chester tapes focus mostly on the Depression and the 1940s and how the color line was broken. The Chester City project includes twenty tapes, which are rich in material dealing with employer-employee relationships, religious life, racial strife, and political corruption. Some of the tapes in the latter collection are restricted.

Three of the collections that include Black history tapes are still growing since the projects continue. These are the Pittsburgh Oral History Project, the Chester County Library Oral History Project, and the Central Pennsylvania Collection. Thirty of the 280 tapes in the Pittsburgh project focus on Black steelworkers in McKeesport, Homestead, and South Pittsburgh. Some of these contain vivid descriptions of neighborhoods, religious life and employment. The Central Pennsylvania Collection produced by the Oral History Project at Pennsylvania State University, Capitol Campus, contains nine tapes on African American life and history in Pennsylvania.

Finally, there are three tapes of interviews with Andrew M. Bradley, the first African American to serve in a governor's cabinet in Pennsylvania. Bradley was secretary of the budget, and later head of the Department of Property and Supplies under both Governors George M. Leader and David L. Lawrence, serving from 1957 to 1963.

Chester, Pennsylvania Project: "Black Experience in Chester." Includes information on long-time residents, the 1917 race riot, local NAACP activities, political corruption, and employer-employee relationships. African American interviewees were: Solomon A. Bouldin, 5/7/77; Tiney Bradford, 12/17/76; James E. Brown, 3/27/77; Stephen E. Ewing, 5/11/77; Emmett C. Grasty, 1/5/77; William W. Grasty, 12/17/76; Bertha C. Green, 5/24/77; Lee S. Holmes, 12/2/76; Helen Hunt, 3/29/77; Charles E. Kincade, 5/18/77; Lois Laws, 4/28/77; Theodore Laws, 4/28/77; George Raymond, 7/6/77; Mamie and William Raymond, 3/24/77; Linwood Rideout, 3/29/77; Horace Saven:, 5/5/77; Alvin H. Swiggett, 2/12/77; Dorothy L. Wilson, 5/23/77; Mary and Robert A. Wright, 5/25/77. Interviewer was John Turner.

Harrisburg Project. Primarily recollections of long time residents of Harrisburg. Included are interviews with African American women who migrated from the South and lived in an uptown neighborhood. African American Interviewees were: Mildred Barber, her autobiography, "I Remember Mama," 7/7/75; Mary Jane Beasley, 7/23/76; Mae Breckenmaker, 5/11/77; Viola Davenport, 8/3/76; Amelia Davis, 1/14/76 and 2/24/76; Rev. George Davis, 2/13/76 and 2/17/76; Margaret Duff, 2/3/76; Hattie Hargrove, 7/27/76; Frederick Jackson, "The Black Chain Gang," 1/132/76; Lilly Jackson, "Slavery in Virginia," 1/19/77; Sarah Jones, 12/16/75, 1/27/76, 3/27/76; James Henry Lee, 3/16/76; /Georgia London, 7/30,76; Mary Elizabeth Moffitt, 8/5/76; Robert Quann, "Blacks in Harrisburg," 2/27/77 and 4/3/77; Florence Roebuck, "Blacksmithing and Growing Up in Harrisburg", 3/7/77.

Cornwall, Pa. Project. Mrs. Warner Franklin was interviewed by Carl Oblinger for the project, "Cornwall: the People and Culture of an Industrial Camelot, 1890-1980" during 1981-1982. She describes the experiences of African Americans who worked in the Cornwall Furnaces and who lived in the community. Mr. and Mrs. Franklin left Virginia in 1916 and he began working in the open pit as a blaster.

Chester County Project: "Yesterdays." Among a body of general biographical information from rural Chester County are interviews providing information on West Chester's Black Community during the Depression. The following African Americans were interviewed: Eroll and Sarah Anderson, Norris (?) Aston, Grace Ann Burnall, Warren H. Burton Sr., Catherine R. Carter, Mildred B. Crawford, Mrs. Davis, Carl E. Durnell Sr., Warner A. Durnell, Ruth Smith Flowers, Cornelius H. Gaither, Howard Grant, Mercedes Greer, Sarah Covety Brown Johnson, Anna Jones, Edith King, Henrietta Mauldin, James McCrea, Charles Melton, Thomas E. Norris, Carita Ponzo, Ida Stuart Ray, Earl Rustin, Helen E. Snyder, Irene Spangler, Robert Spence, Bertha Williams, Mrs. Walter Williams, and Rachel Wilson.

Pennsylvania's New Deal Oral History Project. The project involved eleven individuals who were interviewed from April through September 1990. The following African Americans were interviewed: Samuel J. Brown from Philadelphia; James B. Rowland Sr. from Harrisburg; and Raymond Steth from Philadelphia.

Pittsburgh Oral History Project, 1974-1978. Those interviewed were employed by Carnegie Steel Company, Duquesne Mill of the United States Steel Corporation, Federal Enamel Corporation, Firestone Rubber Company, the Fletcher Henderson Orchestra, Jones and Laughlin Steel Mill, Lockhart Iron and Steel Corporation, McKeesport Tin Plate Mill, Pittsburgh Steel Foundry, Railway Steel Frame Company, Standard Steel Car Company, Steel Tank Company, Clarence Waters Funeral Home, and the *Pittsburgh Courier*. Thirty of the tapes focus on African American workers in McKeesport. Homestead, and South Pittsburgh, providing vivid descriptions of neighborhoods, religious life, and work in the steel mills. The following African Americans were interviewed by Peter Gottlieb: Gordon Mason, Betty Glaze, Lowell T. Williams,

Benjamin Butler, Laval Murray, Henry Coogler, Dennis Schatzman, and Carol Murphy; Jasper W. Adams (Tape 239), Sadie W. Adams (Tape 203), anonymous African American man (Tapes 2-3), anonymous African American woman (Tape 219), George Bailey (Tape 19-2), Samuel Bailey (Tape 47-2), Jean Blair (Tape 210), Henry Brown (Tape 44-1), Homer Brown (Tape 54), Willam Bryant (Tape 46-2), Henry Carter (Tape 49-2), Ethel N. Christian ((Tape 59-2), Samuel Christian (Tape 53), Richard Cobbs (Tape 20-2), Wilbur Collins (Tape 58), Anthony Dawson (Tape 16-2), James Dean (Tape 81), Catherine Benjamin Erving (Tape 7-1), Earnest Freeman (Tape 209), Jerome Goodman (Tape 44-2), Harrison Gant (Tape 7-1), Sylvester Grinage (Tape 59-1), William Harris (Tape 221), Thelma Henry (Tape 50), Mrs. Jackson (Tape 52-2), Carrie J. Jennings (Tape 198), Aaron Jones (Tape 52-2), Keyo Long (Tape 52-1), Merrill Lynch (Tape 11-2), LeRoy McChester (Tape 5-1), Marion M. and Alma McElroy (Tape 80), Art McKissick (Tape 57-2), Frances C. McNairy (Tape 15-2), Hezekiah Mickey (Tape 237), Clarence Myricks (Tape 13-2), Callie Nicholson (Tape 214), James Nicholson (Tape 211), Freeman Patton (Tape 2-1), Mr. Ross (Tape 82-2), Clyde M. Schatzman (Tape 14-1), Reuben Sayles (Tape 45), James L. Simmons (Tape 14-1), Sally Simpson (Tape 222), Lucille L. Smith (Tape 223), Willie Smith (Tape 5-2), Eli Stribling (Tape 57-1), Floyd Thompson (Tape 208), Vernon Urquhart (Tape 57-1), Albert Walker (Tape 46-1), Clarence Waters (Tape 48), Olive W. Wighting (Tape 212), Grant Winston (Tape 218), John Winters (Tape 10-2), Walter Worthington (Tape 83), and Queen E. Wright (Tape 207).

MG-410. PENNSYLVANIA CAMPAIGN FOR NUCLEAR WEAPONS FREEZE COLLECTION, 1982-1987.

The Pennsylvania Campaign for a Nuclear Weapons Freeze was designed to pressure the federal government to halt the nuclear arms race and promoted citizen awareness of the dangers associated with nuclear weapons. The collection contains campaign materials, pamphlets, transcripts of speeches, copies of newspapers such as *The Socialist*, and copies of magazines such as *Freeze Challenger*, *The Pennsylvania Campaign for a Nuclear Weapons Freeze* and *Frontline*. The publications, although collected for their relevance to the nuclear freeze campaign, also contain articles touching on African American issues.

Newspapers. An issue of *The Socialist*, dated April 1987, contains an article about E. D. Nixon, the civil rights trailblazer, discusses his activities in the context of the political structure of the civil rights movement, and his relationship with A. Philip Randolph.

Magazines.

- *Freeze Challenger, The Pennsylvania Campaign for a Nuclear Weapon Freeze:* Vol.. 2, No 1, Feb.-Mar. 1986. The cover was dedicated to the memory of Rev. Dr. Martin Luther King Jr.
- *Freeze Challenger, The Pennsylvania Campaign for a Nuclear Weapon Freeze:* Vol. 2, No 1, June 1986. This issue contains a commentary entitled "Blacks Against the Bomb." The article, reproduced from *Essence Magazine*, Jan. 1985, discusses the organization called B.A.N. (Blacks Against Nukes).
- *Frontline:* April 30, 1987, Vol. 29, No. 18. Contains an article entitled "Our Rage Can No Longer Be Submerged, Rev. Ben

Chavis on Racist Violence and the Fight Back," chronicling the rise of racism in the United States, and a reprint of the Charlotte Perkins Gilman poem "A History Lesson," placing American history in a racial context.

- *Frontline:* April 27, 1987, Vol. 4. No. 21. Contains several articles regarding the plight of the African American in the 1980s. One article entitled "53 Arrested at Columbia U. Anti-racist Protest" discusses the failure of the university to expel a mob of 25 people who beat a black man. A second article, "New Investigations Probe to Police Killing of Black Man," discusses the killing of a twenty-three-year-old black man while he was in the custody of the San Francisco police.

MG-420. JOHN W. HARPER COLLECTION, 1716-1888.

A native of Bellefonte, Pennsylvania, John W. Harper was an avid genealogist who collected *taufschein*, surveys, deeds, patents, and other documents pertaining to his ancestors and for Centre County, Pennsylvania as a whole. Item #44 of the collection is a March 2, 1795 servitude indenture whereby "Negress Dinah" apprenticed herself to Nicholas Young of Philadelphia County for the term of eight years, seven months and ten days. In return for her service, Dinah was to be taught the "Mystery of Housewifery" and given five quarters of schooling. Upon the conclusion of her servitude, she was to receive changes of clothing.

MG-436 THE NATIONAL GUARD OF PENN-SYLVANIA, 2ND REGIMENT, 108TH FIELD ARTILLARY RECORDS, 1847-1947.

The parent unit of this regiment was constituted and organized in Philadelphia on December 11, 1840 as the National Guards.

It was a volunteer militia company assigned to the 1st Volunteer Infantry Regiment of Pennsylvania. Before being reorganized on October 23, 1916 as the 2nd Field Artillery Regiment, the unit was known as the Infantry Corps of National Guards of the City of Philadelphia in 1856; as the 2nd Infantry Regiment in 1861; as the 90th Pennsylvania volunteer Infantry Regiment in 1862; as the 2nd Infantry Regiment (National Guards) in 1867; as the 2nd Pennsylvania Volunteer Infantry Regiment in 1898; and as the 2nd Infantry Regiment, Pennsylvania National Guard in 1899. The collection consists of regimental enlistment books, minute books, photographs, and related records. A group photograph shows two African Americans dressed in gray overcoats that distinguish them from the rest of the group.

MG-449. HARRY SEYLER PAPERS, 1946-1980.

Born in York, Pennsylvania, Harry E. Seyler was a Democratic member of the Pennsylvania General Assembly from 1948 to 1962. Following service in the army during World War II, he was elected to the state house of representatives in 1948. In 1954, he assumed George Leader's vacant seat in the state senate, remaining in that position until 1962. He was appointed a delegate to the White House Conference on Education in 1956, and he was delegate to the Democratic National Convention the same year. Following his legislative career, he was employed in the Philadelphia branch of the Office of Economic Opportunity. He was also a member of the American Civil Liberties Union. The collection consists primarily of newspaper clippings, reference files, and correspondence relating to his political activities.

American Civil Liberties Union of Pennsylvania File, 1963-1965. Contains correspondence and newspaper and other printed articles about the efforts of the ACLU to eliminate discrimination. One case documented by the collection involved the ACLU's pursuance of federal protection for the Baker family, African Americans in Folcroft, Delaware County, whose home was "bombarded with rocks, paint and dead rats" in 1963. Other African American issues referenced in the papers include: Lincoln University, Fisk University, discrimination in public schools, the Commission on Industrial Race Relations, Robert and John Kennedy, and the Council for a Pennsylvania Fair Employment Practices Commission, for the 1950s and 1960s.

MG-451. H. CRAIG LEWIS PAPERS, 1974-1992.

H. Craig Lewis was born on July 22, 1944 in Hazleton, Pennsylvania and served as a Democratic state senator from the 6th District from 1972 to 1992. A graduate of Millersville State College, University of Nebraska graduate school, and Temple University School of Law, Lewis practiced law and served as a member of the bar of the Supreme Court of Pennsylvania, the Pennsylvania Inter-Governmental Council and the State Advisory Committee for Guidance Service. The collection contains legislative papers relating to the service of Senator Lewis. Information focusing on African Americans includes:

General Subject File.

Bensalem Youth Detention Center. This Center is one of eight facilities maintained by the Department of Welfare where juvenile offenders are sent for treatment, supervision, and rehabilitation. Located in Bucks County, it has a 93 percent minority population, many coming from inner-city Philadelphia. The institution has been plagued with numerous problems including inadequate staffing, poor staff training, staff brutality toward inmates, and a high level of inmate violence. This file contains letters, documents, and newspaper clippings relating to African American youth.

Martin Luther King Jr. Expressway, 1987-1988. This file contains letters supporting Senate Bill 741 that was introduced by Senator H. Craig Lewis in 1978 designating a portion of U.S. Route 1 in Bucks County as the Martin Luther King Jr. Expressway. Also included are letters from Senator Lewis thanking supporters of the bill, copies of Senate Bill 741, and a news clipping from an unidentified newspaper entitled "Section of Road Named for Dr. King," by Linda A. Johnson.

Legislation File.

Scotland School for Veterans' Children. Created in 1895 near Chambersburg in Franklin County, this school has a significant enrollment of African American youth. Items relating to Governor Robert P. Casey's proposal to phase out the Scotland School for Veterans' Children in 1991 include:

- Information Pertaining to Scotland School for Veterans' Children," prepared by the Pennsylvania Department of Education, March 8, 1991. The information in this report includes statistical data supporting the closing of the school.
- Letters supporting the appropriation of additional funds to keep the school open. Among the correspondents are: Ruth Ann Shelly, March 11, 1991; Tim E. Cook, a head track coach at nearby Chambersburg Area Senior High School: Edward T. Hoak, state adjutant, American Legion, March 15, 1991; Jeffrey W. Coy, state house representa-

tive of the 89th District, March 18, 1991; and Susan M. Cook, March 19, 1991. A letter from the teachers at the Scotland School for Veterans' Children, dated May 28, 1991, makes reference to all of the above letters as well as to letters of inquiry received from various legislators that the teachers felt were filled with misinformation. This file contains the following items originally enclosed with the teachers' letter to Senator Lewis: "Fact Sheet, Scotland School for Veterans' Children," prepared by the administration on May 10, 1991; "Information Pertaining to Scotland School for Veterans' Children, A Rebuttal to the Pennsylvania Department of Education," prepared by the administration, March 10, 1991; and "Testimonies presented before the Pennsylvania House of Representatives' Subcommittee on Basic Education Pertaining to Scotland School for Veterans' Children," by the following School associates: Interim Superintendent C. Frank Frame, Librarian Richard G. Tarr, student Tara Nicole Smith, and Alumni Association President Robert Shrawder, April 30, 1991.

Camp Hill Riot Transcripts, 1989-1990. Transcripts of hearings and resolutions issued by the House of Representatives, Committee on Judiciary, covering various aspects of the riots at Camp Hill Correctional Institution, October 25-27, 1989. Among these records are the following publications:

After Camp Hill: The Keys to Ending Crisis, a report by the Senate Judiciary Committee, Senator Steward J. Greenleaf, chairman, undated. Topics discussed include: More Secure Institutions/Upgraded Emergency Preparedness; Improved Prison Management; Sentencing Revisions/ Alternatives to Incarceration; and Parole System Overhaul. This report contains information on the riots at the Camp Hill Correctional Institution that occurred October 25-27, 1989. The riot resulted in 120 injuries to prison employees and inmates. Much of the prison was destroyed, requiring the relocation of more than one thousand inmates to other federal prisons in the state. This report also states that during seven months following the October riots, the committee held 117 public hearings and collected over three thousand pages of testimony. A large percentage of the inmates at Camp Hill were African Americans. Causes given for the rioting included overcrowding, understaffing, inadequate infrastructure, shortage of inmate programs and job opportunities, and friction between management and the corrections officers. The committee provided recommendations addressing master planning, public policy, administrative actions, and steps for immediate action. At the time of the riot, there were 2,600 inmates occupying an institution designed to accommodate 1,826.

The Final Report of the Governor's Commission to Investigate Disturbances at the Camp Hill Correctional Institution, December 21, 1989, submitted by Arlin M. Adams, George M. Leader, and K. Leroy Irvis. This report contains an "Executive Summary," chronology of events, analysis, and a set of conclusions and recommendations with regard to riots that occurred at the Camp Hill Correctional Institution on October 25-27, 1989.

Organized Crime in Pennsylvania: A Decade of Change, 1990 Report, Produced by the Pennsylvania Crime Commission. This 364-page report provides an overview of trends in organized crime in Pennsylvania during the preceding decade. Chapter 7 consists of a summary of African American involvement with organized crime in Pennsylvania. Exploring the types of crimes committed and the most frequent modes of organization, the report found African American community involvement in a multi-million dollar numbers racketeering operation and a large drug trafficking network with the major distribution organizations identified in the Pittsburgh, Harrisburg and Philadelphia areas. The report details modes of organization, such as domestic kin and associated networks, and reveals the extent of multi-million dollar drug trafficking networks. Prominent among the organizations reported was Philadelphia's "Black Mafia" and "Junior Black Mafia" whose networks were believed to extend across the state. Names and "street names" of individuals involved in such operations are given together with their addresses, ages, types of crimes, the amount of money involved, whether their activities were part of a family business, and the names of associated family members.

MG-452. PENNSYLVANIA ELECTED WOMEN'S ASSOCIATION RECORDS, 1980-1992.

The Pennsylvania Elected Women's Association (PEWA) is a non-profit, nonpartisan network of elected women and potential women candidates. Rather than offer support or opposition to a political candidate or party, the PEWA works to expand the potential for women in elected offices. The association was created in March 1980 at a conference of elected women sponsored by Carlow College. The PEWA aims to promote better government for all and has established a set of goals designed to increase the effectiveness of women elected to public office, to provide resource and information sharing about campaigns, to improve the process of government, to address the complexities of community management, to increase participation by women in both the political process and in local community affairs, and to achieve greater cooperation and closer communications among women. Among items relating to African Americans are the following:

Newspaper Articles. Harrisburg *The Evening News*, January 26, 1987, contains an article entitled "Local Government to be Fair Topic," announcing details about the Pennsylvania Elected Women's Association's Local Government/Candidates Fair held at Harrisburg Area Community College on January 31, 1987. This article includes a photograph and information on African American Carol Hyman-Huitt, a workshop participant.

President's Book, 1986-1987.

Newsletters. Included are *Keeping in Touch*, prepared by Senator Roxanne H. Jones, an African American woman representing the Third District of Philadelphia, Winter 1985; and *WOMENews*, a newsletter published by the Pennsylvania Commission for Women, Winter 1986, featuring an article entitled "Age Discrimination" by Issie L. Jenkins, Esquire, who at the time was the acting general counsel with the United States Equal Employment Opportunity Commission in Philadelphia. Jenkins was also a member of the Pennsylvania Bar.

Correspondence. Included among the correspondence is a program for the "Local Government/Candidates Fair," sponsored by More Women Candidates, Inc. and Pennsylvania Elected Women's Association on January 31. 1987. The following African American affiliated organizations are listed as co-sponsors: Omnia Bona, Inc., (Harrisburg Chapter), Mitchell Memorial United Methodist Women, Alpha Kappa Alpha Sorority, Inc., Delta Sigma Theta Sorority, Inc., and The Links (Harrisburg Chapter).

MG-454. L. H. KINNARD CHAPTER NO. 7 OF THE TELEPHONE PIONEERS OF AMERICA COLLECTION, 1874-1994.

The Telephone Pioneers of America is an association that was created thirty-six years after Alexander Graham Bell's invention of the telephone. The Pioneers first convened in Boston on November 2, 1911 with the goal of promoting a common bond of fellowship among those who had ushered in this new era of communication. In their own words, "the purpose of the Telephone Pioneers of America shall be to provide a means of friendly association for the longer-service employees in the telephone industry, either active or retired, and to promote among them a continuing fellowship and a spirit of mutual helpfulness, to exemplify and perpetuate those principles which have come to be regarded as the ideals and traditions of the industry, and to participate in such undertakings as may be deemed to make for the happiness, well-being and usefulness of the membership and for the progress of the Association." The L. H. Kinnard Chapter No. 7 originally was established on June 7, 1922 as the Central Pennsylvania Chapter No. 7. The name was changed to the L. H. Kinnard Chapter in 1935 in honor of Leonard Kinnard, who became president of the Bell Telephone Company of Pennsylvania in 1919 and remained in that capacity until his resignation in 1934. The Pioneers are involved in a number of community social activities such as volunteering in walkathons, "bowlathons," telethons, safe-driving transports, and serving the handicapped, and in a wide variety of philanthropic holiday projects. Materials in this collection relating to the African American experience include the following:

A. L. H. KINNARD CHAPTER RECORDS

Photographs. Photographs taken during the 1992 Sports Jamboree include African Americans as subjects.

B. RECORDS OF THE NATIONAL TELEPHONE PIONEERS OF AMERICA

Miscellaneous, [ca. 1941-1987]. Included is the 1984 issue of *The Telephone Pioneer* is a quarterly published by the Telephone Pioneers of America to communicate the goals and activities of Pioneers throughout the United States and Canada. The Winter 1984 issue contains "the Editor's Notebook" written by the *Pioneer's* news editor, Donald Singletary, an African American.

MG-456. PENNSYLVANIA ACADEMY OF SCIENCE RECORDS, 1964-1984.

The Pennsylvania Academy of Science was organized in Harrisburg on April 18, 1924 to promote science and the scientific spirit in Pennsylvania. The academy is affiliated with the American Association for the Advancement of Science and the National Association of Academies of Science. Formally incorporated through the Court of Common Pleas of Northampton County on November 16, 1964, the initial registered office of the corporation was Lafayette College, Easton, Pennsylvania. The corporation was formed for the purpose of encouraging scientific research, promoting interest in the teaching of science, and stimulating the exchange of ideas among those engaged in scientific research in Pennsylvania. When the American Association for the Advancement of Science appointed a national executive to coordinate the various Junior Academies of Science in the United States, the Pennsylvania Academy of Science followed the lead by organizing the Pennsylvania Junior Academy of Science in 1934. The records of the Pennsylvania Academy of Science consist of journals, proceedings, annual reports, newsletters, financial statements, receipts, invoices, audits, photographs, a video, minutes, correspondence, and membership data. The series, **Historians' Publications and Reports,** contains a book list which includes *The Abstracts of Papers* *of the 145th National Meeting, 3-8 January 1979, Houston, Texas*, edited by Arthur Herschman, that summarizes papers relevant to the African American experience:

- "Minority Access and Representation in Higher Education: An Empirical Assessment," by Gail E. Thomas.
- "Institutional Selection Policies and Educational Enrollment Patterns of Black Students," by Edgar Epps.
- "Standardized Testing as a Barrier to Black Higher Education Enrollment," by Charles V. Willie.
- "The Status of Minority Value in Higher Education and Career Outcomes," by Doris T. Wilkinson.
- Access of Minority Students to Professional Schools: Pre- and Post-Bakke Trends and Policies," by James E. Blackwell.
- Increasing Minority Access to College by Increasing the Potential Availability Pool: Some Legislative Remedies," by Frank Brown.

MG-459. HISTORICAL FOUNDATION OF PENNSYLVANIA RECORDS, 1961-1994.
(UNPROCESSED}

Formed in 1961 to promote the preservation of Pennsylvania's rich historical heritage, each year the foundation presents two awards for outstanding achievement in historical education. The S. K. Stevens Award acknowledges achievements of local historical societies and the Philip Klein Award acknowledges outstanding historical writing by individuals. These records contain charters, bylaws, minutes of annual meetings and the executive committee meetings, correspondence, grant applications, project files, newsletters, Internal Revenue Service audit information, bank statements, account books, and membership records of the Historical Foundation of Pennsylvania. In 1994 the S. K. Stevens Award was

MG-465. Capital Area Music Association, 1974-1997.

presented to the Wyoming Historical and Geological Society for a publication entitled *African Americans in the Wyoming Valley, 1778-1990,* "in recognition of outstanding accomplishment in the field of state and local history as certified by the American Association for State and Local History and the Pennsylvania Federation of Museums and Historical Organizations."

MG-465. CAPITAL AREA MUSIC ASSOCIATION RECORDS, 1974-1997. (UNPROCESSED}

Founded November 22, 1974, the Capital Area Music Association (CAMA) is a non-profit interdenominational choral organization based on Christian principles and standards. The organization's first director was John Tungston. Anthony T. Leach served as director from 1975 through June 1998 when Paul McPhail became director. CAMA is composed of persons living in the capital city area, including Harrisburg, Steelton, Carlisle, York, and

MG-467. Ball Family Photograph Collection. Forster Street YMCA
(Colored Branch of Harrisburg), ca. 1930.

University Choir, Morehouse Men's Choir, Washington, D.C.
Chapter of the Gospel Music Workshop of America, and the E. V.
Williams Ensemble.

MG-467. BALL FAMILY PHOTOGRAPH COLLECTION. {UNPROCESSED}

This collection contains thirty-three photographs of the Ball family. These photographs belonged to Lillian L. Ball, an African American musician. Born in 1905, she was a daughter of John S. and Louisa Gaskins Ball of 256 Lincoln Street, Steelton, where she lived her entire life. She began teaching piano in 1928 and later opened the Lillian L. Ball Studio of Music and Elocution. Of special note is a family portrait of Joseph and Ann Gaskins Jackson (Ann was Louisa's sister) with their nine children, and a photograph of the Forster Street YMCA (Colored Branch of Harrisburg), featuring several men thought to be board members and campaign committee members, appearing under a banner that reads "Anniversary Building Campaign Nov. 8-18," circa. 1930.

MG-473. GOSPEL MUSIC WORKSHOP OF AMERICA, HARRISBURG, PENNSYLVANIA CHAPTER, 1991-1999.

Organized September 14, 1991, the Gospel Music Workshop of America, Harrisburg Chapter, is an inter-denominational, interracial, non-profit organization administered by a Board of Directors and administrative officers. The purpose of the Harrisburg Chapter of GMWA is to make persons aware of the benefits of gospel music; to improve the standards of sacred music, directors, musicians and choir members through workshops and seminars; to unite musicians and singers in the Harrisburg area; and give service to the churches and communities whenever needed. A Mass Choir is formed of an unlimited number of dependable, dedicated, volunteer singers and musicians that represent the chapter at the National Convention. The late Rev. James Cleveland of Detroit, Michigan founded the Gospel Music Workshop of America in 1968.

(UNPROCESSED)

Included are legal papers, correspondence, minutes, reports, bills, receipts, cancelled checks, concert programs and bulletins, membership cards, and other miscellaneous records.

MANUSCRIPT COLLECTIONS CONTAINING INCIDENTAL REFERENCES TO AFRICAN AMERICAN MATERIALS IN PENNSYLVANIA AND OTHER STATES.

MG-14. J. SIMPSON AFRICA PAPERS, 1734-1891 (BULK 1772-1891).

J. Simpson Africa (1832-1900) was secretary of internal affairs, 1883-1890. The papers pertain to several generations of the Africa family, of German and Scottish descent, that was prominent in both Huntingdon County and in Pennsylvania. Included are letters, 1794-1807, and a ledger, 1795-1806, of John Cadwallader (d. 1807), a lawyer and Huntington's first postmaster. His papers include drafts of speeches and articles, 1855-90, and a large volume of correspondence, 1855-91, pertaining to politics, business, land transactions, and family affairs. With reference to African Americans, the collection contains a small poster advertising the "Silsby Variety Troupe at Yenter's Hall, March 21, 1873." Appearing was a feature entitled *The Rival Lovers* with one character named Jumbo, a "shrewd nigger," played by W. Maynard.

MG-15. HIRAM C. ALLEMAN PAPERS, 1856-1926.

Hiram C. Alleman was a Harrisburg attorney who served as lieutenant colonel of the 7th Pennsylvania Reserves (36th Pennsylvania Volunteers) and as colonel of the 127th Pennsylvania Regiment during the Civil War. He was also a member of the state House of Representatives from 1864 through 1865. Included in Alleman's correspondence is a petition by the Colored People Union League of Philadelphia, 1877. The petition, from African

Americans of the Philadelphia area, decried the fact that they were not allowed to use local rail transportation—even those who served in the Civil War. John C. Bowers, president of the League, signed the petition.

MG-28. JAMES BUCHANAN COLLECTION, 1815-1863.

James Buchanan (1791-1868) of Lancaster County, Pennsylvania was President of the United States, 1857-1861, a member of the Pennsylvania House of Representatives, 1814-1816, a United States representative, 1821-1831, a United States senator, 1834-1845, and was President Polk's Secretary of State from 1845-1849. This collection contains a letter from then Senator Buchanan to Ovid F. Johnston, Esquire, dated February 2, 1837 regarding a proposal to introduce a bill in Congress appropriating public money for the colonization of American slaves in Africa. In this letter, Buchanan cautioned against raising the proposal made by the colonization society.

MG-32. SAMUEL CALVIN PAPERS, 1850-1856.

Correspondence of Samuel Calvin (1811-1890), lawyer in Hollidaysburg and member of the United States House of Representatives, 1849-1851. Included in his correspondence file is a letter dated September 6, 1850 from W. A. McCarthy requesting a copy of an 1850 speech given by the Honorable Daniel Webster on the slavery question. Also found is a letter dated September 19, 1856 from I. T. Mathews discussing the political scene at the time and "the whigs and the slavery question," with references to Daniel Webster, Henry Clay and Thaddeus Stevens.

MG-33. SIMON CAMERON COLLECTION, 1816, 1835-1875.

Simon Cameron, Abraham Lincoln's first Secretary of War, was noted as a nineteenth-century Pennsylvania political boss. He also built a network of railroads in Pennsylvania and united them into the Northern Central Railroad. Cameron died in 1889, and this collection contains a printed facsimile of his last will and testament. Dated October 2, 1886, the will states ". . . Thirteenth, I give to my colored servant John Campbell one thousand dollars, provided he remains with me until the time of my death."

MG-38. COPE FAMILY PAPERS, 1793-1937.

Correspondence of three generations of an upper middle class Pennsylvania Quaker family having branches in Philadelphia, Chester, Bucks, and Susquehanna counties. William Drinker Cope (b. 1798), son of Thomas P. Cope (1768-1864), kept journals of his travels from 1813 through 1826. In an entry dated September 8, 1813 in Volume 1, William tells of his journey to Lancaster to visit his grandfather, Caleb Cope, stating "when I got pretty near his house, I saw a negro as complete a simpleton to appearance as I ever saw." Included also are some newspaper advertisements: "CASH FOR NEGROES . . . ."

MG-43. DOCK FAMILY PAPERS, 1865-1951.

These are primarily papers of Mira Lloyd Dock (1853-1945). Prominent during the first four decades of the twentieth century in promoting forestry and community improvement, she served on the State Forestry Reservation Commission from 1901 to 1913. Included in this collection are newspapers containing information relating to African Americans:

DOCK PAPERS

No. 65 Miscellaneous

Newspapers and Maps.

- *Valley Spirit*, Chambersburg, Pa., July 31, 1915: "Colored Woman Slain" reports the murder of Susan Jenkins of Fallsington, Pennsylvania. Ms. Jenkins was an eighty-year-old produce dealer from Bucks County.

- *The Patriot*, Harrisburg, Pa., September 16, 1905: May Be Chester Murderer" reports that a negro giving his name as Woodyard and claiming York County as his home was jailed on suspicion of knowing something of the Carter murder at Chester. Two other articles are concerned with the African Methodist Episcopal Church: " At the African M.E. Church, Rev. W.R. Gullins, DD . . . " and "Excavating for New A.M.E Church."

- *The Patriot*, Harrisburg, Pa., September 23, 1905: Under the heading "Church Services" is listed: "Wesley Union Church [A.M.E. Zion], South Street, Rev. W.H. Ferguson, pastor," and "St. Paul's Church, Sixth and Forster Streets, Rev. Leroy F. Baker, rector."

- *Harrisburg Telegraph*, March 7, 1908: Article entitled "Four Negroes Lynched" reports the lynching of four Negroes in connection with a double murder.

MG-44. WILLIAM H. EGLE COLLECTION, 1814-1899.

Harrisburg native, William H. Egle (1830-1901), a Civil War surgeon who engaged in historical research in the years following 1870, served as state librarian from 1887-1899. This collection includes a letter addressed to Leon Englebert in Des Moines, Iowa, citing Harriet Beecher Stowe's book, *Uncle Tom's Cabin*.

MG-48. FALL BROOK RAILROAD AND COAL COMPANY RECORDS, 1768-1938 (BULK 1819-1938).

Records of the business and financial interests of the Magee family of Bath, New York, containing primarily the records of the Fall Brook Coal Company and the Fall Brook Railroad Company. Born near Easton, Pennsylvania, John Magee (1794-1868) took up residence in Bath, Steuben County, New York in 1816. In 1854, John Magee obtained ownership of the Corning and Blossburg Railroad. In 1851, Magee obtained the lease for the coal mines at Blossburg, held earlier by Mallory and Bostwick of Corning, New York. John Magee's son, Duncan S. Magee, discovered coal near Fall Brook, Tioga County, Pennsylvania, and organized the Fall Brook Coal Company in 1859. When John Magee died in 1868, Duncan directed the family enterprises until his death one year later, whereupon he was succeeded by his brother, George J. Magee. In 1897, George J. Magee died and was succeeded as president of the coal and railway companies by his son, also named John Magee.

JOHN MAGEE, 1892-1900

The records of John Magee (grandson of the original) contain minute books, letter press books, general correspondence, and account books. Among the **Correspondence of George J. Magee (1864-1908)** are three letters from George T. Maxwell, a student at Fisk University, Nashville, Tennessee, one of the African American land grant universities, addressed to General G. A. Magee, dated May 8, 16, and 28, 1896, requesting employment from either Magee or his wife for the summer in order to have enough money to return to Fisk University in the fall of 1896. In reviewing Magee's letter press books, no reply to Maxwell was found.

MG-49. JOHN L. FINAFROCK COLLECTION, 1915-1942.

John L. Finafrock (d. 1941) was a Franklin County historian and president of the Kittochtinny Historical Society for many years until his death. The collection contains printed and typewritten material including pamphlets, three issues of the newspaper *Public Opinion*, and a book. In one of the editions of the *Public Opinion* is an article titled "Negroes Held as Suspects in Theft of Coat." Two negro men, William H. Hames of Waynesboro and LeRoy House of Hagerstown, were held in the county jail on charges of larceny and receiving stolen goods.

MG-56. JOHN WHITE GEARY COLLECTION, 1847-1873.

John White Geary (1819 -1873), a native of Mount Pleasant, Pennsylvania, served as governor of Pennsylvania, 1867-1873, and held many other military and public service positions. Most of the thirty two letters were written to his brother, the Reverend Edward R. Geary, an eminent Presbyterian clergyman who served in the Oregon territory for much of his life. Two letters to Edward discuss African Americans.

A letter dated March 5, 1849, from New Grenada, Panama, discusses the town, Chagies: "In many respects the town and its houses resemble a large collection of half decayed hay-stacks. The inhabitants are all black, being negroes, and mestigoes, a mixture of negroes and indians." Another letter dated November 23, 1837, from France, speaks of the elections in Kansas and the "proslavery party" and "constitution with slavery vs. constitution without slavery." In this letter, John Geary expressed his concern about the influence of the southern states on Kansas politics and the subsequent impact on the political situation in Oregon.

MG-58. JOSHUA AND THOMAS GILPIN COLLECTION, 1771-1854.

Thomas Gilpin was a prosperous Quaker merchant in Philadelphia who also owned flour mills on the Sassafras River in Maryland and along the Brandywine Creek. His sons, Joshua Gilpin (1765 -1840) and Thomas Gilpin Jr. (1776 -1853) operated as partners both the Brandywine Paper Mills, founded by Joshua in 1787 and a commission mercantile firm in Philadelphia. The collection consists of two parts, the journals and notebooks of Joshua Gilpin and the miscellaneous papers of Thomas Jr.

Letter Book, 1807-1809. Letter book copies of letters sent by Joshua and Thomas Gilpin and Laurence Greatrake relating to the Brandywine Paper Mill.

- July 12, 1801, a letter from Joshua and Thomas Gilpin: ". . . sent you a sheet of Carey's plate medium made of nothing but thirds as the run in common but very carefully dressed by a Mulatto woman. . . ."
- August 13, 1808, a letter from Laurence Greatrake from Philadelphia expressing concern about Black workers contaminating the paper during the manufacturing process. In a rather awkwardly worded passage he writes that "we want nothing but clean paper to manufacture . . . I am certain that at times many, many blacks get into the engine through the straining bags . . . I have now five mulattos and blacks (whites I could not get) dressing of fine rags (not by the score) but the day in the bleaching house and I attend them as much as possible."
- August 27, 1808, letter to the Gilpin Brothers from Laurence Greatrake: ". . . the rags dressed by the black woman I lately employed . . . is cleaned."

MG-63. GROSS FAMILY PAPERS, 1805-1918.

Legal papers, accounts, correspondence, and deeds relating chiefly to the business activities of David Gross of Winfield, Union County. Included is a book advertisement reading: "1856-Political Discussions-1887, . . . Legislative, Diplomatic, and Popular, upon great questions of national and local interest, including the Anti-Slavery struggle, the issues of the war, the reconstruction period, Chinese Immigration, Civil Service Reform, the great labor question, prohibition . . . By James G. Blaine, signed by H.A. Dutwiler as agent."

MG-108. PETER F. ROTHERMEL PAPERS, 1864-1880.

Letters of acceptance and regret in answer to invitations to attend the unveiling of Peter Frederick Rothermel's painting, *The Battle of Gettysburg*, at the Academy of Music, Philadelphia, 1870. Included also are letters, notes, sketch maps, etc., 1864-80, relating to research on the Battle of Gettysburg. One such letter written to Mr. Rothermel from L. W. Crawford of Huntsville, Alabama describes the formation and movements of his regiment and notes his contact with "Swope," one of the colored corporals.

MG-125. EDWARD SHIPPEN THOMPSON COLLECTION, 1684-1941 (BULK 1746-1904).

Born in 1869, Edward Shippen Thompson of Thompsontown, Juniata County, was an avid genealogist and local historian who assembled an impressive collection of family papers and genealogical notes. The collection chiefly consists of materials relating to the Thompson family, founders of Thompsontown. For more than a century this family remained prominent in the commercial and social life of that community and important portions of the papers also deal with the marriage-connected Burd family of Dauphin County, Shippen family of Lancaster County, and Patterson family of Lancaster and Juniata Counties. The collection includes the following letter and newspaper advertisement that refer to African Americans:

BURD AND SHIPPEN FAMILIES

- A letter to Edward Shippen Thompson from Elsie Burd Peale, of November 11, 1828, refers to the "negro Phyllis" and a letter of April 29, 1854 concerns the death and burial of "Phyllis."
- The following advertisement was taken from a newspaper and used as a backing for a cover of *The Freeman's Journal and Philadelphia Daily Advertisement*, No. 1076, September 5, 1807: "Eight Dollars Reward-Ran away . . . from Hopewell, Huntingdon County, New Jersey, a dark mulatto boy, . . . calls himself Eben Chambers . . ."

MG-149. STEVENS-OUTMAN FAMILY PAPERS, 1856-1972.

Papers of the Outman and Stevens families of Potter County. Prominent among those represented in the papers are Erastus C. Outman (1853-1920) of Harrison Valley, who was a grandfather of Dr. Sylvester K. Stevens, executive director of the Pennsylvania Historical and Museum Commission, and Anna (Outman) Stevens (1873-1950), daughter of E. C. Outman and mother of Dr. Stevens. This collection contains the papers of Dr. Sylvester K. Stevens concerning his book *Pennsylvania: Birthplace of a Nation*. The book, which is not itself included in the papers, contains many references to the African American experience in Pennsylvania history. Also found within the papers is a copy of the *Dickinson Alumnus*, Summer 1967, Vol. 44, No. 3, which contains an article accompanied by pictures reporting "Phi Eps Honor 'Pappy' Hodge for 50 Years at Dickinson." The Phi Epsilon Pi fraternity gathered on May 17, 1967 at the Marriott Motor Hotel, Philadelphia to honor Paul Hodge, and African American, for fifty years of service as house man at their Dickinson College fraternity house.

MG-160 ARTHUR H. JAMES PAPERS, 1937-1943.

A rthur H. James (1883-1974), a native of Plymouth, Luzerne County, served as governor of Pennsylvania, 1939-1943. A 1904 graduate of Dickinson School of Law, prior to becoming governor James was elected district attorney of Luzerne County in 1919, as a Republican lieutenant governor in 1926, and judge of the Superior Court of Pennsylvania in 1932.

A. GOVERNOR'S FILE, 1937-1943

Executive Correspondence, 1937-1943. Included is correspondence written to Governor James or the Governor's Office concerning records of the Bureau of Vital Statistics. One letter from the bureau inquires about regulations regarding birth certificates for African Americans who might potentially work in Pennsylvania's war industries.

MG-164. HIRAM GILBERT ANDREWS COLLECTION, 1890-1964.

H iram Gilbert Andrews (1877-1968), editorial director of the *Johnstown Democrat* from 1928 through 1941, was a prominent spokesman for the Democratic party in the Pennsylvania

House of Representatives from 1932 to 1963, serving at various times as minority whip, minority floor leader, and speaker of the house. Among the books in his collection is William M. Hall's *Reminiscences and Sketches* which includes a chapter entitled "Slave-catching in Bedford County."

MG-166. MATILDA ELLIOTT STUART COLLECTION, [CA. 1701-1902].

Family correspondence and various school, business, and military records of the Elliott family of Sterrett's Gap, Perry County. Included is a February 9, 1895 issue of the *Carlisle Daily Herald*, in which appears an article entitled "Pomfret Street A.M.E. Church." The article announces the 135th anniversary of the birth of Bishop Richard Allen and reports that the pastor of the Carlisle Bethel Church, Rev. J. J. Evans, will speak on the subject "The Need of a Leader."

MG-168. ROBERT E. PATTISON PAPERS, 1855-1904.

Papers of Robert E. Pattison (1850-1904), Philadelphia lawyer and Democratic governor of Pennsylvania, 1883-1887 and 1891-1895. Pattison was named chairman of the United States Pacific Railway Commission in 1887 and was president of the Chestnut Street National Bank in Philadelphia from 1887 to 1891.

General Correspondence, 1882-1896, 1904. Contains a letter dated May 25, 1904, to Pattison from his cousin Thomas R. Stewart. Stewart writes about the genealogy of the family and his recollection of spending time at the family home, "Union Hill," with Pattison's grandfather. He states, "I was at his father's after his negroes all ran away, except for one old colored man . . ."

MG-212. WILLIAM E. STEWART COLLECTION, [CA. 1861-1946].

Miscellaneous printed and manuscript materials relating to military, patriotic, and political matters. Included in the series **Postcards (Novelty Greetings, Special), undated,** is an illustration labeled "Fulton at Clermont Manor (arrival at the Home of Chancellor Livingston), August 18, 1807 on the first trip from New York," which shows in the background a servant of African descent. Found in the series **Newspapers, 1894, 1898, 1943,** are some issues of the military magazine *Victory*. The issue dated January 20, 1943 notes a book entitled *Negroes and the War* that was prepared by the Office of War Information. The January 27, 1943 issue reports the production of a motion picture by the Office of War Information entitled *Henry Browne, Farmer*, "a simple, down-to-earth story of a Negro farmer and his family . . . what they are doing individually and collectively to win the war . . . The film ends with the family visiting the Tuskegee Air Field where they watch the older son soar from the ground and fade over the horizon." The film was directed by Roger Barlow and narrated by Canada Lee. Other items found include *The Soldier's Pocket-Book; The Soldier's Prayer Book*, 1861; *Republican Campaign Text Book: Patriotism, Protection, Property*, 1910; Lincoln Highway Association certificate, 1913; *The Voter's Guide: A Digest of the Election Laws of Pennsylvania*, 1915; and World War II ration books and related items, 1942-45.

MG-213. POSTCARD COLLECTION, [CA. 1880-1974].

Postcards, advertising cards, greeting cards, and political and patriotic pictorial materials arranged by counties and showing urban and rural scenes including historic, public, commercial, industrial, and private buildings, churches; bridges and streams, railroads, and highways. This collection includes a card showing Lincoln University in Oxford, Chester County, and a card announcing a firemen's convention in Beaver Falls, Beaver County, which presents an unfavorable depiction of an African American.

MG-228. WILLIAM C. ARMOR COLLECTION, 1862-1930.

William C. Armor (1842-1911) was born in Westmoreland County and served as a major in the 28th Regiment, Pennsylvania Volunteers during the Civil War. After the war, Armor became a prominent Harrisburg citizen and served six years as executive clerk under Pennsylvania Governor John White Geary. The collection consists of private and military correspondence, appointments, commissions, and miscellaneous items. Included is a page from *The Harrisburg Telegraph*, August 14, 1911, in which the second part of an article entitled "Coatesville Cry for Justice" appears, concerning the lynching of Zachariah Walker in Coatesville.

MG-230. DAVID W. HOWARD COLLECTION, 1863-1889.

Civil War correspondence of David W. Howard, a native of Titusville in Crawford County, served in Company D, 18th Pennsylvania Volunteer Cavalry. Included under the miscellaneous category is an undated poem about Abraham Lincoln, the "one who freedom to all gave."

MG-249. BRADY FAMILY PAPERS, 1814-1964.

Correspondence including typescript copies, clippings, photographs, military commissions, certificates, and related genealogical materials of the Brady family, Scotch-Irish pioneers who settled along the Conodoguinet Creek near Shippensburg around 1750. Also included are newspaper clippings and printed materials pertaining to Captain John Brady, "West Branch Hero of 1776." Found in the series **News clippings** is a December 20, 1888 issue of the Williamsport *Weekly Gazette and Bulletin* which contains articles referring to African Americans.

MG-270. McFARLANE-LITTLE FAMILY PAPERS, 1831-1945.

James McFarlane (1819-1885) was a lawyer, engineer, and businessman in Perry County who authored numerous books dealing with coal and geology in the United States and served as commissioner of the Second Pennsylvania Geological Survey.

Biographical Notes, 1885. On the back of an undated newspaper clipping announcing the death of James McFarlane is an article entitled "The First Colored Man Admitted," referring to Everett J. Warning, the first African American admitted to practice law before the Supreme Court of Maryland. A native of Springfield, Ohio, Warning was a twenty-six-year-old resident of Baltimore who was a pension examiner in the Interior Department for the three years during which he studied law at Howard University.

MG-278. EUNICE MILDRED McCLOSKEY PAPERS, 1931-1979.

Born in 1906 in Ridgway, Pennsylvania, Eunice Mildred McCloskey was a noted writer and painter who was once described as the Grandma Moses of Pennsylvania. Her artistic output included approximately four thousand paintings, and she authored seventeen books. She was a member of the Professional and Executive Hall of Fame, and a Fellow of the International Institute of Arts and Letters. The papers include personal correspondence, scrapbooks, newspapers and clippings, manuscripts of novels, celebrity autographs and magazine reviews. Among the **Newspaper and Clippings, 1958-1977**, which are mostly from the *Ridgway Record*, are two television listings for the program entitle *Black Perspective* dated May 20, 1975, and April 24, 1976.

MG-279. GEORGE N. WADE COLLECTION, 1916-1973.

George N. Wade, a Cumberland County Republican, served as a member of the state senate from the 31st. District from 1941 until his death in 1974. Prior to becoming a senator, Wade was eastern manager of the Ohio National Life Insurance Company and held several positions in Cumberland County including board member of the Cumberland County National Bank and Trust Company. During his years in the senate, he was a member of the State Highway and Bridge Authority and chairman of the Minority Appropriations Committee. The collection includes business records, speeches, correspondence, political items, and photographs. In the series **Pictures, 1946, 1854-1973 and undated** is a folder labeled "Pictures 1967-73;" containing three prints having African Americans as subjects.

MG-289. GEORGE HART PHOTOGRAPHS, [CA. 1860-1960].

Born in 1919 in Doylestown, Pennsylvania, George Hart was the first director of the Railroad Museum of Pennsylvania in Strasburg. Since the 1930s, he has been photographing and collecting photographs of railroads, especially the Reading Railroad. The collection contains forty-seven prints of stereographic views made from original glass negatives, including several photographs of stations belonging to the Pennsylvania Railroad Company. In the Camden and Amboy folder are two pictures of a painting of a station showing an African American servant or waiter. Another photograph in the West New Jersey and Seashore Railroad folder shows the Haddon Avenue station in Camden with a crowd of people and includes one African American man waiting for a train.

MG-294. FRENCH AZILUM COLLECTION, 1781-1934 AND UNDATED.

French Azilum near Towanda, Pennsylvania, was established as a refuge for the former Queen Marie Antoinette and other aristocrats during the French Revolution. Formerly a historic site administered by the Pennsylvania Historical and Museum Commission, it is now in the possession of the Bradford County Historical Society. Two newspapers in the collection contain references to African Americans. The November 21, 1814 issue of the *Albany Gazette* published 1814 census data that included slaves for the New York towns of Whitestown, Utica, Troy, and Johnstown. The Charleston, South Carolina *Gazette and Daily Gazette and Daily Advertiser*, dated June 16, 1802, advertised "Negroes" for sale, persons for hire, and almost two pages of notices of runaway slaves that provide descriptions of the runaways.

MG-302. BOWMAN'S DEPARTMENT STORE RECORDS, 1880-1969.

Originally established in 1871 as a dry good store, Bowman's Department Stoer, Formerly H. H. Bowman and Co., Inc., was located at 314-18 Market Street in Harrisburg, operating as a retail merchandise outlet until 1969. The store had a very active employees' association which participated in sports, picnics, and parties, and which regularly corresponded with employees serving in World War I. The collection includes some of the store's business and financial records, as well as correspondence, floor plans, and materials relating to the 1921 Golden Jubilee.

B: HISTORY, 1895-1963

Golden Jubilee File, June 6, 1921. This file contains letters, advertising items, new first floor plan, sketches and photographs of the store facade, and a copy of the *Harrisburg Telegraph* dated June 4, 1921. The newspaper contains an article entitled "Two Held on Booze Charge" that describes the arrest of two men in Sunbury, one of whom, William Arington, is identified as "colored." The article does not read coherently and appears to be incomplete. The files are arranged alphabetically by subject heading.

Newspaper Clippings, 1897-1963. A *Harrisburg Telegraph* article dated September 29, 1919 contains an article entitled "Negro Lynched," providing details on a lynching that occurred in Omaha, Nebraska. The same newspaper contains an advertisement headed "Homes for Colored Families." Also, there is a copy of the *Penbrook Times* dated June 12, 1897, containing an account of an African American man who was hanged in Virginia after being convicted of raping a white woman.

Pictures, 1895, 1924, 1945, and undated. Includes a photograph dated "June 95" showing an African American man standing on right side of the second row of a group.

MG-313. CENTRAL PENNSYLVANIA QUARRY, STRIPPING, AND CONSTRUCTION COMPANY (CPQSCC) RECORDS, 1903-1961.

Located near Hazleton, Luzerne County, the Central Pennsylvania Quarry, Stripping, and Construction Company conducted quarrying in central Pennsylvania from 1903 to 1961. In 1971 it was renamed Central Pennsylvania Industries, Incorporated. The records were donated by Board Chairman William C.M. Butler Jr. in 1979. **The Workmen's Compensation Case (Accidents) and Accounts Receivable Book, September 1913-December 1916** contains an entry concerning an African American man named John Wilson who was injured at work. The record contains his address, marital status, age, and nationality, as well as employment information and case standing.

MG-330. KNOEDLER FAMILY COLLECTION, 1900-1940.

Treasurer of the Harmony Associates, John Frederick Knoedler was caretaker of the Harmony Society, ca. 1905-1916, and served as justice of the peace and tax collector of Harmony Township, Beaver County, ca. 1891-1908. The collection consists primarily of financial records of the Harmony Society Historical Association as well as personal and legal items.

Personal Letters and Postcards, [ca. 1910-1920]. Included are two seasonal post cards, 1914 and 1915, which show caricatures of African American children.

MG-334. LOWENGARD FAMILY PAPERS, 1905-1930.

Harry and Leon Lowengard were printers and owners of *The Courier*, a weekly Harrisburg newspaper. The collection includes business accounts and related items, as well as a few private materials. One African American appears in an **Advertisement Broadside** depicting the newspaper's employees. Among the **Boy Scout Material and Pictures, [ca. 1918]** are two photographs of Black women at a campsite.

MG-336. HASTINGS-HICKOK FAMILY ESTATE PAPERS, 1766-1901.

Dr. John Anderson (1766-1837) was a county official and land speculator in Bedford County, developer of the Bedford Mineral Springs health spa, and an ancestor of Harrisburg industrialist Ross Anderson Hickok (1876-1943).

General Correspondence, 1777-1834. In the personal letters to Dr. John Anderson that are arranged alphabetically by surname of correspondent, one letter dated October 21, 1821, from James Lytle reveals that he (Lytle) worked with a "black man" who was possibly from Washington, D.C. In another letter, dated December 7, 1818, Mark Richards wrote, "I was sorry to hear that the black boy conducted himself so rascally . . ."

MG-341. FLORENCE AMELIA LINDERMAN PAPERS, 1840-1948.

Florence Amelia Linderman was born July 17, 1893 in Fleetwood, Berks County, Pennsylvania, the daughter of Daniel Boone Linderman and Amelia Shiery. The Linderman family claims kinship with the Daniel Boone family through Florence's grandmother. Consisting primarily of family genealogical materials, this collection contains facsimile copies of three letters written by Abraham Lincoln to A. H. Stephens of North Carolina. In one of the letters, dated December 22, 1860, Lincoln outlined the Republican Party's position on not interfering with slavery in the states where it already existed. Also included in the collection are a number of postcards and greeting cards. A circa 1907 "Thanksgiving Greeting" depicts a turkey and two African American children.

MG-345. M. LEE GOLDSMITH, INC. PAPERS, 1872-1977.

Founded by upholsterer Joseph Goldsmith, M. Lee Goldsmith, Inc. was a furniture store located on Market Square in Harrisburg. In 1881, Goldsmith was in partnership with Amos Fry, but later he acquired sole proprietorship of the business. His son, M. Lee Goldsmith, became a partner in 1919. After M. Lee's death, his sons Richard S. and Joseph K. Goldsmith continued to operate the business under his name until 1981, when it was sold to a New York firm. There are several group photographs of employees that depict at least one African American male with each group.

MG-366. GRAEME PARK COLLECTION, 1743-1918.

Graeme Park, originally constructed by Pennsylvania Governor William Keith, 1721-1722, is the only surviving residence of a colonial Pennsylvania governor. The property was originally intended for use as a distillery before it was sold in to Dr. Thomas Graeme, who renovated it to serve as his country estate. In 1920, Mr. and Mrs. Welsh Strawbridge acquired the land upon which the main house stands and restored the mansion to its original condition. In 1958, the Strawbridges gave the property to the Commonwealth of Pennsylvania. It is currently maintained as a historic site. The collection contains two issues of the *Pennsylvania Packet or, the General Advertiser* containing advertisements for the sale and return of runaway slaves. The issue dated August 29, 1787 has an ad placed for the sale of a "negro man," and the December 7, 1782 issue has an ad placed by Benjamin Rittenhouse seeking the return of a runaway "Mulatto Wench named Chloe."

MG-367. LAWRIE AND GREEN COLLECTION, [CA. 1922-1960].

In 1922 Harrisburg architect M. Edwin Green (1897-1985) joined with Pittsburgh engineer Ritchie Lawrie (1890-1962) to form the Harrisburg architectural firm of Lawrie and Green. Disbanded in 1972, the firm designed several hundred buildings throughout central Pennsylvania, including the North Office Building, the State Farm Show Complex, the Dauphin County Courthouse, and the William Penn Memorial Museum and Archives Building in Harrisburg. Many of the school buildings, such as the Stevens Elementary School in Carlisle, served large numbers of African American students.

MG-375. THE BENJAMIN FRANKLIN FISHER PAPERS, 1862-1881, 1892, 1915, AND UNDATED.

Benjamin Franklin Fisher (1834-1915) enlisted in the 3rd Regiment, Pennsylvania Reserve Corps in April 1861, was commissioned first lieutenant, and transferred to the Signal Corps in 1861. He was captured on June 17, 1863, and confined at Libby Prison until February 9, 1864. Mustered out in 1866 with the rank of brevet brigadier general, Fisher subsequently practiced law in Montgomery County. He died on September 15, 1915 at the age of eighty-one. Two issues of the Philadelphia *Evening Ledger* refer to African Americans: September 10, 1915: a Kemble cartoon strip "GET-RICH-QUICK-WALSINGFORD NO MORE DEMON-STRATIONS FOR SHRIMP" featuring a stereotypical portrayal of African Americans, and articles including "Segregation Brings Protest," "Negro Children Assigned to Old School Building," and "Cop Beaten by Negroes-Camden Policeman in Critical Condi-tion from Fractured Skull"; September 15, 1915, "Church Notice" for the Vincent Baptist Church, Chester Springs, Rev. Samuel Smith, pastor, and a notice of a funeral service for Malinda A. Coleman, wife of Clement Coleman, to be held in the African Methodist Episcopal Church.

MG-387. THE RAYMOND HOFFMAN COL-LECTION, 1918, 1944-1970.

Colonel Raymond Hoffman served as secretary of the Society of the 28th Division, American Expeditionary Forces, which was formed to promote ties of patriotism and comradeship among the men who served in the Keystone Division during World War I. The 28th Division was initially organized as the 7th Division in 1916, serving in the Mexican Border Campaign. In July 1917, the 7th Division was called for active duty in World War I, was reorga-nized into the 28th Division. The 28th Division served in France in World War I, earning the nickname the "Iron Division," and also served in World War II and Korea. In the early 1930s, land in Boalsburg, Pennsylvania was given to the state in order to create a shrine commemorating the service of the 28th Division in World War I. The shrine was officially dedicated in the 1940s, and fol-lowing the Second World War, tablets denoting individual service were placed there by the Society of the 28th Division. One of the photographs in the series **Photographs, 1940**, in the *Boalsburg Shrine* subgroup shows two African American males in uniform.

MG-395. DONALD H. KENT COLLECTION, 1931-1986.

Born in 1910 in Erie, Pennsylvania, Donald Harris Kent was the director of the Bureau of Archives and History of the Pennsylvania Historical and Museum Commission from 1961 to 1975. Prior to assuming the directorship, Kent served as a historian with the commission for more than twenty years, serving as associate state historian, 1945-1956, and as chief of the Division of Research and Publications, 1956-1961. He also edited *Pennsylvania Heritage* for a time and held leadership positions in the Pennsylvania Historical Association. His great interest in Native American history led him to become an expert witness in cases involving Eastern tribal groups. The collection consists of research notes and materials, correspondence, bibliographic note cards, and related papers. In the series **Research Materials-Publications, [ca. 1894-1924]** are: "A Black Bibliography: The Negro in the American Experience" (1968) by Daniel Walker, and the proceedings of the 1957 annual spring meeting of the American Ethnological Society entitled *Cultural Stability and Change.*

MG-397. M. HARVEY TAYLOR COLLECTION, 1896-1982.

A native of Harrisburg, Morris Harvey Taylor was leader in the state Republican Party from 1934 to 1963, chairman of the Dauphin County Republican Committee, and a state senator from 1940 to 1963, when he rose to the position of president pro tempore. He also owned and was president of M. Harvey Taylor Insurance Company. In the series **Photographs** is a folder labeled

"Dinner meetings at Harrisburg Country Club" in which are two photographs showing African American men as cooks, chefs, and waiters in a country club setting.

MG-411. HERSHEY MUSEUM LOCAL HISTORY COLLECTION, 1734-1931.

The Hershey Museum of American life in Hershey maintains collections dealing with early Pennsylvania life and culture. Materials in its custody include American decorative arts, nineteenth-century Pennsylvania German materials and arts, and North American Indian ethnographic and archaeological materials. In addition, the museum houses artifacts relating to chocolate magnate Milton Hershey's life and the company town of Hershey.

LANCASTER COUNTY

Included are papers relating to the McElhenny and Littel families, including wills, estate appraisal, receipts, and probate records. The will of Agnes Littel of Rapho Township, Lancaster County, bequeathed to "Negroess Dinah" a milk cow and five pounds yearly for her support with an allowance for a future increase.

MG-433. THE GEORGE I. BLOOM COLLECTION, 1916-1988.

George I. Bloom (1898-1991) was born in Burgettstown, Pennsylvania and graduated from the University of Pittsburgh School of Law in 1922. He served as secretary to Republican Governor Edward M. Martin, 1943-1946; chief of staff to United States Senator Edward M. Martin, 1946-1956; chairman of the Republican State Committee, 1956-1963; secretary of the Commonwealth, 1963-1965; and chairman of the Pennsylvania Public Utilities Commission, 1965-1975. A member of the American Bar Association, Bloom was admitted to practice before the Pennsylvania Superior and Supreme Courts and the federal courts, and also served as solicitor for West Brownsville, Burgettstown, and McDonald, Pennsylvania. The collection documents Bloom's political career, and includes certificates appointing him to various offices, resolutions honoring him from state and local organizations including the state senate and the Pennsylvania Council for Republicans, and letters from politicians thanking him for his assistance to their electoral campaigns. Also found in the collection are several photographs taken at different awards ceremonies at which African Americans were present.

MG-439. EDWARD R. BARNSLEY PAPERS, 1801-1986 (BULK 1932-1986).

Edward K. Barnsley was a lawyer from Newton, Bucks County and head of the Furnishing Committee of the Pennsbury Manor Reconstruction. The papers relate to Barnsley's early association with Pennsbury Manor from its restoration and inception as a historic site in the 1930's. Included in the series **News clippings, 1908-1972**, is an undated news clipping titled "Penn as a Slave-holder" that was taken from a Philadelphia *Evening Bulletin*. It quotes Hannah Callowhill, the second wife of William Penn as saying: "The young blacks must be disposed to prevent their increasing charge. . . ."

Alston, Junius, 76

American Civil Liberties Union, 357, 439, 510, 511, 522, 531; Harrisburg Chapter Records, 513-4

American Foundation for Negro Affairs, 40, 42

American Revolution, 232: correspondence, 287, 412; documents, 412; forfeited estates, 174, 198; military service, 11-12, 20-23, 61-62, 418; pensions, 11, 21; Pennsylvania Line, 20; Pennsylvania Navy, 21, 22. *See also* Valley Forge Park Commission

Anatomical Board, cadaver books, 51

Anderson, Adilphus W., Sr., 359

Anderson, Betty, 19

Anderson, Eli, 295

Anderson, Eroll and Sarah, 527

Anderson, Felix Adolphus, 191

Anderson, James, 295

Anderson, Jane, 13, 14, 16

Anderson, Maggie, 14, 17

Anderson, Marian, 363, 501

Anderson, Matthew, 321, 509

Anderson, Matt S., 373

Anderson, Sarah A., 362, 376, 385, 468, 509

Anderson, Thomas J., 316, 376

Andrews, Hiram Gilbert, Collection, 553-54

Anthony, Clyde Harrison, 191

Arlene, Herbert, 389, 475, 509

Armor, William C., Collection, 556

Armstrong, Charles, 110

Armstrong Association of Philadelphia, 315, 363

Arnett, Dr. H. Y., 59

Arter, Fannie, 409

Arthursville, 28

Artis, Madella, 404

Asante, Dr. Molefi K., 264

Asbury, John C., 509

Ashby, Linda, 19

associations, 9, 11, 28, 40, 41-42, 64-65, 128, 149, 176, 192-96, 222, 333, 313-14, 315-16, 356, 374, 385, 469,

537. *See also organization names*

Aston, Norris, 527

Athletic Commission, State, 371

Atkinson, Charles Theophilus, 191

Attorney General, 73-74, 376

attorney, letters of, 95

Attucks, Crispus, 176

Atwell, 485

Audio-Visual Collection (motion pictures, recordings, videotapes), 407

Auditor General, Department of the, 10-18

Austin, George, 491

Austin, Nicole Millicent, 404

Avery College Trade School, 321

B

Bacas, Charles, 248

Baer, David, 295

Bagnoll, Rev. Dr. Robert, 175

Bailer, J.W., 310

Bailey, George, 528

Bailey, Samuel, 528

Baily, Albert L., 359

Baily, Albert L. Jr., 361

Baily, Joshua L., 359

Baker, Joseph V., 178, 330

Baker, Rev. Leroy F., 547

Baker family, 531

Bakke, Allan, 436

Balch Institute, 55

Ball, Lillian L., 542

Ball Family Photograph Collection, cover, 542

Baltimore, Mary, 462

Barbee, Darryl, 404

Barber, James D., 460, 468, 472, 475, 476, 477, 509

Barber, Linda Newkirk, 404

Barber, Mildred, 526

Barbour, Rev. J. Pius, 351

Barkley, Rev. H.B., 376

Barnes, Diston, 409

Barnsley, Edward R., Papers, 568

Bostick, Franklin, 181
Boston, T. Clifford, 131
Boswell, William D., 397
Bouldin, Solomon, 104, 526
Bowden, Rev. W.W., 389, 397
Bowers, John C., 545
Bowens, Thomas J., 273
Bowles, George William, 131
Bowman's Department Store Records, 560-61
Bowser, Harry E., 254
Boyer, George, 294
Boyle, Edward Mayfield, 127, 131
Boyle, Dr. Edward Mayfield, 242
Bradford, Tiney, 526
Bradford County, 72, 77, 303, 306, 559
Bradley, Andrew M., 54, 112, 113, 114, 334, 359, 368, 369, 370, 373, 525
Bradley, Erwin S., 420
Bradley, Howard C., 352
Brady, Catherine, 227
Brady Family Papers, 557
Branch, George, 464
Brand, Mary, 11
Branson, Dr. Herman R., 119, 468, 470, 511
Braxton, Alberta J., 351
Breinigsville, 431
Brewer, Charles, 148-49
brewers, 240
Brickerville, 266
Brigerman, John H., 509
Bridgewater School, 292, 293
Brittan, James M., 137, 361
Brooke, Edward W., 378, 453
Brooks, Evelyn, 477
Broomall, C. M., 140
Brown, Bernard, 107
Brown, Charles L., 100
Brown, Charles Leslie, Sr., 199
Brown, Frank, 540
Brown, Henry "Box," 60
Brown, Henry, 528
Brown, Homer, 528
Brown, Homer S., 312, 350, 358, 361, 371, 509

Brown, Mrs. Homer S., 360
Brown, James, 231
Brown, James D., 236
Brown, James E., 526
Brown, John, , 181, 310, 416
Brown, John T., 355
Brown, Joseph E., 107
Brown, Judith Blair, 404
Brown, Martha, 268
Brown, Dr, Richard, 360
Brown, Richard C., 401
Brown, Samuel J., 527
Brown, Maj. Gen. William E., 485
Brown, Rev. William L., 371
Bruff, Thomas, 103
Brumbaugh, Gov. Martin G., Papers, 499-500
Bryan, George, 92, 115
Bryant, William, 528
Bryn Mawr, 354, 357
Buchanan, James, 424; Collection, 545
Bucks County, 23, 33, 77, 198, 235-6, 293, 419, 532, 547, 568; Human Relations Council of, 372; tax list, 273
Bull, Leland H., 8
Bullard, Aaron, 98
Bullard, James, 98
Bullard, John, 98, 99
Burden, W.F., 348
Bureau of Markets, 8, 9. *See also* market houses
Burgettstown, 567
Burke, Dr. Selma H., 472
Burleigh, Harry T., 273-74, 275
Burnall, Grace Ann, 527
Burns, Levi, 21
Burns, Lewis R., 236
Burrows, Thomas H., 180
Burton, Warren H., Sr., 527
Business Records Collection, 265-67
Butcher, Alice B., 140
Butler, Benjamin, 528
Butler, Sarah Ann, 268
Butler County, 84, 326
Byers, Elizabeth and William, 227

Byron, Fletcher L., 462

C

Cahill, Phadrig, United Press International Photographs, 520
Caldwell, Bishop J. S., 59
Calloway, Irene F., 253
Calvin, Samuel, Papers, 545
Cambria County, 84, 395; Bloom Almshouse, 173
Cameron, Simon, 417, 420; Collection, 546
Camp Curtin, 271; YMCA, 381, 398
Camp Hill, 432; White Hill Industrial School, 74, 258; Correctional Institution, 75, 465, 534-35 (riots)
Camp William Penn, 96, 98, 280, 312, 398, 441
Campanella, Roy, 364, 380
Campbell, Ann, 294
Campbell, John B. 461, 464
Camps for Underprivileged Boys, 371
Canonsburg, 194, 316
Capital Area Music Association Records, 540-42
Carbon County, 201
Carlisle, 68, 99, 193, 297, 395, 409, 487-88, 541, 554; school alumni registers, 253; Stevens Elementary School, 564
Carlisle Barracks, 396, 508
Carlisle Indian School Collection, 396
Carn, Andrew J., 37
Carnegie, 200, 306
Carr, Benjamin, 277-78
Carr, Rev. L.G., 364
Carter, Anna Lucille, 501
Carter, Carol Lynn, 403
Carter, Catherine R., 527
Carter, Cornelius Lennon, 131
Carter, Henry, 528
Carter, Ivan L., Photographs, x, 487-89
Carter, Lewis J., 359

Carter, Matthew, 267
Carter, Nancy, 19
Carter, Robert, 84
Carter, W. Beverly, 360
cartoons, political, 421
Carver, George Washington, Day, 353, 363, 370, 379
Casey, Gov. Robert P., 36-39, 42, 43, 532; Family Collection, 520-21
Cassatt, A. J., 439
Cayce, Rev. James B., 360
Census: 1970, 248; 1980, 248; 1990, 249, 263; employment data, 42; Septennial, 32-33; slaves, New York towns, 1814, 559
Censors, State Board of (motion picture), 122-23
Central Pennsylvania Quarry, Stripping, and Construction Co. Records, 561
Centre County, 72, 77, 236, 310, 330, 401
certiorari papers, 207
Chalfont, 364
Chambersburg, 14-17, 69, 444
Chapman, Betty, 354
Chapman, William, 409
charitable foundations, 205
Charitable Organizations, Commission on, 191-94
Charles, Albert J., 361
Charming Forge, 266
Chatman, Rev. Jacob L., 462, 464
Chavis, Rev. Ben, 530
Checks, John, 108
Chester, 337, 372, 382, 383, 384, 468, 525; School District, 454
Chester, T. Morris, 273, 411
Chester County, cover photo, 32, 33, 47, 48, 50, 77, 193, 199, 210, 211, 212, 303, 315, 556; Library Oral History Project, 526
Cheyney University, 19, 34, 37, 41, 60, 117-21, 135-7, 138, 140, 193, 221, 255-56, 299, 313, 321, 322, 333, 334, 335, 349, 352, 355, 361 (trustees),

363, 373, 378, 382, 383, 384, 385,
450, 462 (trustees), 464 (trustees),
466, 469. 476, 511, 522
children, juveniles, 64-5, 149, 192-3,
268, 294, 314, 326, 384, 489, 522,
523, 561, 565
Children and Families, Governor's
Commission for, 43
Children and Youth, Governor' Committee on, 351, 359
Chisholm, Shirley, 423
Choate, J.N., 409
Christian, Ethel N., 528
Christian, Samuel, 528
Christiana, 417
Chud, Earl, 367
churches, 11, 29, 40, 57, 59, 60, 64,
66-9, 95, 96, 113, 175, 192-96, 316,
320, 333, 334, 335, 336, 354, 362,
371 376, 393, 394-95, 396, 397, 409,
410-11, 433, 446-67, 452, 461, 477,
502, 507, 519, 527-28, 547, 554, 565;
cemeteries, 66
civil liberties, 485
civil rights, 331, 332, 334, 337, 338,
359, 378, 383, 390, 416, 452, 510,
522, 528; legislation, 335, 336
Civil Rights Act, 122, 378, 453; of
1963, 420; of 1964, 137, 452; of
1968, 391
Civil Service Commission, 18-19 (employees), 40, 466
Civil Tension Task Force, 457
Civil War, 13, 124, 271, 280, 330, 341,
408, 411, 429, 448, 490-91, 515; correspondence, 100-1, 285-86, 400;
military service, 96-99, 100-1, 185,
280. See also Battle of Gettysburg;
United States Colored Troops
Civil War damage claims, 288;
Chambersburg, 14, 16, 17; Adams,
Bedford, Cumberland, Franklin,
Fulton, and York Counties, 15
Civilian Conservation Corps, 487-88,
508; Pine Grove Furnace, 31
Claborne, William, 295

Clairton, 395
Claremont, 341
Clarion County, 201
Clark, E.W., 321
Clark, Edward, 12
Clark, Mrs. Jesse, 461
Clark, Joseph S., Jr., 362
Clark, Lucille, 463
Clark, Mrs. Nathan, 316
Clark, William S., 397
Clay, William, 423
Clearfield County, 32, 72, 84, 315
Clelence, Henry J., 294
Clelence, Samuel, 294
Clement, M. W., 439-40
Cleveland, Rev. James, 543
Clifton, Alice, 197
Clinton, Pres. William J., 38
Clothier, Clarkson, 321
Coatesville, 193, 299, 316, 376, 556;
lynching, 310, 556
Cobb, Ivory, 175
Cobbs, Richard, 528
Cohen, Herbert B., 376
Cole, Addie B., 315
Cole, Pat, 443
Cole, Rebecca, 72
Cole, William Durant, 371
Coleman, Alexander, 100
Coleman, Maude P., 313, 316
Coleman, Robert H. 328
Coleman, William T., 381
colleges and universities, 9, 40, 41, 51,
116-21, 354; Land Grant, 8. See also
Students, Commonwealth Associa-
tion of; higher education; Pennsylva-
nia State System of Higher Educa-
tion; and names of institutions
Collins, Wilbur, 528
Columbia, 69, 301
Columbia County, 33, 77
Commerce, Department of, 204-5
Commission for Children and Fami-
lies, Governor's, 43
commission books, 92-95
Commonwealth Court, 435

patients, 142-43; burials 143-44
Darby, 476
Daroff, Samuel H., 356
Dauphin County, 23, 33, 52, 65, 77, 193, 238, 239-43, 286, 288, 291, 389, 395; Court of Common Pleas, 240; Folk Festival, 480-1, 482; poor relief, 242-43; school children, 268
Davenport, Violet, 526
Davis, Amelia, 526
Davis, Edward, 109
Davis, Rev. George, 526
Davis, Hannah, 14, 17, 18
Davis, William R., 254
Dawson, Anthony, 528
Day, William Howard, 273
Dean, Andrew, 408
Dean, James, 528
Dearing, J. Earl, 452
debtors, 210
de Coy, Robert, 376
Delaney, Martin Robinson, 273
Delaware County, 33, 37, 77, 220, 285, 315, 531
Delaware River, Navigation Commission for the, 224-26
Delaware River Port Authority, 385
Dellmuth, Terry, 454, 455, 463, 466
Denford, David, 268
Denford, Margaret, 268
Denford, Palm, 268
Dennis, Shirley M., 254, 464
Dennis, William C., 387
Denny, Rose, 376
Dental Council and Examining Board, State, 134
dentists, 125, 238, 239, 366. *See also* National Dental Association
Denton, Dr. Stanley E., 262
Derry, Anna E., 236
Derry, Elizabeth, 236
Derry, John, 236
desegregation, 454
Desmond, Carolyn, 190
Devlin, William J., 380
Dick, "Governor," 340, 341, 346

Dickerson, Carl O., 462
Dickinson, John, 401, 496
Dickinson College, 553
Diggs, Catherine, 294
Diggs, John, 14, 17, 18
Dilworth, Richardson, 362
Discrimination, Governor's Task Force to Combat, 454
discrimination, state, 204, 355, 454, 463
distillers, 23, 240
Dix, P.C., 348
Dixmont State Hospital, 144-49, 157, 161; patients, 145-48
Dixon, Marie Vernon Patricia, 299
Dobson, John R., 110
Dock, Mira Lloyd, 546
Dock Family Papers, 546-47
Donaldson, Nathaniel, 352
Dorset, 215
Dorsey, Lewis, 310
Douds, Charles T., Papers, 483-85
Douglas, Phoebe, 180
Douglass, Frederick, 185, 416
Douglass, Frederick, Memorial Exposition, 320
Douglass, Frederick, Memorial Hospital and Nursing School, 326
Doylestown, 559
Dowling, Ruth B., 137
Downingtown, 193
Downingtown Industrial School, 314, 355
Drayton, Willie, 459
Drew, Clarence Edward, 100
Drug and Alcohol Abuse, Governor's Council on, 44
Duckery, Marjerie, 462
Duckrey, Dr. James H., 135, 136, 335, 349, 364
Dudley, John R., 357
Duff, Gov. James H.: Papers, 330-33; Jean F. Gerdes Collection of Photographs, 499
Duff, Margaret, 526
Dumas, Aljia, 475

Duncan, B.J., 316
Dunston, Dr. Joseph N., 125, 238
Dunston, Dr. Walter Thurston, 134
Duquesne, 395
Durnell, Carl E., Sr., 527
Durnell, Warner A., 527
Durnin, Thomas, 84
Duss, John, Papers, 477-78. *See also* Harmony Society Papers
Dykes, Sylvia, 465

E

Eames, Edwin, 114
Earle, Gov. George H., Papers, 294-95
Eason, W., 377
East Stroudsburg University, 299, 450
Eastern State Penitentiary, 77-81, 418-19; medical records, 79, 80, 81
economic development, 468
Edinboro University, 450
Edmonds, Calvin C., 463
education, higher, 416, 539
Education, Department of, vi, 115-41, 456, 476, 533
Education, State Board of, 138-39
education, multicultural, 122, 263-64
Educational Equality League, 362, 376
Egle, William H., Collection, 547
Eisenhour, John, 493
Elizabeth Furnace, 266
Elizabethtown Hospital for Children and Youth, 45-46
Ellington, Duke, 399
Elliott, Theodore, 372
emancipation, 32, 58, 59, 124, 308, 335, 336, 416; Day, 379
Emergency School Aid Act, 122
Emerson, Junius, 509
employment: minority, 8, 42, 43, 44, 74, 89, 221, 228, 298, 380, 385, 388, 430, 436, 454, 455, 473, 472, 479, 482, 510, 512, 519, 523, 548, 550, 553, 559, 563, 567; Governor's Conference on, 390, 391, 392; age, 365;

state, 19, 40, 74, 228, 331, 368, 369, 388, 456, 463; statistics, 89, 329
Energy Conservation Work Camp: Licking Creek, 30; Clear Run Road, 30
Engle, Horace M., Collection, 341
English, Phobe, 212
Environmental Resources, Department of, 228-29
Epidemiology and Disease Prevention, Burreau of, 46
Epps, Edgar, 540
Epps, Jacqueline, 354
Equal Education Opportunity, Office of, 121
Equal Employment Opportunity Commission, 43, 121
Equal Employment, President's Commission on, 112
Equal Opportunity Employment Office, 457
Equal Rights Amendment, 43, 290, 475
Equal Rights Day, 460, 468
Equal Rights Task Force, 40, 456
Erie, 68, 305, 332, 389, 455, 566
Erie County, 9, 40, 84, 201
Erving, Catherine Benjamin, 528
escheat papers, 208-10
Ethics Commission, State, 254
Ethnic Culture Survey, 56, 58-59
Ethnic Groups, Coalition of, 42
Ethnic Studies Collections, 393-95
ethnicity, 407, 511, 522; Governor's Conference on, 263
Evans, Dwight, 37, 187, 254
Evans, Rev. J.J., 554
Evans, Samuel, 524
Ewing, Stephen E., 526
Exum, Marone Wilson, 446

F

Fair Employment Practices Commission, 311, 332, 351, 355, 356, 357,

360 (members), 361, 372, 374, 531
Fairchance, 69
Fairview State Hospital, 157
Falco, Dr. Maria J., 437
Fall Brook Railroad and Coal Company Records, 548
Fallsington, 547
farmers, 8
farms, 23
Father Divine, 63
Fattah, Chaka, 37
Faulcon, Clarence Augustus, 277
Faulk, Harry R., 467
Fauset, Crystal Byrd, 509
Fayette County, 23, 33, 72, 84, 243-44, 266
Felton, William McDonald, 486
Fenn, George Washington, Papers, 490-92
Ferguson, Rev. W.H., 547
Fields, Barton A., 189, 387, 397, 398, 466
Fillkill, Jane, 14, 18
Fillmore, Pres. Millard, 124
Finafrock, John L., Collection, 549
Fine, Gov. John S., Papers, 348-58
Finley, Joyce, 19
Fischer, Bertha P., 468
Fisher, Benjamin Franklin, Papers, 564-65
Fisher, Gov. John S., Papers, 313-16
Fleetwood, 562
Flemming, Charles, 108
Flood, James E., 54
Flowers, Ruth Smith, 527
Floyd, Clarence, 522
Floyd, Homer G., 463
Floyd, Samuel, 373, 509
Fogelsanger, Berkely R., 464
Foggie, Rev. Charles H., 336, 360, 361
Folcroft, 382, 383, 531
football, vi, 331, 520-21
Ford, C. W., 8
Ford, Corey, 231
Ford, Henry, 521
Forest Academy, Mont Alto, 30

Forests and Waters, Department of, 29-31
Forney, John W., 285
Fort Indiantown Gap, 480
Forton, James, Sr., 273
Foster, David C., 72
Foster, Evelyn Louise, 131
Foster, Henry D., 420
Foster, James Edward, 128, 131
Foster, Dr. James Edward, 242
Foster, Julius, 376
Foster, Pearl, 316
Foster, Rev. Peter, 367
Foster, Stephen Colliins, 274-77
Fox, Alma Speed, 461
Fox, Solomon, Collection, 400
Frame, C. Frank, 533, 534
Francis, John, 21, 22, 23, 62
Franklin, Jacob, 462
Franklin, Mrs. Warner, 526
Franklin County, 23, 30, 33, 72, 77, 549; tax records, 269
Frasier, Ella, 480, 501
Frazer, James, 77
Frazer, Reah, Papers, 284
Frazer, William, 284
Frazer, William Clark, 284
Frazier, Joe, 522
free persons, 23, 24, 246, 284
Freedom Day, 37, 39
Freeman, Charly, 403
Freeman, Earnest, 528
Freeman, John, 403
Fremont, John C., 420, 424
French, Paul Comly, 361
French Azilum Collection, 559
Frey, Oscar N., 136, 135, 136
fugitive slave laws, 32, 217, 284, 301, 310, 413-14, 416, 417; *Commonwealth vs. Prigg,* 217. *See also* Christiana Riot
Fuller, William Harvey, 509
Fulton, J. Alexander, Papers, 285
Fulton, Robin, 404
funeral directors, 128, 356; State Board of, 128, 190, 360, 462

Furguson, Lydia, 216
Furness, William Eliot, 101

G

Gaither, Cornelius H., 527
Galamison, Rev. Milton A., 423
Gallagher, James J. A., 229
Gant, Dawson, 369
Gant, Harrison, 528
Gantz, Jacob, 227
Garris, Presto, 98
Garvin, Jesse, 231
Gates, Eli, 14, 18
Gates, Louisa, 14, 18
Gates, William, 72
Gatewood, Harold Cook, 100
Gatewood, Thomas J., 322
Gatter, Carl W., Architectural Research
  Books, 495-97
Geary, Gov. John White, 184; Collec-
  tion, 549
General Assembly, 31-33, 36, 399;
  Collection, 508-9; African American
  legislators, 509 (1911-74), 523; leg-
  islation, 1973-79, 474-75; women's
  legislation, 509
General Services, Department of, 111-
  14
General State Authority, 33-35
Georges, Dr. Thomas W., Jr., 397
Gettysburg, 273, 279
Gettysburg, Battle of, 551; 50th Anni-
  versary Commission, 174
Gibson, John, 310
Gillespie, Rev. G.T., 377
Gillison, Rev. Horace W., Jr., 469
Gilmore, Bruce, 521
Gilpin, Joshua and Thomas, Collec-
  tion, 550
Gilson, Malachi, 253
Girard, Stephen, 391, 392; Collection,
  404-5
Girard College, 331, 379, 382, 383,
  390, 391, 392, 405

Gittins, William W., 316
Glaze, Betty, 527
Gloster, Hugh, 114
Goldsmith, M. Lee, Inc., Papers, 563
Goens, Arthur, 84
Goode, Wilson, 38, 477
Goodman, Jerome, 528
Goodridge, Glenalvin J., 78, 181-82,
  186
Goodwin, John S., Collection, 285-86
Gordon, Noah, 267
Gordon, Pauline H.L., 128
Gordon, Sylvester, 181
Gospel Music Workshop of America,
  Harrisburg Chapter, 543
Governor, Office of the, 35-44, 520
Graeme Park Collection, 563-64
Graham, Gwendolyn, 354
Grant, Howard, 527
Grasty, Emmett C., 526
Grasty, William W., 526
Gray, Robert, 295
Gray, William H. Jr., 28, 29, 349, 351,
  356, 509
Grayson, Ida S., 316
Great Depression, 63, 105, 526-27
Green, Bertha, 526
Green, John, 294
Green, Thomas, 310
Green, William J., 359
Green Circle Program, 263
Greene, Isaiah, 338
Greene, William, 72
Greene County, 72, 84
Greenfield, Mrs. Albert M., 381
Greenfield, Elizabeth, 273, 462
Greenleaf, Steward J., 534
Greenough, A. J., 440
Greer, Mercedes, 527
Gregg, Theodore, Collection, 401
Griffin, Mrs. Albert, 316
Griffin, Dorothy R., 299
Griffin, John Howard, 386
Grim, Harold F., 338, 352, 365
Grimke, Charlotte, 273
Grinage, Sylvester, 528

Huggins, T.V., 377
Hughes, Helena G., 254
Hull, Gillmore, 181
Human Service Integration Project, 467
Humphreys, Richard, 256, 363
Hunn, Lydia J., 269
Hunt, Alfred H., 462
Hunt, Helen M., 128, 526
Huntingdon, 81, 82, 297
Huntingdon County, 23, 33, 84, 301, 544
Huston, Charles L., III, 462
Huston, Joseph M., Collection, 290
Hutchinson, Vincent G., 111
Hutton, Herbert, 462
Hyman-Huitt, Carol, 537

I

Illery, Dr. Erma Johnson, 353, 363, 366, 379
illustrations, 124, 273. *See also* cartoons; posters; postcards; trade cards
Indiana County, 84, 201, 483
Industrial Race Relations, Governor's Commission on, 221, 349, 351, 356, 357, 531
Ink Spots, 398
Insurance, Department of, 223-24, 466
intermarriage, 32
Interracial Cooperation, Commission on, 332
Internal Affairs, Department of, 71-2; Bureau of Statistics, 71-72
Irvin, James H., 348
Irvis, K. Leroy, 28, 29, 37, 43, 59, 187, 254, 336, 436, 457, 467, 470, 473, 474, 475, 510, 511, 512, 535
Irwin, William, 209
Isele, John A., 480

J

Jack, Andrew, 266
Jack, Edward, 266
Jackson, Barbara, 403
Jackson, Byron, 398
Jackson, C. Sylvester, 347
Jackson, Charles, 240
Jackson, Frederick, 526
Jackson, Inez, 354
Jackson, Rev. Jesse, 251, 469, 470
Jackson, Lewis/Louis, 14, 16
Jackson, Lilly, 526
Jackson, Walter K., 510
Jackson, Webster D., 128
Jackson, William J., 295
Jacobs, James, 310
Jacobs, John W., 491
James, Gov. Arthur H., Papers, 553
James, Harold, 37
James, Milton, M., 363
James, Vernon R., 139
Jassum, Abraham, 98
Jassum, Edward, 98
Jeanes, Samuel, 184
Jeffers, Dr. Benjamin Butler, 242
Jefferson, Benjamin, 14, 16
Jefferson, F. L., 319, 320
Jefferson, George, 354
Jefferson, John H., 461
Jefferson, Ralph T., 510
Jefferson County, 30, 84
Jenkins, Beau, 398
Jenkins, Rev. C.F., 316, 348
Jenkins, Issie, L., 537
Jenkins, Susan, 547
Jennings, Carrie J., 528
Jiggetts, Mary, 19
Joanna Furnace, 57
Johnson, Abraham, 236
Johnson, Amos, 409
Johnson, Dr. Burrell K., 357, 358
Johnson, Cordelia Greene, 352
Johnson, Dorothy, 465
Johnson, Elliot, 100
Johnson, Emer, 236

582

K

L

Labor and Industry, Department of, 88-91, 178, 466; Division of Negro Research and Planning, 178, 330
labor: coal and coke, 507; migratory, 8, 9, 228-29, 334, 338, 362, 374, 379, 501 (female); Governor's Committee on Migratory, 219, 349, 351, 382, 383, 461, 463; health, 8, 48, 49, 89, 229; Interdepartmental Committee on, 361; movement, 8, 372, 376, 484; relations, 89, 90, 436, 461, 464, 525; steel mills, 527-28; strikes, 61, 89, 201-2, 311; war industry, 62
Lackawanna County, 471
Lamb, Samuel, 446
Lambert, Eugene, 258
Lampkin, Daisy, 55, 57, 336
Lancaster, Andrew, 294
Lancaster, 51, 69, 246, 301, 304, 476: Farmers' Market, 9
Lancaster County, 23, 33, 43, 52, 77, 199, 207, 209, 210, 211, 214, 244, 266, 284-85, 287, 304, 310, 327, 381, 413, 437, 510, 545, 546
Land Records, Office of, 91-96
Lane, John, 295
Lane, Moses Charles, 100
Lane, Robert, 84, 295
Larris, Anne, 246
Larris, John, 246
Larson, Stanley, 399
La Rue, Alphonso, 372
Laurel Furnace, 266
Lawler, Pamela Rainey, 466
Lawrence, Gov. David L., 114, 525; Papers, 333-39
Lawrence, William J., 393
Lawrence County, 201, 321
Lawrie and Green Collection, 564
Laws, Lois, 526
Laws, Theodore, 526
Laws Funeral Home, 190
Lawson, Paul M., 510
Lawson, Samuel, 294

Lawson, Stanley, 398
Layton, Morris Hallowell, Jr., 128, 242
Layton, Dr. Morris H, Sr., 96
Leach, Anthony T., 541
Leach, James, 408
Leader, Gov. George M., 358, 525
Lebanon County, 77, 448, 498; Historical Society Deposit, 327-28
Leboo, Levi, 236
Lee, Edward, 462, 464
Lee, James Henry, 526
Lee, Jarena, 273
Leeds, Mrs. Morris E., 351
Leetsdale, 489
Leftwich, William "Mike," 19
Legislative Affairs, Secretary for, 36
Legislative Reapportionment Commissions, 247-49
Legislative Reference Bureau, 220
Lehigh Coal and Navigation Company Records, 478-79; employment records, 479
Lehigh County, 77; Almshouse, 173
Lehigh Valley Railroad Company Records, 429-30
Lemon, Harriet Wright, 357
Lench, Ronald G., 463
Leonard, Ruth, 95
Levinson, Aaron, 360
Levittown, 362, 375
Levok, Samuel J., 36
Lewis, Charles, 19
Lewis, Charles Anthony, 127
Lewis, Evangeline, 14
Lewis, H. Craig, 531, 533
Lewis, Dr. Stephen Johnson, 125
Lichtenberg, Philip, 464
Lieutenant Governor, Office of, 259-61
Lilly, 200
Lincoln, Abraham, 32, 124, 300, 339, 421, 556, 563
Lincoln School, 94
Lincoln University, cover photo, 8, 43, 60, 114, 117-20, 137, 221, 303, 331, 332, 336, 338, 353, 357, 363, 365-

66, 379, 383, 384, 387, 392, 450, 462, 464, 467, 470, 472, 473, 474, 476, 511, 512, 522, 531, 556

Linderman, Florence Amelia, Papers, 562-63

Lindsey, Ben, 295

liquor licenses, 240

Little, Jo Ann, 453

Lloyd, Charles, 404

Lloyd, John, 182

Local Government Commission, 251-52

Lock, Thomas, 182

Logan, Algernon Sydney and Robert Restalrig, Papers, 401-3

Logan, Floyd L., 376

Logan, James, 496

Logan, James A., 439

Logue, Thomas A., 494

London, Georgia, 526

Long, Charles, 461

Long, Keyo, 528

Lotman, Arlene, 463

Love, George, 263

Lowengard Family Papers, 562

Luzerne County, 33, 77, 348, 553, 561; Almshouse, 166, 167; Central Poor District, 167

Lycoming County, 33, 77, 193, 395

Lynch, Merrill, 528

lynching, 310, 547, 556, 560

M

MacDonald, Ernest R., 127

Mackae, Mary M., 366

Mackey, Mayor Harry, 175

Mackey, Margaret C., 227

Mackey, Philip, 100

Mackley, Crawford, 464

Maclay Family Papers, 501-2

Mahony, Joseph L., 321

Mahonney, Joseph, 28

Maier, William M., 361

Manfrey, Eugene R., 464

maps, 273, 278, 304

Marietta, 69, 341

market houses, 9

marriages, 71-72, 211; interracial, 512

Marshall, Dr. Alexander L., 242, 480

Marshall, Commander John, 21

Marshall, Samuel, 326

Martin, Aaron, 462

Martin, Gov. (Gen.) Edward, 60, 356; Papers, 311-12

Maso, Alonzo, 84

Mason, Gordon, 527

Mason, Dr. Joseph J.B., 125, 127

Massell, Gertrude Bustill, 273

Massell, Nathan Francis, 273

Mathis, Johnny, 398

Mauldin, Henrietta, 527

Maxwell, George T., 548

Maxwell, J.E., 139

Maxwell, William, 372

May, Mrs. Herbert, 462

Maydon, George, 268

Maydon, Isaac, 268

Maydon, William, 268

Mays, Benjamin E., 484

Mayview State Hospital, 157-60; burials, 160; patients, 158-60

McAllister, Col. Richard, 291

McAllister Family Papers, 291-92

McBride, Thomas, 364, 376

McBride, William, 398

McCallum, Duncan C., 350

McCard, J. Phillip, 227, 409

McCard, Maria Randolph, 409

McCauley, E. Grace, 313

McCauley, Thomas, 303

McCauley, W., 183

McChester, Leroy, 528

McClintock, Jenny, 393

McCloskey, Eunice Mildred, Papers, 558

McCloud, Dennis, 444

McCormick, Robert C., 384

McCormick, William M., 466

McCoy, Julius, 398

McCrea, James, 439, 527

Morgan, Samuel, 111
Morris, Alfred, 466
Morris, Robert, 458
Morris, Walter T., 110
Morrison, Clarence C., 398
Morrison, James E., 111
Morrison, John, 111
Morse, Otis B., 376
motion pictures 122-23
Mott, Lucretia, 416, 501
Mount Braddock, 266
Mount Joy Forge, 299
Mount Olive Baptist Church, 518
Mount Pleasant, 549
MOVE, 512
Municipal Governments, Records of, 245-46
Munick, George E., 108
Muncy Women's Facility, 501
Murphy, Carol, 528
Murray, Laval, 528
music, 277-78, 309, 345, 407, 480, 542: minstrel songs, 274-76; negro spirituals, 123, 481; recordings, 541
Musmanno, Dr. Neal V., 121
muster rolls, 12, 21, 61, 96-98, 102, 107-10, 418. *See also* military service *and names of wars*
Myers, F. T. D., 439
Myers, William and Daisy, 375
Myhan, Lee, 510
Myricks, Clarence, 528

N

Nanticoke, 348
National Achievement Clubs, 366, 379
National Association for the Advancement of Colored People, 19, 40, 42, 43, 44, 61, 203, 249, 263, 311, 331, 335, 336, 337, 357, 358, 362, 373, 374, 376, 377, 379, 384, 387, 391, 420, 454, 455, 457, 461, 466, 470, 471, 473, 477, 484, 523, 525
National Association for the Advance-

ment of White People, 391
National Association of Colored Women's Clubs, 473
National Conference for Human Rights, 375
National Dental Association, 366
National Freedom Day, 312, 358, 366, 370
National Guard. *See* Pennsylvania National Guard
National Negro Congress, 331
Native Americans, 396, 402
Nauman, Gertrude Howard, Papers, 344-45
Neal, Mildred, 389
Neff, Lawrence W., 377
Negro, Cezar, 20
Negro History Week, 337, 380, 388, 460
Negro jokes, 483
Negro Life and History, Association for the Study of, 337, 380, 388
Negro Trade Union Leadership Council, 40, 372, 464, 473
Neighborhood Youth Corps, 382
Nelson, D.N., 316
Nelson, Louisa, 14
Nelson, Robert J., 319, 320
New Castle, 455
New Kensington, 315
New York Tribune, 416
Newman, Jerry M., 439
Newville, 68
Newton, Huey, 423
Newton, 568
Niagara, U.S. Brig., 12
Nichols, Bishop Roy, 462
Nicholson, Callie, 528
Nicholson, James, 528
Nicholson, John, 209
Nickens, Osward J., 129
Nipson, John W., 315
Nix, Robert N. C., 40, 54, 389, 464
Nixon, E.D., 529
Norris, Nancy, 14
Norris, Rebecca, 14

Pennsylvania Hall, 179, 300
Pennsylvania Heritage Affairs Commission, 262-64, 511
Pennsylvania Historical and Museum Commission, 52-71, 394, 485, 524, 566; Bureau of Archives and History, 56-62
Pennsylvania Historical Association Papers, 318
Pennsylvania Historical Commission, 62-71
Pennsylvania Historical Records Advisory Board, 59
Pennsylvania Human Relations Act, 252, 382, 455, 474, 475
Pennsylvania Human Relations Commission, 40, 43, 55, 74, 334, 335, 338, 378, 382, 387, 391, 392, 454, 457, 459, 460, 461, 467, 470, 473, 474, 511
Pennsylvania Industrial Reformatory, Huntingdon, 81-84; physicians' records, 83
Pennsylvania Industrial School, 74
Pennsylvania Medical Society, 126, 127
Pennsylvania Military Museum Collection, 428-29
Pennsylvania militia, 22; fines, 174
Pennsylvania Minority Business Development Authority Act, 252
Pennsylvania National Guard, 106-11, 312, 355, 357, 388, 391, 428-29, 514; 104th Cavalry Veterans' Association Collection, 506 (photographs); 2nd Regiment, 108th Field Artillary Records, 530. *See also* State Fencibles
Pennsylvania Post-War Planning Commission, 178
Pennsylvania Public Television Network Commission, 258-59
Pennsylvania Railroad Company, 372, 439-46; mechanical drawings, 445
Pennsylvania, Records of the Proprietary Government, 114-15; Provincial

Council, 115
Pennsylvania Sesqui-Centennial Commission, 178
Pennsylvania State Library, 123-24
Pennsylvania State Lunatic Hospital, 172; patients 172-73. *See also* Harrisburg State Hospital
Pennsylvania, State Museum of, Collection, 426-27
Pennsylvania State Police, 199-203, 355, 357, 375, 379, 388, 389, 391, 456, 466; Memorabilia Collection, 506-7
Pennsylvania State System of Higher Education, 41, 255-57, 391, 449-51, 454, 465, 470
Pennsylvania State University, 263
Pennsylvania Supreme Court, 11, 459; Records of the, 206-17; of Nisi Prius, 210-11
Pennsylvania Turnpike Commission, 369
Pennsylvania Veterinary Medical Association Collection, 517
Pennsylvania Women's Legislative Exchange Collection, 505
Pennsylvania Writers Collection, 273-78
Pennsylvania's Revolutionary Governments, Records of, 196-99
Pennypacker, Gov. Samuel W., 59; Papers, 319-22
Pernell-Arnold, Anita, 262
Perry, Christoper James, Jr., 273
Perry, William, 236
Perry County, 77, 515, 557
Peters, Charles, 310
Peterson, Agnes, 19
Peterson, Lois G., 464
Peterson, Philip, 14
Peterson, William F., 403
Pettigrew, J. Thompson, 510
Petty, Walter M., 368, 369
Pharmacy, State Board of, 132-33
Philadelphia, 23, 28, 32, 37, 38, 42, 54, 56, 59, 61, 63, 69, 77, 93, 128, 175,

225-26; health, 225-26
Porter, Charles M., 464, 465
Porter, Dr. David H., 467
Postcard Collection, 555-56
postcards, 426, 428, 429, 561, 563
Poster Collection, 344
posters, 273, 344, 544
Potter, Dr. Ellen, 315
Potter County, 84, 552
Potts Family Papers, 299
Pottsville, 203
poverty, 9, 384, 390
Powel, John, 294
Powell, Adam Clayton, 423
Pratt, William A., 315
Preston, Arianna, 350, 352
Preston, Henry, 236
Prise, John, 268
Prise, Sarah, 268
prisons, 35, 74-75, 152, 207, 323, 338, 342-43, 418; health, 419. *See also names of prisons*
Probation and Parole, Pennsylvania Board of, 461
Proctor, Boyd L.
Proctor, Edward, 14
Proctor, Dr. Ralph, 512
Profator, Carl Victor, 100
Profator, LeRoy, 84
Professional and Occupational Affairs, Bureau of, 189-91
Professional Health Services, Bureau of, 49
Project Head Start, 382
Property and Supplies, Department of, 113-14
Proud, Robert, 272
Prout, Leon K., 361
public assistance, 243, 436
Public Charities, Board of, 149, 152, 161, 171-72
public housekeepers, 211
Public Instruction, Superintendent of, 134-41. *See also* Education, Department of
Public School Employees' Retirement

System, 246-47
Public Welfare, Department of, 141-73, 313-14, 466; Office of Public Assistance, 323
Pullman Standard Car Company of Butler, Pennsylvania Records, 517-19; employee records, 519
Pulpress, Benjamin L., 14, 16
Purvis, Robert, 273

Q

Quann, Pat, 463
Quann, Robert, 526

R

race relations, 485, 524, 529
racial integration, 376
Railroad Museum of Pennsylvania, 559; Collections, 343-44
Ramey, Felicenne, 39
Ramsey, George, 408
Randall, David V., 359, 374
Randall, P. J. Clyde, 175
Randleman, Edward E., Jr., 403
Randolph, A. Philip, 529
Randolph, Armistead, 77
Rawlins, Gladys, 263
Ray, Ida Stuart, 527
Ray, Michele, 403
Rayburn, John F., 321
Rayhauser, William, 465
Raymond, George, 526
Raymond, Mamie and Wiilliam, 526
Reading, 200, 319, 320
Reber, James D., 360
Rector, Lewis, 267
Reed, Lewis, 408
Reed, Gen. William B., 179-80
Register General, Office of the, 173-74
Rehabilitation, Bureau of, 90
Reichley, James, 382

S

Saven, Horace, 526
sawmills, 23
Sayles, Reuben, 528
Scaife, Richard Mellon, 462
Schadd, Charles S., 72
Schatzman, Clyde M., 528
Schatzman, Dennis, 528
Schmidt, Judge Harvey, 462
School Districts, Records of, 252-53
School Equity, Office of, 121-22
schools, 253, 293, 314, 321, 337, 393, 397-99, 416, 478, 531, 564; integration, 121, 122, 338, 386, 391, 392, 454, 475, 476, 487-88, 505, 510, 513, 522. *See also* Scotland School *and other names*
Schultz, George W., Collection, 300
Schuylkill County, 31, 77
Schwartz, Frances Toby, Collection, 428
Scotland School for Veterans' Children, 39, 101, 327, 334, 349, 350, 352, 373, 382, 383, 464 (board), 532-33
Scott, Bernard, 376
Scott, Rev. Dr. D.S., 321
Scott, Elizabeth, 461
Scott, Sen. Hugh, 437
Scott, William, 295
Scranton, 51, 221, 521
Scranton, Willliam W., 462; Papers, 377-84
Scudder, Walter H., 131
Seamen's Aid Society, 149
segregation, 322, 338, 362, 377, 383, 392, 445, 450, 519
Selinsgrove, 273
Sellers, George, 477
Sellers, Karen, 19
servitude, indentured, 529
Settlers, Laura, 227
Sewickley: YMCA, 347
Seyler, Harry E., 376; Papers, 530-31
Shafer, Gov. Raymond P., 8, 251; Papers, 384-92
Shain, Joseph, 464

Shapiro, Harry, 373; Collection, 322-23
Shapp, Gov. Milton J., 251, 450, 454, 456; Papers, 460-77
Shaw, Rev. Dr. William J., 368, 477
Shawn, Shirley, 376
Sheasley, Gerald, 258
Shelly, Ruth Ann, 533
Shelton, Ulysses, 510
Shepard, Marshall, 510
Shields, Jesse J., 373, 510
Shier, Richard F., 135
Shimmell, Lewis Slifer, Papers, 300
Shippensburg, 557
ships, 21, 69-71, 225-26, 430; captains, 70; masters, 69, 71, 225-26; owners, 71
Short Creek, 283
Shorter, Charles A., 376
Shrawder, Robert, 534
Shrewsbury, 200
sickle-cell anemia, 470, 471
Simmons, James L., 528
Simpson, Sally, 528
Singelton, Henry, 521
Singleton, Wilbert F., 398
Sipes, Thomas Henry, 100
Skillington, R.M., 408
Slater, Peter, 14
Slaughter, Mary, 313
slavery, 63, 175, 272, 280, 285, 309-10, 356, 406, 413-15, 416, 417, 423, 424-56, 430, 448, 490, 492, 496-97, 545, 549, 563; Act for the Gradual Abolition of, 187, 211, 243; West Indies, 281
slaves, 23, 24, 32, 70, 71, 82, 124, 207-8, 210-15, 216-17, 225-26, 232, 234-35, 236-39, 243-45, 266, 272-73, 278, 281-82, 286, 288, 291, 294, 296-97, 298, 299, 304, 305, 317, 329, 345, 402, 405, 411, 413, 415, 419, 421, 497, 506, 515, 545, 554, 564; manumissions, 92, 93-95, 301; owners, 32, 70, 211-15, 216-17, 232, 234, 236-39, 243-45, 272, 289, 291, 297,

564, 568; New York, 559; South Carolina, 559; Virginia, 272
Slippery Rock, 444
Smallwood, Eunice, 131
Smith, C. Milbourne, 361
Smith, Charles, 14
Smith, Griffith, 11
Smith, Henry R., 361, 362
Smith, Henry R., Jr., 360, 376
Smith, James, 491
Smith, Jonathan, 236
Smith, Julius, 59
Smith, Mrs. Lawrence M. C., Collection, 300-1
Smith, Lucille L., 528
Smith, Rev. Robert Johnson Smith, 461
Smith, Samuel, 100
Smith, Stephen, 302
Smith, Tara Nicole, 534
Smith, Willie, 528
Smithy, Margaret, 294
Snowden, Elizabeth Ruth, 227
Snyder, Helen E., 527
Snyder, Richard A., Papers, 510-12
Soldiers and Sailors Homes, 327
Somerset County, 33, 84, 338
South Pittsburgh, 527-28
Sowers, William K., Collection, 508
Spangler, Irene, 527
Spanish-American War, 506; military service, 102-4
Special Commissions, Records of, 174-78
Special Health Services, Bureau of, Genetic Disease Program, 50
Speedwell Forge, 266
Speller, Dr. J. Finton, 463
Spence, Robert, 527
Spencer, John, Papers, 301
Spanish-American War, 102-4
Stackfield, Frank, 100
Standford, Julia A., 14
Stanton, John T., 227
State, Department of, 179-96
State Fencibles Collection, 514-15
Staub, Shalom, 263

Steelton, 541
Steese, Dr. Ruth Miller, 465
Steth, Raymond, 527
Stevens, Andrew F., 510
Stevens, G,E., 100
Stevens, Dr. Sylvester K., papers, 552-53
Stevens, Thaddeus, 300, 416, 545; Papers, 415-17
Stevens, Thaddeus Jr., 416
Stevens Dr. Willard Montgomery, 349, 373
Stevens-Outman Family Papers, 552-53
Stevenson, Diana, 14
Stevenson, Lillian W., 350, 352
Stevenson, Robert, 295
Stevenson, Rev. William P., 354
Steward, Rowena, 262
Stewart, Col. Alexander, 101
Stewart, Capt. John H., 271
Stewart, William E., Collection, 555
Still, William, 273, 318
Stokes, Louis, 423
Stone, Gov. William A., Papers, 326-27
Stouch, Samuel G. III, 200
Stover, Edward, Papers, 482-83
Stowe, Harriet Beecher, 414
Streets, William, 295
Stribling, Eli, 528
Strickler, Daniel B., Collection, 504; photographs, 504
Striplin, Benjamin A., 240
Strohm, John, Papers, 301-3
Stuart, James, 253
Stuart, John, 84
Stuart, Matilda Elliott, Collection, 554
Stuckey, Edward, 181
Students, Commonwealth Association of, Records, 449-51, 454
Stuyter, Charles, 214
Stuyter, Margaret, 214
Sudarkasa, Dr. Niara, 262, 263
suffrage. See voting rights
Sullivan, Andrea D., 466

for, 501
Wood, Anne Brancato, Papers, 508-9
Wood, Barbara, 354
Woodard, Elon A., 417
Woodfork, Frank, 240
Woods, David, 294
Woods, Jesse, 464
Woods, Mary Jane, 294
Woods Family Collection, 330
Woods Farm, x
Woodson, Lewis, 28
Woodville State Hospital, 157, 169-71; patients, 170-71
Woodward, John, 286
workers, 297, 345
Workmen's Compensation, 561; Bureau, 89
Workmen's Insurance Fund, 89
Works Progress Administration, 62-63, 67, 480; American Guide Series: Pennsylvania Anthracite, 63; Dauphin County, 65; Negro in Philadelphia, 63-65; Negro in Pittsburgh, 65
World War I, 506: conscientious objection, 437; Draft Board Records, 99, 271; draft boards, 499; First Colored Regiment, 500; military service, 99-100, 104, 146, 271; Pennsylvania War History Commission, 105; workers, 429
World War II, 60, 62, 506, 519, 555; Pennsylvania State Defense Corps Auxiliary, 110-11; Post-War Planning Commission, 178; Veterans Compensation Applications, 106
Worthington, Walter, 528
Wright, Emmanuel C., 357
Wright, Emmanuel E., 358
Wright, Helen J., 461, 463
Wright, Mary and Robert, 526
Wright, Queen E., 528
Wright, Mayor Robert, 312
Wright family. *See* Haldeman-Wright Family Collection
Wyalusing, 303
Wyoming County, 33

Wyoming Historical and Geological Society, 540
Wyoming, Pa., 407

Y

Yarnell, Stanley Y., 138
Yeates, Jasper, 299; Family Papers, 304
York, 194, 316, 354, 395, 476, 530, 541
York County, 23, 33, 51, 77, 194, 198, 199, 209, 211, 213, 214, 215, 358, 395, 547; teachers and school directors, 253
Young, Edward C., 510
Young, George "Toby," 19
Young, Harriet, 299
Young, James Garfield, 247
Young, John, 11
Young, Scipio, 298
Young, Toby, 389, 399
Young, William P., 219, 251
Young Men's Christian Association, vi, 123, 193, 335, 381, 398, 484, 542; Pennsylvania Records, 347-48
Young Women's Christian Association, Phyllis Wheatley, 411

Z

Zachery, Sam, 210